Major League Stadiums

For Conor:
official hot dog taster

Major League Stadiums: A Vacation Planning Reference to the 26 Baseball Parks

by Dan Dickinson *and* Kieran Dickinson

McFarland & Company, Inc., Publishers
Jefferson, North Carolina, and London

Cover photo by Jerome Kelly

British Library Cataloguing-in-Publication data are available

Library of Congress Cataloguing-in-Publication Data

Dickinson, Daniel, 1950–
    Major league stadiums : a vacation planning reference to the 26
baseball parks / by Dan Dickinson and Kieran Dickinson.
      p. cm.
    Includes index.
    ISBN 0-89950-610-0 (sewn softcover : 50# alk. paper) ∞
    1. Baseball fields – United States – Guide-books. 2. Baseball
fields – Canada – Guide-books. 3. Stadiums – United States – Guide
-books. 4. Stadiums – Canada – Guide-books. I. Dickinson, Kieran,
1972– . II. Title.
GV879.5.D53 1991
796.357′06′873 – dc20   91-52509
                                                        CIP

Manufactured in the United States of America

McFarland & Company, Inc., Publishers
  Box 611, Jefferson, North Carolina 28640

Contents

Contents

Acknowledgments

We began the research on this book with a rushed trip to Baltimore in June 1990, after learning, to our horror, that the night game at which we had expected to begin our investigations was in fact scheduled for 1 P.M. Three months and twenty thousand miles later, on a hot night in Arlington, Texas, the research for *Major League Stadiums* ended and the writing began.

We knew when we started this project that putting together a book on all the baseball parks was going to be a gargantuan task. Getting it done at all would have been impossible without the help we received along the way from fans, stadium officials, security officers, medical personnel, and the major league teams. Literally hundreds of people answered our questions, mailed us information, and shared with us their insights on why this crazy, awkward game called baseball has such a compelling hold on us.

The following are among the folks who were especially helpful: Rick Vaughn, Baltimore Orioles; Dr. Mike Foley and Bob Brasciani, Boston Red Sox; Greg Smith, California Angels; Judy Orbzut, Chicago White Sox; Bob DiBiasio and John Adams, Cleveland Indians; Dan Ewald, Dr. James Lowe, and Diane Krzynstun, Detroit Tigers; Dean Vogelaar, Kansas City Royals; Jon Greenberg, Amy Shaffer, Milwaukee Brewers; Tom Mee, Minnesota Twins; Bob Pellegrino, New York Yankees; Darold Cox, Oakland Athletics; David Aust, Seattle Mariners; John Blake, Texas Rangers; Howard Stackman, Toronto Blue Jays; Sam Stokes and Carolyn Sloss, Atlanta Braves; Jon Braude, Cincinnati Reds; Rob Matwick, Houston Astros; Mike Williams, Los Angeles Dodgers; Larry Shenck, Philadelphia Phillies; Donna Kraniak, Pittsburgh Pirates; Mike Williams, Tammy Fichtman, and Sherryl Ward, San Diego Padres; John Wilkerson, St. Louis Cardinals; and Karl Schachne, San Francisco Giants. There were others who were equally willing to provide assistance whose names we did not get or somehow lost. Their help was equally appreciated.

It goes without saying that none of the above are responsible for either the opinions or the facts contained in *Major League Stadiums*. The views in

vii

this book as well as any oversights or mistakes are solely the responsibility of the authors.

During the six months that it took to write this guide the other Dickinsons, Kelley, Megan, and Conor, have had to do without, respectively, a husband, father, and a brother. The willingness of the three of them to put up with half a year's effective absence while we pursued this project was and is deeply appreciated.

Introduction

It is a basic principle of physics that everything must have a beginning. This book began at Wrigley Field.

In April 1990, one of the authors visited Chicago on business and decided he would like to go to a Cubs game. He had never been to Wrigley, and like most fans he wanted to see those celebrated vine-covered walls.

After buying tickets over the phone he asked for directions to the stadium, but found that no one at his hotel knew precisely where Wrigley Field was, although they all agreed that it was on the North Side of Chicago. Heading out in the general direction of the park, he had to contend with bad traffic, rapacious parking space owners, and the maze of confusing streets in Wrigleyville. After the contest he managed to duck just in time to avoid a beer bottle dropped out of the second story window of one of Wrigley's horde of bars. Then he proceeded to spend the next half hour trying to find the dark spot behind a florist shop where he had left his car.

Despite it all, he had a wonderful time. For any fan there are few experiences more evocative of what baseball is all about than a game at Wrigley. The place's intensely partisan fans, its attractive old scoreboard and beautiful brick walls, the vibrant Wrigleyville scene, and the appeal of the Cubs themselves make going to the game an unforgettable event. Still, some aspects of the trip could have been more pleasant had the traveler known more about the stadium and the area around it.

When the author returned home, he was determined to buy one of what he was sure were dozens of travel guides on the market specifically focused on visiting the major league ballparks. There weren't any to be had—not a single one. That set the wheels turning for both writers.

This is not the first guide to the baseball parks. Although they are no longer in print, a few other books have talked about such aspects of stadium life as the food that's available in the various facilities or the statistics of the clubs that play in them. *Major League Stadiums*, however, is the first volume that takes a comprehensive look at the parks. Here you will find information on how to get to the games, where to sit, what the stadiums are like, food, features — in short, most of the things you will need to know to make your baseball vacation experience as rewarding as possible.

As you read, you should understand a few things about what you will find in this book and what you won't.

First, every chapter is in two parts. The first section provides an overview of the baseball park, the team that plays in it, some highlights that have happened in the facility, and the nature of the fans that come to watch the game. We regard this last area as very important, for one of the subthemes that you will encounter in this volume is our belief that baseball audiences frequently create their own "fan cultures" that often mirror the beliefs and values of the various communities where the parks are situated.

The second part of each chapter amounts to a "practical guide." This is where you will find directions on how to get to the stadium, where to buy tickets, how to find good seats, and what sorts of foods are available in each park. We also provide information on security issues, parking, health, and where you can find souvenirs and autographs. The prices we quote are what we found them to be in 1990. Assuming they will be a bit higher by the time you get out to the ballpark, they will still give you a good idea of what to expect. Costs at the two Canadian parks are given in Canadian dollars. Normally, the Canadian dollar is valued at about 10 to 15 percent less than U.S. currency, so if you are traveling to Montreal or Toronto from the U.S. you should take this into account when budgeting for your trip. By contrast, of course, if you are traveling from Canada to the U.S. parks you will need to add another 10 to 15 percent to your expected costs.

Just a word on two other issues: accuracy and objectivity. We have tried our best to insure that the figures we have supplied, the phone numbers we've listed, and the addresses we have given were right at the time this book was written. Unfortunately, parks add and take away seats and phone numbers change or are disconnected. Accordingly, some of what you read will already be wrong by the time you pick up the volume; this is inevitable with any travel guide. All we can say is that we will try to correct these things as the book is later revised. And as much as we would like to believe that we have put every player on his proper team, placed each club in its proper standing, and related each hoary baseball anecdote exactly as it was supposed to have happened, we know full well that there are going to be some errors in this book that rank right up there with Bill Buckner's. Let us know and we will try to get it right next time.

The issue of objectivity was a matter of much discussion when we began this project. We did not see our role in compiling *Major League Stadiums* to be that of a critic. Nor did we want to get into the business of rating the hot dogs at each park and awarding stars to stadiums for their accomplishments in providing inexpensive parking or comfortable seats. At the same time, though, we didn't want this to be one of those gosh-wow travel books in which all the sights are equally spectacular, all the locals are invariably friendly and interesting, and all the meals are both tasty and nutritious. You deserve better than that. The fact of the matter is that, just as is the case with teams, not all baseball parks are created equal. And while there is not a single one of the twenty-six baseball stadiums that we would not on the whole be happy to visit again, some are prettier than others, some have better food than others, and some sell tickets at lower prices than others. You ought to know which parks have which strong points so that you can do your baseball vacationing on the basis of what is important to you.

Whenever you get into the business of making distinctions, you cannot help bringing your own values into play. As you will soon see, we like natural grass, blue skies, involved audiences, and baseball parks in which there is a sense of communion between the players and the fans. We are less enthralled with concrete sports palaces, astroturfed playing areas, and "baseball as entertainment" management philosophies, even though we would admit that some of these things have a role to play in the sport. If you share our basic perspective, you may agree with many of our views. If you can't go along with us on these things, you will find us consistently wrong-headed on many issues. We have made our calls in writing this book. Now it's your turn to make yours in reading it.

A final point. If we wanted to convey one thing in writing *Major League Stadiums* it was that visiting North America's stadiums constitutes just about the most consistently rewarding vacation that any fan could possibly have. We had fun traveling to the ballparks. We know you will have a great time going to them too.

The Stadiums

ATLANTA BRAVES
Atlanta–Fulton County Stadium

Major league baseball includes three kinds of teams.

First are the clubs that everyone knows, the historic squads such as the Yankees, Dodgers, Red Sox, and Cards that have dominated and shaped the game for decades.

Then there are the newer, sometimes more aggressive, expansion squads. Many of these have yet to see their days of glory, but others—the Royals and Blue Jays, for example—demonstrated their winning ways fairly early on.

Beyond these, however, is another group of teams that seem to have been around forever, but that rarely win a pennant. Most have had their place in the sun for a moment or two, only to have receded into perpetual shadow. Their players are little known, their box scores are often not run, and nonbaseball fans are often barely aware that these teams exist. Even in their home towns, the reaction to these squads can be tepid: the local newspapers don't report on them as well as they should, attendance is low, and in some places admirers of visiting teams come close to outnumbering fans of the home club.

Yet these teams do serve a purpose. First, they bring professional ball to areas of the country that otherwise might not have it. They also provide a convenient stopping spot for rookies on their way up and superstars on their way down. Finally, they supply us with living proof of an important but somber message: persistance doesn't always pay off.

The Braves are a classic case of this phenomenon. Possibly the worst still-active team in baseball history (there are several other contenders), the Braves have nevertheless soldiered on through the decades, always showing, occasionally winning, hoping for that season when tenacity will be rewarded, and, at last, "we'll turn it around." Well, maybe someday.

Oddly, though the Braves have one of the poorest records in the majors, they have fans all over the continent thanks to the wonders of technology. TBS Superstation magnate Ted Turner—who also owns the Braves—has decided to make this sorry squad "America's Team." Accordingly, Turner broadcasts the team's schedule across the U.S. *and* abroad: when we visited Cancun, for example, we found that Mexican fans knew the stats of the whole Braves team but had never heard of Rickey Henderson or Roger Clemens. This interest has certainly improved the Braves' recognition. It has not, thus far, seemed to have had an appreciatively positive impact on their play.

We'd like to tell you that attending Braves games has great compensations other than the play, either in the beauty of the stadium, the quality of the food, or the excellence of seating. Alas, it isn't so. Though it's by no means the poorest in any of these categories, winning percentage is not the only area in which Atlanta remains an "also ran." Still, the Braves serve one essential purpose in today's world: they bring major league ball into the South.

Few areas of North America have contributed more to the game in the way of providing great players than the South, and no area has been more shamefully neglected by the majors when it comes to siting teams. California has five clubs, while New York, Texas, Ohio, Illinois, Pennsylvania, and Missouri have two each. Meanwhile, Florida and North Carolina, the fourth and tenth largest states, do not currently have a single one, though Miami was recently awarded an expansion franchise which will begin play in 1993.

It's sometimes argued that baseball has no following in the South—indeed, that the Atlanta Braves' poor attendence shows that there isn't much of a baseball market in this region. Yet Florida has a long baseball tradition, spurred by spring training contests which grow more popular each year, while North Carolina's "A" league teams, the lowest level in the minors, have the best attendence in the states. While relatively few do turn out for Braves games, that wasn't the case when the franchise moved to Atlanta. It's doubtful that any team could post the kind of record the Braves have had and expect to do significantly better in drawing fans.

Baseball likes to claim that it's "the national pastime." Certainly this was the case forty years ago when the other contenders weren't even close. Not so anymore. While baseball rested on its laurels, football blanketed North America with franchises. An even more aggressive NBA—probably the best managed sports organization in the U.S.—strategically invaded regions with its game, to great effect. If football can make it in Green Bay and basketball can succeed in Salt Lake City, why can't baseball make it in Tampa, Nashville, or Raleigh?

If baseball wants to really be the nation's sport, it's got to be willing to take some risks for the future of the game. In the meantime, while southern fans wait for baseball commissioner Fay Vincent and his minions to come to their senses, they'll have to continue to hustle hundreds of miles down I-75 and I-20 once

a year or so to attend the games of the Atlanta Braves.

The Team

The Braves are one of the oldest teams in baseball. Braves history—and baseball history—in effect started when the Cincinnati Red Stockings, the first professional team, made its celebrated tour around the nation in 1869, offering to play against all comers and dispatching absolutely everybody—usually with lop-sided scores.

Baseball enthusiasts across the nation were impressed, none more than in Boston. When the Red Stockings collapsed, some of their players were invited to Beantown to join a new squad being formed by local boosters. Set up in the early 1870s, that team is the franchise we know as the Braves today.

Of course, it wasn't called the Braves then. In fact, few teams have gone through a more bewildering collection of monikers: Red Stockings, Beaneaters, Red Caps, Doves, and Rustlers were some that were used before the squad finally settled on the name "Braves" in 1912. (By the way, the rubric had little to do with Indians, despite the tomahawks that grace Atlanta uniforms today. The name came about because the team's owner was an official of New York's Tammany Hall political club. Such people were called "Braves.")

As the "Red Stockings," the Braves were pretty good. And though it may be the worst major league name ever, the term "Beaneaters" proved a charm for the Bostonians in the 1890s. They collected half the National League pennants of that far off decade.

Since then, though, it has been mostly downhill for the Braves, marked by an occasional blip upward. Over a seventy-six year career in Boston, the Braves went to the Series twice.

1914 was the glory year. Then, the Braves climbed out of the last-place cellar in mid–July to win the National

League pennant, an event regarded as a miracle. When in the Series the Braves took the mighty Philadelphia Athletics in four games, they registered the greatest upset of the era, and maybe of all-time World Series play.

Unfortunately, that didn't change things. The Braves didn't get hot again until 1948. That year, the Braves' drive to the pennant was headed up by two pitching aces to such an extent that Bostonians came to mutter a little prayer before going to the stadium: "A day of Spahn [Warren], a day of Sain [Johnny], and two days of rain!" Spahn, Sain, and the elements conspired to get the Braves to the Series. But this time their luck ran out. Their rival was Cleveland, a team they resemble in other ways than sharing a Native American reference in their name. The Indians won that lackluster contest 4–2.

A losing record, poor attendance, and the always invidious comparisons with the more glamorous AL Red Sox, drove the Braves westward to Milwaukee in 1953. It was there that the team had its brief moment in the sun.

The 1950s were without a doubt the best decade in the Braves' 120-year history. Driven by Warren Spahn's consistent 20-win seasons, Eddie Mathews' spectacular slugging, and the great hitting and fine fielding of a last-minute, off-the-bench outfield replacement named Hank Aaron, the Braves at last gave their fans something to cheer about. Milwaukee did well nearly every year in the decade, bringing the pennant home in 1958 and taking all the marbles in 1957 versus Casey Stengel's powerful Yankees. That particular contest featured that rarest of all baseball events, an umpire admitting he made an incorrect call. In the fourth game, Braves player "Nippy" Jones claimed that he'd been hit by a ball, but the ump said he had not. Jones retrieved the ball and showed an incriminating streak of his shoe polish across it. Jones got his base.

Unfortunately, the Milwaukee Braves couldn't continue their winning ways into the 1960s. As losses mounted and attendance declined once more, the Braves looked for a new home.

They found it in Atlanta in 1965. There, a booming sun belt city was willing to invest millions in a new stadium to attract a major league team. Boasting a population much in excess of Milwaukee's, Atlanta could provide the people to make the Braves a financial success—if the Braves could supply the victories.

As it turned out, Atlanta did supply the attendees, at least for awhile. But the Braves rarely supplied the wins.

In truth, the Atlanta Braves match has not been serendipitous. There have, over the past twenty-five years, been moments of glory. The Braves have won two NL Western Division titles in Atlanta (1969, 1982), but lost both playoff series in three straight. Phil Niekro's outstanding pitching excited crowds in the 1970s, while double MVP winner (1982–83) Dale Murphy's all-around excellent play kept fans happy in the 1980s. Of course, the greatest moment in baseball in recent decades occured in Atlanta on April 8, 1974, when Hank Aaron broke Babe Ruth's "unbeatable" record of 714 home runs.

On the whole, though, it has not been an outstanding record. Twenty-five years of play without a single Series appearance and final standings in the second division almost every year are not the sort of statistics a fan can brag about.

Right now, the Atlanta Braves seem to be in more turmoil than usual. Dale Murphy's departure leaves them, for the first time, without a single identifiable star. It's not that everyone on the squad is second-rate; actually, Atlanta has some good players, such as outfielder Ron Gant, pitcher John Smotlz, and 1990 Rookie of the Year Dave Justice. The problem is that there is not a single player on the team just now that will set the turnstiles rotating. That won't matter if the Braves surprise everyone and start to win which is just what they started doing early in 1991. But if they perform as usual, Atlanta's already low box receipts could sink a good deal lower.

The temptation for the team may be to move again. That probably would be a mistake. While some teams, such as the Pirates, do seem to suffer from indifferent fans, this isn't the case in Atlanta. The problem is not an apathetic audience, it's management that, for whatever reasons, fails to get the job done. If the Braves really want to "turn it around," working at the problems from that level — and right at the top — would most likely be the place to start.

The Stadium

Thousands of business travelers each year see Atlanta–Fulton County Stadium as they ride into the center city from Hartsfield International Airport. There it stands as the capitol of the New South swings into your view: a majestic, airy circle set against Atlanta's equally impressive skyline.

Atlanta–Fulton County Stadium is really quite a sight. Whether it's a good place to play baseball is another matter.

On the whole, the park is well situated. Located just south of the Georgia State Capitol in downtown Atlanta, the stadium rests at the intersections of Interstates 20 and 75, making the park easy to reach by car. And although Atlanta's efficient MARTA subway line doesn't stop at the stadium, well-planned bus connections make it possible for you to reach a Braves game from most city locations and from the airport for a minimal charge. The downtown setting means that you are within minutes of good restaurants and

the city's exciting new "Underground Atlanta" nightlife area.

So what's to be faulted? Frankly, the neighborhood around the park isn't all that safe. That's a matter of some concern since the stadium's parking, though policed and lighted, is not secured.

The stadium itself has the familiar circular concrete design. Opened in 1965, it is yet another of that long series of multipurpose (read: football) stadiums constructed by municipalities during the sixties and seventies. Not particularly big, and not particularly small (it seats 52,007), Atlanta stadium is neither better nor worse than a half-dozen other sport palaces in the majors. It's strictly standard issue.

Outside the park are ramps leading up to the main concourse, as well as shaded greenspaces at the corners, which some fans use for picnics before the game. On the exterior concourse itself are three items of interest. At the top of the main ramp, between gates J and K, is an attractive statue of the Braves' greatest star, Hank Aaron. It shows him hitting home run 715 and shattering Babe Ruth's mark. To the north of the park, by gate P, is another statue. This one has Phil Niekro curling one of his knuckleballs. The best of this bronze cast trio is the tribute to Ty Cobb outside Gate M. Here Cobb is in characteristic pose, sliding into base with his spikes flaring, a half-sneer on his lips, a look of cool calculation in his eyes — probably a pretty accurate picture of what the "Georgia Peach" was like.

Inside, the stadium has wide public areas that are relatively clean and spacious. Concession stands, are well-spaced, though not particularly attractive. With attendance what it is, stands in outlying areas tend to open late and close early. Altogether, the place could be tidied up a bit. Boxes sit on the open floor, garbage bags are allowed to overflow, and there are sections of the park that could use a coat of paint. Nor is the playing area exempt from this worn look. The natural grass is brown and thin in places, and there are a number of bare spots. Atlanta Stadium isn't dilapidated. But neither does it have the freshness that you see at Yankee or Dodger stadium. This is compensated for by stadium personnel that are uniformly helpful and courteous.

The seating arrangements are blessedly simple. There's a long terrace of seats sliding back from the field, topped by a steeply pitched upper deck. Indented between these two is the club level, where you'll find the press area and corporate suites as well as some box seats (see "Seating"). As in all the multipurpose stadiums, many seats in this park are quite distant from the action.

The field is designed for hitters. The right and left foul poles are set fairly short at 330′, while the center field wall is at 402′. Beyond the right field wall is "Rally Alley," a platform with a cannon on it which is is set off by one of the Braves' three mascots (generally "Homer the Brave") when the club hits a home run. Over the center field wall are placards bearing the Braves' retired numbers; from left to right, they are: #21, pitcher Warren Spahn; #41, third baseman Eddie Mathews; #44, home run king Hank Aaron; and #35, pitcher Phil Niekro. Above these is a modest "diamond vision" style video display screen and an electronic scoreboard. Both run interesting trivia questions and decent baseball jokes during the game.

One of the most popular stories the Braves like to run used to be told by Joe McCarthy, of Yankee's fame. It seems that McCarthy had a dream one night in which he died and went to heaven. Once there, God told McCarthy that he was to coach the Paradise ball club. Looking around, Joe couldn't believe the talent he had to draw from: Ruth, Gehrig, Cobb, Cy Young, Satch Paige, Honus Wagner — all the departed greats were there.

McCarthy had no sooner made his selection when he got a call from Satan. Would McCarthy, the devil wondered, like to have a challenge match against his team?

"Sure," Joe replied. "But you haven't got a chance. I've got all the players."

"That's true," Satan allowed. "But I have all the umpires."

In actuality, Atlanta Stadium is neither heaven nor hell. Like the earth it sits on, it's somewhere between the extremes.

Highlights

Since the Braves have not reached the World Series since moving South, Atlanta–Fulton County Stadium is a bit short on highlights, though there are some. Phil Niekro pitched a no-hitter in the park on August 5, 1973. The Giant's John Montefusco performed the same feat on September 26, 1976.

Of course, the one major landmark associated with the park is probably the game's premiere moment of the past quarter century. That was Hank Aaron's record shattering 715th home run blast on April 8, 1974. On that day, across the U.S. and Canada, TV stations stopped their broadcasts when Aaron stepped up to bat to cover what they hoped would be the big moment.

Hank didn't disappoint. With the Dodgers' Al Downing pitching, Aaron sent a fastball arching into the Braves' left field dugout. Typical of the man, Hank was among the last to know that he had achieved the mark. It had been his practice over the years to reach first before he looked for the ball, and he wasn't going to abandon that habit now. Still, well-before he touched that bag, the roar of the crowd must have told him that, after nearly forty years, Ruth's "unbeatable" record had fallen.

Fans

Who would go out of their way to attend the ball games of a team that usually loses? The answer is simple: people who care about baseball.

Atlanta Braves fans may not be baseball's most colorful audience. They have, for example, few distinctive fan traditions. Nor is this a crowd that's especially enthusiastic. In fact, attendees at the games may not even be Braves admirers: popular clubs like the Mets, the Dodgers, and the Cubs seem to draw nearly as many enthusiasts as the home team does. Yet, while this may not be baseball's most intense crowd, it does pay attention. Plays are watched and discussed, socializing and beer drinking is minimal, and a procession of two or three poor plays by the Braves—a not unheard of occurrence—will bring forth howls of agony from the audience, while a fine fielding effort or a home run will be met with appreciative applause. Braves fans are, indisputably, down. But they still care.

Who goes to the game? Families, mostly. These are working and middle-class sorts, some of them transplanted northerners working for Atlanta's thriving corporations and factories, others, southern baseball fans drawn from a wide region; cars from Tennessee, South Carolina, Florida, and Alabama crowd the parking lots. Since the stadium can get very, very hot during the humid Atlanta summer, fans like to dress down for the game, though this being "Southern Baptist" territory, never beyond the bounds of propriety. Bringing a cooler along is popular; so is carrying in take-out orders from the *The Varsity*, a 1950s style "car hop" restaurant that's a local institution. As with so many things that can be said about Atlanta–Fulton County Stadium, there are no extremes in this audience. These are simply down home folks out to have a good time at the ballgame.

Getting There

One of the advantages of the newer generation of ballparks is that most are centrally located. Atlanta–Fulton County Stadium is certainly no exception. It can be conveniently reached by car, cab, and mass transit from most locations.

By car. Car is generally the best option for vacationers coming into town from the surrounding states to see a game or two. It's also an option for those arriving at the airport.

If you're coming from such *north* locations as Chattanooga, Knoxville, Charlotte, or Greensboro, take either I-75 (through Tennessee) or I-85 (through the Carolinas) to where they join in downtown Atlanta. Follow the joined routes to Exit 91 Fulton Street/Stadium. At the end of the exit ramp, turn left on Fulton Street. Parking is ahead on the right.

From such *east* locations as Augusta and Columbia, take I-20 west to Exit 24 Capitol Avenue. Go to the end of the exit ramp and on to Capitol Avenue. Parking is on the right.

People coming from such *south* areas as Macon, Jacksonville, and Orlando should take I-75 northbound to where it merges with I-85. From there, take Exit 90 Georgia Avenue/Stadium. Turn left at the stop sign on Washington Street. From Washington, turn right on Georgia Avenue. Parking is on the left.

Those coming from Birmingham, and other points *west* should take I-20 east to Exit 22 Windsor Street/Stadium. At the first light go right on Windsor Street. Turn left on Fulton Street. Parking is ahead on the right.

People arriving at *Hartsfield International Airport* who want to reach the park by rental car should take I-85 northbound to where it joins I-75. Proceed to Exit 90 Georgia Avenue/Stadium. Turn left at stop sign on Washington Street. From Washington, turn right on Georgia Avenue. Parking is on the left.

By cab. A cab is a good option from any of the downtown hotels. All cabs in Atlanta operate on a zone system, and thus the flat fare from this area to the stadium is $4 for the first person, one way, and $2 for each additional rider.

Taking a cab from the airport is more expensive. Most drivers will say that the stadium is in the hotel zone and will charge $15. Occasionally, drivers can be persuaded that it's nearer than that (which it is) and will ask for $9.

Mass transit. Atlanta's MARTA subway system presents the cheapest, and, in many ways, the best means to get to the game. From any area served by MARTA, including the airport, take the train to Five Points Station. Make sure you get a transfer. From there, shuttle buses are waiting to whisk you to the game. The cost, even from Hartsfield, is a very reasonable $1 each way.

After the contest, go back to the buses, which wait outside Gate A. You'll be whisked back to Five Points, from which you can head for home. On the other hand, you might want to stop here to join fans for dancing, drinks, etc.— Five Points Station is right next to the popular "Underground Atlanta" the restaurant and nightlife district.

MARTA, at (404) 848-4711, would be happy to supply further details.

Parking

Atlanta–Fulton County Stadium is surrounded with facility owned parking spaces north, south, and east of the stadium. All are uniformly priced at a very reasonable $3. There are also some neighborhood spots in the area for $2. While parking occasionally can get tight during Atlanta Falcons football games, no one can recall parking for baseball ever running out.

Security is a problem. While the stadium lots are well lighted and policed, they are not secured. Neighborhood lots are generally neither policed nor lighted. During day games, this isn't much of a concern. During nights, the neighborhood lots should be avoided. You would probably do well to arrive early to get a closer-in parking spot.

Tickets

As at most stadiums, you can order tickets by mail, call in orders, pick them up in person, or buy them at the game.

In truth, the Braves' attendance figures are so low that mail orders are hardly necessary. There are good seats available for nearly every game. Still, the prudent might well want to send in advance. To do so, write: Atlanta Braves, Ticket Orders, PO Box 4064, Atlanta GA 30302-4064. Indicate the number of tickets you want and for what games. Be sure to include your check, which should include a $2 service charge. We feel it is only fair to warn you that our attempts to get schedules and other information by mail from the Braves were fruitless. Hopefully, you won't have a similar experience.

Phone orders are also accepted. In the Atlanta area, call 577-9600; outside it, punch 1-800-322-7767. Be prepared with the location you'd like to sit in, plus the number and the expiration date of your major credit card. You'll be hit with a service charge here, too.

Particularly if you're arriving in Atlanta a day or two before the event, going to the advance ticket office may be your best option — you'll be able to see a seating chart before you put your money down. It's located at Gate G of the stadium and is open from 8:30 A.M. until 5 P.M., Monday through Friday. During the season when the team is in town, the office is also open on Saturday 8:30 A.M. to 5 P.M. and on Sunday 1 P.M. to 5 P.M.

You can also buy tickets directly before a game. At many parks this isn't a good idea. In Atlanta, you should have no problem doing this if you find you are pressed for time.

Availability. The Atlanta Braves occupy a large stadium and have one of the worst attendance records in baseball — they didn't crack even a million attendees in 1988. What this means is that you will have no problem getting tickets for any game on the schedule.

For most contests, any prior planning will net you very good seats as well. Cubs, Mets, and Dodgers contests tend to bring in the fans: if you want to go to one of these, consider ordering your tickets ahead of time. For other games, a visit to the advance ticket booth a day or so before the game should net you within the baselines club or field seats if you're willing to pay the price.

Costs. Braves tickets are uniformly priced based on stadium level *and* view. This system leads to less disparity than in most parks. Generally speaking, tickets are worth about what you pay for them.

During 1990, Braves ticket charges were as follows: Dugout Level ($9.50); Club Level ($9.50); Field Level ($8); Upper Level ($6); General Admission (Adults [$4]); (Kids under 11 [$1]).

Rainouts. Rainouts happen with some regularity in Atlanta, generally a couple of times a year. Unfortunately, management's attitude towards them is pretty hardnosed. While they are perfectly willing to exchange rainout tickets for future games, there are NO REFUNDS (their caps, not ours). So if you flew in from Buenos Aires just to attend a Braves home game, and you got rained-out, and you are never coming to America again — well, you're just out of luck.

Actually, people traveling to the game from long distance might want to consider the rainout issue when ordering tickets. Specifically, they might want to consider whether it might be best *not* to order and to wait until they got into town before deciding whether to buy. Normally, this wouldn't be a good idea — and, should the Braves get hot, it will not be a wise move. But if things stay as they are, you will probably get nearly as good a selection of seats when you get into Atlanta as you would have gotten if you'd paid in advance. You'll also avoid getting stuck.

Seating

The news regarding seating at Atlanta Stadium is both good and bad.

The bad news is that the stadium has a high proportion of poor spots. The good news is that you probably won't have to sit in them.

The inside of Atlanta Stadium makes you wonder what went through the minds of the architects when they designed the place. The front rows of seats (called "Dugout" here) are wonderful, of course — they are in every park. And, as you'd expect, the seats in the field level, slanting back from the action, get progressively worse the further you move from the diamond. No surprise there, either.

But then there's the upper deck. Is it projected way over the field seats, so people in this area get a bird's eye view of the proceedings? No! Instead, the thing is set back to the point that it overhangs the field level by only a few rows. Not only does that put anyone who sits in this area a long way from the batter's box; it also denies shade to the lion's share of the people paying top dollar in the field level. But, then, why would anyone want shade in Atlanta in August?

To make matters worse, whoever designed the place put their corporate customers and many of their top dollar season ticket people not close to the action, but at the abutment where the field level cuts off and the upper level begins! Apparently some corporations will still pay thousands to buy a suite,

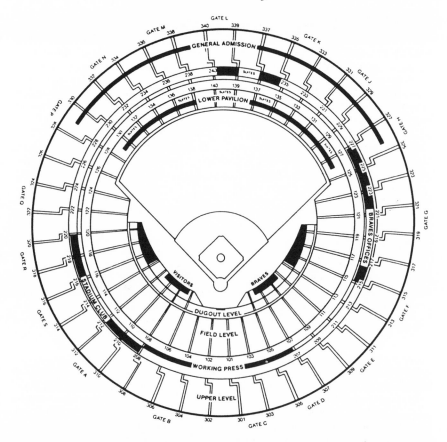

Seating chart, Atlanta–Fulton County Stadium.

even knowing that it was more than a hundred feet from the field.

All of this brings up something that is a sore point with fans — and shouldn't be. Many baseball admirers feel that most of the new stadiums are being built with the needs of big corporations in mind, rather than those of the average fan. It's certainly true that considering how many corporate suites can be sold, where an exclusive restaurant can be located, and — most of all — how much revenue this can generate are very much on the minds of team officials when they plan new facilities. Baseball, after all, isn't a crusade. It's a business.

But the next time you go to the stadium, think first about where you sit and where Mr. Corporate Executive sits. If you're really objective about it and remove from the picture the expensive frills he or she is paying for — phones, liquor service, and buffets — that have nothing to do with the game, you're usually going to reach a startling conclusion: "Hey, I've got a better seat than he does!" And, in most stadiums, you'll be right.

What happens in the ballparks is the same thing that happens on an airplane. The people in First Class get the legroom and the drinks, and they pay royally for it, effectively subsidizing the rest of us. In baseball, the system works even better, because "coach" seating, at least in the better sections, generally has the superior view.

The seating system at Atlanta Stadium is arranged as follows:

The Dugout level's dark blue plastic seats ($9.50) are simply wonderful, particularly within the baselines, which run from odd section 109 (first base) to even section 110 (third base). This section, only eleven rows deep at its widest point, directly faces the field. Those seats in double lettered rows — AA, BB, and so forth — are just about close enough to touch the players. Unfortunately, most of the spots in this section are snapped up fast by season ticket holders — you can't even order them by mail. Still, there's nothing to stop you from asking for one at the advance ticket booth. You might get lucky.

Next best is the "family reserved areas" which are dugout level seats located beyond the baselines to the right and left of the field (aisles 11# to 120). You won't be allowed to drink or smoke here, and there will be plenty of kids. You will get a superior view of the game at the price of a field level ticket ($8). Since not that many fans are aware of the existence of these sections, you have a reasonable shot of getting a spot here, even on the day of the game.

Field level seats ($8) are just that, somewhat worn light blue plastic seats overlooking the field, just past the dugout level areas. These are good spots if you follow the basic provisos: stay in the baselines, which are set at odd 109 (first base) to even 110 (third) and in the lowest rows possible. Rows 2 to 15 are best. Rows 23 to 30 are questionable as box seats, although they do get some shade from the upper decks' slight overhang. Unfortunately, rows in this area are *very* long — 25 seats is not unusual — and people getting in and out of their chairs can be quite distracting.

Upstairs, the seats progressively deteriorate. The Club level is a case in point. Charging the same as Dugout seats ($9.50), these sun-baked red chairs are located in the abutment over the back of the field level, sharing this space with the press box (which hogs the home plate area) and the corporate suites. Three rows deep, these aisles offer privacy and some shade. However, the view is not the best — at least not for $9.50. The food selection at this level is limited as well.

The upper level ($6) is worse. Cramped, with smallish red, orange, and yellow seats offering limited legroom and long rows, these spots are strictly for those who want to spend less. That many fans who sit in this area bring binoculars to the game says all that needs to be said about the view. Still, if you need to save a buck, the best spots are in the lower rows and within the baselines, aisles 310 (third) through 307 (first).

Pavilion seats ($6) are located beyond the oufield wall at the field level. They're OK. While the view is reasonably good (probably better than the upper level), so few fans sit there that it's hard to get any real enthusiasm going.

General Admission seats ($4), available the day of the game, fill in the higher spots in the upper level. If you go, bring your binoculars. You'll need them.

There's a factor you should take into consideration no matter where you sit, and that's the sun. Most of the stadium is sun-exposed, and the right field side of the park gets the biggest share of the heat. If you're sun sensitive, try to sit along the third base line.

Special Needs

Parking. Parking for the physically disabled is available directly south of the stadium, next to the players' parking lot. To get to it, pull into the parking lot north of Georgia Avenue and show the attendant your handicapped sticker or plate. You'll be pointed to the lot.

Seating. Handicapped seating is available, too, though it's not the best. These spots are simple wheelchair parking spaces at the ends of row 27 throughout the field level. Though the view isn't bad, handicapped people who "park" in these places will be in danger of being bumped by passing fans. They may also be asked by others to move repeatedly so people can get in and out of their seats.

Atlanta–Fulton County Stadium is one of the increasing numbers of parks that has a "family reserved section." Both alchohol and tobacco are forbidden here, and the spots are in one of the best sections of the stadium.

Food and Features

Food. The food situation at Atlanta–Fulton County Stadium is grim. The selection is poor, costs are not particularly good, and the quality is iffy.

Of course, there's the standard ballpark fare, including "plumper" hot dog, "Super Dogs," and a wretched "corn dog." Other selections include personal pizza (a frozen minipie), chicken sandwich (not recommended), and outrageously priced peanuts. Potato chips and popcorn are a bit more reasonable.

The South has America's best regional foods. But you wouldn't know it from Atlanta Stadium. The sole bow in this direction is a "BBQ Rib" sandwich. Bearing no relation whatsoever to real southern BBQ (which is delicious), this is a fried patty chiefly composed of fat and grizzle. It's a real horror.

Drinks. This being Atlanta, the soft drinks are Coca-Cola products, reasonably priced. Iced tea, the real southern specialty, is unobtainable.

Miller Lite beer seems to be the standard choice of the concessionaires. Oddly, the vendors in the stands have a better selection; some carry Coors and Busch in addition to the Millers. Wine — "Master Cellars Chablis" — is available solely from the nacho stands scattered throughout the park.

As you might expect given the heat, ice cream is popular. Unfortunately, the few ice cream stands attract huge crowds, while employees at the other concessions stand around with their hands in their pockets. So why doesn't management open more ice cream spots? You've got us.

You might want to do what many Braves fans do and skip the stadium food scene altogether. You could, for example, pack a lunch. Coolers can be brought into the facility, as long as they're small enough to fit under your seat and contain neither bottles nor alcoholic beverages. Another possibility is to carry in take-out foods. Two popular spots that cater to this market are the *Kentucky Fried Chicken* outlet that you'll find southeast of the park and *The Varsity*.

Features. As befits a family ballpark, Atlanta Stadium has some features to edify and amuse the fans. An attractive bust of Hank Aaron is located behind Aisle 115 on the lower concourse. The lower concourse also has a speed pitch concession behind aisle 127, while there's a small, closed-in picnic area at the Club level's aisle 227.

Particularly popular with the younger set is the *Kid's Corner*. Here, between the 4th and 8th innings kids (and adults) can come down to meet and be photographed with the Braves' three mascots. These are "Homer the Brave" (a sort of Indian who shoots off a cannon when a home run is hit); "Rally" (a fuzzy baseball, we guess); and the "Furskin Bear" (don't ask us what he's got to do with the game). Anyway, kids like these characters, so you might want to drop by if you have any in tow.

We admit that we're rather partial to "Homer" ourselves.

Assistance

If you are having problems with drunken fans (not likely), seat-jumpers (fairly likely), or simply want to have questions answered, be sure to make a stop at the Guest Relations booth, which can be found behind Aisle 119 on the lower concourse. Even given the fairly high standard of these offices throughout the majors, the Braves assistance people are unusually knowledgeable, friendly, and helpful. You may end up concluding, as we did, that the best thing about the Braves experience is not the team, the stadium, nor (God forbid) the food. Rather, it's the positive, polite attitude of the people who work in the park.

Safety and Security

Safety. Atlanta Stadium has two sides in this area. Inside the park, you are a good deal safer than in the average baseball facility. Outside, you should exercise caution.

The biggest security problem in ballparks relates to alcohol and its side-effects. In Atlanta Stadium, despite a liberal drinking policy that allows in-the-stands sales and has a four-beer per purchase sales "limit," that problem is minimal.

It's really a question of social pressure. In the Midwest, heavy drinking is acceptable, sometimes even encouraged. That, after all, is the German heritage that many Midwesterners were brought up with.

Not so in the South. This is the "Bible belt," and drinking is frowned upon. Accordingly, while alcohol is as accessible in this park as in many others, there's just about no drinking problem to speak of. As a result, swearing

(another Southern "no-no"), fights, abusive language, and obnoxious behavior are rare indeed. If you are unfortunate enough to run into any of these things, a word to any usher will insure that the offender will be told in polite but very direct terms that he or she is to straighten up or leave.

The situation outside the park is another matter. Atlanta, like any big city, has its high-crime neighborhoods. Atlanta Stadium sits in the middle of one of them, though during and after games the area is heavily policed.

We asked an Atlanta police officer whether this was a matter of concern. He seemed a bit offended. "Not at all," he declared, "just as long as you remember to bring a little something with you."

And what was that, we wondered? "A .357 magnum," the officer replied.

Of course, it was meant as a joke. Still, you'd be well advised, especially for night games, to err on the side of caution. If you drive, park you car near the stadium, and (particularly if you're female), go back to it with the crowd. If you're taking the bus to Five Points Stations, move along; don't hang around. Don't decide that it would be a good idea to walk to "Underground Atlanta." If you're dumb enough to try it, a logical route will take you past a street full of 24-hour "Bail Bond" offices; the crowd of people you'll see hanging around these storefronts aren't there because they've got nothing else to do on a summer evening.

We realize that we are overstating Atlanta Stadium's security problem. Yet it's probably better to overstate than understate the difficulty. By all means, go to the game. Just use common sense in leaving it.

Health. Atlanta's hot summer sun is the biggest health hazard in the stadium. Scratches from missed foul balls, indigestion from "BBQ Rib" sandwiches, and the usual spills, falls, and overindulgences are the other threats to your welfare.

The Braves first aid office, behind Aisle 113 on the lower concourse, has a full complement of medical professionals prepared to handle most of these difficulties. Should your needs exceed what they can do, there is an ambulance on site to whisk you off to nearby hospitals. This is the place to report to if you have a baby that needs nursing, a cut that needs bandaging, or if you just want a cool place to sit down.

Mementos

Souvenirs. Braves fans are not big on team-embossed shirts and caps. Still, if you want these things, they're available in the park at a variety of places. Prices are what you'd pay just about anyplace else.

The team also has a "Clubhouse Store" with a much wider selection in downtown Atlanta at the CNN center. It's hours are Monday–Saturday, 10 A.M. to 6 P.M., and Sunday, 10 A.M. to 3 P.M. (404) 523-5854.

Foul Balls. Atlanta–Fulton County Stadium has fairly wide "foul" territories

on its field, so foul ball catching opportunities are somewhat limited. The best spots seem to be in the field level, along aisles 109, 110, 111, and 112.

Autographs. The Braves go out of their way to arrange public autograph sessions, which helps to make up for the limited signing opportunities otherwise available. Generally speaking, Sunday home games in Atlanta feature a structured chance to collect autographs from several players, who will stand in a booth and sign for early-arrivers until about ninety minutes before the game.

Other than that, your chances of getting a signature aren't all that good. Some fans like to stand near the dugouts during batting practice. Occasionally, players will walk over and sign. Outside, after the game, fans collect around the inner-stadium parking ramp, which is between gates H & J. Most of the Braves have their cars inside the stadium; you may get to see a few roaring by. Sometimes players park above, in the secured lot near the ramp. You can occasionally get them.

As far as the visitors go, forget it. Their bus pulls into the stadium, picks people up, and rolls back out.

BALTIMORE ORIOLES
Memorial Stadium

Baseball isn't just a sport of great players and fine plays. It's also an athletic contest in which the interaction between participants and fans is integral to the game.

That certainly isn't the case in most sports. Stuffed into helmets and pads, the gladiators of football are only

barely aware of the crowds, while to the swimmer, runner, and bicyclist, the audience exists only as an indiscriminate blur and roar near the finish line. In some sports, overt reaction from the crowd is not even acceptable. In skating, cricket, and tennis (at least until recently), the audience is allowed, at best, to recognize good performance with polite applause. Comments — especially of the critical kind — are strictly *verboten*.

Baseball was like that at first. In the nineteenth century, fans (then called "kranks") were invited to pay and sit quietly, saluting plays in the same way that you'd recognize a good piano recital. Some of the kranks would get excited even then, of course, and they would fill their parks with cries of approbation — or its reverse. Such emotional outpourings were frowned upon and were the subject of disapproving newspaper editorials and much hand-wringing by owners.

Then one man changed that. In the 1890s, former baseball great Ned Hanlon became manager of the National League Baltimore Orioles. In an exciting decade, Hanlon revolutionized the way the sport was played, turning the game's "gentlemanly" traditions inside out and, in the process, helping to create the game we know today.

At the same time, Hanlon realized that rooting crowds, far from an annoyance, could be a potent offensive tool: they could build morale in his players, help sustain momentum, and leave opponents wishing they were anyplace but Baltimore. Hanlon broke ranks with everyone else in the League and went out of his way to encourage Baltimore kranks to let their feelings be known, preferably as loudly as possible.

Hanlon's innovations caught on, including the one about encouraging fan participation. Thus, baseball moved from being purely a spectator sport to a game at which everyone in the stadium could, at least to a small degree, affect the outcome of the contest. Even if (improbably) Cooperstown is where baseball began, Baltimore was where the cheering started.

Despite some ups and downs in recent years, the cheering in Baltimore continues to this very day. In truth, Memorial Stadium is not the best facility

in baseball, nor is it easy to get to. In terms of comfort and convenience it offers fans, the Oriole's ballpark rates pretty low. But never mind that. In more important other areas, Baltimore excels. Its management is customer oriented and is commited to creating a "family" baseball atmosphere, while its fans are among the most knowledgeable and welcoming in the game. This is one of those parks where "the baseball tradition" is very much a part of the consciousness of those who attend.

In other towns, people go to the game because they want to have a good time. In Baltimore, people trek out to Memorial because they love baseball. There is a difference.

The Team

The story of the Baltimore Orioles is the story of a team, or perhaps a dream, that would not die.

When most people think of the Orioles, they think of the current franchise (since 1954), one of the more successful ballclubs of the modern era. Yet there have been two other "Oriole" teams, dating back to the earliest days of the game. Both made baseball history in their own way.

Baltimore entered baseball in 1872 with a team called the "Lord Baltimores," but that squad failed to make an impact. It was in its later incarnation as the National League Orioles in the 1890s that the team first made history.

The operational genius behind the O's of that era was manager Ned Hanlon, a profane, hard-bitten former Pittsburgh player. During his first season with the club, Hanlon set out on a quest for the tough, no-holds-barred players he'd need for the squad he intended to build. And he found them; the Orioles line-up during that decade included hard-slugging hitters Dan Brouthers and Joe Kelley, diminutive precision slugger "Wee Willie" Keeler (famous for "hitting them where they ain't"), and all around tough-guy third baseman John McGraw. This was a team that, according to one commentator, "breakfasted on gunpowder and warm blood."

Their style of play was creative, dramatic — and downright dirty. When a ball was hit, Hanlon's Orioles snapped to action: bases were covered, positions shifted, and runners were interfered with, if the umpire wasn't watching. Should an umpire make calls against the Orioles, the crowd, with Hanlon's blessing, would howl its displeasure. Fan intimidation became a tool of the game. When the O's came to bat, men on base stood ready, using threatened steals to move opposition players out of position: the hit-and-run play, which had barely been practiced before, became a science in Baltimore.

Occasionally, things got out of hand. Once, an enraged Baltimore fan rushed onto the field, grabbed an ump, and tried to toss him into the stands. The official was rescued in the nick of time. Sometimes, the tricks of Hanlon's crew backfired as well. One of the favorite stunts of John McGraw (first in a long series of great Baltimore third basemen), was to hold onto a runner by the belt for a few seconds after the ball was hit, costing the man several yards. Louisville's great Pete Browning got wind of this and thoughtfully loosened his belt just before tagging third. As Pete sped into home, McGraw was left with Browning's belt hanging incriminatingly from his hand!

Still, this style of ball produced excitement and results: the Orioles won the pennant for three years running (1894, 1895, and 1896) and revolutionized baseball. Six members of Hanlon's original nine ended their careers in Cooperstown.

The fun stopped in 1901. That year, Baltimore joined the American League. After two dispiriting seasons, Balti-more's franchise was sold to New York under mysterious circumstances, and the team thus created later became the Yankees.

Major league ball had left Baltimore, but the game itself, and the Orioles name, refused to die. In its second manifestation, the Orioles emerged as an International League franchise. From the 1900s through the early 1950s, minor league ball had an enthusiastic following in the town, and for good reason: during many of these years (and especially from 1920–25) the Orioles were better than some of the major league teams. Two pitchers in particular excited Baltimoreans; Lefty Grove (who spent much of his career here) and local boy Babe Ruth, who tore up the International League (a 14-6 record by July 1914) during his brief stay with the Orioles.

Major league action returned to Maryland in 1954 when local boosters succeeded in hooking the franchise of the St. Louis Browns, that storied squad that was "first in booze, first in shoes, and last in the American League." The Browns' record as the worst team ever to play in the major leagues was, at first, simply continued in Baltimore. In 1954, the Orioles finished the season 57 games back (but not in last place; that honor was reserved for Philadelphia).

Things stayed bad for a long while. Though the Orioles threatened with a second place finish in 1960, their record continued to be undistinguished. Yet during these years of frequent humiliation, the squad managed to attract some solid talent. Future Hall of Fame players Brooks Robinson, Luis Aparicio, and Frank Robinson came on board, as did long ball hitter "Boog" Powell and pitchers Dave McNally and Jim Palmer.

Then, in 1966, to the surprise of the Orioles and everyone else, they won the American League pennant. The Series, against the powerhouse Los

Angles Dodgers, was expected to be one of the most lopsided in history—and so it was, but it was the Orioles who shut down the Dodgers. While the entire baseball world sat in stunned amazement, the unheralded O's swept the fall classic 4–0. Suddenly, the Orioles had come of age.

Over the next fifteen years, the Orioles, principally under manager Earl Weaver, established one of baseball's great teams. Driven by pitchers Palmer (1990 Hall of Famer), McNally, Mike Cuellar, and, later, Mike Flanagan, and backed by Powell, Ken Singleton, the two Robinsons, and, later, Eddie Murray and Cal Ripken, Jr., the O's won AL East Divisional titles in 1969, 1970, 1971, 1974, 1979, and 1983, pennants in 1969, 1970, 1971, 1979, and 1983, and they took all the marbles in 1970 and 1983. During that era they compiled the best win-loss record in the majors.

With Weaver's departure in 1982, though, things began to go downhill. Sure, there was the 1983 Series victory under Joe Altobelli, but that proved to be a brief Indian Summer before winter set in.

The team continued to have stars. Quality pitchers like Mike Bodicker and Dennis Martinez, great players like Murray and Cal Ripken, Jr., continued to turn in outstanding individual performances, but the team as a whole failed to jell. In 1988, the O's hit rock bottom, setting the all-time record for consecutive losses at the beginning of a season and finishing last. Finally, in 1989, management shed itself of most of its stars (it kept Ripken), brought in a new squad of untried players, and hired former Oriole great Frank Robinson as manager.

At first, this radical approach yielded results. In 1989, the Orioles astounded baseball by finishing a close second in the AL East. In 1990, the team's lack of talent was more apparent. Though the Orioles threatened several times, they faded badly in the last months of the season.

Prospects for the Orioles are currently uncertain. They have a sound manager, one certifiable star (Ripken, a certain Hall of Famer), one good relief pitcher (Gregg Olson), and a bunch of sincere Wannabees who try hard, but too often come up short. Are young players like sluggers Joe Orsulak and Randy Milligan and pitchers Ben McDonald and Dave Johnson really the Robinsons, Powells, and Palmers of their generation, waiting for their 1966? Or are they also-rans? Time will tell.

In the meantime, the Orioles would do well to keep in mind the words of Yoda from the *Star Wars* films. "Do or do not do. There is no try."

The Stadium

Baseball has experienced two great stadium-building periods and may now be at the beginning of a third.

The first period started in the 1910s when it became apparent that the sport was here to stay. Beautiful "neighborhood" parks rose to accommodate the crowds who were flocking to the games. Built mainly by private enterprise at the expense of owners who, for the most part, had once been ball players themselves, these places rarely reveled in conveniences. What they did feature, in compensation, were designs truly amenable to the sport. Only a few of these parks remain today: Wrigley Field, Fenway Park, Yankee and Tiger Stadiums. It is a sad commentary on architecture since then that these remain, in most ways, the best ballparks in operation.

Starting in 1960, the "bigger is better" municipal ballpark movement took hold. Since plenty is said elsewhere in this book about these stadiums, it's only worth mentioning here that most of these parks did provide more convenience and comfort than their predecessors, but at a cost in baseball "feel."

Of course, several stadiums were built between the initial surge of park construction in the 1910s and the second spurt in the 1960s and '70s. One of these parks is Memorial Stadium, which opened in 1954.

It must be admitted right off the bat that, in many ways, Memorial Stadium is one of the poorest facilities in the major leagues.

Its first problem is location. Though set in a nice-enough (though deteriorating) urban neighborhood, Memorial is not near any major roads or highways. Getting there by car can be a pain in the neck.

Once there, parking is a problem, too. Though Memorial has lots, they are small, inconvenient, and designed in such a way as to put your car at risk. Given that Oriole games are pretty popular, space even in the most distant lots has a tendency to run out. That leaves late-comers to seek neighborhood parking, which has problems of its own (see "Security").

So you'll take mass transit? If you live outside of Baltimore, forget it. The transit system is very confusing for any outsider. Even transportation by cab can be a problem: Memorial Stadium is not very near downtown, and it's quite a distance from the airport.

Once at the stadium, you will be standing before an imposing building built out of those institutional red and yellow bricks so popular in the forties and fifties. Outside there is nothing to hold your interest save some lettering on the face of the building, dedicating the stadium to the veterans of World War II.

Inside, darkness predominates. Corridors are dank and fairly dreary. Restrooms are old (though some offer free cologne, and have, a la country clubs, attendants to dry your hands!), and everything looks worn out. Though the food at Memorial Stadium *is* good, concession stands have no overall motifs and look anything but appetizing.

Seating areas of the stadium also do not appeal. As in all stadiums, there are plenty of good seats up close, but in Memorial the number of bad seats truly astounds — over 5,000 have serious (and we mean *serious*) pole obstructions, while thousands more are mere benches set in the boiling sun. Even in the better areas, rows are often long and legroom can be tight.

Memorial's best feature is its field. It's a nice egg-shaped expanse of natural grass, very well-maintained, with, if you can believe it, a small, productive tomato patch running just beyond the left field line. It's there for the benefit of the groundskeeper and his family, who passes out tomatoes to team members from time to time.

This is a pitcher's park. Its lines are regular (indeed, Memorial is reputed to be the hardest place to hit an inside-the-park homer; no one has done it since 1974), with the right field pole set at 387', the left at 376', and the center at 405'.

Memorial is a hard place to "hit the ball out of the park." In fact, in the team's history, only one person — Frank Robinson — has ever done it. That's saying quite a bit when you consider that Mickey Mantle, Boog Powell, Roger Maris, Reggie Jackson (briefly an Oriole), and Bo Jackson are among the long-ball hitters who've played here.

New Stadium

As many fans are aware, the limitations — and heritage — of Memorial Stadium will soon be a memory. Currently, the Orioles are building a new stadium, which will be located in downtown Baltimore in the "Camden Yards" section, just south of the trendy "Harbor Place" district. It will feature easy access to highways, mass transportation, hotels, and restaurants. Scheduled to open in 1993, center field in the new park will be located directly over the remains of "Ruth's Cafe," one of the Bambino's numerous boyhood homes in the town.

The Orioles' plans for this new facility have attracted even more than usual interest. That's because it is the stated intention of the club and the state of Maryland to create a park that will capture both the spirit and the design features of the classic stadiums of the 1910s, bringing into the park at the same time the conveniences fans have come to expect in the 1990s.

Will the Orioles succeed in accomplishing this? At this point, no one can say. However, if they can pull it off, the Birds will do baseball a singular service.

Highlights

Given its six World Series appearances, Memorial Stadium has seen lots of moments of baseball history.

Few Baltimore fans will ever forget the fourth and final game of the 1966 Series (October 9, 1966), where the Dodgers bowed to the Orioles, thanks to a shut-out delivered by Dave McNally and a game winning home run courtesy of Frank Robinson. In the third game of the 1970 series versus Cincinnati, McNally showed that he knew one end of a bat from another, too, driving in three runs on a homer and delighting the crowd.

Equally memorable was Frank Robinson's whole 1966 season. Traded to the Orioles by the Cincinnati Reds for some minor players, it seemed as if Robinson was washed up. "He's an old 30," the Reds manager said, justifying the swap. Robinson went on, that year, to win the Triple Crown and to become the first and only player to win MVP in both leagues.

There has been no-hitter action in the park as well. Hoyt Wilhelm, during his stay with the club, pitched the stadium's first no-hitter on September 20, 1958, versus New York. Jim Palmer hurled another on August 13, 1969, against Oakland.

There have been moments of humor, too. During one game, champion Oriole jokester John Lowenstein was hit by a savage pitch. Dropping like a rock, it looked as if Lowenstein had gone down for the count. Thousands stood in horror as a stretcher rushed to carry him to the ambulance. Just before the stretchers headed out the gate, Lowenstein bounded off the bed, raised his hands, and bowed to the crowd. The audience went wild.

Fans

What makes a baseball fan? It's an appropriate question to ask, for Oriole admirers are pretty much conceded to be among the most committed baseball people around. What, therefore, makes a Bird fancier different from the sorts of people who like the Padres or the Twins?

One clear characteristic is his or her knowledge of the game. In some parks, the complaints or praise are merely general statements: "Boy, they stink tonight!" or, "Gee, they're really hot!"

Not so in Baltimore. At Memorial, every action, every decision that is made — or not made — is subject to analysis and scrutiny, most of it surprisingly informed. It's not just, "boy, they stink"; in Baltimore, it's more like, "Robinson never should have traded Bradley. What did Kittle do for the White Sox, that's what I want to know?" or, "I told you they were smart in bringing up Leadfeet from Rochester. Who says the guy can't run?"

The hard-core fans, too, know that true enjoyment of the game comes only with a little work. In many stadiums that serve a middle class audience, people are happy to put down their pens and go to the ballpark. In places like Baltimore, where the audience is largely — but by no means exclusively — working class, fans go to the game to pick their pencils up. Many fans buy scorecards in Baltimore, and this is one park where, when you do buy a program, you're often handed a sharpened pencil without asking for it. The idea is that of course you'll want to keep score. Many Baltimore fans also wear a Walkman so they can listen to the play-by-play.

A third characteristic of the devoted baseball zealot is a certain sociability. Go to an Oriole game and, unless you make it clear you'd rather be left alone, you are very likely to be drawn into a conversation about the team, their prospects, and their players. Real fans are almost always polite (they are outstandingly so in Baltimore) to outsiders — excepting, of course, the umpires.

Finally, the true fan is loyal. They may curse their team (in Philadelphia, another den of the baseball zealot, fans seem to take a perverse joy in doing this), but they will not abandon it. Although you will not likely see much of this behavior in Baltimore, which tends to identify with the more courteous South, in many of the stadium's where "baseball fans" are strong (Fenway, the Vet, Yankee) you will see much booing and hostility directed toward poorly performing players, or even toward the home team itself. Nevertheless, you will almost never see these cross-grained fans leave the stadium before the last ball has been pitched. The thought that they might miss a 9th-inning rally which would lead to victory is just intolerable to them.

Who are these Baltimore baseball purists? They're a largely male, mosty working class group of folks, with better minority representation than in most parks, and with a sprinkling of yuppies and even some Washington politicos and intellectuals thrown in (conservative columnist George Will is at most games; George Bush shows from time to time). Thanks to clever marketing plans, they are drawn from a wide geographic area. Plates from Delaware, Virginia, Pennsylvania,, and the District of Columbia are common in Memorial's bulging parking lots, while those from New Jersey and even North Carolina are not unknown. Though it was not always so (see "Security"), this is now a very "family oriented" crowd. There are a fair number of mother-father-kids combos, and a lot more father-son units. Nor are fathers carrying their babies around in backpacks all that unusual here, either. Memorial Stadium is one of the few parks that has diaper-changing tables in the men's restrooms as well as the women's. They get used.

If baseball, to the Baltimore fan, is a sort of male bonding rite (and it is) it's a social ritual as well. Not only does the Bird admirer like to drink beer and chat about the game but also he enjoys feeling a part of it. Though it is not one of the older parks, Memorial is rich in baseball traditions. When the fans sing the "Star Spangled Banner" (which was written in Baltimore), they often make a circle with their arms at "O say" — as in Orioles. During August and September, if the Birds are still in contention, they also give an extra shout to "still there!!!" in the line "and our flag was still there," just to let the nation know they're still around. When a fan barehands a foul ball (a frequent ocurrence here; people take pride in making the catch), you will sometimes hear people chant "Contract! Contract!" Sure enough, someone from a local radio station will rush into the stadium and sign the alert fan to an Orioles contract, requiring that he or she report for spring training on request.

To the die-hard baseball fan, and

especially to the Bird admirer, loyalty to the team is driven by an innate recognition that, as important as the game is to the fan, the fan is pretty important to the team, too—and not simply because of economics. Oriole fans believe that, in essence, they share a oneness with the team, that their relationship is shared, and, in a way, mutually complementary.

A number of years ago, Orioles fans gave a beautiful example of how real this feeling is in this baseball-obsessed city. In 1982, the Birds faced the Brewers in a last-game-of-the-season contest that would decide the AL East championship. It also happened to be Earl Weaver's last game.

The Birds lost. Nevertheless, 51,000 Oriole fans stayed in the stadium for a quarter of an hour, mutually refusing to leave, chanting "We Want Earl!" until Weaver came out to accept their grateful, tumultuous applause. As Howard Cosell put it, "It was a moment for Baltimore to show the world that there's something more important than winning."

Getting There

Memorial Stadium is one of the harder parks in the majors to get to. If you are able to find it, parking can be difficult to locate. The car is probably your best option, though you can also get to Memorial by cab and, with some difficulty, by bus.

By car. Those coming from Washington, D.C., northern Virginia and other *south* destinations should take I-95 north to the Baltimore-Washington Parkway (Exit 22), heading toward Baltimore. Follow the B-W Parkway into Baltimore city. Once there, make a right on Pratt Street, then a left onto Calvert. Finally, make a right on 33rd Street. Memorial Stadium is nine blocks down.

From Wilmington, Philadelphia, and

points *east*, take I-95 west to the Baltimore Beltway (I-695), heading toward Towson. Proceed to Exit 30 Perring Parkway, and follow Perring (which, after awhile, becomes Hillen Road) south to 33rd Street. Turn right on 33rd and follow to stadium.

From Harrisburg, York, and areas *northwest*, follow I-83 south to I-695 (Baltimore Beltway), toward "Baltimore." From I-695, take Exit 23 Jones Falls Expressway. Follow the Jones Falls Expressway to the 28th Street East exit. Follow 28th Street East to Calvert Street. Make a left on Calvert, and follow to 33rd Street. Make a right on 33rd and follow to ballpark.

From Hagerstown, and other *west* points, take I-70 to I-695. Go north on I-695, then exit south onto the Jones Falls Expressway. Follow to Exit 7 (28th Street East), and proceed on 28th until you hit Calvert, where you'll turn left. Follow Calvert to 33rd. Turn right on 33rd and proceed to stadium.

By cab. It isn't cheap to take a cab to the stadium, but it's an option. A cab from the Baltimore-Washington Airport should run $17 or so one way. From the downtown hotels, the fare will be about $7 one way.

By bus. Though it isn't easy, you can take a Baltimore Mass Transit bus to the game. Take bus #3 (33rd Street) from the downtown area and ask the bus driver to let you off at Memorial Stadium. The BMTs number is (301) 539-5000.

Parking

The parking situation at Memorial Stadium is not great. Altogether, the team has four lots and about 3,500 spaces total—not nearly enough for the crowd.

The best spots are those around the stadium. They, however, are limited to season ticket holders and the handicapped. Also OK are the Venable and

South lots across 33rd Street from the park. At these places you'll be asked to park bumper to bumper—no spaces between cars. Predictably, this area turns into a zoo when the game is over. If you get out with your car and temper intact, you will have done well. The charge is $4.

The last official parking option is to drive down 33rd to the lots at Lake Montebello. In some ways, the situation here is better than it is at the other lots, but you end up half a mile from the stadium. There is an often crowded $.25 shuttle bus to the game. The parking charge is $3.

Beyond these options, you could try parking in the surrounding neighborhoods. All we can say is, lots of luck. Though some area residents offer decent parking in their yards at reasonable rates, watch out for scams. Some people will stand outside someone else's home with a sign, charge you to park in the driveway, and then disappear. When the enraged owner comes home, you're likely to be towed. To make matters worse, the Baltimore police patrol the area heavily during the game, ticketing or hauling away the auto of anyone who isn't parked where he should be.

Our advice is to arrive early, get a close-in space, and have a bite to eat while watching batting practice.

Tickets

Oriole tickets can be ordered by mail, phoned for, picked up in person, or purchased at the game.

Mail orders are probably a good idea here, given that really fine seats can be tough to find during popular matchups. To order by mail, send your check or money order to Ticket Office, Baltimore Orioles, Memorial Stadium, Baltimore, MD 21218. Be sure to give the dates and sections you want, and include an extra $1 for the Orioles' service charge.

Phone orders are accepted, too. Call the Ticketcenter line at (301) 481-6000 from 10 A.M. to 10 P.M. to get your seats. Be prepared with your major credit card. A service charge is assessed here as well.

Visiting the advance ticket office is a good idea, too, since you can look at a seating chart before making your selection. The advance ticket window at Memorial Stadium can be found at gate W-2. It's open from 9 to 6, Monday through Saturday.

Availability. Despite its poor performance in several of the last few seasons, the Orioles are still a pretty hot ticket. They've racked up attendance figures in the very respectable 2.5 million range in recent years, and they usually sell about 15,000 season tickets.

As a result, though Memorial Stadium is big (53,371 seats), the place can get pretty packed during popular matchups (particularly against New York, Boston, and Toronto) and on weekend day games. Thus, if you show up intending to buy your tickets at the game, you could end up broiling on an aluminum bench out in the bleachers or sitting behind a pole.

Generally, however, you *will* get a ticket—for a simple if inconvenient reason. That's because Memorial runs out of parking spots long before it runs out of seats. So if you are able to find a spot outside the stadium, you'll likely find one inside as well. (On the other hand, if you come late, you may join those who spend a frustrating hour or two finding neither.)

Costs. Oriole tickets aren't all that cheap for what you get. Terrace boxes, for example, go for $10, even though they are fairly far from the field. Still, at least the ticket pricing pattern makes sense. Inexpensive tickets provide poor or obstructed views, while high-priced spots let you see the action.

The Orioles' 1990 price schedule was as follows: Lower Box Seats ($11); Mezzanine Box Seats ($10); Terrace Box

Seats ($10); Upper Box Seats ($8.50); Lower Reserved ($7.50); Upper Reserved ($7.50); Lower Grandstand Reserve ($6.50); General Admission (Adult [$4.75]); (Child/Senior [$1.50]); (Student [$2.50]).

It should be noted that the Orioles, though they tell you in advance that you are getting one, sell their "obstructed view" tickets for the same prices as their regular tickets.

Rainouts. You can generally count on several rainouts in Baltimore each season. Should it happen to you, your ticket can be exchanged for another game. If you live 75 miles or more outside of Baltimore, however, you are eligible for a refund. Just write to the ticket office explaining the situation.

Seating

Seating really runs the gamut at Memorial Stadium, from fine spots close to the action to aluminum benches under a broiling sun. Happily, ticket prices bear some relation to value.

Lower box seats are the most expensive spots ($11) and the best. Coded blue on the map, these are comfortable chairs, rising gradually back from the field. If you're able to get a seat here (not always easy, thanks to the large

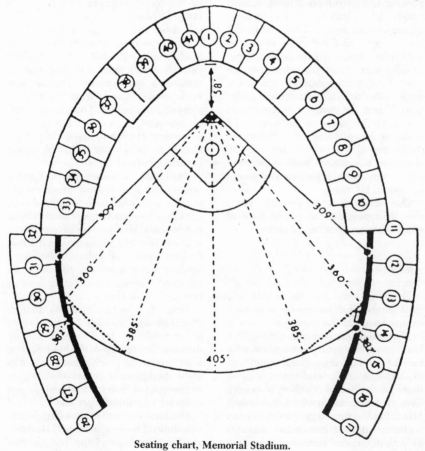

Seating chart, Memorial Stadium.

number of season ticket holders), try to stay in the baselines, which run from sections 1 to 7 on the left field side and 41 to 37 on the right field line. (These are the baseline dimensions throughout the park.)

If you can't find something in the baselines in the lower box seats, you might want to check out the Mezzanine boxes ($10), which are a level upstairs. These are comfortable wood and metal chairs, painted yellow. Thanks to the design of Memorial Stadium, this middle deck hangs out pretty far over the boxes—if you get a spot in rows A or B within the baselines, you will be close to the action indeed. Be careful, however, when you order seats on this mezzanine level: past the baselines on either side you will not, in rows C and D, be able to see all of the field.

Terrace boxes ($10) are available, too. Dark green seats a section across from and directly behind the box seats, these are perfectly acceptable spots, though a bit far from the action. Baseline seats, as always, are best.

Upper box seats ($8.50) are not for those who fear heights. Located way above the action, these spots would not even be termed "boxes" in most stadiums. However, the design of Memorial does put you closer to the action here than in the upper deck of many other parks. Also, all of the upper boxes are set in the baselines.

Beyond these areas, seats decline rapidly in quality. Lower reserved spots (light green wooden chairs, $7.50) are beaten up seats on the first level. Thousands of these spots have pole obstructions; the rest are really packed in. Upper reserved seats ($7.50) are likewise not up to snuff. Aluminum benches with backs, these spots are practically in the clouds: you may see more of the feathered sort of orioles here than the ones with bats. Lower grandstand reserved seats ($6.50) are bleacher spots behind right and left field that you can reserve—at a much higher price. Aluminum benches very exposed to the sun, these seats are very hot but are reasonably close to the action. Accordingly, we like them better than the more costly upper reserved chairs. Those located in left field (sections 12–15) are to be preferred, as they are less exposed to the sun. Past the lower grandstand, and at the far extremes of the upper deck, are the general admission seats ($4.75). Distant from the action and uncomfortable, their relatively low price is all that recommends them. Those in the bleacher sections are better than those on the top deck.

Special Needs

Parking. Handicapped parking is available in the East lot, which is located directly to the east of the stadium. Simply pull into the area and show your sticker or plate; you will be pointed in the right direction. The charge is $4.

Seating. Handicapped seating is set in two areas. The first of these is the lower boxes ($11), directly behind home plate. These seats are some of the best spots in the park. Also available are other seats behind the lower grandstand area ($7.50), past the baselines in right and left field. These places aren't nearly as good. Since there are only 42 handicapped spots in the park, it is almost always essential for you to reserve in advance.

Food and Features

Food. The food at Memorial Stadium is pretty good. There's decent variety, good quality, and prices that are no worse than in other stadiums.

Standard ballpark fare can be found throughout the facility: hot dogs (unaccountably, "Kosher hot dogs" available at "Fan Fare" cost less), pizza slices, soft serve cones, nachos, peanuts, and popcorn.

Beyond traditional ballpark fare, there are a number of specialties. These include "Maryland Crab Cakes," grilled sausages and bratwurst, chicken fillet sandwiches, and garden salads. Probably the standout item is pasta with red or white sauces, which is surprisingly good and reasonably priced.

Drinks. Of course, the usual Coke products are on hand, and Busch is the standard brew. At the "Beers of the World" stands located throughout the main concourse you can get such import brews as Heineken, Becks, Corona, and St. Pauli Girl. Wine drinkers will find Inglenook chablis available at "Fan Fare" outlets.

Features. Memorial Stadium isn't loaded with features, but there are some. A "Speed Pitch" concession is located behind section 11 on the lower concourse, while a "player photo booth" can be found behind section 8. Occasionally you'll also run into the Baltimore "Oriole," the team's popular mascot. The bird has a great costume, and looks cute when he rides around the field on his motor scooter. However, the Oriole doesn't seem to play as big a role in the game as, say, the Philly Phanatic.

Probably Baltimore's best feature, and an idea other teams would do well to emulate, is the kid's playground behind the scoreboard in right field. Open just before and during the contest, this is the place to take little kids for an inning or two if they're getting restless. You'll find the entrance to the park behind section 27 (right field) on the lower concourse.

Assistance

The Orioles' fan assistance office is located behind section 41 (home plate) of the main concourse. This is the place to go if you're being bothered by obnox-ious fans or have questions or suggestions.

Safety and Security

Safety. For some time now, employees at baseball parks have been seeing a horror film that shows what can happen in a park if you let drinking get out of hand. In the movie, a wild, drunken band of fans are shown to have virtually seized control of a stadium section; they shout curses at opposing players, dance on the dugouts, and seem dedicated to making themselves as obnoxious as possible. These scenes were filmed at Memorial.

Some years ago, a group of Oriole admirers, lead by a particularly rambunctious fan, almost single-handedly turned Memorial into a "problem park"—the kind of place that families weren't sure they wanted to go to. To be fair to these fans, they certainly provided some entertainment—but many Baltimoreans considered their antics a pain in the neck.

Orioles management decided to regain control. On the alcohol side, they banned tailgating in the parking lots, cutoff alcohol sales in the seventh inning, and insisted that vendors stop serving to people who had clearly had enough. On the family side, the team brought in the Oriole mascot to keep the children entertained, featured a lot of kid promotions, and established a playground (see "Features").

These techniques worked. Today, although drunkeness and rowdyism are not totally absent from Memorial, the place can truly be said to be a "family park." More important, the Orioles established a pattern for reform that has had a profound effect on improving alcohol control and safety in parks throughout the leagues.

Outside the park, the security situation is also good. Though they are not secured, the parking lots are reasonably safe, as is the neighborhood around Memorial.

Health. Fans at Memorial face three health threats. First, many of the seats — particularly in the right field bleachers — get a lot of sun. Bring a cap and plenty of lotion if you intend to sit there. Second, the upper reserved section is really high here. Though there are escalators to this area, it's a tough climb to most seats even from them. Thus, if you have a heart condition or a few extra years, you might want to choose a spot on the lower level. Finally, a lot of foul balls tend to land in the upper deck box seats: the temptation to reach over to catch one is great here, and it would be all too easy to go over the rail. Be careful. Should you have a scratch that needs bandaging or if you simply need to get out of the sun for awhile, the first aid office is behind section 3 on the lower concourse. There's another office at the upper deck, behind 41, that's also open when the crowd is particularly big.

Mementos

Souvenirs. Orioles fans like to wear them. The best selection in the park is behind lower concourse section 36. Prices are moderate.

Foul balls. Barehand one here and you may end up with an Orioles contract as well as a ball. However, you'll have lots of competition in trying to snag one — half the future Babe Ruths of Baltimore attend every game, glove at the ready.

Lower sections 6 and 7 (left field) and 37 and 38 (right field) are good places to sit, but the best area may be upper boxes 39, 40, 41, 1, 2, and 3, which are wrapped behind home plate.

Autographs. Baltimore is a good place to get signatures. Orioles leave the stadium for their parking lot from Gate W-2. Visitors board their bus at Gate E-2.

BOSTON RED SOX
Fenway Park

What makes a ballpark, or for that matter any public building, beautiful?

For most of the past fifty years or so, architects seem to have operated on the assumption that if something is useful and maybe impressive, it is therefore attractive as well. Believing that "form should follow function," builders have filled our cities with tall dark boxes and called them skyscrapers, loaded our suburbs with short narrow boxes and called them homes, and inundated our metropolitan centers with huge concrete circles and styled them baseball

parks. Everywhere the emphasis has been on symmetry, uniformity, and keeping everything in balance.

This idea of architectural balance is so deeply set in our minds now that most of us believe it to be a requirement of art. The theory is that such "balance" is necessary to please and satisfy the mind. But uniformity doesn't delight the mind; it deadens it. Happily, our great grandparents did not subscribe to modern theories. They lived in a day when most builders would probably have agreed with poet Alexander Pope's dictum that "He gains all points who pleasingly confounds, Surprises, varies, and conceals the Bounds." Following no strictly "right" way to make a building, they strove to create edifices that would delight as well as serve, and that, most importantly, would bear the mark of their creator. These people built many ugly buildings to be sure, and some ugly ballparks as well. But they created many others that were uniquely beautiful.

One of these is Fenway Park. After the recent destruction of Comiskey, Fenway now shares with Tiger Stadium the distinction of being the oldest park in baseball, for, at least officially, both were opened on the same day in 1912. These two, along with Wrigley Field (1916), now constitute the remaining "classic" parks in the game. Though Tiger Stadium certainly has many strengths, most people who have been to the three would admit that Fenway and Wrigley are, overall, more appealing facilities. Of these two, a case could be made that Wrigley is the more beautiful. It would be hard to believe, though, that anyone would dispute that Fenway is the most interesting stadium in the game.

Tell people that you've attended a game at Fenway and the first thing people ask is generally not "Did Clemens pitch?" Or "How'd Boggs do?" Rather, you'll be asked your opinion of "the Green Monster," Fenway's famous outfield wall, which is the most familiar architectural feature of any ballpark. Stick around for awhile and your questioner, if he or she is a baseball fan, will certainly ask about Fenway's twisty outfield, its diminutive size, and its old-fashioned scoreboard with the names of the team's owners written in Morse code on it. Fenway is a stadium that has captured the imagination of fans across North America.

So, for that matter, has the team that plays in it. The Boston Red Sox may not be the most popular team in baseball, but only the Yankees and perhaps one or two other squads can be said to have had an equal power to keep fans fascinated for so long. Part of the interest is caused by the legendary players who have, over the decades, taken the field at Fenway, a list that includes Ruth, Williams, and Yastrzemski, to name but a few. Yet at least as compelling for fans is what has come to be called "The Curse of the Bambino," the fact that the often spectacular Sox have not won a World Series since Babe Ruth and Carl Mays each put two games away for them in 1918. Shortly thereafter, the Sox sold their star Ruth (and traded Mays) to the Yankees. The Sox have not won a Series since.

Did Ruth really put the hex on Boston? There's no record of it. We can, however, tell you for a fact that everyone in Beantown believes the story. One more finish like the Sox had in their 1986 Series against the Mets and we will believe it, too.

A few years ago, in an ad campaign, Swiss authorities adopted as their slogan "Switzerland. It's worth it." The phrase was intended to counter the principal objection people had to taking an Alpine vacation, which was that the country had gotten too expensive. The slogan, though, is something you should keep in mind when you visit the Sox. We'd like to be able to tell you that your visit to Fenway will be pure enjoyment, with few or no inconveniences. It just isn't so. Boston traffic is terrible, the parking situation at the stadium is bad, Red Sox ticket prices are high, Fenway's food isn't all that good, and the Sox's management is less than totally committed to customer satisfaction.

Should you therefore stay away? Heck no. Even with these difficulties, attending a game at Fenway has got to be among the finest experiences a baseball fan can have. Boston, in turn, is one of the most exciting, attractive, and interesting cities to visit on the continent. Is Fenway worth it? You bet.

The Team

The Red Sox may not be the oldest team in baseball, but as far as the American League goes, they can truthfully say that they were there at the beginning. One of the original American League franchises, the Bostonians—then styled the "Puritans"—quickly displayed the fine play that marked their first two decades in the majors. The Puritans placed second during the AL's first campaign, stayed competitive in the second, and went on to take a pennant in 1903.

That was the year of the first World Series. Before the start of The Classic, all the money was on the Sox's opponents, the long established Pittsburgh Pirates led by the great Honus Wagner. Boston, behind the stellar pitching of Cy Young, carried the contest 5–3 in a result that so infuriated the Nationals, who had expected an easy win, that they refused to participate in a 1904 contest.

Boston stayed close to the pack for the rest of the decade, but did not return to the Series until the 1910s, a decade that would prove without a doubt the greatest in the Sox's history. Powered by such great pitchers as Smoky Joe Wood, Carl Mays, and Ruth and outfielders Harry Hooper and Tris Speaker, the Sox made four trips to the Series (1912, 1915, 1916, and 1918) and came home with the trophy each time. Little, of course, did the triumphant Bostonians realize that, having won four Series in seven years, they would not win another for seventy-two years—at least.

This was an interesting time in the sport, and the Sox had their share of colorful players, of whom Ruth was one of the most consistently fascinating. Normally a pleasant man, Ruth could get hot under the collar when umpires made what he considered bad calls. Once in 1917, while pitching against Washington, the Bambino got in a dispute with umpire Brick Owens, an argument that resulted in the star rushing the batter's box and getting at least one good punch in before being carted away by the police. Brought in to relieve Ruth, Ernie Shore than proceeded to pitch a perfect game, the only one ever hurled in Fenway.

Starting in 1918, Boston's owner, hungry for cash, began selling off his best players one by one. Ruth and Mays went to the Yanks, others headed elsewhere, and the team's standing sank accordingly. During his last year with the club, the Red Sox decided to throw a "Babe Ruth Day" celebration to honor their star. Charging for the affair, the Sox pulled in 15,000 fans and then proceeded to give the Babe a cigar in the ceremony. They also charged him for his wife's ticket. If Ruth didn't put a curse on Boston, he should have.

If the 1910s were the Sox's golden years, the next two decades were the team's dark ages. During twenty dismal campaigns the Sox placed in the lower division virtually every year, taking as their sole compensation the fact that during most of this period they were somewhat less pathetic than the Boston Braves. Sure Boston had some stars during these times, such as pitchers Lefty Grove and sluggers Jimmy Foxx and Bobby Doerr, but they were unable to bring the Sox back to their glory days.

With the appearance of Ted Williams in 1939, things started to improve. Saying to the press before his first Boston plate appearance that his goals were modest and that he just wanted people to say when he walked by, "there goes the greatest hitter that ever lived," Williams single-mindedly pursued his goal to become just that. No player in the history of the game ever made a more intensive study of the art of slugging than Williams did, and probably only one player (Ruth) can seriously challenge Williams' claim to being the greatest hitter. Williams' 1941 mark of

.406 is the highest of modern era, and it seems likely to remain unmatched for many years to come.

You would think that Red Sox admirers would have been gleeful to have Williams on their side, but actually Ted had a difficult time with the fans throughout his career in Boston. An intense and sometimes moody man with a decided loner streak, Williams managed to alienate much of the Boston sports press early in his term of service, and many local journalists proceeded to cast everything Williams said or did thereafter in the worst light. Before he had been with the team for very long, Williams was sometimes booed at Fenway while being treated to rapturous applause elsewhere. Thus began what has, since, been a feature of Boston baseball: the fact that Red Sox enthusiasts sometimes take a dislike to some of their team's greatest stars.

Whether Williams was liked or disliked, there is no question that his performance and presence energized the club. After years in the doldrums, Boston pennant races got exciting. The team went to the Series in 1946, and, though they fell to the Cardinals 4–3, at least the team had shown the world that they were alive. The team also, though, established a pattern that has bedeviled them to this day: doing well through most of the season, only to fall apart at the end.

The 1950s and 1960s brought such great new players as Jackie Jensen, Carl Yastrzemski, Rico Petrocelli, and Tony Conigliaro to the squad. These years also brought close but ultimately unsuccessful pennant challenges. Boston did manage to go to the classic in 1967, but it was against the same team (the Cards), with the same outcome. Worse yet, Tony Conigliaro's career was cut short in a tragic beaning incident.

Red Sox admirers had every reason to believe that the 1970s would be their decade. After all, not only did they still have Yastrzemski; they also had en-rolled such standout players as pitcher Luis Tiant, catcher Carlton Fisk, and sluggers Jim Rice, Fred Lynn, and Dwight Evans. Yet once again, ultimate victory eluded the squad, even though in 1975 they and the Cincinnati Reds gave baseball what may have been the finest Series of all time.

During the 1980s, the Red Sox put on one of their most aggressive campaigns ever, winning AL East championships in 1986, 1988, and 1990, and enduring a horrible 4–3 Series loss to the Mets in 1986, in which they literally came within one strike of capturing the prize that has eluded them so long.

Currently, Boston is fielding one of the strongest teams in baseball. Standout players include future Hall of Famer Wade Boggs, who presently stands fourth on the all-time batting average list, MVP and double Cy Young–winning pitcher Roger Clemens, hard playing sluggers Jack Clark, Ellis Burks, Tom Brunansky, and Mike Greenwell. There is no doubt that these people have the ability to take the Red Sox all the way. The only question is, will they? Or will "the curse of the Bambino" once again stand between Boston and victory?

The Bible tells us that "the sins of the fathers are inherited by the sons, unto the third generation." If that's true, then the Sox's term in baseball purgatory should be just about over.

The Stadium

Like the other classic ballparks, Fenway is located neither downtown nor in the suburbs. Rather, the stadium is set in an urban neighborhood of the sort that millions of Americans lived in prior to the Second World War. About two miles southwest of downtown Boston, just past student-dominated Kenmore Square (which is close to Boston University), the area around the park is known to Bostonians as "the Fens," which is an English term that means marshes. At the time of the American Revolution, the neighborhood was just that, a marshy area that was part of the nearby Charles River. Various projects over the years reclaimed the land and made this part of Boston possible. When the baseball park was located in this area, it was named after this section of the city.

It is, overall, a fairly pleasant place. The area directly surrounding the park is a not especially attractive mixed commercial area of warehouses, souvenir stands, and nightclubs. On the other hand, a few blocks south of the facility you'll find a nice section of middle class homes, student apartments, and some good, inexpensive restaurants.

Approaching Fenway, you'll be surprised at the suddeness with which the place appears. The only real one-deck stadium in the majors, Fenway is set low to the ground and is only a bit higher than the surrounding buildings. If you are coming from the Kenmore Square subway station, for example, you'll first see it only when you cross the bridge over the Massachusetts Pike a few hundred yards from the gate. If you are talking with a friend, you may not really catch it at all.

One thing you will certainly notice is the crowd. Before every Red Sox session, a veritable festival occurs outside the stadium as food vendors fry sausages and bark them to the fans, as souvenir sellers try to hawk "genuine" balls signed by the Sox, and as Boston's ferocious scalpers weave through the patrons muttering under their breath, "You buyin'?" and, if you ignore that, "You sellin'!?" People line up for clam sandwiches at "The Batter's Box" on Yawkey Way, party at "The Cask and Flagon," and argue with street sellers over how much a Topp's Clemens "rookie" is really worth. We strongly suggest that you tarry awhile and take all of this in before going inside the stadium. Fenway has, along with

Wrigley, the most vibrant pre-game "street scene" in baseball.

Once past the gate at Fenway, you may wonder what the fuss over this stadium is all about, for the bowels of this park are singularly unattractive. The facility's one corridor is dark and dank, the restrooms are less than immaculate, and the lines you'll see at the concession stands will usually be long—though why anyone would wait in line for Fenway food beats us. Is this the great Fenway Park everyone talks about?

Once you move to the seating area, though, your doubts vanish like fog under a blazing sun. Stretched before you will be that crazy, challenging field that's like no other in the game. Wrapped to either side will be seats so close to the action that you'll wonder that play isn't interrupted by fans grabbing in-play balls more often than they do. Just what shape is Fenway? That's hard to say. It certainly isn't a circle, nor is it a "U," nor even a rectangle. We guess it must be a sort of irregular hexagon, though it's probably more accurate to say that it is "Fenway-shaped."

The seating areas will cause you either to whoop for joy or to gnash your teeth, dependng on where you get put. Fenway's tiny size (with 34, 182 seats it is the smallest park in baseball) insures that every chair has a great view—if it has a view at all! The problem is that Fenway's Reserved Grandstand area is littered with obstructing poles. In some places in the park, seats are literally right behind a pole, something we have seen at no other facility. Nor is there any absolute guarantee that, if you are to be seated behind an obstruction, you'll be told that before you buy your ticket: sometimes the fact is mentioned, and sometimes it isn't. So you should always ask. As for the chairs themselves, many are fairly comfortable plastic and metal seats, though some sections still have the old-fashioned (and hard) wood and metal ones.

The field is, along with the Sox, what you came to Fenway for, and it is a wonder. A tidy expanse of natural green, the place has the shortest left field in baseball, with the foul pole set at 315'. Running from the left field pole to center field is the celebrated "Green Monster," which turns what ought to be a home run heaven park into something less than that. Rising 37' over the field, the wall is baseball's most formidable obstacle. Hardly a game passes in Fenway, in fact, when an in-play ball doesn't hit the wall, sending the Sox's left fielder scurrying to catch the bounce while opposing players try to figure out whether they should try for an extra base or not.

Were it not for the "Monster," center field is what would catch everybody's attention at the stadium, for the simple fact that is has a crazy indentation. Starting at 379' on the left, center rapidly sinks to 420', and then, at a virtual right angle, soars forty feet back to 380'. The effect of all this is that balls in deep center can smack one of the walls and, in effect, act like pinballs, bouncing from side to side while Sox outfielders futilely try to grab them. On the other hand, visitors can crack one out to center and take a leisurely tour of the bags, confident that they've homered, only to find out that they have—damn Fenway!—put a live one "in the hole." It's little wonder that opposing players either hate or love this park. Absolutely no one is ever moderate on the place.

By contrast, right field is at least somewhat more regular, though the field does dive in shockingly at the last moment to a foul pole set at a short 302'.

In addition to the field itself, which is Fenway's main feature, there are some other things about the place that you should note. On the "Green Monster" is mounted Fenway's famed old-fashioned hand-operated scoreboard, one of only two left in the majors (the other is at Wrigley). It is, by the way, one of only three scoreboards that is in play. Sure enough, if you know your Morse Code, you'll note that the unobtrusive dots and dashes on the board do spell out Tom and Jean Yawkey, the ownership team that took the Sox out of the doldrums and brought them back to greatness. Over the roof near the right field wall are four circular plaques with the Sox's retired numbers: #9, Ted Williams; #8, triple crown winner Carl Yastrzemski; #1, second baseman Bobby Doerr; #4, shortstop and former manager Joe Cronin. Now if they would just have the sense to put the Babe up there, maybe he'd leave them alone.

Highlights

With the disappearance of Comiskey, the number of ballparks where Babe Ruth, Joe DiMaggio, Lou Gehrig, and the other American League greats of the thirties played is now down to a handful: Yankee, Tiger, Cleveland, Fenway, and Wrigley—for the Cubs competed against the Yankees in the Series during these years. Go back a generation further, when such stars as Nap Lajoie, Christy Mathewson, and Honus Wagner took the field, and you are down to just Fenway, Tiger, and Wrigley. Thus the biggest highlight about these parks is simply that these are the places where these now almost mythical figures strove, swore, sweated, and swatted their way into history.

Still, there are a few Fenway dates that you should be aware of. June 23, 1917, was the day when Babe Ruth was ejected for punching an umpire, and Ernie Shore stepped in to pitch the park's sole "perfect." (The baseball experts will point out that Cy Young pitched one for the team in 1904. True, but he didn't do it in Fenway.) September 11, 1918, may be the greatest and the most painful date of all, for that's when, behind hard-hurling Carl Mays, the Sox last won a World Series. Another highlight occurred on July 9, 1946, when the American League, behind Bob Feller's searing pitching and a two homer performance by Ted Williams, beat the Nationals 12–0 in the most crushing defeat in All-Star game history. Yet another Williams date of note is September 26, 1960, when Ted homered in his final at bat but refused to acknowledge the Boston fans' cheers. "I thought about tipping my cap," he later recalled, "you're damn right I did . . . but by the time I got to second base I knew I couldn't do it."

Carlton Fisk's game-winning twelfth inning home run off the left field foul pole in game six of the 1975 World Series ended one of the most exciting Series games in history. On April 29, 1986, Roger "the Rocket" Clemens stopped TV broadcasts across the nation as he gunned down 20 batters in a contest against the Mariners, setting the all-time one game strikeout record.

Fans

What makes the Boston's fans almost as legendary as their teams?

One thing they have going for them is knowledge, which is hardly surprising in this education-obsessed town in which the question of "What does he know?" is often the first thing that is asked about someone. Boston fans know their sport to a degree that's almost unheard of elsewhere. Talk to almost any Red Sox admirer and he can give you stats on the team, its history, and its prospects. In this respect, only fans in Baltimore, and, perhaps, New York can be said to be their equal.

Knowledge brings with it power, and, in truth, a certain degree of arrogance. Few are the Boston fans who do not know in their hearts that they could do an infinitely better job of running the club than the present mana-

ger. Nor are fans in Boston shy about letting Mrs. Yawkey know of their availability for the managing position. At every Red Sox game, fans feel free to stand up at any point in the contest and scream their recommendations toward the field; during any summer night, the lines at Boston's many radio talk shows will light up with callers who will confidently read off lists of who the Sox should trade, play, sit — and shoot.

If knowledge is one attribute of the Boston fan, partisanship is another, and it is a partisanship that goes far deeper than the sport. Boston rather modestly styles itself "the Hub," as in "the hub of the solar system," and that catches the local attitude perfectly. Bostonians are aware that other cities exist, to be sure — and they are especially aware that New York is around — but as far as they are concerned, any place that isn't Boston can only be a pale reflection their home's glory. Thus teams that come from the places that Beantown-ites think of as nowheres-villes — hick towns like Cleveland and Minneapolis — are treated well: after all, that's *noblesse oblige*. Those from cities with pretensions to excellence, most especially those from New York and Los Angeles, however, drive Bostonians to distraction. The long-standing rivalries between the Red Sox and the Yankees in baseball and between the Celtics and the Lakers in basketball are among the deepest felt in professional sports.

The final thing that sets the Boston sports fan apart is the fact that he or she is finicky, and sometimes fickle. Bostonians like their sports heroes to be modest sorts, who put — or at least seem to put — the needs of the team before their own careers. Brash, bragging stars, in the Reggie Jackson or Jose Canseco mold, set Bostonians' teeth on edge. Loners of the Ted Williams or Jim Rice sort are equally distrusted. Finally, Red Sox fans don't like anyone that they feel isn't pulling his weight; and, given the salaries that players get these days, Boston fans can reach a negative judgement on someone very quickly.

All of this has resulted in the frequent love-hate relationship between the fans and the club. Players like Williams and Rice, who would have been worshipped anyplace else, were frequently booed in Fenway. Other stars who fit the mold, like Carl Yastrzemski, were demigods in Boston. Fans got so down on well-paid pitcher Bob Stanley, who, in truth, did disappoint, that management after a while took to bringing the reliever out mainly when the team was on the road.

These attitudes persist even now. In recent years in Fenway, two fine "team" players with little national following— Dwight Evans and Marty Barret—received rapturous applause whenever they stripped up to the plate. Today, so does the big star, Roger Clemens. Wade Boggs, one of the greatest hitters in the game, is, on the other hand, treated with less than idolatry. Don't get us wrong, Boggs isn't disliked, as Rice often was—but he has yet to really win these folks over.

Probably the most dramatic example of the Boston fan showing his true colors occurred during the 1990 season. The Red Sox, in a surprise move, acquired Bill Buckner, the man whose celebrated sixth game error cost the team the 1986 Series. Commentators on opening day braced for boos and abuse as "Billy Buck" took the field. Instead, he was greeted with the greatest applause of the day. Why? Are Boston fans, like Cubs admirers, baseball masochists who love a loser more than a winner? Not at all. The Sox crowd simply wanted to show Buckner, a "team" player of the sort that Boston admires, that they appreciated what he'd done in the past, and that they didn't hold his one mistake against him. It wouldn't have happened that way in most ballparks.

At any Sox game you are liable to note the above attributes on display, usually in bold colors. There are some other things you'll catch, too. One is the composition of the audience: there are lots of females. In fact, the Red Sox seem to us to have a higher proportion of women fans than just about any other team. You'll also note the existence of fan traditions. Beach balls and "the wave" are common here. So are letter signs in the bleachers that, when put together, spell out something like D . . . I . . . E . . . O . . . R . . . I . . . O . . . L . . . E . . . S. Whenever Roger Clemens is on the mound, fans show up with "K" signs to count the strikeouts, whereas at every game a contingent of fans sits behind the backstop and do anything they can think of to distract visiting pitchers. It's all quite a spectacle, and it's a heck of a lot of fun.

So what is the most rewarding part of a baseball visit to Boston? Is it the fans, Fenway, or the Sox? We'd rate them all about equally appealing, and taken together they may well constitute the sport's finest viewing experience.

Getting There

The best piece of advice we can give about going to Fenway Park is that if you are thinking of driving, think again. Located in a mixed commercial and industrial neighborhood southwest of downtown, Fenway is fairly hard to find if you don't know the area. Once you do get there, you will find the parking situation terrible. As for Boston's traffic and drivers, they are both the worst north of Mexico City—and saying that may be unfair to the Mexicans.

The best way to get to Fenway Park by far is to take the MTA, Boston's subway. There are several points outside of town where you can park your car and ride into the game. Other options are cab and auto.

By MTA. If some of its cars are a bit creaky (Boston's subway system predates

New York's), the MTA at least provides fast and efficient service to all parts of Beantown. All you really have to do is enter any subway station and take a train to Kenmore Square, which is on the Green Line. No matter which point you are entering from, you will have to change trains no more than once. Once you get to Kenmore, just follow the crowd to Fenway, which is at the corner of Brookline Avenue and Yawkey Way, a two-minute walk from the station. The current cost is $.75, but that may be increased by the time you read this.

Here are directions for those coming from specific areas.

In town: If you are traveling from *downtown*, pick up the outbound green Line at the Park Street Station and take it to Kenmore Squre. Those arriving at *Logan Airport* will want to take the free MTA bus (outside the baggage claim area) to the Airport Station. From there take the Blue Line inbound to Government Center, then shift to the Green Line outbound to Kenmore Square.

Out of town: People traveling from such west locations as Worcester, Springfield, and Albany should take the Massachusetts Turnpike (I-90) to I-95 South. From I-95 South, take the Grove Street/MTA exit and follow the sign to parking, which is at the Riverside MTA station. From Riverside, take the Green Line inbound to Kenmore station. You'll pay $3 or $4 for parking plus $1.50 per person for the train.

Those coming to Boston from such *south* points as Providence, New Haven, and New York should take I-95 north to the Grove Street/MTA exit and follow the directions above.

By cab. Taxis in Boston are pretty pricey. To go the short distance from Fenway to downtown expect to pay about $12. From the airport, the cabbies will soak you for $24. The MTA fare from these locations is $.75 and the service is quicker.

By car. If you insist on taking your auto, here are the best routes.

Those coming from Providence, New Haven, New York, and other *south* points should take I-95 north to I-93 north, driving through downtown Boston. From there (be careful to stay in the right hand lane), exit at Storrow drive and follow Storrow Drive to the Fenway/Route 1 exit. When you go around the ramp, bear right toward Fenway, then turn right at Beacon Street. Follow Beacon to a five-way intersection, and bear left down Brookline. Fenway is two blocks away on the left.

Travelers from such *north* points such as Salem and Concord should take I-93 south to the Storrow Drive exit and follow the above instructions to get to the stadiums.

Fans coming *west* from such spots as Springfield and Albany should take the Massachusetts Turnpike (I-90) east to the Storrow Drive exit, and then should follow Storrow Drive east to Fenway/Route 1 exit. From there you should follow the directions above.

Parking

Built at the time (1912) when automobiles were a toy for the rich, the planners of Fenway made no provisions for parking. That's an oversight fans continue to pay for today.

The parking situation at Fenway is horrendous. There are three tiny lots near the stadium, two on Brookline and one on Yawkey Way across from the gates. Beyond these spots, which cost $10 and generally fill up at least an hour before the game, you are entirely on your own. In the neighborhoods around the park every gas station, vacant lot, and space behind a bar becomes a parking facility, and every kid, clerk, and housewife in the vicinity can be seen standing in the middle of the road with a red flag, trying to coax you into their lot. Prices vary from a low $6 to $10 and even more.

Our advice on how to handle the situation is two-fold. First, arrive early and get a spot without having to hassle with traffic. Fenway has one of the most exciting pre-game "street scenes" in baseball, and you won't really have the complete Fenway experience unless you are part of it. Second, accept the fact that since you brought your car, you're going to have to pay for the privilege. If you find one of the cheaper spots quickly, fine: but don't keep looking forever. Park in a convenient spot, pay up, and go and enjoy the game.

Tickets

You can buy Red Sox tickets by mail, by phone, or you can pick them up at the advance ticket office.

To order tickets by mail, write to the team at: Boston Red Sox Tickets, 4 Yawkey Way, Fenway Park, Boston, MA 02215.

When you order by mail, be sure to include the dates, the number of tickets, and the locations you'd like to have. Remember to include payment in full by check or money order, along with an extra $2 for the Red Sox's service charge. The Sox would also like you to include your phone number so they can call you if all the tickets you want are sold out.

Phone orders are accepted at (617) 267-1700. Have your MasterCard or Visa and a seating chart ready when you order by phone. You'll pay a service charge if you do it this way too.

The Red Sox advance ticket office is located at the park, near the corner of Brookline Avenue and Yawkey Way. it's open from 9 A.M. to 5 P.M. Monday through Friday and 9:30 A.M. to 2:00 P.M. on Saturdays throughout the season.

Availability. Fenway, with only 34,182 seats, is the smallest park in baseball. More than half the seats in the park go to season ticket holders. Ticket availability, therefore, is a big problem. If you want any tickets at all to match-ups against such rivals as New York and Toronto, you should order *months* in advance. The New York games always sell out, and the Toronto ones usually do. Match-ups against Baltimore, Oakland, and Kansas City can also be extremely tight. These tickets should be purchased well ahead of time, too.

For most other games you should be able to find a spot somewhere if you call in a few days before the game, but there are no guarantees. If you show up directly before a contest you may get in or you may not. If you are willing to purchase seats from one of the hordes of scalpers that mill around outside the gates before each contest, you'll certainly find something. However, you'll also run the risk the scalper's tickets are counterfeit or that he or she is an undercover police officer.

Costs. Red Sox tickets are very nearly the most expensive in baseball. Are they overpriced? Well, all that can be said is that, even at the outrageous rates the team charges, the Sox seem to have no problem selling seats. All of which means that if you want to go to Fenway, you're going to have to pay what the squad charges.

As everyone knows, every seat in Fenway has a great view because the park is so small. Generally, that's true as long as you aren't sitting behind a post, which the facility has a mighty host of. When buying tickets, specify that you do not like sitting behind poles, or you could end up assigned to one.

In 1990, the Red Sox ticket prices were as follows: Field Box Seats ($16); Infield Roof Box Seats ($14); Rightfield Roof Box Seats ($12); Box Seats ($12); Reserved Granstand ($10); Bleachers ($6).

Rainouts. We lived in Boston for ten years, and our son/brother Conor was born there. If you asked Conor up to age six what color the sky was, he'd routinely answer "grey."

It rains a lot in Boston. And even when it doesn't rain, it often looks like it is about to pour. As a result, rainouts are pretty common in Beantown. And though the Sox are pretty reluctant about giving out an exact figure, we'd guess that postponements probably happen five or six times a year.

The Sox's basic policy regarding cancelled games is to exchange your ticket for a future contest. However, if you are coming from out of town and have no plans to return to "the Hub," you can write to the ticket office explaining this, being sure to enclose your ticket stubs, and you may well get your money back.

There's one thing we want to caution you about: make sure your game is formally cancelled before you leave Fenway. The Sox will often delay play for several hours to try to wait out a storm and get a game in. If they take the field after you've departed, you'll be out of luck.

Seating

Since you are going to pay through the nose at Fenway for your seats, you'll want to make sure you get good ones. Happily, most of the spots in the park have wonderful views, and just being a part of the game at Fenway is one of baseball's most rewarding experiences. Still, this stadium is also a place where ticket-buying fans can get badly burned if they don't do their research before plunking down their money.

Field Box Seats ($16) are the most expensive spots in the park and are among the best chairs in baseball. Composed principally of the seats wrapped around the infield, most of these chairs are right on top of the action. Those spots in the low rows of, for example, section 19, are so close to home plate that you can practically hear the whistle of Wade Boggs' bat. Lots of luck in trying to get one of these

spots — they are mostly sold to season ticket people. However, if you do get one, you'll have a great view of the game.

Infield Roof Seats ($14) sit on top of the stadium's roof, and are odd in the extreme. If you sit here you'll be far from the concessions and from the majority of fans, but the view is still pretty fine. On the other hand, the Right Field Roof Seats ($12) are a bit too far down the right field line for our likes. You could probably do better by booking spots below.

Box seats ($12) run from the sublime to the ridiculous. If you can find spots in the infield sections, which run from 14 (first base) to 27 (third base), you'll be well situated indeed. Beyond those sections, though, things are less good. Particularly to be avoided are sections 1 through 7, which are past the right field foul pole and are little better than "bleacher" seats.

Reserved Grandstand seats ($10) present both problems and delights. Composed of old-fashioned wood and metal seats, this is the area in which Fenway's famous poles intrude. The numbering system for the rows, moreover, makes it tough to say which seats will have vision problems and which won't. If you luck out and have an unobstructed view, you'll have a great spot. But you can really lose here, too.

Our best advice for this situation is to try to book spots in the baseline areas (14 to 26), making it very clear when you purchase your seats that you want them obstruction free. If you can't find spots at least reasonably close to the baselines, think about going for the bleachers.

The Bleachers ($6) at Fenway attract a pretty lively crowd, and they also get plenty of sun. All seats offer a full view of the field, and the action is closer in this park than it is in bleacher sections in most other stadiums. The chairs in this area are the same ones you'll find in the box seats and are reasonably comfortable. Accordingly, sitting here is probably a pretty good alternative for those who want to save a few dollars or who simply can't find chairs elsewhere in Fenway. If you do decide on the bleachers, arrive early so you can get a seat in one of the lower rows.

Special Needs

Parking. There is no special handicapped parking, although the handicapped may be dropped off at the front gate.

Seating. Handicapped seating is available in sections 21 and 22 of the reserved grandstand behind homeplate. These can be purchased at the advance ticket office or by calling (617) 267-8661.

The Red Sox also offer a "no alcohol" family reserved seating area. Located in sections 32 and 33 near the left field foul pole, these are terrible spots, set far from the action.

Food and Features

Food. There is lots of good food to be found around Fenway Park. Specifically, you will find the bulk of the truly tasty things to eat offered by the street vendors who clog the streets around the stadium before, during, and after the games. Accordingly, you'd be wise to snack before you enter the park.

Inside Fenway, the food is second rate. The selection is limited, the quality is so-so, and the prices are pretty high . . . in truth, the dining situation in the park is a real bummer.

Choices at Fenway are limited to "baseball" fare: nachos, sports ice cream bars, chicken wing dings, peanuts, pizza, and the famous "Fenway Frank." We have had dozens of the latter over the years, and as far as we're concerned this celebrated sausage is just another steamed weiner.

There is one aspect of the food situation at Fenway that we do like, and that's the ingenious technique the in-stand vendors use to collect the money that's owed to them. After passing your hot dog to you, they toss a tennis ball with a slit down the middle of it. You tuck whatever you owe into the ball and toss it back. Surprisingly, the vendors almost never miss the return pass, and the fans usually catch the initial one.

Drinks. The drink situation is equally unimaginative, offering beer or Coke products.

Features. The principal feature at this park is the opportunity to attend a game at America's oldest and most intriguing baseball stadium. For most fans, that's feature enough.

Assistance

The basic attitude at Fenway Park, as at Wrigley Field, all but says "Hey, you're getting to watch a ball game in this classic old park. You want service, too!?" Managements in both parks don't knock themselves out for the attendees—and given the fact that both parks fill most of their seats every game, the owners of these teams are probably right in thinking that a focus on customer service doesn't matter for them. Fenway, like Wrigley, has a modest "information stand" to provide help to fans. The Sox's stand is a portable booth that is usually situated at the main concourse behind home plate, though it occasionally gets moved to other locations. If you can't find it, ask an usher and you'll be pointed in the right direction. Once you get there, the staff will try to be helpful. Don't, however, expect the same kind of "red carpet" treatment that you receive in some of the other stadiums.

Safety and Security

Safety. Though the drinking situation is in no way as bad as it is in some of the other parks, inebriation, shouted abuse, and fights do happen at Fenway—particularly during games against the Yankees. You can usually avoid these problems by staying out of the bleachers, but even there these difficulties are by no means so common that you should go out of your way to avoid the bleachers because of them. The Boston Police, who handle security in the park, are experts at spotting troublemakers and hustling them out of the stadium before most people even realize there is trouble.

The neighborhood around Fenway is well-patrolled and reasonably safe, but not totally so. Though you should probably feel free to hang around for the nightlife opportunities provided by such places as the *Cask and Flagon* and *Cite* after an evening game, it would be a good idea, particularly if you are female, to travel with friends back to your car and to stay on well-lighted streets.

Health. The climate is the big problem at Fenway, for Boston's weather is capricious and often damp. During the spring, and particularly in April, Fenway can be cold and wet. Bring a sweater and perhaps even a coat if you are going to the park at this time. In the summer both rain and sun can be problems. Bring an umbrella if the skies look threatening, and, if you are heat sensitive, avoid the bleachers on sunny days. Even if the sun doesn't especially get to you, if you plan on sitting in this area, bring some tanning lotion along.

Those with health related problems should repair to the park's first aid offices, which are located behind first and third bases on the main concourse.

There you will find a very professional staff well-prepared to handle most problems.

Mementos

Souvenirs. Within Fenway, the best place to buy souvenirs is *The Landsdowne Shop*, which is located behind section 38 on the left field side of the lower concourse. There you will find an extensive selection of baseball goods at moderate prices. A nice hat, for example, goes for $7. You'll find an even broader choice at *The Souvenir Store*, 19 Yawkey Way ([617] 437-1384), across from Fenway. This place has one of the most extensive selections of baseball goods we've seen and is open all year. Hours are 9 A.M. to 5 P.M. Monday through Saturday and 12 P.M. to 5 P.M. on Sundays. On game days, the store is open until a half hour following the game's completion.

Foul Balls. Strays are best snagged in the box seats just past first and third. If you want a souvenir from Wade Boggs or Mike Greenwell that you'll always remember, try sitting in Boxes 26-29 (left field) and 12-15 (right field).

Autographs. Fenway isn't a great place to collect signatures, but that doesn't stop a mighty horde of fans from trying to get them. Before and after each game a crowd gathers at the corner of Yawkey Way and Van Ness, to the south of Fenway, which is where the players enter and leave from their parking lot. Mostly, the players just drive by the fans, but every once in a while someone will stop to sign a few.

CALIFORNIA ANGELS
Anaheim Stadium

What is baseball? Is it a game? A sport? Or is it simply a form of entertainment?

Initially, of course, it was a game. A century or more ago, it was something groups of men did for fun between shift changes at the factory, after the harvest had been brought in, or even in the long lulls after battles; the Civil War probably did more to spread "baseball"— or at least a version of the game—than any other event. If one's friends, especially the distaff side, wanted to watch the match, that was fine too.

With the birth of professional ball, baseball emerged as a full-fledged sport. Rules were standardized, records were established and broken, training became regularized and stressed. Fans prided themselves on knowing who were the league leaders in a bewildering variety of categories. This is still the way of baseball in many of America's small towns.

The past few decades, though, have seen the growth of a third style of baseball, one that sees the great game principally as a form of entertainment, an activity that competes directly for the recreation dollar with beaches, amusement parks, and the movies. Instead of statistics, teams that stress entertainment try to offer their customers a spectacle. Rather than an organ, their soundtracks boogey to the sounds of rock, while on increasingly frequent occasions, fireworks light up the skies. Instead of trying to keep ravenous fans happy with hot dogs, they offer a lavish selection of food choices to lure into the stadium those who might be tempted to spend their money elsewhere.

As is so often the case with North American trends, the move toward "baseball as entertainment" was galvanized in California. Though he wasn't the first owner with the idea (maverick proprietor Bill Veeck tried to push the concept in the 1950s), California Angels chairman Gene Autry was certainly among the first of baseball's leaders to see the inherent possibilities in baseball as diversion.

Who among owners could be more appropriate to head the game in this direction? Though it's hard for anyone under forty really to understand, Gene Autry, "the singing cowboy," was a very popular star in the 1930s and '40s. His movies, largely forgotten today, scored big: even now, Autry is still number four on the all-time box-office list for actors. His recording career was even more spectacular. One of Autry's 600-plus records was the first "gold" disc. Another, the ubiquitous "Rudolph the Red-Nosed Reindeer," was the first platinum single. Probably more to the point, Autry has long ranked high among Hollywood's most successful businessmen.

Starting with an impulse buy of the American League's new expansion Los Angeles club in 1960—a radio station owner. Autry had showed up at the meeting to award the franchise in hopes of getting L.A. broadcasting rights; he wound up with the whole team—Autry has persistently pushed his vision of what baseball must be if it wants to attract audiences for decades to come. Following four frustrating years in Los Angeles, he moved the club to Anaheim, a booming town that shared his futuristic outlook and his commitment to provide a baseball experience that kept "convenience, comfort, and courtesy" in mind.

The California Angels today are nothing more nor less than a reflection of Autry's pioneering vision. Few baseball clubs or stadium managements in either league have gone so far out of their way to make going to a game a pleasant experience than the Angels and the people at Anaheim Stadium. And while the baseball-as-entertainment idea has been growing, particularly among the newer franchises, few indeed are the teams that so fully realize that amusement is their purpose, or so fully fulfill that realization.

The reward of this approach has been, for the Angels, a fair degree of public acceptance for their team. Attendance, even in bad seasons, is pleasingly high. They are recognized everywhere as a well-run organization. Their stadium, a huge "sports palace" in the cookie-cutter concrete mold, is pretty much recognized as a model of its sort.

Yet this direction has, to the frustration of Angels fans, not led to all that many victories. The Angels have had stars like Reggie Jackson, Nolan Ryan, and Rod Carew. They have had moments of baseball drama, too: if there has ever been a better playoff than their heartstopping American League 1986 contest against the Red Sox, we don't know of it. What they have not had in thirty years of baseball is a single World Series appearance.

Gene Autry, now in his eighties, is said to be somewhat discouraged about this. Yet who knows? He may still see that victory. In the meantime, Autry can take some satisfaction in being one of the few owners in the history of baseball who can be said to have truly shaped the game.

The Team

Over their thirty years of existence, the California Angels have given their fans everything but victory.

During the 1960s, the Angels had the typical deplorable expansion team record. Though they twice finished in third, they wound up in the second division every other year. Still, California pitcher Dean Chance's Cy Young award–winning performance in 1964 gave fans something to cheer about.

Things got better in the 1970s. For one thing, the team started to attract some of baseball's superstars. Hall of Famer Frank Robinson joined the squad and thrilled the crowd with a home run during his first at bat. Mickey Rivers, one of the game's certifiable "characters" (he liked to call everyone "Gozzlehead") also did a turn with the club. Two pitchers, Frank Tanana and Nolan Ryan, supplied the thrills, with Nolan racking up 138 victories in his seven years on the team, the club record. Finally, in 1979, the Angels copped their first divisional title, but lost the pennant to the Orioles, 3–1.

The 1980s proved to be the best decade in the franchise's history. The team won two divisional titles (1982, and 1986), and they finished in the first division five times. Not a fantastic performance, but a definite improvement over the past. The trek of superstars out of southern California continued. Rod Carew tore up the American League for the Angels with his matchless hitting in the early eighties. Don Baylor also put his solid skills to work. Following his bitter feud with owner George Steinbrenner, Reggie Jackson left the Yankees to join the Angels. On his first appearance back in the "Big Apple," Jackson hit a game-winning homer. The appreciative Yankees fans began chanting "Reg-gie! Reg-gie!" — until it dawned on them that their hero was playing for the *other* team. Whereupon the crowd broke into a chorus of "Steinbrenner sucks! Steinbrenner sucks!"

A disappointing year was 1990 for Angel fans as their squad finished well behind. Still, they currently have one of the better teams in baseball, a team that includes such standout players as veteran pitcher Bert Blyleven, first baseman Wally Joyner, catcher Lance Parrish, and pitchers Mark Langston, Jim Abbott, and Kirk McCaskill. Thus, they have every reason to believe that the 1990s will be their best decade yet.

The Stadium

Imagine you were the officials of a mid-sized but rapidly growing city, determined to show the world that your town was "first class" in every way. Imagine you had ample financial resources, lots of architectural expertise to draw upon, and a major league franchise in hand. What sort of stadium would you build?

You'd certainly want to make it grandiose. You would, after all, defeat your own purpose to attract attention if you skimped on comfort and convenience. You'd also want to put the palace where it would be remarked upon. Finally, if you had the funds, you'd want to make it a model of its kind.

The town fathers of Anaheim, California, we suspect, approached the task of creating a stadium for the California Angles with at least some of these thoughts in mind. Of the huge, multi-purpose "sports palaces" built by government officials during the 1960s and 1970s, Anaheim Stadium is the very biggest — it seats 64,593 — and is certainly among the most impressive. More important than that, it is also among the best.

The reader will not have to look far between the lines to understand that concrete and steel stadiums like Anaheim (and Candlestick, Three Rivers, Riverfront, and so on) are not to the taste of the authors. These places were constructed more as expressions of urban pride than as places to play the game of baseball — they are in most ways inferior to such early parks as Comiskey, Wrigley, and Fenway. Still,

it must be said that if you are still determined to build one of them, you could do worse than imitate Anaheim. It's one of the best in its class.

One of the real pluses of the place is location. Sited in a pleasant suburban neighborhood on the east side of Anaheim, the park is convenient to freeways, hotels, restaurants, and other entertainment centers — Disneyland is right down the street. Ingress to the stadium couldn't be easier; exits are well marked, and there are many access points to the stadium parking lots. If you *do* run into traffic problems (a distinct possibility), it will be because of freeway rather than game traffic.

The stadium itself is *big*. Happily, it isn't round; rather, the shape is a modified oval form — not ideal for baseball, but an improvement over the usual circle. On the outside are two features to attract your attention. The first is an enormous electronic scoreboard-sign, designed in the shape of a big "A," with a halo wrapped around the top of it. This sits next to the freeway, and the halo lights up whenever the Angels win. On the southwest side of the park is a tasteful monument to Gene Autry, outlining his accomplishments in films, TV, radio, and recording.

The public areas of Anaheim stadium are immaculate. The concourses are wide and well-lit, aisles are easy to reach and well-marked, concession stands are attractive and well-spaced. Chairs in the park are the usual plastic and steel combinations. They're fairly comfortable and have decent legroom.

The field is, thankfully, natural grass. Foul ball territories are purposefully short, which makes for better viewing for fans and more lively foul ball catching, while the field lines are fairly long. It's 362' out to either right or left field, while center is set at 404'. Finally, the field has one of those oddities that you occasionally come upon in baseball: the pitcher's mound floats! Incredible as it may seem, the thing actually is suspended over 3,500 gallons of water, which in turn is encased in a concrete container.

Why, you might ask, would anyone want a floating pitcher's mound? The idea is to make the park easily convertible to football (the Rams play here). You simply drain under the mound, dropping it below field level, landscape over, and presto—you have a football stadium!

Theoretically, the water is packed in so tight that the pitcher feels no movement whatever. Still, the next time you hear some TV announcer say that the Angels' pitching staff is a bit shaky, you'll know there could be some literal truth in the statement!

Highlights

Anaheim Stadium and the Angels have not been around long enough to rack up a lot of baseball milestones. Still, there have been some.

Nolan Ryan pitched two of his six no-hitters here. The first came on September 28, 1974, versus Minnesota, while the second was on June 1, 1978, against Baltimore. Nolan also accomplished an even more singular feat when, during a game, he hurled a ball 100.9 miles per hour (August 20, 1974)—it was the fastest major league pitch ever clocked.

For many baseball fans, the most memorable moments in Anaheim Stadium occurred during the 1986 American League playoff series. In a nerve-racking contest that went down to the wire, Boston denied the Angels their shot at a series appearance, largely thanks to the hitting of the Sox's Marty Barrett and Dave Henderson. Still, after the battle was over, one commentator summed up the thoughts of millions when he said that "this was a playoff that both teams deserved to win."

Fans

If you build a baseball park that stresses that it's in the entertainment business, what kind of fans do you get? It's simple: those who want to be entertained.

No one would accuse an Angels fan of being a baseball nut. If a scorecard were thrust into his or her hands, an Angel fan would probably wonder what the thing was. Nor will you see many Angel fans with headphones tuned in to the play-by-play. If anyone has a radio, you can bet its tuned to a rock station rather than to the game. And should things get boring on the field, the creative Angels admirer can keep himself amused. The "wave"—that curse of baseball—is very popular here. Legend has it that it once got so distractingly bad that the umpires stopped the game until it was brought under control. Of course, if no one wants to do the wave, then it's "break out the beach balls, dude."

Who comes to the games? Families and young people mostly, with a scattering of senior citizens. These are well-dressed, middle-class sorts, fairly sober, friendly, willing to watch the contest if something interesting is going on—usually just as willing to talk with their friends or you if the play is slow. They love to eat, and God knows they have a lot of eats to choose from. They don't mind a drink, either, but the drinking is rarely excessive.

"Laid back" is the overused term for Californians—and it certainly doesn't fit the fans in either San Francisco or Oakland, who are anything but "laid back." But its a pretty apt description of Angels admirers. They're certainly happy if their team wins, but if they don't, it's no big deal.

Any eastern fan will find this attitude a bit disturbing. If you're from New York, Cleveland, Boston, or Baltimore, it may leave you talking to yourself. "Don't they realize," you'll grit your teeth, "that this isn't just a game. Don't they know that it's war!"

Actually, they don't know that in Anaheim. They think baseball is just — *entertainment*. Moreover, the stress reduction crowd tells us that such relaxed folks live longer than we more involved types. Which goes to show that God may not be just after all.

Getting There

As is true with most of southern California, Anaheim Stadium is best reached by private or rental car. Other options include cab and train.

By car. Anaheim Stadium is located near the junction of I-5 (the Santa Ana Freeway), Route 57 (the Orange Freeway), and Route 22 (the Garden Grove Freeway).

All of these are big, busy roads. If you are going to a game, study a map carefully before you go: it can be difficult changing lanes to reach an exit in heavy traffic.

Here are the best approaches:

From Los Angeles, San Francisco, and the *north*, take I-5 south to the State College Boulevard/The City Avenue Exit. Bear left on State College and follow to stadium parking.

From San Diego and the *south*, take I-5 north to the Chapman Avenue/State College Exit. Then follow South State College to stadium parking.

By cab. Cab is a good option from the downtown Anaheim area (about $8, one way), and an alright choice if you are arriving at John Wayne airport (about $20). From either Los Angeles or LAX airport, the cab fares are prohibitive . . . you would probably do better to rent a car.

By train. You can take Amtrak to the Angels games! Amtrak's Anaheim station is directly across the parking lot from the "Big A," and it provides convenient and regular service to Los Angeles, San Diego, San Francisco, and

most other points on the Amtrak system. From most areas served in California, it's entirely possible to train to the game, spend the night in one of the nearby hotels (a few are within walking distance), and either go to nearby Disneyland or return home in the morning. Call Amtrak at (800) 872-7245 for current schedules and fares.

Parking

Anaheim Stadium has ample, well lighted, on-site parking.

Altogether, there are 16,100 spaces wrapped around the park, all priced at $4. R.V. parking is available, too, though at a much higher rate. This is enough to handle all Angels crowds. However, if you don't mind walking and would like to save $4, there is plenty of free parking in the neighborhoods surrounding the park.

Tailgating, though not a big thing at Anaheim Stadium, is allowed in designated areas. If you intend to tailgate, mention it to the parking attendant as you pull in, and you'll be directed to the appropriate sections. Barbeque grills and the usual tailgating paraphrenalia is allowed, though alcohol in any form is strictly forbidden.

Tickets

Angels tickets are available by mail or by phone and can be picked up in person or bought at the game.

To order by mail, write down the area and the category of seats you'd like and send your check or money order to: Angels Tickets, PO Box 2000, Anaheim, CA 92803.

Also be sure to include $3 extra for the "service charge" that the Angels require.

Phone orders are handled by Ticketron at (714) 634-1300 and (213) 410-1062.

When you call, be prepared to designate where you want your seats and have a major credit card handy. You'll also be hit with a service charge. These lines are open from 9 A.M. to 9 P.M., Monday through Saturday, and from 10 A.M. to 8 P.M. on Sunday.

The Angels' advance ticket office will give you the opportunity to look at a seating chart before you buy your tickets. It opens on March 17 and is located outside gate 1 of the stadium, at the field level. Its hours are 9 A.M. until 5:30 P.M., Monday through Saturday.

Seats are also available before and during the game on a "first come, first served" basis.

Availability. If the Angels played anyplace other than Anaheim Stadium, ticket availability might be a problem. Though their record isn't all that great, the Angels currently rank sixth in major league attendance. They sell about 20,000 season tickets a year, and they have an average attendance of over 32,000 per game.

However, even a crowd of 32,000 doesn't come near to filling the "Big A." For most contests, a call or mail order even a few days in advance will net you good seats. If you're pressed for time and decide just to show up, you'll almost certainly find a decent spot.

Cost. Angels tickets, like those of their Interstate 5 neighbors the Dodgers, are very reasonably priced. Splitting up the pricing system by charging less for box seats in the centerfield area than for those along the baselines adds a measure of fairness to pricing that not all parks provide.

In 1990 Angels prices were as follows: Field and Club Box ($9); Terrace Box ($8); Centerfield Box ($7); View Level, Reserved ($6); Family Section (Centerfield Box [$5]); General Admission (½ hour before game [$3]); Kids General Admission (Monday–Thursday, 15 and under [$1]).

Rainouts. Rainouts are exceedingly rare in arid Southern California. Specif-

ically, they happen about once every three years.

If a rainout happens to you, your ticket will be exchanged for another Angels game. Should a return trip to Anaheim not be in your plans, jot a short note to the Angels explaining this, and your money will be refunded.

Seating

Anaheim Stadium has unusually good seating for a multi-purpose municipal sports facility (the L.A. Rams play here, too). Thanks to short foul territory lines, the good seats are often very good indeed. And thanks to what must be one of the most extended tiers in the major leagues, at least some of the "bad" seats are very acceptable as well.

Anaheim Stadium is a three-tiered park with an oblong design — on the inside it bears an uncanny resemblence to Tiger Stadium, which is the second oldest arena in the majors. What this design means in practice is that many of the seats in the outfield area, particularly at the view level, are very far from the action. On the other hand, those seats along the foul lines are closer than they are in most of the more modern, round parks.

Many of the most expensive seats are at the Field level ($9). This is a simple deck that slants back from the action on the diamond. The key is to see to it that you get seats in low rows, within the baselines. These run, roughly, from odd aisle 31 (third base), to even aisle 30 (first base). Behind the field seats are those designated terrace ($8). These are further yet from the action, yet within the baselines (same as above) are still quite acceptable.

Club box ($9) seats are a level higher. Though the same price as some of the field seats and not quite as close to the action as some of those spots are, club boxes are excellent seats with a fine

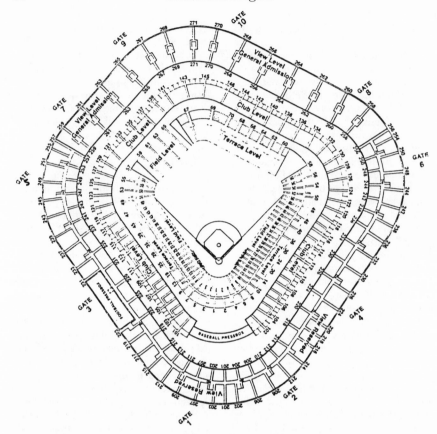

Seating chart, Anaheim Stadium.

view of all the action, particularly if you snag one in the baselines, which at this level run from 121 (third) to 120 (first). In our opinion, *club boxes* in these areas are worth the extra buck as compared to the terrace spots.

Centerfield boxes ($7), on the other hand, are not great buys. They're nice enough seats, but they're simply too far from the action for our liking . . . these spots would be termed "bleachers" in other stadiums. The Family Reserved Seats ($5) are cheaper and probably just as good. This is a no-alcohol section that tends to be inhabited by the kiddie corp. The spots are behind the left field wall and have a nice view of the visitors bullpen. General Admission seats ($3),

rest in the upper deck area, above both these sections and also along the foul lines. It goes without saying that these are not very good seats. However, for $3 you'll at least get to see major league ball.

We've saved the best for last. These are the view level reserved seats ($6). Although perched on top of Anaheim Stadium, these seats, thanks to unusually sound design, are surprisingly close to the action: from home plate to the upper deck is a short 95'. Thus, a low row spot in upper reserved will be closer to the action than a fair number of the seats in the terrace area. And just about *any* in-the-baselines-view box seat (aisles 223, third base, through 224, first) will have a better view than any of the more expensive centerfield boxes. Up here, of course, you'll have to do without some of Anaheim Stadium's amenities. You'll usually run into a more boisterous crowd than you'll get below. Still, particularly if you sit in the view level aisles wrapped around home plate (201 to 209), you'll find yourself sitting in seats that are among the best bargains in the majors.

Important seating note. Try to wander around Anaheim Stadium and you'll soon get an idea of what it's like to cross an Eastern European frontier without a visa. No matter where you go, security people very politely ask to see your ticket stub — even (or especially) if you are burdened down with four drinks and six hot dogs.

This fixation on security can get excessive. During a game we attended, a boy in the family reserved section caught a ball hit out of the park during batting practice. Before the urchin could hoist it for his parents to see, a security guard rushed out of nowhere, grabbed the ball out of the kid's hands (while the fans booed) and threw it back onto the field.

Happily, a merciful White Sox player, watching this scene, tossed the ball back into the stands. Still, we can only hope that this was an isolated incident.

Special Needs

Parking. Officially, Anaheim Stadium has no designated "handicapped parking." This probably reflects the fact that Anaheim is in highly conservative Orange County, a land where specific catering to "special interests" gets people's backs up.

Yet if you are physically disabled, have no fears. Simply point out your handicapped sticker or plate to the attendant when you come to the park, and you'll be pointed to "reserved park-

ing" areas appropriate to your needs. Should you require wheelchair service, just have whoever is with you speak to an usher. You'll be efficiently taken care of.

Seating. Inside the stadium, handicapped seating is provided in aisles 1–6 on the terrace level. These are fine spots, directly behind home plate. The fact is that Anaheim Stadium, quietly and without specific policies, does a better job in providing for the physically disabled than a lot of parks that like to boast about all the great things they're doing in this area.

Food and Features

Food. As befits its status as a park that offers an "entertainment" experience, Anaheim Stadium puts a lot of emphasis on providing good food choices for its guests. In fact, stadium officials like to brag that the average fan at Anaheim spends more money on things to eat here than at any other stadium. Wander around its terrace level and you won't wonder why.

The Angels offer their fans some of the best food in baseball. The variety is great, prices are reasonable, and the quality is uniformly good. Even if you don't like baseball (and God knows there are enough people in the park who don't seem all that interested in the game), you'll certainly enjoy browsing around, seeing what Anaheim has to offer.

There is, of course, the usual baseball food. It seems offered here mostly as a bow to tradition or even as an afterthought. Still, if you want to eat what your grandpa ate at the ballgame, you'll find it at Anaheim. The hot dogs are reasonable in price, while sausage and pepper sandwiches, bratwurst, knockwurst, and polish sausage all go for a bit more. You can get popcorn, peanuts, and nachos, too.

Anaheim, though, specializes in more exotic choices, many of which can be found on the field/terrace level behind home plate. Everyone's favorite seems to be the fresh baked cinnamon rolls; you'll be surprised (unless you've eaten one) how many people will be lined up after the game to get a "take home" pack. Other popular stops include the "Potato Hut," which offers delicious stuffed potatoes; the fish and chips stands, which will give you a portion you'll have trouble finishing; "Pasta House," which features a wide selection of Italian specialties; and the "Cantina Old El Paso," which has Mexican favorites at fair prices.

And, yes, we can confirm it: Anaheim Stadium does indeed have a "Sushi Bar." Here you can get raw fish specialties along with such less daring entres as "Yakitori" (B-B-Q chicken on a stick) and "Yahisoba" (noodles in broth). All we can say about the raw fish is, don't knock it until you've tried it.

Most of Anaheim's best food spots are on the terrace/field level. However, there's a major exception to this rule, and that's the "Seafood Bar," located behind aisle 101 at the club level. Here you can find "raw bar" items, as well as such things as shrimp cocktail and seafood salad. The place also has a wide selection of drinks. Getting to the club level, if you're not seated in it, is the problem: security people may well try to stop you from going there. Our suggestion is that you tell them—very politely—to get stuffed. Park policy allows fans to visit this concession, make their purchases, and return to their seats.

As good as the food situation at Anaheim is, it may soon get even better. Current plans call for the opening of a full-service restaurant open to all fans over the Angels bullpen sometime in the next year or two.

Unlike may parks, Angels fans seem to like to arrive at the stadium early to take advantage of the dining opportunities. You might want to do likewise.

Drinks. As at all the stadiums, you can get the usual selection of soft drinks at the usual high price.

Anaheim Stadium, on the other hand, excels when it comes to offering alcoholic beverages to its guests. Indeed, in this area, it without a doubt has the widest selection in the Majors. Most parks limit fans to beer. Some have wine tucked away in a place or two. A few served mixed drinks to season ticket holders and those who know where to look.

At Anaheim, however, you can get it all. At the terrace level, a wide selection of beers, wines, and mixed drinks is offered throughout the game. Moreover, you can bring any of the above back to your seats. Further, there's no official shutoff time, though management will close outlets down if things seem to be getting out of hand.

Yet as liberal as this policy seems, there are restrictions. Fans can buy no more than two drinks at any one time, and there are no vendor sales of alcoholic beverages in the stands.

Does such a "mixed" policy regarding alcohol control work? All that can be said is that it seems to be successful. At any rate, if there's any serious drinking problem in this stadium, it was not apparent to these observers.

Features. Anaheim Stadium has relatively few features.

There's a nice "hall of fame" style display of famous Angels in the lobby near Gate 2. Players featured include slugger and 1981 home run champ Bobby Grich (#4), player-manager Jim Fregosi (#11), and all-around great player Don Baylor (#25). While these fine players sit in the "hall of fame" though, the Angels have only retired the numbers of two people: Rod Carew (#29), and Gene Autry (#26). Carew has the distinction of being the only American League player ever whose number has been vacated by two teams: he's also been "retired" by the Twins.

Anaheim Stadium's biggest feature is probably the tour it runs of its own facility. If you want to see the inside of a players' clubhouse, would like to find out what the stadium looks like from the press box, or want to know how the Angels' floating mound actually works, this excursion may be for you. Offered daily on the hour, the tour costs $3 for adults, $2 for seniors, and $2 for kids under 16. Since weather and day games can interfere with schedules, you should call (714) 937-7333 before setting out to make sure that the tour you want is actually on.

Assistance

Anaheim prides itself on its well-trained staff. According to its officials, people at the stadium are expected to treat fans as "guests," extending to them the same sort of courtesy they'd receive if they were visiting the employee's own homes.

Actually, Angels people are a pretty friendly and helpful lot. Ushers are knowledgeable and efficient—they are able to solve most of the problems you'll have in the park on the spot. Should you need additional assistance, a visit to the fan accommodation office, which is located behind home plate on the terrace/field level, will insure a quick resolution to whatever is bothering you.

Safety and Security

Safety. No big city is crime free, but Anaheim comes about as close to that ideal as any American town.

Within the park, your only security risk is the occasional drunken fan or fight. These things don't happen often, and when they do happen, security usually will solve the problem before you are even aware there has been one. Still, if you find security unresponsive,

a word to any usher will quickly set matters to rights.

Safety in the parking lots and in the neighborhood around the park likewise presents few difficulties. If you feel in the mood to walk back to your hotel or to a local restaurant after a game, you should go ahead. Though robberies and the like can happen anywhere, you are about as safe in Anaheim as you are likely to be anyplace.

Health. The biggest health threats in Anaheim Stadium are the sun and injuries from foul balls.

If you're sun sensitive, try to avoid the upper deck—particularly the General Admission seats over the field and the first base line. If you do sit in this area on a bright day, bring sun screen and drink plenty of water.

The park's short foul territories lead to exciting—and dangerous—foul ball play. If you're in field level seats near or just past first and third, either stay alert or move elsewhere.

Should you neglect our advice and end up with burns or bruises, a visit to the First Aid office should put you to rights. It's located at the terrace/field level, just to the right of home plate.

Mementos

Souvenirs. Angel fans aren't that big on wearing Angels paraphernalia. Still, should you want to show the locals up, you can suit yourself in proper fan style at "The Souvenir Shop." Located at the terrace/field level at gate one (it has entrances inside and outside the stadium), this enclosed store has a large selection of baseball goods offered at the usual prices. It's open before, during, and after Angels games, and is also open whenever the advance ticket box office is.

Foul Balls. Anaheim Stadium is a great place to either catch or be battered by foul balls. Given the closeness of the seats to the action here, specific aisle recommendations aren't that meaningful. Sit in the field, terrace, club or view sections near the baselines and keep an eye out.

Autographs. Signatures are also reasonably easy to obtain in Anaheim.

You can try hanging around the dugouts during batting practice; players sometimes walk over to sign. After the game, both Angels and visitors leave from around Gate 1. This is a good place to catch them.

CHICAGO CUBS
Wrigley Field

Change may be a wonderful thing, but it instinctively arouses suspicion in baseball people.

When the overhand throw came into the game more than a century ago, the "kranks" fought it. Why couldn't people toss the ball in the normal, underhand way? Equipment was likewise scorned, and decades after gloves and chest protectors had become standard issue, people could still be found who yeared for the "good old days" when "real men" played baseball. Even now, metal bats, the proud possessions of every Little Leaguer, remain banned in the Major Leagues.

In fact hardly any baseball innovation wasn't resisted, from night ball games, to television coverage, to allowing players some measure of freedom in deciding what team to serve with.

This innate conservatism has in some ways inhibited the game. Many of the changes that ultimately made their way into the sport, particularly those that affected the style of play, clearly made baseball more exciting and interesting. The contests of the 1880s would seem to us static and pedestrian. The integration of baseball, thanks to the courage of Branch Rickey and Jackie Robinson, greatly enhanced the quality of performance in both Leagues. It's no coinci-

dence that baseball entered one of the greatest decades in its history in the 1950s, thanks in part to such players as Hank Aaron, Ernie Banks, and Willie Mays. Is it possible to imagine the sport without them?

Yet because some changes are good, does that make all of them worthwhile? Has baseball really benefited from astroturf, "multipurpose" stadiums, and sportswriters who feel it's their duty to expose to public view the intimate details of player's lives? Does a free agency system that starves poorer teams for talent really enhance the game's intrinsic interest? Do bidding wars between prestige-seeking cities and bored millionaires over franchises insure that new teams will be sited in the areas where fans will be most likely to support them?

The average Chicago Cubs fan would probably say no to those questions. That's because Cubs admirers worship most days during the regular season at what is without a doubt the temple of baseball conservatism, Wrigley Field.

For decades, the Cubs were just about the most determinedly unfashionable club in baseball. While other teams ripped up their old parks in order to build new, gleaming facilities near major expressways, the Cubs clung to their ancient, beloved sports palace, which is among the more inconvenient parks to get to in the Majors. While other organizations rolled out the astroturf, Wrigley kept planting grass. As ballparks trotted out sushi bars, "speed pitch" concessions, and mascots to keep attendees amused, the Cubs stuck to the notion (questionable, actually, in their case) that fans come to the park not to dine or watch some character cavorting in a ridiculous costume, but to see a ball game. Decades after lights had been installed in every other park, Cubs admirers resisted night baseball, contending that the great game should be played under the sun, as God intended. Actually, the fans lost that contest, but only after a prolonged battle with mutual intransigence on both sides. It can be fairly predicted that, should a move ever be made to retire Wrigley, blood will flow in the North Side streets of Chicago.

For a long time, the Cubs were something of a joke in baseball: they were the team with the old-fashioned ways that always lost. But if the Cubs weren't a winning team, at least they played in a place with a warm, human feel to it — not to mention those beautiful vines!

Not long ago, interest in all the old ballparks picked up. Instead of going to Yellowstone yet again, families decided that it would be a great idea to go to see the classic ballparks. The Smithsonian Institution, of all places, began conducting tours of them. The problem was that few were left, and those that had survived had problems. Comiskey, though beautiful, was run down, Yankee Stadium had been changed, and Tiger Stadium was really a collection of ballpark pieces assembled over decades. The real seeker of the pure baseball park of the past was left with two choices: Fenway and Wrigley. People headed for both, and they are still heading for them today.

As a result, Wrigley, which a decade or so ago was decidedly un-chic, is now very much an "in" place. This fact has aspects to it that are good and bad, which we will be getting to later.

In truth, for baseball fans, there are four "must" experiences. One, of course, is to visit Cooperstown. The other three, in no special order, are to attend games at Fenway Park, Yankee Stadium, and Wrigley Field. These three are truly the parks where the "baseball tradition" (believe it, such a thing *does* exist) finds its fullest living expression. These are the places where baseball history was largely made.

Note well: we do not contend that these are the three best stadiums. Though all have strong pluses, they have some drawbacks as well. If you seek perfection rather than just tradition, you might try games in Los Angeles or Kansas City. But, if you want to understand what the game is all about and what it has meant to fans over the decades, these three parks, above all others, are the places to go.

Wrigley Field has another attribute beyond the role it played in defining the sport. Many teams boast of "a winning tradition," whether justified by the stats or not. Cub fans are among the very few who loudly boast of "a losing tradition!"

It is not that the Cubs are the only team in baseball that regularly loses — far from it. But when the Braves collapse, they hear about it from the fans. As for the Indians, the howl of agony that reverberates through the stands at Cleveland Stadium upon each Indian loss is a thing both wondrous and terrible to behold: if wanting to win were the key to success, Indians fans would bring home the pennant every year. No, it is only on the North Side that defeat is worn as a sort of badge of honor.

We suppose it represents a certain Chicagoan practicality. If you cannot brag about the Cubs wins (and they haven't won a Series since 1908), then why not make a kind of virtue out of their losses? Well, we guess, that makes some sort of sense. Yet the irony of it is that the Cubs have not always been losers. Initially, they were far from it, indeed.

The Team

Ask any baseball fan "What has been the greatest baseball team in the twentieth century?" and you will generally get a quick, easy, and correct answer: "The Yankees." As fine as some of the other teams, such as St. Louis and Oakland, have been, there is simply no way to compare their records with the Bombers of the Bronx.

Ask "What was the greatest team of the nineteenth century?" and you'll get confusion. For good reason. Leadership in that time of changing leagues, poor record-keeping, and shifting franchises is difficult to pin down. Still, a pretty good case could be made that the best team then was the Cubs.

One of the original National League clubs of 1876, the Chicago "White Stockings" (the 1901 AL franchise would later steal the name; the NL team became "Cubs" in 1902), the Chicago team won the first national pennant ever that year. After that, the Chicagoans racked up an impressive series of wins. They copped the pennant five times in the 1880s, and kept close on the heels of the opposition through the 1890s. During this period, they boasted one of the great lineups in baseball, including Hall of Famer Cap Anson, Billy Sunday (later, the prominent evangelist), and Hall of Fame catcher Mike "King" Kelly, certainly the most colorful player of the period, and probably baseball's first "superstar."

The first decade of this century was another great period for the Cubs. Behind the pitching of Mordecai "Three Finger" Brown, who even today boasts the third lowest ERA in history,

the Cubs went to the series four times in the decade, winning in 1907 and 1908 (it would turn out to be their last victory) and losing in 1910, and, surprisingly, in 1906, when they bowed to their South Side neighbors the White Sox in one of the greatest upsets in baseball history.

After that, the pattern of losing set in. In 1918, the Cubs reached the Series again, this time against Boston. But they were bombed out 4–2, thanks largely to the stellar pitching of Babe Ruth. Eleven years later, in 1929, they were back in the series again, this time bowing to the Athletics 4–1. The 1930s proved probably their best decade since the glory years of the 1900s: they made three trips to the fall classic (1932, 1935, and 1938), but they lost each time. Finally, in 1945, they gave it their last and closest shot. Still, they folded 4–3 to the Athletics in a close contest that broke Chicago hearts.

During these years of disappointment, though, the Cubs had a series of outstanding performers. The 1910s were graced by the famed "double play" combination of Joe Tinker, Johnny Evers, and Frank Chance. Even though two of the team, Tinker and Evers, were not close friends (to put it mildly), they still understood each other's moves. All went into the Hall of Fame on the same day. Hack Wilson, not one of baseball's nicest players, nevertheless gave Cubs fans much to cheer about during the twenties and thirties. His 1930 total of 190 RBIs remains the all-time single season record. During the otherwise dismal 1950s, the greatest Cub was undoubtedly hard-hitting shortstop Ernie Banks, who won back to back MVP honors in 1957–58, and who was probably the greatest player never to appear in a World Series. "Without Banks," the White Sox's manager Jimmy Dykes once said, "the Cubs would finish in Albuquerque."

Currently, the Cubs have one of their

best teams ever. Standout players include second baseman (and 1984 MVP) Ryne Sandberg, shortstop Shawon Dunston, and outfielders Andre Dawson and George Bell. Until now this first class combination has yet to produce a pennant, but if the Cubs continue to attract competitors of this caliber, it may be only a matter of time before they become winners again.

The Stadium

Wrigley Field may be the best loved park in baseball. If that's so, it's easy enough to understand why. In practically all of its magnificently maintained details, this place is a classic.

Wrigley is located in "Wrigley-ville," a middle-class commercial and residential area on the North Side of Chicago, located perhaps a half mile or so from Lake Michigan. Driving there you may well find yourself wondering if you're going the right way. The surrounding neighborhood is a simple stretch of nice homes and small, mostly ethnic restaurants and shops. Until you are practically on top of the place, there is absolutely nothing to prepare you for the presence of a 39,000-seat stadium in the midst of this pleasant, pedestrain area.

And suddenly there it is, rising in all its green and gold glory. Even from the outside, the place looks, well, irregular. It is not possessed of a soaring height: it does not dominate the skyline. Nor is it round or square. Rather, Wrigley's lines are rather like those of a ballfield: the place is rounded behind home plate and angled off at the back. Modern stadiums are often built to impress, and impress they do. Wrigley was clearly designed to fit into the neighborhood setting in which it was placed, and it does.

Wrigley's integration into its setting is even more apparent as you walk around the place. To the south and west of the park are a huge collection of bars, restaurants, and souvenirs shops, all reflecting the status of the Cubs' home as a leading tourist attraction for baseball travelers. The Cubs run a very pleasant sidewalk cafe in this area, right outside the park. To the north and east are townhouses, nearly all of which have seating arrangements on their roofs for those who want to view the game without paying—or at least without paying the Cubs! Signs on some of the doors outline what a "season ticket" costs for what is really the "upper deck." To complete the "feel" of the place, there's an old-fashioned fire station just past the right field wall. The firemen sit outside their station, during many games, hoping that someone will "put one over the wall" and into their hands.

Wrigley, opened in 1916, was the second stadium built by Zachary Taylor Davis; the first was Comiskey Park. Both were built to provide comfort and baseball viewing convenience for average fans as those concepts were understood in the early years of this century. Accordingly, public areas in the park are reasonably wide, most of the seats are exceptionally close to the action, and thought was clearly given to keeping the sun off the backs of most attendees. Even so, though, in keeping with turn-of-the-century design practice, some spots have serious pole obstructions while the chairs in many sections, though models of comfort when they were first installed, are somewhat less than ideal now. It's part of the price you pay for going to an older park.

One price you won't pay, though, is to sacrifice cleanliness and safety. Unlike Comiskey, which was allowed to decay in its last few decades, Wrigley is immaculate. Everything is well-maintained, concession stands are attractive and bright, and everything looks—and is—freshly painted.

The field is a thing of beauty—a

smooth, natural grass expanse, surrounded by a brick wall. The brickwork
snakes across the outfield wall, loading
the park with those irregular nooks and
crannies that add dynamism and surprise to a ball game. The wall itself, as
every baseball fan knows, is wreathed
in ivy. This actually was not an original
feature; the idea came in the 1930s
from a teenaged Bill Veeck, Jr., later
White Sox owner and baseball in-
novator, whose dad owned the Cubs for
a while.

The field lines suggest the outfield
wall's oddities. The left field pole is set
at 355'. On top of this pole you'll see
flags celebrating the Cubs' pennant
wins, as well as a banner with Ernie
Bank's retired #14. After the pole, the
field juts out a bit, then in, then reaches
its its maximum depth in center of 400'.
There's another dramatic inward cut
toward the right field foul pole at 353'.
On top of that are more flags, as well as
retired #26, Hall of Fame outfielder Billy
Williams. Altogether, this is the place to
go if you like a hitting game.

Beyond the outfield are Wrigley's
famed (and wild) bleachers. Past them
is probably the park's best feature of all,
its beautiful, hand-operated scoreboard.
Standing some 25' high, this classic
device gives National League scores on
the left and AL results on the right.
You'll find the Cubs totals on the bottom left-hand side. To the top is a clock
(which, of course, is not digital), and,
over that, a sailing mast topped by a
flag. Why the sailing mast? We don't
know, but we are sure some of you can
enlighten us. What we can attest to is
that once you've seen this board, you'll
wonder why anyone would want one of
those electronic visual displays. For our
part, should the Cubs ever decide to
scrap it, we hereby volunteer to lie
across the intersection of Clark and Addison until they relent or we are sent to
that great diamond in the sky, where,
we have no doubt, the grass will be
natural, the hot dogs will be a foot long,

and the umpires will be willing to over-
rule each other.

The fact that Wrigley, Fenway, and
the rest are now being appreciated may
be good news for the sport. "Baseball,"
says columnist and fan George Will, "is
learning not to try to improve what is
right." Wrigley Field, as it is, is very
"right" indeed.

Highlights

The Cubs have gone to the Series ten
times. Moreover, nearly every great
modern era player of note appeared in
the park at one time or another, if only
because Wrigley has been a popular site
for All-Star Games. Thus, the baseball
highlights from Wrigley Field are many.
Yet all recede into the twilight by one of
those few incidents that moves baseball
from sport to mythology.

On October 1, 1932, the Cubs faced
the Yankees in the World Series.
Already down two games and angered
over a disagreement concerning how to
split the Series proceeds, the Cubs fans
and players were even more over-
wrought than usual.

Accordingly, when Babe Ruth stepped
to the plate, he was greeted with howls
from the Cubs' dugout and a shower of
lemons thrown by fans in the stands.
Twice the Bambino took mighty
swings, and twice the ball flew by. The
Cubbies, sensing blood, rose from their
bench and started shouting abuse at the
Babe.

What happened next is the subject of
a controversy that will never end. Many
of the fans and the Yankees saw Ruth
point to the center field bleachers. The
manager of the Cubs swore to his dying
day that it never happened. With one
swing left, the "Sultan of Swat" drove
the ball into the center field bleachers.
It remains among the longest homers
ever hit in the park.

Did Ruth "call his shot?" His own
comment about the affair probably tells

us the most about it. When asked what he thought while rounding the bases, the Babe recalled "I just said to myself, 'you lucky, lucky dog!'" He'd called the shot, alright, and was as surprised as everyone else when he pulled it off.

Fans

At most stadiums, most fans come to the game, watch it, and then go home. At others, a bit of socializing occurs before and after the contest.

Not at Wrigley Field. Every game, day or night, is to the Cub fan an excuse for a party that starts early and often lasts long into the night. Friends meet, have some laughs, dance to the music, consume great quantities of beer, and might even watch a few innings of baseball. Cubs contests are really "happenings" where people gather and anything can, and does, occur. In other cities, to be a baseball fan simply says that you like to follow the game. Being a "Cub fan" however, suggests that you're a participant in a distinct way of life, with its own code, rituals, and rites.

For many fans, Cub contests start perhaps an hour before the game in the bars and eateries around the park where you meet up with "the crowd," who rarely miss a game. You discuss the Cubs, throw some darts, and generally try to impress with what a great car, job, or girlfriend you have. After a beer or two and maybe a sandwich, it's over to Wrigley, where the party continues.

The baseball portion of the festival consists largely of drinking more beer and chatting up young women, while joining in fan rituals. Indeed, fan traditions are probably richer at Wrigley than at any other park. Probably the best known of these is the habit Cubs bleacher fans have of throwing back into the field home run balls hit by the opposition. Should anyone resist giving up their treasure, fans will break into chants of "Throw ... it ... back!!" —

and woe betide those who don't comply. Fans here also like to break out into chants regarding the particular merits of other sections of the park, along the lines of "Bleachers s____!" "Boxes s____!" In another tradition the bleacher fans rise as one and bow to fielders who make spectacular catches; they will even do this for opposing fielders on occasion, although that's atypical. Generally speaking, opponents, and especially umpires, are subjected to many boos and some abuse. You never have any doubt where Cubs admirers stand.

When Cub fans are not booing or chanting, they like to sing. The "Star Spangled Banner" gets a good response here, but it's nothing compared to "Take Me Out to the Ballpark," which is sung during the seventh inning stretch when Cubs announcer Harry Caray sticks his head out of the booth and mike in hand, leads the assembled thousands. Holy Cow!

After the game is over (or, perhaps, a bit before; the Cubs fan's celebrated loyalty doesn't prevent some from cutting out early if their team is losing), it's time for stage three of the party to begin. Within minutes after the game's end, the dozens of bars around the park are filled. At many of them, the good times continue far into the night.

Just who are these people? Mostly, Cubs fans are young adults, middle class, generally well-dressed (scouting out the opposite sex is a big part of the scene here), and fairly equally divided between males and females. Some of these people are college students, some have working-class jobs, and there is a large contingent of Yuppies from the wealthy Lake Shore Drive district nearby. While older people and kids are always present, their numbers do not compare with the party folks. In truth, Wrigley is one of the least family oriented parks in baseball.

It's important, too, to point out that these folks are "Cub" fans, not baseball people per se. Since socializing is a big part of the experience at Wrigley, the fine points of the game are often lost on fans—not that this especially seems to bother anyone. If you want to be surrounded by folks who know a lot about the sport, you might be better off at the new Comiskey Park.

Thus spending an evening with Cub fans can have its pluses and minuses. On the negative side, parents with kids may well find some of the language used in the park offensive—people without kids may not care for it, either. Those who come to a game principally to watch baseball may find some aspects of the Wrigley experience off-putting, too. To be frank, the biggest obstacles to seeing the contest in Wrigley are not the poles, as bothersome as they can be. The problem is fans who persist in constantly getting up and down, standing in the aisles talking, or even sitting on the guard rails between you and the field.

And yet, having said all this, we have to point out that however annoying Wrigley fans can be, this is still one of the most exciting and interesting audiences in baseball. Like the stadium that they sit in, Cubs fans are one of a kind. They, too, are classics of a sort.

Getting There

Built in an era when most people lived in cities and when cars were owned mainly by the upper class, Wrigley Field is one of the toughest parks to get to in baseball. Options for travel to the park include car, train, and cab. Particuarly if you are coming by car, patience and a good map will be required if you want to get to the game with your temper intact.

By car. Wrigley Field is located in a plesant middle-class neighborhood on the North Side of Chicago, near Lake Michigan. Accordingly, there is no direct expressway approach to the park

whatsoever. The closest major road to Wrigley is Lakeshore Drive. That, however, moves very fast—or, alternatively, slow when it is choaked with traffic. If you go to Wrigley any other way than by Lake Shore, you'll be spending time in stop-and-go traffic in unfamiliar Chicago neighborhoods. At any rate, here are some routes:

From South Bend, Gary, Indianapolis, and other *south* and *east* areas, take I-90/94 (the Kennedy Expressway) north to Exit 45 B Addison Street. Turn right on Addison. Follow about 2½ miles to Wrigley, find parking, and follow the crowd to the park.

From Milwaukee, Madison, and other *north* locations, take the Edens Expressway (I-94) south to where it joins the Kennedy Expressway (I-90). Proceed to Exit 43D Irving Park Road and follow Irving Park left. Drive 2½ miles to Wrigley, park, and follow the fans.

From *O'Hare* and points *west*, take the Kennedy Expressway (I-90) east to Exit 43D Irving Park Road, and follow the above instructions. From Midway airport, follow the Stevenson Expressway (I-55) east to where it joins the Dan Ryan expressway (I-90/94). Drive north on the Ryan (it soon becomes the Kennedy) and exit at 45B Addison Street. Turn right on Addison and follow 2½ miles to Wrigley.

From *the Loop* (downtown), take Lakeshore Drive (Route 41) north to Addison. Turn left, travel ½ mile, and start looking for parking.

By cab. Taking a cab to Wrigley isn't an especially cost-effective option. From downtown, expect to pay about $12 one way. From O'Hare it could cost $15 or more.

By train. Train is a better option for getting to the park than car, if you happen to be near a train station! From the Loop, take any Howard-Englewood/Jackson Park A or B train north to the Addison Street Station. Wrigley Field is at the station. The cost is $1.25. It's a bit trickier to take public transit from O'Hare to Wrigley, but it's do-able. From the airport, take the Douglas "B" train to Addison Station, making sure you buy a transfer. From the Addison Station, grab the 152 RTA bus going east and get out at Wrigley. The total cost from O'Hare is $1.50.

Parking

Parking at Wrigley Field is a nightmare. The stadium has two small lots at 1140 West Eddy Street and at 1126 West Grace (both are off North Clark), which are expensive ($10) and fill up fast. Once these places close— usually long before the game starts— you have to look for parking in the neighborhood.

The way the system works it that you drive towards the park by any route you choose. When you get within, say ⅓ of a mile of Wrigley, you'll see people standing on the edge of the streets, waving red flags and trying to coax you into their vacant lot, apartment parking spot, or their driveway. Sometimes they'll have prices posted, sometimes not; and believe us, they'll tell you where to go—whether you decide to park with them or not! Generally speaking, prices run from a low of $5 for spots about halfway back to the Loop to $15 for something quite close to Wrigley.

Some pointers. First, come early: it's the best way to get a space easily and avoid a lot of hassle. Second, don't be too choosy. The longer you wait before deciding, the fewer spaces there will be, and you'll encounter more traffic problems. Third, watch out for rip-offs. One trick played here is to coax you into a lot with reasonable rates, and then tell you, once you get out of the car, that the cheap spots are all gone and you are in one of the unposted expensive places. Should this happen to you, we suggest you get back in your car and

drive out, preferably over the attendant. Finally, be sure to mark down where you are. It's incredibly easy to get lost in the Wrigley area after the contest.

Tickets

You can get Cubs tickets in the usual way: by mail, phone, or through the advance ticket office.

Mail is an option—if you don't intend to buy very good seats! Under Cub rules, club and field box seats (see "Seating") are not sold by mail, no matter how early you order, while terrace and upper deck box seats can only be ordered for weekday day games. "So why bother ordering by mail?" you might ask. Good question. Still, if you are looking for inexpensive seats and you'd like to have them well in advance, send a note including the type of ticket you want, the general location, and your payment in full (plus $2 service charge) to: Chicago Cubs Ticket Office, Wrigley Field, 1060 West Addison Street, Chicago, IL 60613.

Buying tickets by phone is probably just as good a choice. To order tickets that way, call Ticketmaster at (312) 559-1212 within Illinois or (800) 347-CUBS (outside the state) to order. Be prepared with the sections you'd like and a major credit card. Phone lines are open Monday through Friday from 8 A.M. to 9 P.M., on Saturday from 8 A.M. to 8 P.M., and on Sunday from 9 A.M. to 6 P.M. You will be hit with a service charge here, too.

The advance ticket office is your best option—if you come *well* in advance. It's located at the corner of Addison and North Clark from 9 A.M. to 6 P.M. Monday through Friday, and from 9 A.M. to 4 P.M. on Saturday and Sunday.

Availability. At some point during the 1980s, Cubs games became the "in" place to be for thousands of Chicagoans. Until that fashion changes, good tickets for Cubs games will continue to be hard to come by, whether they win or lose.

In 1990, for example, the Cubs attendance was 2.5 million at a time when the team performed miserably. Since Wrigley Field, with 39,012 seats, is the second smallest park in the majors, those numbers mean box seats are very hard to get and that there are frequent sell-outs. At many parks, if you show up at a game without tickets, you won't get good seats. At Wrigley, it's quite likely you won't get any chair at all.

How can you avoid being disappointed? Simply by ordering early. If you get into the Chicago area with any frequency, visit the advance ticket office and get the seats you want for later in the season. If you live outside of town, call for tickets well before you plan to be in the Windy City. If this isn't possible, showing up for weekday games, or contests against less popular teams (such as Atlanta or Houston), will greatly increase your chances of finding a decent spot.

What if you are completely shut out? We will point out that the area around the park is simply crawling with scalpers. We don't recommend that you do business with them: scalpers push ticket prices up, and the spots they sell can be counterfeit, in which case you'll be totally out of luck. However, it's an option that, given Wrigley's situation, you may want to consider. If you do buy from scalpers, make sure you do it away from the stadium — say across Addison or Clark from the park. Buying from scalpers on Wrigley's property gets management's nose very out of joint, and you could end up having some unpleasantness with the authorities.

Costs. Cubs prices are very popular — with Cub's management. Other people might consider them a bit high. But, then, since the Cubs are hav-

ing no trouble filling their stadium at their current fee schedule, there is little to motivate them to roll back prices. Since attending a game at Wrigley is one of the premier baseball experiences, we suppose you have to expect to pay for it.

Within the various price ranges, too, there is a great diversity in the quality of the seats (see "Seating"). This is a park where it would be a very good idea to have a seating chart by you while purchasing spots. At Wrigley Field, all seats are decidedly not created equal.

In 1990, the Cubs' price schedule was as follows: Club Box ($13); Field Box ($13); Terrace Box ($10); Upper Deck Box ($10); Terrace Reserved ($7); Upper Deck Reserved (Adults [$5]); (Child [$3]); Bleachers ($5); Standing Room* ($5).

Rainouts. Chicago is not an outstandingly wet place, but rainouts — and snowouts — happen. Cubs written policies allow ticket exchanges only for future games if a "called" game happens to you.

Seating

A small park built in the classic modified "U" design, Wrigley Field has some of the best seats in baseball. However, it has its share of bad ones, too.

Club boxes ($13) are the most expensive spots in the park, and they are worth the extra money. These are super spots located directly off the field. In rows 1–10, for example, you can practically touch the players. The whole key to getting the best spots here lies in selecting within the baselines (section 11, third, to section 32, first), and in the lowest rows possible. However, these seats are so good that any spot in this area will give you an excellent view. The problem is in finding any such

*Offered after sellouts.

spaces: these seats are usually bought by season ticket holders well in advance of the season.

Field box seats are a bit farther from the field and are the same price as the Club Box spots. Hence, they are not quite as good a bargain, but at least are somewhat available. Here, the same rules apply: stay in low rows within the baselines, which here run from section 111 to 132.

Terrace boxes ($10) slope up behind the field boxes, and are among the better bargains in the park. Located just past the field seats, these spots are a ways from the action, but they boast an unobstructed view of the field. Not so in the Terrace Reserved ($7). Here, there are serious pole obstructions. If you must sit in this area, try to get seats in the middle of the rows, as the pole problem is lessened considerably. However, if you sit there, bring plenty of food and drink with you: rows are long in this area, and it is tough to get in and out. As always, the best seats are in the baselines, which in both sections run from 209 (3rd) to 233 (1st).

Upper boxes ($10) consist of the first ten rows of the top deck. These are fine spots when they're close to home plate and get progressively worse the further you move from the batter's box. For this price, you should certainly insist that you be given a seat within the baselines (boxes 431, first base, or 413, third base). If you're given a choice, try to favor the left field side if attending a night game — the setting sun can be a serious view problem on the right field side.

Ditto with the upper deck reserved seats ($5), which are located above the upper boxes. These are among the cheaper seats in the park, and they should be. Having serious pole obstructions and being located quite far from the field, these spots are none too good. Middle of the row baseline seats (530 to 512) are the best of an undistinguished lot.

Bleacher seats ($5) are, to our minds,

preferrable to the upper deck reserved ones, although you'll find yourselves sitting in the middle of a wild and crazy crowd. Consisting of green benches located under a glaring sun at the end of center field, these spots are still fairly close in, if only because Wrigley is a small park. If you're coming for a night game, select aisles 150 to 153 and you'll avoid some sun. If you're coming for a sunny day game, bring shades and lotion.

Last and least are the "Family Reserved" spots. Located at the end of left field, these are practically the worst seats in the house. Nevertheless, you'll be expected to pay twice the price of bleacher seats (hence, $10) for the "privilege" of sitting in an alcohol-free environment. It's an outrage.

Special Needs

Wrigley Field was built long before concern about the handicapped was a consideration. Accordingly, facilities for the physically disabled are limited.

Parking. Handicapped parking is located right next to the park. However, you must call (312) 404-4077 to reserve a space. The charge is $10.

Seating. There is one handicapped seating section, which is located in aisle 120, directly behind home plate. These are excellent spots, but their numbers are few. If you want one, you should reserve well in advance.

Food and Features

Food. Food is pretty good at Wrigley Field, although not outstanding. Prices are moderate to high and the selection is decent, if not great.

Standard ballpark fare can be found throughout the park. The list includes hot dogs, jumbo hots, potato chips (they like them here), Italian sausage, carmel corn, nachos, and pizza.

The big specialty at Wrigley is "Italian Beef," which is pretty good. The "Italian Beef" stand can be found to the right of home plate on the main concourse.

Drinks. Drinks available include beer (Bud or Old Style) and Pepsi products, reasonably priced.

Beyond this, the park boasts two restaurants. *The Friendly Confines* offers light pre-and-during game dining in a pleasant atmosphere. It serves food until the 8th inning or until 9 P.M., and is located mid-way along the first base-line. The *Sheffield Grill* at the end of the right field line on the main concourse is a pleasant, enclosed spot with tables and nice wall plaques outlining the careers of famous Cubs. Served here are grilled items and deli sandwiches. The place also has a very wide selection of imported beers which go for the same price as the domestic brews.

Dining note. Lines at Wrigley are often long. One way of avoiding them is to buy your food at the Sheffield Grill. Lines are often shorter, prices are the same as in the stands, and the place has TV monitors so you can keep up with the game.

Features. Wrigley Field has no features, the attitude here being that attending a game in this classic old park ought to be a feature enough. It is.

Assistance

Wrigley has a small "Customer Relations Booth" located behind Aisle 118 (home plate) on the main concourse. During our visits, this locale was occupied by an employee who seemed far more interested in getting in some reading than in helping fans. Possibly, this was not typical of how this operation is run.

However, it is also possible that this was all too typical of Wrigley. Like that other great "classic" ballpark, Fenway Park, the attitude here too often tends to be almost dismissive of the customer. Stadium personnel here can be curt (there are, of course, many courteous ones), requests for routine information are ignored or not complied with, and management policies such as the restriction on buying box seats through the mail and the lack of decent numbers of handicapped seats bespeak a disinterest in the fan. Of course, as long as fans keep coming—as they indisputibly do—there's little reason for Wrigley to change things.

Safety and Security

Safety. Cubs fans may not be the biggest drinkers in baseball (their peers at Comiskey and in Milwaukee could give them a run for their money), but it's a sure thing that after any Cubs game the alcohol level in Lake Michigan rises perceptibly. Beer controls are minimal here (there is a four beer per-person per-purchase "limit"), and in the stands beer vendors are very aggressive. Within the park, therefore, drunkenness and the problems that come with it—obnoxious behavior and fights—are all too common. Most of these problems seem to be confined to the bleachers, but elements of it can be found anyplace else. If you find drinkers are causing troubles in your section, you should bring the matter to the attention of the ushers. If you find bad language and loud behavior particularly offensive and can't get seats in the more sedate boxes, you might want to consider sitting in the overpriced "Family Reserved" area.

Sun is the next biggest problem. You can avoid most of it by staying out of the bleachers and the end sections along the right field line. In spring, cold can be a problem, too. Bring a coat or a blanket along.

The area outside the park is reasonably safe, particularly in the main business sections along North Clark. However, if you know that you will be returning to your car late, you might want to seek out a lighted lot along a main street rather than a dark alleyway, particularly if you are female. Crime isn't common here, but it happens. Don't let it happen to you.

Health. Should you get too much sun or have too many Buds in the general merriment, the First Aid station can be found behind home plate on the main concourse.

Mementos

Souvenirs. The *Official Cub Gift Shop* has three Cubs souvenir stores at Wrigley. The biggest one is behind home plate on the main concourse, while the others are at the ends of left and right fields. The selection is good, and the prices are moderate to high.

Sports World, across the street from Wrigley at 3555 North Clark (312) 4720-7701, has an even bigger selection of baseball goods. It's open Mondays to Fridays from 9 A.M. to 8 P.M., and on Saturday and Sunday from 9 A.M. to 5 P.M.

Foul Balls. Wrigley, a small park, is a good place to snag fouls. You will have lots of competition here, though. This park, which attracts lots of young men,

is full of folks who think that they should be suited up and down on the field. They try to prove it by barehanding balls. You can take your chances at outdoing them by sitting in aisles 110–113 on the lower deck.

Important note. If you're in the bleachers and the Cubs' opponents hit a home run ball to you, for God's sake stand up and throw it back into the field. Should you try to keep it, we can take no responsibility for your well-being.

Autographs. While Wrigley may be a classic old park, it takes a decidedly modern view toward autograph seekers. Specifically, it does what it can to keep fans away from any contact with the players.

As a practical matter, your best chance here probably consists of standing near the dugouts during batting practice. Players sometimes stroll over and sign a few. Large numbers of fans gather outside the players' parking lot after the contest (located on the North Clark Street side of the stadium), but as it is totally fenced in, few ever get an autograph.

The situation with visitors is even worse. They exit from Gate D and, to shelter them from their admirers, their bus will actually pull over the curb and park kittycorner to the door, eliminating all possibility of fans getting anywhere near or even seeing the stars. We think this stinks.

CHICAGO WHITE SOX
Comiskey Park

When did baseball become the national sport? Surely by the Civil War it was already a popular game, and by the

1890s few indeed were the large towns that did not have a team of one sport or another. Yet, in those years, attendance at baseball parks was minimal, leagues came and went with startling regularity, and only a handful of players (Mike "King" Kelly, Cy Young, and Willie Keeler perhaps) could truly have been said to have captured the public's imagination.

In truth, the creation of a real two-league structure with the formation of the American League in 1901 gave baseball the momentum to push it foward. With two great contending leagues, baseball touched a far greater number of towns than ever before with truly professional action, and competition was greatly enhanced. With separation, too, it became possible for fans in different leagues to argue about the respective merits of their players, without fear of direct, on the field contradiction—at least until the Series! Thus, as fans compared notes on Ed Delahanty, Tris Speaker, Honus Wagner and Tyrus Cobb, commitment and enthusiasm deepened.

The National League bitterly protested the creation of their American rivals, particularly after the Americans resorted to the underhanded tactic of paying ballplayers a living wage. Authorities in the press confidently predicted that "too much baseball" would water down talent and interest. In fact, the creation of the second great band of clubs was the making of both leagues, and of the sport.

Byron "Ban" Johnson was the founding genius of the American League. Standing by his side right at the beginning, though, was Charles Comiskey, son of an Irish Chicago "wardheeler," a former St. Louis ballplaying great, and, at the time the AL was founded, owner of a minor league club in St. Paul, Minnesota. A close friend and drinking companion of Johnson, Comiskey shared the older man's dreams of what baseball could become. Accordingly, when the initial AL franchises were awarded, Comiskey signed up for the new Chicago club. The "White Stock-

ings" (later shortened to "Sox," supposedly because it was easier to set in type) were born.

Over the next two decades, Charles Comiskey—known as "The Old Roman" because of his stoic bearing—forwarded the game of baseball, showing a sense of vision that had rarely been seen in management before or since. While other owners focused their attention on the turnstile, or, at best, labored to put together solid teams, Comiskey had an eye on the big picture. Convinced that baseball could be an international phenomenon, "the Old Roman" launched world tours, strutting baseball's best stuff to the bemusement of Britishers and Egyptians. He also initiated "Ladies' Days," when women—suitably escorted, of course—could come to the ballpark at no charge, the idea being to "civilize" the Great Game. Finally, over a nine-year period, he pulled strings, hired and fired promoters, and smooth-talked bankers and politicians, all with the idea of building a stadium that truly would mirror in its dimensions the magnificence, and future, of his sport. At last, in 1910, with the help of architect Zachary Taylor Davis (who would later design Wrigley Field), "The Old Roman" built, in a cabbage field in the heavily Irish neighborhood of Bridgeport, the self-proclaimed "Baseball Palace of the World." Fittingly, Comiskey laid the first green brick for the foundation while kneeling on a piece of turf especially brought over from the "old sod" of Ireland.

The Team

The team that occupied Comiskey Park for its eight decades of existence is one of the older clubs in baseball, but its record is not distinguished. After an initial strong start, the Chicago White Sox succumbed to the biggest scandal in the history of the sport. Since then, the Sox have lived in a kind of perpetual baseball twilight; though the team has had moments of glory, they have been perpetual also rans. Now, it seems as if the White Sox may finally be moving out of the shadows and into the light.

During the first two decades of this century, the White Sox were one of the better squads in baseball. They took the first American League pennant in 1901, they won the first "Streetcar Series" in 1906 when they beat the Cubs, and in 1917 they took a second fall classic against the Giants. It would be their last.

Many stars played with the team in these years, but the greatest of all was the all-but-illiterate "Shoeless" Joe Jackson, currently number three on the all-time batting average list.

In 1919, the White Sox went to the Series again, matched against the underdog Cincinnati Reds. Before the Series, there were rumors of a "fix." But, then, such rumors in the sport were common enough, for a simple reason: throwing games happened with some frequency in the early years of the sport. During the first game, played in Cincinnati, Chicago pitcher Ed Cicotte intentionally beaned a player. Gamblers throughout the park nodded their heads in satisfaction—it was a prearranged signal, on the part of the Sox, that they had agreed to throw the Series.

Which was exactly what they did. Cincinnati won the classic, 5–3. But the fix was so obvious that suspicions were aroused. Chicago sports columinst Ring Lardner was one of the first to catch on. On the train back to Chicago after the game, he stumbled drunkenly through the players' car, singing:

"I'm forever blowing ball-games
Pretty ball-games in the air.
I'm forever blowing ball-games,
And the gamblers treat us fair."

The Sox were not amused. Other people began to ask questions, too. Soon, one by one, the Sox began to crack.

Eventually, eight players were indicted for attempting to throw the Series, including Jackson. That was not the whole team: some players refused to get involved with the scheme. All eight were later acquitted, thanks to some suspiciously missing evidence, but none ever played baseball again.

There has been a tendency in recent years to sympathize with this group. In particular, Jackson has often been treated as a kind of folk hero, a martyr to the greed of owners and the "capitalist system." It has been suggested that he ought to take that place in the Hall of Fame that his records indicate he otherwise deserves.

But the "eight men out" were guilty by their own confessions, as well as by the testimony of the honest players. The law may have been forced to let them go on technicalities; baseball was under no such obligation. Bill James, in his great *Historical Baseball Abstract*, gets it exactly right when he says, "The only injustice that was done to Joe Jackson and friends is that the sons of bitches were allowed to walk the streets, rather than going to jail where they belonged."

The "Black Sox" scandal seemed to take the heart out of the Chicago crew for a good long time. Through the twenties, thirties, and forties, they were the team that wasn't there: no Series appearances, few close races, poor attendance, and only a handful of certified stars, principal among these slugger Luke Appling. Finally, after nearly sixty years of control, the Comiskey family sold the team to the only man in baseball capable of breathing life back into a corpse.

That was Bill Veeck. Over the next few years, and then again in the late 1970s, baseball's most idiosyncratic and best loved owner left no stone unturned in his attempt to bring fans to the park. He refurbished the place top to bottom, installed Comiskey Park's famous "exploding scoreboard" (which bursts into swirling colors and bursting fireworks every time a home run was hit), and even installed a shower and a barber chair in the center field bleachers to keep fans cool and clean-cut during games! To keep the fans amused, Veeck was not adverse to stunts, either. Once he dressed up as the "Spirit of '76," and led an impromptu parade through the stadium. On another occasion, he had midget (Veeck's former St. Louis Browns' major leaguer!) Ed Gaedel "fly" into center field dressed as a Martian, supposedly intent on taking diminutive Sox players Luis Aparicio and Nellie Fox back to the "Red Planet" with him.

Beyond the games, though, Veeck was also commited to building a winning team. He recruited one of the best White Sox squads ever, including Aparicio, Minnie Minoso, and Hall of Fame pitcher Early Wynn. In 1959, after a forty-year drought, the White Sox went to the Series, bowing on this occasion to the Dodgers, 4–2.

Unfortunately, Veeck could not keep the magic going. In failing health, Veeck sold the team. It soon returned to its familiar pattern of failure.

In 1990, however, things changed. A long period of rebuilding at last started to pay off as quality players like catcher Carlton Fisk, shortstop Ozzie Guillen, and single-season save leader Bobby Thigpen drove the Sox to a second place divisional finish and its best showing since 1983.

Does this season mean that things are finally turning around for the Sox? At this juncture, it's hard to say. The Sox's performance in 1990 showed that the team has the will to win, and, as the saying goes, where there's a will there is usually a way.

The Stadium

Where previous stadiums had been ramshackle wooden affairs that tumbled down with discouraging regularity, the new stadium was a magnificent brick and steel edifice. Whereas seating in Comiskey's predecessors had consisted mainly of hard wooden benches, the new palace was filled with handsome wood-and-metal chairs, exceedingly comfortable for their time. While the older parks had often been constructed with little thought to such matters as view angles, Comiskey constructed his place with the goal of insuring that the "krank" in a 25-cent seat would have as good a view as the "swell" and the alderman. Henry Ford was then bringing the auto to the average worker. Thinking in a similar fashion, Charles Comiskey wanted to bring the best in baseball to everyman.

Comiskey Park was not perfect. Taylor, for example, had supplied "The Old Roman" with a pioneering "cantilevered" design that would have eliminated all the poles—and, thus, all the obstructed seats—from the park, two generations before such plans became common elsewhere. Comiskey, a tight man with a buck, did not want to spend the extra money. Comiskey also took special pride in locating his "baseball palace" in the Irish neighborhoods of South Chicago, forgetting that most of the people in the area worked in the nearby slaughterhouses and their accompanying stockyard. Over the next several decades, fans would have frequent occasions, whenever the wind changed, to recall exactly where they were.

Still, despite its limitations, Comiskey Park revolutionized the business of stadium constructiuon throughout the United States. Clubs rushed to bring new parks on line modeled after the "baseball palace," and such famous ballparks as Fenway, Tiger, Yankee, and Wrigley entered the lexicon of the game. Other managers can say they did more to influence how the game was played than Charles Comiskey. But no one had a greater influence on where it was played.

Having said all this, we have to conclude on what we regard as the saddest note in this book. As this volume was being written, Comiskey Park, "the greatest baseball palace in the world"—and one of the most historically significant parks—was headache-balled to serve as a parking lot for the brand new stadium to be located directly south of the old facility. That such a thing could be allowed to happen in the 1990s, when citizens are supposedly aware of the need to preserve buildings that have significance to the history and development of this country, seems to us a thing both incredible and horrible. But it happened.

At the beginning of our researches, as, we suspect, for many another fan, Comiskey Park was "the other ballpark in Chicago." It was the one that was not Wrigley Field. In writing this book, we learned to love the deteriorating old place. Sure it had seen better days. Nor do we especially doubt management's claims that Comiskey was structurally unsound. But if Comiskey Park was a ruin, it was a magnificent one. With its beautiful arches and its simple, two-tiered construction, the place had an airiness and a feeling of majesty missing in the other older parks. With its close-to-the-lines true baseball design, an incredible number of seats really did provide great views, even if there were also some that did not. Had the "baseball palace" been as well maintained as Fenway or Wrigley, it might be recognized today as having been the greatest stadium of them all.

As we go to print, the new Comiskey has been introduced, to generally glowing reviews. We discuss some aspects of the new stadium in the "Seating," and "Features" section of this guide. Basically, the new Comiskey has succeeded in maintaining a fair position of baseball "feel."

In the "comfort and convenience" areas—those double-headed gods of the modern baseball fan—the New Comiskey is certainly superior to the old. Yet in a larger sense, baseball on the South Side can never again be the same. Gone are wonderful arches that let in the sun—and helped you forget about the stockyard smell. Gone too is that vast expanse of soil and grass, upon which Luke Appling, Babe Ruth, Lou Gehrig, Joe DiMaggio, Joe Jackson, and Ty Cobb ran, sweat, lost, and won . . . all of them living the ultimate male fantasy, which is to be well-paid to do those things that we loved doing as little boys.

Sentimentality? You bet. But as someone once said, "it's all part of the game."

Fans

The Chicago White Sox may not be the most remarkable team in baseball, but it does have some of the most remarkable fans.

White Sox admirers stuck with their squad after the "Black Sox" scandal, an event that probably would have sunk another team. And though their numbers went down, fans continued to trolley to Wentworth and 33rd through the long decades of defeat and disappointment that followed that event. When Bill Veeck appeared among them, they forgave the fact that Veeck's dad had owned the Cubs (which is damn near unforgivable on the South Side) and took the new owner and his antics to their heart. In fact, the White Sox may be the only team where a former owner may be the most loved person ever associated with the organization. When current Sox management announced plans to destroy their beloved, deteriorating Comiskey, the fans rose in righteous indignation. Of course, since they were White Sox fans, it was an effort tinged with futility.

Who are these people? It is something of a theme in this book that fans often mirror the cities they live in. In the case of the White Sox, though, the reflection is not of a city, but of a neighborhood. Specifically, that neighborhood is Chicago's South Side.

The South Side of Chicago was where the slaughterhouses and steel yards were located. It was where the immigrants first arrived, and continue to arrive. It's an area where the church is Catholic, politics are Democratic (though many liked Reagan), and where someone having trouble with his English might chew you out if you bought a foreign car. Initially the home of the "Windy City's" shanty Irish and Italians, these groups were joined some time ago by much of Chicago's black and Hispanic population. Harold Washington, the City's first black mayor, was from this area. So was Mayor Richard J. Daley, who lived within walking distance of Comiskey and could be spotted at many games.

Like the people of the South Side, Comiskey fans are mainly a working class, ethnic crowd: there are many people of Irish and Polish descent, some Germans, blacks, and Hispanics. Distributed about evenly among the age groups and not especially well-dressed, this is a tough, passionate, loud, mostly male audience that likes beer (in fact, it likes it a bit too much), hates umpires, loves and knows baseball, and is willing to let its feelings be expressed without worrying about subtlety. Go, for example, to a game against Milwaukee, and you will likely see many sweatshirts advising the Sox to "S_____ the Brew Crew!" We will leave it to you to figure out what these sweatshirts say about Oakland when the Sox play the As.

Fan traditions, many of them centering around Nancy Faust's organ playing (see "Features"), abound here. When a home run is hit, just after the "exploding scoreboard" settles down, the crowd belts out a chorus of "Hey, Hey, Hey, Goodbye!" Departing oppos-

ing pitchers get the same treatment. For that matter, just about every opportunity to sing is seized upon: the "National Anthem" gets a rousing rendition, while "Take Me Out to the Ball Game" is given its loudest chorus in the majors, even without the help of Harry Caray. Unison chanting of "whiff!! whiff!!" greets opposing batters after two strikes, combined with deafening, accelerating applause—it's got to be really intimidating, which is why they do it.

One tradition you will not see is the habit of throwing home run balls hit by opposing players back into the stadium. That practice is associated with Wrigley Field, and if there is one thing the White Sox is sure of in this world, it is that he is not a Cub fan. To the Cubs admirer, Sox fans are, well, lower-class. To the White Soxers, Cubbie lovers are a bunch of quiche-eaters who know nothing about baseball. A bumper sticker we saw in the Comiskey lots pretty much sums up the feeling. It says simply, "Die, Yuppie Scum."

Going to a White Sox game is an experience. It's not entirely positive, for Sox admirers often drink too much and swear too much, and fights in the stands happen more often here than in most places. But beyond these things, if you go to a White Sox game you'll be surrounded by fans who really know the game, who care about it passionately, and who invest that emotional energy necessary to really create that sense of communiation between the players and the fans that alone can make baseball a transcendent experience. Even with its problems, the White Sox audience has to be rated one of the most electrifying in baseball.

Getting There

Though old Comiskey Park will be gone by the time you read this,

Chicago's newest baseball facility will be open for business right across the street. Both parks are just south of Chicago's downtown. Easier to get to than Wrigley Field, new Comiskey Park will be accessible by car, train, or cab.

By car. Chicago is a big city with terrible traffic during rush hours. Accordingly, if taking the train is an option for you, it's probably the best way to get to the park. That being said, however, reaching Comiskey by auto presents no special problems.

If you are coming in from Milwaukee, Madison, and other points *north*, take I-94 south to the John Kennedy Expressway (I-90) east. Follow the Kennedy south as it merges with the Dan Ryan Expressway (you'll still be on I-90). Exit the Dan Ryan at Exit 54 31st Street. Follow two blocks to Comiskey Park.

From *O'Hare Airport*, simply take the John Kennedy Expressway east, and follow the above instructions.

From Joliet, St. Louis, *Midway Airport* and points *west* and *southwest*, take I-55 North to its junction with the Dan Ryan Expressway (90/94), and then head south (towards Indiana) on the Dan Ryan Expressway. Bear left and take Exit 54 31st Street. Proceed two blocks to the stadium.

From Indianapolis, South Bend, Detroit, and other *south* and *east* areas, take I-90 north until it becomes the Dan Ryan Expressway. Take Exit 55A Comiskey Park/35th Street. Go up ramp and turn left. Park is two blocks west.

By cab. If you are staying in the downtown hotels, taking a cab is a good way to get to the game. You should be able to get to the park for under $10 from most of them. A cab from Midway Airport will run about $16, while one from O'Hare could run from $25 to $30.

By train. If you are staying in downtown Chicago, taking the train is the best way to get to Comiskey Park. However, the park can be reached by train from most sections of the city, as well as from O'Hare Airport.

If you are traveling from the *downtown area*, take any southbound Dan Ryan elevated train and get off at the Sox-35th Street Station. Comiskey Park is on the west side of the tracks, as you leave the station. Trains on this line leave every few minutes, and the fare is $1.25.

From *O'Hare Airport*, take the CTA train to downtown Chicago, making sure that you pick up a transfer. Exit the O'Hare train at the Lake Transfer Station. At this point, take the Lake and Clark Street exit to the street level, where you'll see an entrance for the elevated train. From here, take the Lake Dan Ryan A or B train going toward 95th Street. Exit at the Sox-35th Street Station. Comiskey Park is one block to the west.

Parking

Parking had been a problem at old Comiskey Park. Although there were enough spaces for most games, lots were spread out over a wide area around the park, in locations that were none too secure. While the "unsafe" feeling was probably more a function of emotion than reality, this parking situation was a considerable disincentive to attending games: during our research on this book, we had fans in Atlanta, Montreal, and Los Angeles tell us about how frightened they were in walking back to their autos after a game at Comiskey — although none reported any actual difficulties.

One of the principal promises of management in the plans for the new park is the creation of thousands of new, lighted and secured parking spaces. This will certainly help to alleviate fan concerns. Unfortunately, one of these new lots will be directly over where the "baseball palace of the world" sat in all its ruined majesty.

Tickets

Tickets to White Sox games can be ordered by mail, phone, picked up at the advance ticket office, or bought directly at the game.

To get tickets by mail, send the dates you want, location of seats, and your payment in full to: Chicago White Sox, Ticket Office, 324 West 35th Street, Chicago, IL 60616.

Be sure to include the White Sox's $2 service charge with your order.

You can also get tickets over the phone. Call Ticketmaster at (312) 559-1212 to order. Be sure to have a major credit card on hand. You'll get hit with a service charge here, too.

In the new park, the advance ticket window will be located at the stadium, at the corner of 35th Street and Sheilds (therefore, around home plate). This office will be open from 9 A.M. to 5 P.M. Monday through Friday during the off-season, and from 10 A.M. to 6 P.M. Monday through Friday and 10 A.M. to 4 P.M. Saturday and Sunday during the regular season.

Of course, as in the past, you will also be able to buy your tickets at the game.

Availability. Historically, ticket availability has been no problem whatsoever at Comiskey Park. For years, attendance — and performance — has been pretty low. On most nights, you could walk up to the gate on the night of the game and get pretty good spots in most sections of the park.

Last year changed that. A hot team and a vibrant pennant race sent ticket sales soaring. Sellouts were still rare, but you could no longer count on getting a decent seat near the baselines at the last minute, either.

How will it be in the new Comiskey Park? It's hard to say. The new stadium will have just about the same number of seats as the old. However, it will also, at least at first, have the fact of newness working on its behalf. Lots of folks will probably come in the first season or two, just to "check it out."

In the past, matchups against the Yankees and Oakland were consistently among the most popular. If you attend one of these in particular, you should probably get your tickets well in advance.

Costs. White Sox ticket prices have, in the past, been moderate. Plans for the new stadium have not, at this writing, been announced, but we would be surprised if prices dropped.

In 1990, White Sox prices were as follows: Golden Box ($11.50); Loge ($10.50); Upper and Lower Boxes ($9.50); Mezzanine Terrace ($7.50); Reserved Grandstand ($6.50); General Admission ($5).

Rainouts. Rainouts aren't all that frequent in Chicago, but they happen. Snowouts, though rare, occur too. In either case, you can exchange your stub for tickets to another game.

Seating

Given the new Comiskey's status as a just opened park, we can only make a few comments on seating.

The club's promise that the new Comiskey wouldn't have "a single obstructed view seat in the house" has been kept. That's certainly an improvement over the old park. The wooden chairs of the old stadium have been replaced by more comfortable, contour plastic ones, while the bleacher benches in new Comiskey Park will at least have backs on them (they didn't in the old).

This is all very fine. Still, we are a bit concerned about the overall layout. The new park has a deck that is spaced fairly far from the action, while the new Comiskey is a much higher stadium than the old one. Thus, upper deck fans find themselves more distant from the field in the 1990s than they were in the 1910s.

Over the past three decades, new ballparks have been sold to the public on the basis that they'll provide more comfort and convenience than the old ones. Usually, they have. Unfortunately, they have rarely provided as good a view of the ballgame. As fine as the new Comiskey is, it still adheres to this general diction.

Special Needs

One area in which new stadiums have made vast strides over the old ones has been in providing facilities for the handicapped.

The old Comiskey Park had both handicapped seating and parking, but they were limited and difficult to get to. The new park has 400 handicapped spots, among the highest proportions of handicapped seats to regular seats in baseball. Special elevators are convenient to both seating and handicapped parking.

Food and Features

Food. One thing management preserved from old Comiskey Park is the stadium's food. And that's great because the food at Comiskey Park was one of the place's best attractions. Though the concession stands in the "baseball palace" were unsightly, they variety of things to eat was excellent and the prices were very reasonable.

Comiskey has the usual ballpark fare, of course: very good hot dogs, kosher hots, cotton candy, pretzels, pizza, and an excellent grilled "super hamburger."

The place is also strong on specialties. These include "tropic ices" (fruit flavored), deli sandwiches, excellent bratwursts, and Polish sausages. Probably best of all is the Mexican food: tasty tacos, burritos, and tostadas.

You'll, find all of these in the new park, along with other selections as well. The park also has a "Stadium Club" restaurant and lounge, which is located over the right field section of the park. The Club, we are informed, has "everything to accommodate even the busiest executive," including private phone booths, fax machines and "coat and briefcase" checking. Unfortunately (though unsurprisingly) it's limited to members only . . . so if you were planning to watch a Sox game while faxing your latest corporate takeover bid to Tokyo, well, you can forget it.

Drinks. Drinks of all sorts have always been a part of the scene at Comiskey Park—in fact, the place once had its own soda bottling plant in the basement! Miller beer was the standard brew at the old park, while Coke products were the soft drinks, including a reasonable "Souvenir Cup." The same things are available in the new edifice.

Features. The greatest feature of both the old Comiskey Park and the new, and one of the best in baseball, has been the organ music of Nancy Faust. For several years, Mrs. Faust, a pixieish young woman, has played her instrument at Comiskey Park—not in a box up in the press booth somewhere, but out in the stands, where fans can walk up, watch, and listen.

And walk up they do. Throughout any White Sox game, you'll see quite a crowd around Nancy, and for good reason: she's just great at what she does. Boasting a repertoire of hundreds of songs at her fingertips, Mrs. Faust seems to have a sixth sense about knowing what to play to express the emotions of the crowd and to needle the opposition, particularly during pitching changes and after errors. We guarantee that something she plays will have you laughing out loud at least once in the game. Happily, Nancy will be coming over to the new park.

The other feature the old Comiskey was famous for was Bill Veeck's celebrated "exploding scoreboard," which would burst into a shower of fireworks and a brilliant blaze of colored lights everytime the Sox hit a home run. The crowd, as you can imagine, just loves it. This will be a feature of the new stadium, too.

New features are planned as well. There will be a White Sox "Hall of Fame," a kid's play area, and two on-site White Sox souvenir stores.

Assistance

The folks at the Customer Service office at the old park were outstandingly helpful and knowledgeable. They will no doubt do an equally fine job in the new facility.

Safety and Security

Safety. Safety was a concern at the old stadium, and it may remain one in the new.

The biggest problem at White Sox games is drinking. White Sox fans like beer, and they consume quite a lot of it. And while management has pious statements posted everywhere encouraging sobriety, beer vendors in the stands are among the most aggressive in baseball. While in most parks beer sales are cut-off in the seventh inning, at Comiskey vendors are out in force yelling "last call" at the end of the ninth.

The results of this policy (or lack of a policy) are predictable. While most fans are well-behaved, obnoxious drunks are encountered, and fights break out with some regularity. Security does a good job in controlling these problems, but a better approach to alcohol control would do more to straighten things out than billy clubs.

You can generally avoid this problem by staying out of the bleacher areas, where the worst offenders seem to congregate. However, there is no guarantee that you will sidestep these people anyplace in the park. We do not want to discourage going to Comiskey, or bringing your family. We basically like these fans very much. And even if you should run into some folks who've had a few too many, outside of hearing some abusive language shouted at the umpires, you are unlikely to encounter any problems. However, you should be aware of the situation.

There are difficulties outside, too. Both the old and new Comiskeys are located in a tough area of the South Side. To the north and west of the park is a mixed residential and commercial area that is fairly safe. To the south and east are housing projects, which should be avoided. Our best advice is, if you decide to have a drink after the game in one of the local spots, go with a friend, particularly if you're leaving the game late. Since this area is heavily patrolled by Chicago police before, during, and after the contest, going to and from parking lots should present no concerns if you head out directly after the game.

Health. New, modern, and fully equipped first aid facilities are planned for the new Comiskey. The design of the park suggests that sun is liable to be a problem in the bleachers—bring lotion and drink water if you plan to sit there. Particularly in the early spring, it can get cold in Chicago. Make sure you dress warmly, especially if you are going to a night game.

Mementos

Souvenirs. The new Comiskey will have two on-site souvenir stores.

Foul Balls. Design maps of the park indicate that the best spots to snag foul balls in the new park will be just past first and third on the lower deck.

Autographs. The old Comiskey park was one of the easiest places in baseball to get signatures; quite the reverse of neighboring Wrigley Field, which is one of the hardest. Where the new park will stand in this area is anyone's guess.

CINCINNATI REDS
Riverfront Stadium

What is the best known line of American poetry? Some might recall Robert Frost's "the road not taken," or Poe's archaic "Quoth the Raven, never-more!" But it's a good bet that the line correctly identified by more folks than any other would be a humble one: "The outlook wasn't brilliant for the Mudville Nine that day. . . ."

Most wouldn't know who the author was (it was Ernest Thayer), but just about everyone would recognize the phrase as the opening of "Casey at the Bat." In truth, "Casey" isn't great poetry, a fact that Thayer knew as well as anyone. But the darned thing, now a century old, has proved incredibly durable and it no doubt will still be among the most known poems another hundred years from now.

Why has "Casey" proved so popular? In large part, because it recalls a simpler America, an age that was dying even when Thayer wrote his verse. It was a time when most Americans lived in small communities or on the farm, when heroes were people we could look up to, and when baseball wasn't just a game: it was a contest that gave expression to people as members of a community. "Casey" isn't a poem about Casey at all; it is about what the sport

means to Mudville. Though the poem has the sense to end on a melancholy note ("There is no joy in Mudville"), it nevertheless implied that an age in which people's biggest problem is a lost ballgame is a pretty good time in which to be alive.

Did such an America ever exist, after all? Probably not in the real world. But it certainly existed in our hearts, and it continues to dwell there today.

Should you visit Cincinnati to attend Reds games, you may well be reminded a bit of the world of "Casey." Certainly Riverfront Stadium won't recall the Mudville milieu, for it is yet another monumental "cookie-cutter" concrete sports palace. Cincinnati itself is another matter. One of the smaller cities represented in the majors, "The Queen City" has taken the Reds to its heart in a way that is close to unique in the sport. Nearly everyone in town watches the Reds games, either in person or on television. In schools, offices, and on the farms, the Reds prospects are a principal element of concern; indeed, the interest in the team is so common that it's a conversational bridge between the classes. People who, on being thrown together, find they have nothing to talk about can always be assured of getting a discussion going by asking "Do you think the Reds can do it again?" So all embracing is Reds-mania in Cincinnati that "Opening Day," which is celebrated with an enormous parade, is the biggest event of the year in this river town. So wrapped up in the team are townspeople that in most Cincinnati schools, a kid's possession of an "Opening Day" ticket is written up as an excused absence.

If it all sounds very neighborly, it is. Cincinnati is one of the few teams where the owner sits in the stands with the fans (specifically, in Blue 108), rather than in an enclosed corporate box somewhere. Not only does Mrs. Schott consort with the audience (all of whom call her Marge), she also loves to do "the Wave," and frequently shows up at games accompanied by "Schott-zie" ("sweetheart," in German), her 170-pound St. Bernard.

The Cincinnati baseball tradition isn't just deeply felt, though. It is also "time honored." Though there are a good number of squads in baseball that have a better overall record than the Reds, only one other team—the Yankees—can claim to have played an equal role in this history of the sport. The Yankees brought baseball excitement to everyone. The Reds may very well have invented the game as an organized professional sport.

The Team

The Reds are the proud possessors of one of the oldest franchises in baseball. While one team may be just about as old (the Indians), and another has used the same name for a longer period (the Phillies), few would question that league baseball started in Cincinnati.

Just after the Civil War, local Cincinnati boosters latched onto the East Coast practice of paying baseball players, and they began to build a team that they thought would be capable of

taking on such eastern powerhouse squads as the New York Mutuals and the Troy Haymakers. Under manager Harry Wright a team came together that was named the "Red-Stockings" in honor of their colorful hosiery. In 1869, the new squad set out upon what is certainly the greatest road trip in all baseball history, offering to play against "all comers" at their home parks.

For the next few months, the budding baseball world stood in amazement as the Red Stockings beat every team of note in the country, generally by incredibly lopsided scores. Retiring undefeated in their first season, their players had become national sports heroes—probably the first in the country's history. The next year, they started out winning again. Finally, two years and 130 games after their streak had begun, the Red Stockings were stopped by the Brooklyn Atlantics.

The excitement generated by the Cincinnati tour led to the creation of the "National Association" in 1871, a predecessor to today's major leagues. Cincinnati's team had broken apart by that point, though, so it didn't join. It reappeared in time to be a charter member of the National League, and then defected for a while to the new American Association—largely because the Nationals did not allow beer sales! By the 1890s, the Reds were back in the National League to stay.

Over the next several decades, Cincinnati had a record that was undistinguished. The Reds were rarely last, but they were rarely first, either. They had been in major leagues of one sort or another for forty years before they finally won a pennant, in 1919. They won the series, too, with the timely help of several members of the opposing White Sox: this was the Series of the "Black Sox" scandal.

After that, it was twenty years before the Reds got good again. Though they took a beating at the hands of the Yankees in the 1939 classic, losing 4–0, they won the next year over the Tigers in a 4–3 heart stopper. During these years of many disappointments and some successes, the Reds enrolled such sound players as hard-hitting outfielder Edd Rousch, "bottle bat" slugger Heinie Groh, and pitchers Bucky Walter and Johnny Vander Meer.

There were moments of history, too. In 1934, the Reds became the first team to use a plane to get to games—though some of the players refused to travel in it! On May 24, 1935, the Reds moved baseball into a new era when they held the first night game ever. In 1938, Johnny Vander Meer hurled the only consecutive no hitters in baseball history.

Still, it was not until the 1950s and 1960s that Cincinnati baseball really got interesting. During these years, two players drove the team, both powerful sluggers. One was Frank Robinson, the celebrated Hall of Famer. The other was Ted Kluszewski, who could pound a ball about as hard and as far as anyone.

"Klu" was an enormous, impressive guy, whose biceps were so large that the sleeves of his uniform had to be sliced with a razor to allow his arms to fit through. Normally—and happily—of a pleasant disposition, Kluszewski lost his temper in baseball only once. During a game against Milwaukee, pitcher Ernie Johnson very nearly beaned Klu with a ball behind his head. That made the big Pole mad. Ted then drove out a drive down the right field line, and, while the first baseman chased it, Johnson covered. Klu was ready with his spikes, giving the Milwaukee pitcher a memorable laceration.

Johnson wanted to retaliate, but thought it over. "I looked up at Klu," he later recalled, "standing there and waiting for me, and I said to myself 'You're smarter than this.'" As anyone who can remember Klu will attest, that was a very wise decision.

If the 1960s were interesting, the 1970s were incredible. During that decade the Reds won their division six times, went to the Series on four occasions (1970, 1972, 1975, and 1976), and won twice. They enlisted one of the greatest teams in baseball history ("The Big Red Machine") and won a fall classic against Boston (1975) that may well be the best Series ever.

Who were these Reds? In the line-up were the "Big Four," catcher Johnny Bench, second baseman Joe Morgan, infielder Tony Perez, and the multi-talented Pete Rose. Two of these are in the Hall of Fame, and the other two will probably get there, sooner or later. Beyond the four, though, other members of "the Machine" were only marginally less talented, if that. These included George Foster, the last National Leaguer to hit over fifty home runs, standout shortstop Dave Concepcion, outfielder Ken Griffey, and pitcher Don Gullett. Altogether, this group of superstars collected six MVP awards in an eight year period.

More than anyone else, though, it was Rose who captured the public's imagination. "Charlie Hustle" may not have been the greatest baseball player of all time (though there are many in Cincinnati who would dispute that statement), but few indeed are the players who more wanted to win, or had more of that combination of guts and sheer ability that makes victory possible. No matter what the score was, no matter what the situation was, whenever Rose got up to bat, you sensed something was about to happen. With amazing regularity, it did.

As the 1970s progressed, Cincinnati fans—and baseball enthusiasts throughout America—got caught up in a drama that went beyond the league championships that the Reds were winning with regularity. Always a consistently outstanding player, it was confidently predicted that Rose, like just about everyone, would see his hitting pace slow down dramatically as he got older.

But in Rose's case, it didn't happen. On May 5, 1978, Pete slugged out hit number 3,000, and he was still going strong. People began to wonder if it was possible that "Charlie Hustle" could top that all time "Holy Grail" of baseball records: Ty Cobb's mark of 4,191 hits. At the time, Rose himself didn't think it was possible. But he kept slugging away.

As Rose got closer to the mark, excitement grew. Rose began asking everyone he knew what they had heard about Cobb, and in time he became an authority on the "Georgia Peach." When Pete was asked if he thought Cobb was "looking down from heaven at him," as Rose pursued the record, Pete gritted his teeth and said "From what I know about Ty, if he's lookin', he's lookin' up." Rose kept on swinging. Finally, on September 11, 1985, "Charlie Hustle" went over the top, setting an all-time record that, whatever difficulties he's experienced since then, neither time nor memory will erase.

As the seventies ended, so did the glory days for the Reds. The team stayed good, but, until 1990, it seemed to be not good enough.

Then magic happened. Confounding the predictions of the experts, who felt that the Reds' untried squad and Pete Rose's difficulties would result in a poor 1990 Cincinnati performance, the Reds came out of the box swinging early in the season, establishing a commanding lead in the National League West. They didn't always wow everyone after the first few months; following the All-Star break, the Red's record wasn't great. Nevertheless, the Reds hung on to win the division. They convincingly beat the Pirates for the pennant and then astounded the baseball world with their four game sweep of the mighty Oakland A's in the fall classic.

Is this the beginning of a new "Red Machine?" Time, of course, will tell. However, with such sound players as outfielder Eric Davis, shortstop Barry Larkin, third baseman Chris Sabo, and pitchers like Jose Rijo—to say nothing of such "Nasty Boy" relievers as Rob Dibble—they have the troops necessary to make 1991 every bit as exciting a year for Cincinnati fans as 1990 was.

The Stadium

If baseball parks could be judged merely by how they looked on the outside, Riverfront Stadium would rank as one of the most impressive in sports. Rising just south of Cincinnati's magnificent and attractive downtown on the north bank of the Ohio River, Riverfront is postcard pretty in its circular concrete splendor. It's location is great, too. Set at the junction of the major interstates linking Ohio, Indiana, and Kentucky, and placed within an easy and pleasant walk of the "Queen City's" offices, shops, and restaurants, Riverfront is easy to get to, and is set in a pleasant place to be once you are there.

If you are arriving at Riverfront by car, you will most likely park either in the stadium or in the parking lots around the base. From there, you'll be directed to escalators to the Plaza level, which is where the entrances are. If, on the other hand, you end up walking to Riverfront from downtown, you'll simply end up in this area as you take the "Skywalk" bridge from town. In either case, don't rush into the building. There are a few things here you should see.

Along the bridge to downtown, which is at the northeast corner of the park, are a series of attractive signboards that outline key events in the history of the Reds. Celebrated in this area are such things as the emergence of the Reds as the first professional team, the establishment of the rules for the World Series by Reds' owner Garry Hermann, the Reds' role in establishing night baseball, and such key moments in Reds' history as Johnny Vander Meer's 1938 consecutive no-hitters and Pete Rose's 1985 smashing of Ty Cobb's lifetime hits record.

The stadium itself has some monuments, too. Outside Gate A, you'll see plaques commemorating Hall of Fame catcher Johnny Bench and "Red Machine" general manager Bob Howsam. Easily viewable from this area is a classic old suspension bridge across the Ohio. Pre-dating the Brooklyn Bridge by two decades, it was one of the country's first.

Inside, the park is modern and convenient, as you would expect. Aisles are wide and well marked, concession stands are well-spaced, color-coordinated, and attractive. There is some evidence of wear and tear in the place, and litter pick up, even before the game, is not all it could be. Nevertheless, the place looks at least resonably spiffy.

Appointments in the seating areas follow the same pattern. The chairs are all plastic. They are reasonably comfortable, though by no means exceptional. As we describe in some detail elsewhere (see "Seating"), the design of the stadium doesn't provide the best views possible. But if you can't always see what's happening on the field, at least your back will not ache.

The field area itself is strictly standard issue. The right and left field poles are set at 330', while the center field sits at 404'. The bullpens consist of benches and mounds set in the right and left field foul territories. Above the center-field wall is an electronic scoreboard and a good-quality visual display, that, unfortunately, seriously obstructs the view of several hundred seats. Whoever handles the display does a good job; many of the cartoons played on it are funny, and the use of the "William Tell Overture" at key dramatic moments is a good idea.

Nevertheless, if all of this makes Riverfront seem like a standardized place with little individuality, that's because it is. No doubt the Reds paid their architects a fair amount of money to design this park, but they could have saved themselves all that change simply by borrowing the drawings for Three Rivers, Atlanta Stadium, or the Vet — there is that little difference among them.

It's an irony, really. Cincinnati has fans that are warm and neighborly — but the Reds have provided them a stadium that is monumental and cold.

Highlights

Riverfront has seen more baseball history within its confines than just about any of the newer stadiums. In truth, only Dodger Stadium and the Oakland Coliseum can compare among the more modern parks for racking up recent baseball highlights.

For any fan, the premiere moment has to be Pete Rose's hit number 4,192, smashing Ty Cobb's record, which occurred on September 11, 1985. It was one of the great events in baseball in the postwar period.

Nearly as memorable, though, was Rose's game-winning crash into catcher Ray Fosse that gave the National Leaguers the 1970 All-Star game, 5–4. And it was in Riverfront, on April 4, 1974, that Hank Aaron tied the Bambino's home run mark of 714.

There have been pitching feats aplenty, too. The biggest of all was undoubtedly Tom Browning's perfect game, which he pitched against the Dodgers on September 16, 1988. The great Tom Seaver also hurled a no-hitter here on April 18, 1981.

World Series action has been a particular strength at Riverfront; altogether, thirteen Series contests have happened in the park. And as memorable as 1990s sweep of the A's was, for most fans the 1975 contest against the

Red Sox set an all-time standard for
thrills, chills, and classic baseball excitement. The Riverfront highlight in that
contest was game three, a heartstopper
that the Reds pulled out of the hat only
after ten innings of white-knuckled
play. The Reds, of course, went on to
Boston to win what many fans think was
the best Series ever.

Fans

Cincinnati, like most of the Midwest,
is a place that's solid, not flashy. It's a
basic values sort of town where schools
are good, "culture" is encouraged, a
sense of community reigns, and overt
individualism and antisocial behavior is
frowned on. Though the town has produced a few celebrated nonconformists,
most of its famous people are solid
citizen types, such as Presidents Grant
and Taft, singers Andy Williams and
Doris Day, and Daniel Beard, founder
of the Boy Scouts, USA.

People work hard in Cincinnati, but
they never work with that frantic drive
and ambition that you see in New York
or Philly. People like having a good
time, too, but they rarely go overboard.
And though Cincinnati is a city where
there are plenty of rich people, thanks
to its wealth of corporate headquarters,
few of them show up at work in chauf-
fered limos. Most drive themselves to
their offices and factories, just like
everyone else.

Reds fans are pretty much like other
Cincinnatians. They are generally
white, middle-class folk, more male
than female, although families predominate. Most Reds fans are Midwesterners, though there's also a significant element of "hill" people from
Kentucky and West Virginia. These
people come to the games well-dressed
but not overdressed, they are unfailingly
polite to outsiders, and save their abuse
for the umpires. They like drinking
beer (this is, after all, a German town),
but are rarely drunken. They are very
vocal and enthusiastic, but almost
never swear. You will rarely hear Reds
fans boo specific players, either from
visiting teams or their own. You will on
occasion catch them applauding good
plays handled by opponents, while
standing ovations for visitors who really
do something spectacular are not
unknown.

This is not a crowd with any perceiv-
able quirks or customs that are not
familiar in other parks. Beyond having
an excessive fondness for "the wave"
(and an excessive fondness for the Reds),
this is an audience that's focused on
what's happening on the field, rather
than what's happening in the stands.

Many teams have famous fanatical
fans—people who are known to just
about everyone, who rarely miss a
game, and who epitomize the club's admirers with their fervent enthusiasm.
The Reds have one of these fans too,
with a slight difference: this enthusiast
happens to own the team. Her name is
Marge Schott.

If you want to really understand what
Cincinnati fans are all about, watch
Mrs. Schott. It really isn't hard to do—
alone among all the current club owners,
Mrs. Schott sits among the fans (usually
in blue section 108), where she can see
them and they can see—and talk with—
her. More often than not Marge will be
accompanied by her 170-pound St. Bernard "Schottzie," the unofficial mascot,
who is a lot more popular than most
teams' official ones. During the game,
you'll see Mrs. Schott doing "the wave"
(she says she loves it), talking animatedly
with those around her about good
plays, and springing to her feet on a
long ball, craning to see if it's going to
make the wall. Indeed, Marge Schott
jumping up and down after a Reds
homer is one of television baseball's
most popular clips, for good reason.
The sheer triumphant joy we see in her
eyes is a reflection of the way we feel
when our team does the same thing.

Mrs. Schott has said for years that her life would be complete if the Reds could only win the Series under her leadership. Now, they have. It was, for us, among the principal joys of that contest to see Marge achieve her goal. In a world of big money contracts, TV rights negotiations, and faceless managements, Mrs. Schott is a throwback to a time when owners and fans shared the mutual communion of the game, when team owners were motivated as much by love of the sport as by the money a team could generate. In a sense, Mrs. Schott — and, indeed, the whole approach of Cincinnatians to the game they did so much to promote — is an anachronism. But if the Reds keep winning, and if they keep filling their oversized stadium, Mrs. Schott may succeed in accomplishing something a lot more important than winning a Series. She may get other owners to reflect on what approaches to the *game* at baseball are really consistent with producing happy fans — and full coffers.

Getting There

Located on the north bank of the Ohio River in downtown Cincinnati, Riverfront Stadium is easy to reach by car or cab. It's also within walking distance of all the major downtown hotels.

By car. Convenient to all the major expressways in the area, Riverfront Stadium is easy to reach. However, since traffic can get bad in Cincinnati around the rush hours, you should allow a little extra time getting into town if you are coming for a night game.

If you are traveling from such *north* destinations as Dayton, Toledo, or Detroit, follow I-75 to the intersection for I-71 north. Proceed east for ½ mile and exit at signs for Riverfront Stadium. Follow to stadium parking.

From such *northeast* areas as Colum-

bus and Cleveland, take I-71 south to downtown Cincinnati. Exit at Riverfront Stadium and follow signs to parking.

From such *south* locales as Lexington and Knoxville, proceed on I-75 north until you cross the Ohio River and then head up I-71 north toward Columbus. Exit I-71 at Riverfront Stadium and proceed to parking.

Those driving in from the *Greater Cincinnati Airport* will want to head east on I-275 to the point where it merges with I-75 north. Then follow the above directions to Riverfront Stadium and parking.

By cab. Cab service from downtown is available. You should be able to taxi to Riverfront from anyplace in the central business district for $5 or less. Cab service from the airport is considerably more expensive. It runs about $20 one way.

By bus. Mass transit opportunities to get to the game are few. However, those arriving at the airport might want to consider taking the Jetport Express bus, which serves the downtown hotels. Simply ask to be dropped off at the Westin and take a short, covered stroll to Riverfront Stadium from there. The charge is $8, and the service is very regular.

By foot. Thanks to its innovative Skywalk system, you can take a pleasant, elevated, and climate controlled stroll to the game from most of the downtown hotels. The Skywalk system runs throughout the central business district and connects all points to Riverfront — just follow the conveniently sited maps.

Parking

Located in downtown Cincinnati, Riverfront is literally surrounded by parking lots of all shapes, descriptions, and sizes.

Within the stadium are 3,100 covered spaces, which go for $5. If you want one, come early . . . they tend to fill up fast. To the east and west of the park are outdoor, stadium-controlled lots that are cheaper ($3.50).

During night games and weekend contests, you should have no problem finding parking, particularly if you arrive early. However, during the Reds' relatively rare weekday contests, parking is a major problem. You will often find the stadium lots filled with cars belonging to people working in the downtown offices. Other downtown lots may be filled, too.

Under these circumstances, it is essential to come early. If you still find Riverfront's lots full—a distinct possibility—try parking somewhere within reach of the Skywalk system and take it to the game. Cincinnati is a pleasant and attractive city to stroll through.

Tickets

You can get Reds tickets by mail, by phone, or you can pick them up in person at the advance ticket office.

Though it is rarely necessary to buy tickets far in advance of games, if you want the best seat selection, it's probably a good idea. To order by mail, select your day of game and the number of tickets you want, and send your order to: The Cincinnati Reds, PO Box 1970, Cincinnati, OH 45201-1970. Be sure to include your check for payment in full, plus the Reds' $2 "postage and handling" charge.

You can also get tickets by phone. To order this way, call (513) 421-REDS within the Cincinnati area or (800) 829-5353 outside of town (but not throughout the country), and be prepared to pay with MasterCard or Visa. You'll also be hit with a service charge.

Normally, we like to see fans head for the advance ticket office, but getting to

this one is a major hassle! Although it's located directly at the stadium, just try to get a car to it, and you'll see what we mean . . . we spent forty minutes trying to find the way in, and we had been given directions.

At any rate, the best means of approach seems to be to take Pete Rose Way (the road directly north of Riverfront) to Broadway, going north. From there, turn left onto Fourth. Travel one block and turn left on Sycamore. Just after you turn on Sycamore, you'll find an unmarked side street on your right. Go down it. That will lead you to the plaza level of Riverfront Stadium. (These are also the directions to handicapped parking.)

Even when you get to the edifice, though, the office will not be in sight. You'll need to walk around the building to the "home plate" area which is between gates 1 and 13 of the plaza level to find the office, which is located at the southwest of the building, overlooking the Ohio River. After all this effort, you will at least be able to check out a ticket chart as you purchase your spots. The advance ticket window is open from 9 A.M. to 5:30 P.M. all week when the Reds are in town, and during the same hours from Monday through Friday when they are not.

Availability. Seating 52,392 people, Riverfront is about medium-sized, as multipurpose stadiums go. Its attendance has also been about medium-sized, or perhaps a little better, in recent times. During most years, the Reds attract a little shy of 2,000,000 fans. What that means as a practical matter is that seats for Reds games are almost always available, though really good seats are limited for popular matchups against such squads as the Dodgers, Mets, Cubs, and Cards.

The World Series victory of 1990 will certainly boost attendance. Accordingly, if you are planning to attend games against any of the above teams, you would be wise to order well in advance.

Should you be planning to go to contests against less popular squads, a phone order a few days in advance would be prudent, though, as in the past, if you simply show a seat will probably be available for you.

Costs. The good news about fees is that the Reds have some of the lowest seat prices in baseball. The bad news is that Riverfront Stadium, a multipurpose facility built to accommodate football as well as baseball, has some of the worst chairs in the majors. Unfortunately, pricing is in no way a certain guide to quality. Accordingly, make sure you check the seating chart in this book as you order your seats.

In 1990, Reds ticket charges were as follows: Blue Level Box Seats ($8.50); Green Level Box Seats ($8); Yellow Level Box Seats ($8); Red Level Box Seats ($7); Green Level Reserve Seats ($6); Red Level Reserve Seats ($5.50); "Top Six" Reserve Seats ($3.50).

Rainouts. An astroturfed facility, Cincinnati doesn't have as many rainouts as some of the other parks, but they still happen from time to time. Generally speaking, the Reds' rainout policy is strictly exchange. However, if you're involved in a cancelled game and have no plans to return to town, you might want to try writing to the Reds, explain the situation, and request a refund. You are likely to get it.

Seating

During the 1990 National League championship series, the wives of the Pittsburgh Pirates caused a brief flurry of controversy when they complained that the seats they had been assigned at Riverfront Stadium were far from the action and up in "nosebleed country." No doubt thousands of Reds fans, on reading that, said to themselves, "Welcome to the real world, ladies!"

Riverfront Stadium, viewed from across the Ohio, is one of the most impressive looking athletic facilities in North America. It is also, however, a pretty deficient place in which to watch baseball.

The problem is simple. Baseball is a game that's played in a diamond, to which is attached a fan. Ideally, a stadium's form should, then, look something like the "bell" of a fluted champagne glass: it should be narrow around home plate, bulge out slightly at the baselines, and curve back in a bit just past the outfield wall. In the real world, a few parks actually do look like that: Dodger and Yankee Stadiums are two of them.

The difficulty with Riverfront is that it isn't "fluted" (the ideal), nor even "U" shaped. It is round. What that means as a practical matter is that those folks caught in the bulge just past the baselines find themselves pretty far from the action. And while the Reds have compensated for this unpleasant effect by building their more expensive "blue" box seats into a "U" around the field, the rims of the two upper decks maintain the imperfect perfect circle. As a result, there are few "good" seats at all in the first level, and not a single one in the second. Which was probably why the Pirate wives were dissatisfied; but then, they weren't having a good series anyway.

The Reds' most expensive seats are classified "Blue Level Box Seats" ($8.50), and at that price they are certainly a bargain. These are comfortable, plastic and metal chairs with decent legroom and good to great views of the field. Seats within the baselines, which is to say 113 (first base) to 152 (third base) would be best here, but seats further along the baselines should also be good, given the price. To be avoided, though, are Blue Boxes 125–132. These are glorified (and overpriced) seats beyond the right field wall that would be called "bleachers" in most other parks.

"Green Level Box Seats" ($8) are

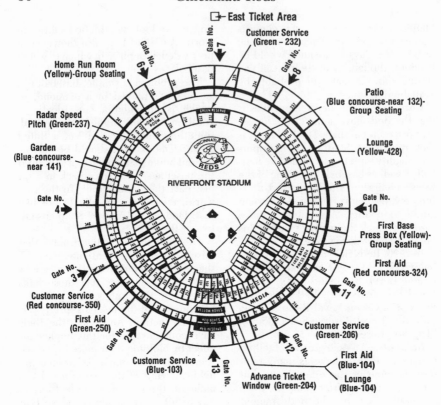

Seating chart, Riverfront Stadium.

next in quality, and they are certainly not as good as the Blue spots. These seats slope back behind the blue area and track the circle design of the park. Accordingly, getting in the baselines is important. Sections 216 (first base) to 248 (third) are the most desirable. You should also try to get a low row; 7 or less would be best.

"Yellow Level Box Seats" are a tier up, and at $8 they don't have a lot to recommend them. Sure, the seats are comfortable and the rows are short, but not a single seat in this "box" section is within the baselines. They'd probably do in a pinch, but otherwise, to heck with 'em say we.

"Red Level Boxes" ($7) are yet another tier up, and, as far as we are concerned, they're too far from the action to be considered good seats. Still, it's quite possible you'll end up sitting here. If you do, get as close as you can to the batter's box (312–361 would be best) and sit as low as possible.

Better yet, consider the "Green Level Reserve Seats" ($6). These spots are what most parks would designate as "bleachers." The chairs are comfortable, and the action is fairly close, though the price is perhaps a dollar too high. Sections 237–239, close in on the left field side, are probably the best of the lot.

After this point, the situation deteriorates considerably. "Red Level Reserve

Seats" ($5.50) are real cloud scrapers, the sections 310 through 362 are the best of a sorry lot. The "Top Six" Reserve Seats are, at $3.50, overpriced. They occupy the top rim of the stadium, and you will find that you are closer to God than to Eric Davis. At least you'll be able to say "I was there."

Special Needs

Parking. Parking for the physically disabled is available at the plaza level of the stadium. To get to this area, follow the directions for the advance ticket office (see "Tickets") and be prepared to show your plate or sticker. The charge for parking is $5.

Seating. Wheelchair seating in the stadium is available on both the green and blue levels. In the green areas, this seating is provided behind sections 228, 229, and 230. These are bad spots past the centerfield wall. Information on where the blue area wheelchair spots are located is hard to come by: no one seems to know just where these seats are.

Purchasing tickets is a problem, too. Ticketmaster is not allowed to sell handicapped seats, nor will they tell you where these seats are located. Instead, they refer you to the Reds' box office. The Reds' box office line is answered by an automatic phone machine that says nothing about handicapped seating. Call then the Reds' offices, and they insist that they can't enlighten you; you must talk with the automated phone system. If you try to get directions to the handicapped parking (which is hard to find), you'll also be referred back to the phone system, which in turn sends you on to the Cincinnati police, who don't know anything about it. If it all sounds like an outrageous run-around, that's exactly what it is.

Food and Features

Food. The food situation at Riverfront is good but not great. Selection is

decent, prices are very reasonable, and quality varies pretty widely.

Food stands are located throughout the park. Though they tend to congregate behind the home plate areas, you'll not be too far from food in any area of the park. Mostly, they sell standard fare. The park's standard dogs — Kahn's — are quite good. You can also get Kahn's "super dogs," a tasty bratwurst. Other favorites include popcorn, pizza slice, nachos and pretzels.

There are some specialties, too. At the *Plaza Bar* (see "Drinks") and a few other spots you can get a decent chicken hoagie. Also available in several locations is a "Bar-b-Que" beef sandwich, if you want it. It looks pretty repulsive, and we can assure you that it tastes every bit as bad as it looks. The big specialty at Riverfront, though, are "Cincinnati Coneys" — the regional treat. These are small hot dogs smothered in chili, shaved cheese, and mustard. "Coneys" can be found at the "Gold Star Chili" stands throughout the park — try one, you might like it.

Drinks. The usual soft drinks can be found at Riverfront Stadium, and the prices are more reasonable than at most places.

Cincinnatians also relish beverages of the alcoholic kind. Beer stands are all over the place, and sell a 20-ounce cup of beer (often Bud Dry) at decent prices. "Margaritaville" stands offer margaritas. Those looking for a bigger selection of mixed drinks should repair to the *Plaza Level Bar*, which is located behind Green section 254, where you'll find mixed drinks and wine.

Features. Riverfront Stadium has only one feature, a "Speed Pitch" concession behind Green section 237.

Assistance

Rather than maintain an office, the Reds have four "customer service" booths where you can have questions answered, get assistance regarding unruly fans, and find out a bit more about the park. These are located behind Blue aisle 103, Behind Green aisles 206 and 232, and on the Red level behind aisle 350.

Safety and Security

Safety. Reds fans, many of them German midwesterners, don't mind hoisting a few. As a result, a fair amount of drinking goes on at Reds games, and this can lead to some obnoxious, rowdy, and annoying behavior in the park. This being said, though, the problem is pretty minor; it would be unusual for you to run into it. If you do have any problems, a word to the usher will insure that the difficulty will be straightened out.

In the parking areas and in downtown Cincinnati, you should have no problem at all. One of America's more civilized cities, Cincinnati is well policed and quite safe.

Should you decide to visit the Riverboat restaurants and lounges on the Kentucky side of the Ohio, though, keep in mind that nearby Covington has something of a "roughneck" reputation, an image in no way hurt by its many strip shows and topless bars. You should be careful if you're walking around this area.

Health. Cincinnati can get quite humid and unpleasant in the summer, and much of the stadium is exposed to the sun. If you are attending a sunny day game, you should bring sun tan lotion, a hat and drink plenty of water.

Climbing to the top of Riverfront is a recipe for stroke. If you have heart trouble or are getting up in years, you might want to avoid "Top Six" seats. Also, be especially careful on the top deck stairs: if you trip in this area and take a "header" (particularly going down), you are likely to get seriously messed up.

We also learned from the first aid people that one of the biggest causes of problems at the park are blisters businessmen get from wearing new shoes and then walking from their downtown offices to the stadium! If you are in town on business and are planning on strolling down to the game after your meetings are over, you might try a trick your secretary has known about for a while: pack a pair of sneakers and switch over to them before you head out the door.

Should you run into these or other difficulties, the Reds' first aid offices are located behind aisles 104 (Blue), 250 (Green), and 324 (Red).

Mementos

Souvenirs. Cincinnati fans love to wear Reds paraphernalia. The biggest selection in the park is behind aisle 148 (Blue), but there are at least a half dozen other souvenir stands in the facility.

If you are looking for a bigger selection yet, you should visit the Cincinnati Reds' *Official Gift Shop*, which is located in the Hyatt Regency Hotel at Fifth and Elm (513) 651-7200. Among other things, you can pick up a "Schottzie" plush doll here ($20). The shop is open all year from 9 A.M. to 5:30 P.M., Monday through Saturday.

Foul Balls. Foul ball catching competition in Cincinnati is pretty fierce. About half the kids in town show up at each game, mitt in hand, ready to snag one off the bat of Eric Davis. If you think you can outcatch or outfox them, try sitting in Blue aisles 152, 151, 150, and 144 or Green Boxes 201 to 207.

Autographs. Riverfront Stadium is not a good place to get autographs. The players have their own parking area, which is outside Gate B inside the stadium. The place is difficult to get to, and once you get there you'll find police and gates standing between you and the Reds. Still, some players may walk over and sign.

You might have better luck trying to get signatures at batting practice, which starts about an hour and a half before the game. Experience indicates that at least some players will walk over

to sign a few during this period. If you don't have seats in the Blue level boxes, go to any customer service stand and you'll be issued an "autograph pass." This will allow you to go to the dugouts and seek signatures until a half hour before game time.

CLEVELAND INDIANS

Cleveland Stadium

"Try, try, and try again," goes an old saw, "and you will succeed."

Noble sentiments, certainly. And as the life careers of people like Thomas Edison and Abraham Lincoln attest, this advice sometimes proves to be true. But the fact is that for every Edison who tried one thousand filaments before he found the one that would illuminate his electric lamp, there were an unknown legion of other scientists who worked just as hard as Tom did and did not succeed. For every bestselling writer who finally sold his book to a publisher after it had been rejected twenty times, there were other writers who never got published at all. Persistence does not always pay off.

No one knows this better than the Cleveland Indians. They may not be the worst team in baseball, but they are one of the worst. They also aren't the poorest squad in the history of the sport; that honor belongs to the St. Louis Browns. But it can be fairly said that no team now in existence has been so bad for so long as the Tribe.

The Indian's doggedly substandard performance has, over the years, assumed mythic porportions. Fathers tell their sons "I'm so old that I can

remember when Cleveland won a pennant," and coaches snort, "You couldn't get a contract with the Indians!" at hotshot college pitchers. When Tinseltown wanted to make a movie about a hopeless team with hopeless players winning a pennant, what squad did they portray? The Tribe, of course. Although *Major League* wasn't one of the better baseball flicks, it did have one of the genre's funniest lines. In the film, the Indians' catcher is trying to rekindle a romance with a young woman who's engaged to a stockbroking Yuppie. Barging into her apartment, he finds that the Yuppie is visiting, along with another couple.

Trying to make the best of the situation, the woman introduces her ex-boyfriend to the group. "He's a catcher with the Cleveland Indians.

"My gosh," says the second woman, "I didn't know we still had a team!"

Actually, they do know that they have a team in Cleveland, even if they are quiet about it. And while attendance at Cleveland Stadium isn't all that hot, it's better than you'd think when you consider that the team hasn't won a pennant in thirty-six years, and that in most seasons a fifth place finish is regarded as pretty good. Cleveland fans may not have seen much of victory over all these many years, but they haven't lost their taste for it.

Still, the question must be posed: Is it worthwhile for you to go out of your way to attend a series of Indian games? If you are looking for spectacular baseball action, a beautiful playing facility, great food and drink, and a fun time in a fine tourist town, the answer is no. Unless the Indians change a lot, they will continue to finish well down in the standings, their ancient stadium is proof positive that people knew how to construct ugly parks before Candlestick, and their concession operations are second rate. As for Cleveland, while it is not nearly as bad a place as rumor would have it, a vacation mecca it ain't.

If, on the other hand, you have any interest in the history of the game, Cleveland Stadium is someplace you'll want to be. A substantial number of baseball's most memorable moments have happened in Cleveland, and a surprisingly large proportion of the game's greats, particularly pitchers, have spend much of their careers here.

Beyond that, there are the fans. We have no idea if cartoonist Charles Schultz is from Cleveland, but when he has Charlie Brown say of his ball team, "How can we lose when we're so sincere?" it's hard to believe he wasn't talking about the Tribe's admirers. Boy, these people want to win! And the slightest ray of hope springing off the Tribe's bats will bring such paroxysms of joy ringing from thousands of Cleveland throats that you'll swear you'd just watched the Indians clinch the pennant.

By objective standards, attending Indian games cannot rate among baseball's great experiences. Still, we had fun in Cleveland. Maybe you'd have fun, too.

The Team

Baseball has been around so long in this city on the lake that it can fairly be said to have an integral part of the town's character. In 1869, before Cleveland was Cleveland and before their were any leagues, the "Forest Citys" became one of the first professional teams in the history of the sport. Over the next thirty years, the Clevelanders went through a bewildering number of name changes and franchise shifts, but baseball kept its place in town. Finally, in 1902 Cleveland (by this time the Bronchos), entered the American League to stay.

The first two decades of this century were glory years for Cleveland baseball fans. Some of the greatest players of all time—Tris Speaker, Napolean Lajoie, Addie Joss (who pitched a perfect game for the squad in 1908), Joe Jackson, and Cy Young—played for the team. Popular, too, was Luis Sockalexis, one of the first American Indian players in the major leagues. In 1915, shortly after Sockalexis died, a Cleveland fan wrote that the squad ought to be named after him. The "Cleveland Sockalexis" being thought something of a tongue-twister, the term "Indians" was settled on. Cleveland remains the only team in the majors named to honor a specific player.

This "Golden Age" for Cleveland baseball ended in the 1920 World Series against the Brooklyn Dodgers, which for thrills, chills, and outlandish occurrences must set some kind of record. Early in the contest, ace Brooklyn pitcher Rube Marquard was arrested for scalping tickets. Later on, Dodger owner Charles Ebbets was picked up by federal agents for passing out test tubes of whiskey; this was, of course, during Prohibition. But the cake was taken during the fifth game in Cleveland when the Indians' second baseman Bill Wambsganss executed the first and only unassisted triple play in World Series history. The fans, of course, went wild. Brooklyn player Clarence Mitchell was the person who hit into the triple play. The next time up, he managed to slice into a double play; Mitchell's boxscore, two at bats, five outs. Not a good day for Clarence!

The Indians went into a tailspin of sorts after that. Yet even if the final results weren't always great, there were moments of excellence. A good many of them surrounded Cleveland pitching great Bob Feller.

Among pitchers, Feller is one of the most storied of all, for a simple reason: he was colorful, and very, very fast.

Recruited as a junior in high school in 1936, Feller was literally too young to go into the majors. Afraid to lose him to another squad, though, the Indians put the young speedball artist in the concession department, where, it was thought, he could pedal popcorn and practice pitching.

The precocious seventeen-year-old pushed for a start. Finally, sick of hearing about it, the Indians' management suited Feller up for a relief situation in an exhibition game against the Cardinals. Maybe, the Indians manager thought, the Cards would pin the whippersnapper's ears back and send Feller back to his popcorn.

Instead, down the batters went, most of them ducking away from the plate rather than taking a swing, as jaws dropped along both benches. Finally, after six strikeouts, the Indians' catcher, Sam O'Neil, had had enough. "He throws too hard for me," he declared as he stalked back to the dugout. O'Neil had his name scratched from the line-up. An inning later, Feller had won the contest, burning down eight of nine batters.

Though Feller was allowed to go back to Iowa to finish high school, the Indians were smart enough to know they had a star. Over the next twenty years, Feller had the fastest fastball in the sport, and possibly the fastest of all time. Perhaps his greatest moment came when, in 1940, he ruined opening day for the Chicago White Sox by pitching a searing no-hitter at Comiskey Park. One disgruntled Sox spoke for hundreds of other players when he questioned an official's call. "What was wrong with it?" said the ump. "It sounded a little high," the Sox declared.

Yet Feller was far from the only great Indian of these decades. Also on the squad were Hall of Famer pitchers Bob Lemon, Early Wynn, and Satch Paige, and hard slugging shortstop Lou Boudreau.

Boudreau etched one of his own niches in baseball history in Cleveland Stadium on July 17, 1941, when the great Joe DiMaggio hit a line drive to him in the late innings. Boudreau turned a bad hop into a double play, and the Yankee Clipper's 56-game hitting streak was over.

Cleveland's last moment in the sun came in the late 1940s and early fifties, powered by Boudreau, Feller, Lemon, Paige, and a creative new owner named Bill Veeck.

Veeck, as at St. Louis and Chicago, engaged in his usual crowd pleasing promotions. When the team lost a close pennant contest in 1949, he had the pennant ceremonially buried before an Indians game. It was delivered to the gravesite in a horse-drawn hearse, and Veeck presided over the festivities in a mortician's outfit. Later, when a Cleveland nightwatchman named Joe Early wrote to a local newspaper complaining that the Indians were doing everything to honor players while doing little to show appreciation for average fans like himself, Veeck promptly declared "Good Old Joe Early Day." He filled Cleveland Stadium with folks who attested to Early's great contributions to the game and then presented the nightwatchman with a new car and other presents. It was Veeck, also, who came up with the grinning Indian logo that Cleveland is known for.

Yet as much as Veeck concentrated on keeping fans amused with gimmicks, he also worked to give them victories.

In 1948, he did just that, as Cleveland won the Series 4–2 over the Boston Braves. The fifth game of that contest scored the highest paid attendance ever at a baseball game: 86,288.

Veeck soon sold the team, but it would have one more moment of glory before the darkness. In 1954, the Indians again captured the pennant, setting the all-time record for both leagues in season wins at 111. Nevertheless, the Indians folded in four games to the New York Giants, thanks in part to Willie Mays's spectacular running outfield catch in the first game.

Everyone knows what happened after that. The Indians fell apart, and have, sad to say, never rebounded. There are good players on the current team, including catcher Sandy Alomar, Jr. Whether these stars, and a generally untried bench, represent enough horsepower to bring the Tribe the pennant they have long coveted remains to be seen.

The Stadium

Cities, as well as people, have dreams. In the early 1930s, as the Depression settled over America, Cleveland felt that if it could only show the world what it had to offer, industry and new jobs would beat a path to its door. Accordingly, the Forest City made a bid for the 1932 Summer Olympics. To convince the Olympic committee of their sincerity, Cleveland built a magnificent new stadium by Lake Erie for the track and field events.

As it turned out, Los Angeles rather than Cleveland got the games. The Indians got Cleveland Stadium.

In truth, the place is a sort of booby prize. A huge facility resting a few hundred yards off the shore or Lake Erie, Cleveland Stadium is the biggest park in baseball with 74,483 seats. That's 10,000 more spots than the next largest park, which is Anaheim. As a result of this anomoly, the Indians, whose attendance figures are among the smallest in the majors, also have attracted many of the biggest crowds in baseball history, mainly for Series and All-Star contests.

The fact is, Cleveland Stadium is just too big for a game that runs some 162 contests a year and depends on some intimacy between player and fan. It also lacks an identifiable baseball design. Though there are many good seats in the stadium, there are thousands upon thousands of terrible ones. Happily for the fan, though, the Indians' poor attendance means that you don't have to sit in any of the poor spots. Still, like baseball's other track-and-field facility, Montreal's Big "O," Cleveland Stadium just isn't all that suitable for the game.

Cleveland Stadium is located downtown, just south of Lake Erie. This should be a super spot, for Erie is a pretty body of water. Unfortunately, Cleveland—unlike Chicago—is a town that has never utilized the potential of its lakefront. As a result, the area is fairly run down, composed of railroad tracks, warehouses, and rusty port facilities, although there's a nice bit of park land fronting the north side of the stadium.

The place itself is, from the outside, an unsightly old monstrosity, built primarily out of those institutional yellow bricks so popular during the thirties and forties. If the original designers had thought to cut down on the walls and allow, from the inside, views of the lake and downtown, the place could have been pretty. As it is, the stadium looks boxed in and somewhat forbidding.

The view from the inside isn't a lot better. The concourses are pleasantly wide, but there are cracks on the floor and litter pick up is not what it should be. Windows are unusually dirty, and they don't let in much light, which adds to the gloom. Chairs in the stands are color-coded, but many, particularly in the cheap seats, could use a coat of paint.

The field itself is unexceptional. It is natural grass, seems well-maintained, and has unusually short foul territories, which make it a good place for fans to catch foul balls. Field lines are at 320' at the left and right field poles and 400' at the back of the center field wall. Beyond that wall are the center field bleachers, which are a considerable ways out—so far, in fact, that no one has ever put a ball into them. That's quite a feat when you consider that Babe Ruth, Lou Gehrig, Joe DiMaggio, and Ted Williams all played here.

Overall, this is a pitcher's park. The walls are fairly far away and the weather helps. Normally speaking, winds blow off Lake Erie into the face of batters. The winds also have a habit of swirling around the place, pulling balls into the stands, all of which can make trying to get on base something of a challenge here. It's no wonder that this is the place where DiMaggio's streak ended.

New Stadium

In May 1990, a proposal went to the voters of Cleveland to fund the building of a new baseball stadium in the city. The proposal passed by a razor-thin margin after months of controversy and debate. A goundbreaking has taken place, but as of this writing little construction has started.

The new park will be located just south of downtown. That means that the next home of the Indians will be nearer to highways, but also farther from the lakefront. Cleveland Stadium itself will not be torn down. It will remain as the home of the Cleveland Browns football squad.

Cleveland was the first baseball city to fall victim to the disease of sports giganticism. Though plans at present are unclear, it can only be hoped that the Forest City's new facility will absorb the lessons of the past and will be a place of human—and humane—dimensions.

Highlights

As befits its status as one of baseball's oldest facilities, Cleveland Stadium has hosted its share of memorable baseball moments.

The most important date was probably July 17, 1941. That was when Lou Boudreau, catching a ball on a bad hop, put an end to Joe DiMaggio's hitting streak at game 56.

Given Cleveland's fantastic pitching stats (Cleveland pitchers have had more 20 win seasons than any other squad), much hurling history has happened here. Though Addie Joss' "perfect game" actually happened at another Cleveland park, Len Barker's May 15, 1981, "perfect" did occur here. Bob Feller threw a no-hitter in the park on June 30, 1948. So did Dennis Eckersley, back in the days when he was a starter for the Tribe. That milestone happened on May 30, 1977.

There have been moments of tragedy, too. During the 1950s, many thought that Cleveland's pitching ace Herb Score would match the marks set by Feller and Lemon. In 1957, a line drive off the bat of the Yankees' Gil McDougald hit Score in the right eye, cutting short a promising career. Today, Score broadcasts the Tribe's games.

Fans

Who would attend the games of a team that has been losing for thirty years? The answer's simple: people who care very much about baseball.

One Indians observer we spoke to put it very accurately. "At the other parks, people come to watch a game," he said. "At Cleveland Stadium, it's life and death every night."

We don't care whether you go to New York, Minneapolis, or San Diego, you will find no baseball fans as much into the game as that small band that assembles nightly in Cleveland. You'll also find no group of people so emotionally drawn into the contest than the Tribe followers. Just about everyone in the park seems to have a box seat on an emotional roller coaster. When the Indians lose, as they usually do, the moans are heartfelt and piteous, the recriminations are biting and targeted: God help the overpaid superstar who lets these people down consistently. Defeat, inflicted so terribly often, still has an incredible power to draw blood from these downtrodden, always loyal fans.

Ah, but let the Tribe win, and then you'll really see something! Games in Cleveland begin and end with fireworks, but the flashes and explosions in the sky are nothing compared to what you will see in the stands should Cleveland, miracle of miracles, start to win. Then you will be expected to do "high-fives" with those around you, you'll hear Indian war whoops, and strangers will hug each other. Even though it's August, you'll ask yourself, "Did they clinch the pennant, for cripes sake?!" and you will wonder where the heck you have been.

Who are these people? They are working and middle class folks, mostly. Lots of them are old timers . . . some can even remember back to when the Indians used to win. There are quite a few kids, too. This is really a very family sort of place. The "in" crowd is largely absent from Cleveland Stadium: it became uncool to be a Tribe enthusiast some time ago. Virtually all of these fans, including the kids, are real baseball people, very knowledgeable and well-informed about the sport. If, after all, you didn't know and love the game, what other possible motivation

would you have for coming to Cleveland Stadium?

"Characters" also are a prominent part of the Indians scene. Many vendors, stripped of the conformity required by sophisticated customer service schemes, often have clever and funny ways to get you to buy their wares. Fans, too, are often "originals" who decide that Cleveland Stadium is a good place to let their real selves out. Mostly, these are good humored, fun sorts of people.

Probably the most famous of the bunch is John Adams, a friendly fellow who sits in right field (section 2), and beats on an enormous drum every time the Indians do something right. Like Betsy Chattsworth ("the Dodger Momma") and John Wilkerson, the "Mayor of the Bleachers" at Busch Stadium, Adams is no oddball at all. He's simply a real baseball fan who has decided to hang his love for his team on his sleeve. "I get a kick out of beating the drum," John says. The truth is, we get a kick out of it, too.

"Victory," says an old saying, "has many fathers. Defeat is an orphan." Actually, that's not so. Defeat may not have many fathers, but it does have a few. They are the parents who, when all is said and done, show themselves through all storms to be honest, loyal, tried, and true. The Indians do not have many fans. But those that they do have are some of the best.

Getting There

An urban ballpark located downtown on the shores of Lake Erie, Cleveland Stadium is nevertheless pretty easy to get to. You can access the place by car, though cab, train, and even private boat are additional options.

By car. Cleveland Stadium is directly north of the Terminal Tower, easily the most prominent building in Cleveland's skyscape. If you keep this fact in mind, you'll have little trouble reaching the park, even if you mislay these directions.

Here are the best approaches: From *Hopkins Airport*, Columbus, Cincinnati, and points *south*, take I-70 north into Cleveland. Exit unto East 9th Street, and follow north until you hit the Erie lakefront. The stadium will be on your left.

If you are heading in from such *west* destinations as Toledo, South Bend, and Chicago, head east on I-80, exit north on I-71, and follow the above directions to the park.

From *east* and locations, such as Youngstown, Williamsport, and New York, take I-80 west to where I-80 becomes the Ohio Turnpike. Proceed on the Turnpike to Exit 13 Streetsboro. Follow signs to I-480 West. Take I-480 to I-77 north, and follow that to the East 9th Street. Proceed north on East 9th to the stadium area.

Those coming from such *northeast* destinations as Erie, Buffalo, and Rochester will want to take I-90 west to the Ohio Route 2 Exit, going west. Follow the East 9th Street Exit. Proceed north on East Ninth to the lakefront.

By cab. Cab rates in Cleveland are fairly reasonable. It will cost you about $10 to get to the game from the airport and a few bucks from any of the downtown hotels.

By train. Taking public transit to the stadium is also a possibility. Cleveland's Regional Transit Authority offers convenient train service from Hopkins Airport to downtown, departing every twenty minutes or so. To get to the stadium this way, follow the signs marked "Rapid Transit" from the baggage claims area and take the train to Cleveland. Exit at "Tower City." When you come out of the station, you'll find yourself on Superior Avenue. From there, walk down West 3rd Street to the park; it's about five blocks down. The charge is $1.

Important note: While getting to the stadium this way is easy, getting back to the airport area may not be: the last train leaves at 9:55 P.M. The RTA offers a shuttle bus service to the airport after that time, but if you intend to use it, you should call in advance to get its schedule. The RTA's number is (216) 621-9500.

It is also possible to take Amtrak to the games from Chicago, Buffalo, New York, or anyplace else along its system: Amtrak's Cleveland station is directly across from the stadium. Call Amtrack for details on schedules and fares (800) 872-7245.

By boat. If your vacation plans include sailing the Great Lakes, you might want to consider cruising into Cleveland for a game or two. North Coast Harbor, located a short walk east of the stadium, offers docking services for those wishing to attend a game. Slippage fees run from $6 to $12 depending on the size of your boat. Call (216) 241-2060 for details. Additional anchorages can be had in the Mud Flats entertainment district to the west of the park.

Parking

There's plenty of parking in the Cleveland Stadium area. The biggest lot is located to the west of the facility. Additional lots are north and east of the place. All charge $4.

Tickets

Although there's rarely any need to get your seats in advance at Cleveland Stadium, you can still order tickets by mail or phone, or you can pick them up in person at the advance ticket office.

To order by mail, send your seat selection, dates, and numbers of tickets to: Cleveland Indians Ticket Office, Cleveland Stadium, Cleveland, OH 44114. You can either include your check or money order or attach your

MasterCard or Visa number and expiration date to your order. In either case, be sure to include the Tribe's rather stiff $3 service charge.

Phone orders are handled by Ticketmaster at (216) 241-5555 in Cleveland, or (800) 729-6464 outside of town. Be sure to have your Visa or MasterCard ready, as well as the sections you'd like seats in. You will, of course, be hit with a service charge here as well. Ticketmaster's hours are 9 A.M. to 11 P.M. Monday through Friday, 9 A.M. to 10 P.M. on Saturday, and 10 A.M. to 7 P.M. on Sunday.

The Indians' advance ticket office is located at Gate A of the stadium, which is at the southwest corner of the building. Here, you can check out a seating chart before you buy. The office is open from 9 A.M. to 5 P.M. on weekdays and from 10 A.M. to 4 P.M. on Saturday.

You can, of course, also buy tickets at the game. However, you should be aware that these sales are cash only.

Availability. The Indians, for three decades one of the worst teams in baseball, occupy the biggest stadium in the major leagues. What this means as a practical matter is that, save for Opening Day, when the park is crowded, you will have no problem whatsoever in finding a seat. With an attendance that averages in the 1.2 million range, Cleveland has more excess spaces on any given night than any other team in baseball.

You are also likely, even at the last minute, to find a very good seat if you're willing to pay the extra money. The Indians sell only about 5,000 boxes to season ticket holders; that leaves an additional 11,000 available for single game purchasers. During contests against Oakland, Detroit, and the Yankees, finding first rate box seats can still be tough. On other occasions, one will almost certainly be available for you.

Costs. Indian ticket prices are

moderate. They're below those of such popular parks as Fenway and Wrigley, but, surprisingly, they're a bit higher than such other stadiums as Atlanta and Dodger.

Happily, though, charges are almost always a reasonable guide to seat quality. Basically, if you pay for a good seat at Cleveland Stadium, you'll get one.

In 1990, these were the charges: Field Box ($10.50); Lower Box ($10.50); Upper Box ($10.50); Lower Reserved ($8); Upper Reserved ($8); General Admission* (Adult [$4.50]); (Youth/seniors [$3]); Bleachers (when open)* ($3).

Rainouts. Rainouts occur with some regularity here—some would say that it's been raining on the Tribe for decades! Should you be caught in a cancellation, the Indians' official policy is that you can exchange your ticket only for another game. "There are," says their Fan Guide, "no refunds." Still, we are informed that, if you write and explain that you are from out of town and have no plans to return to Cleveland, you'll probably get a check.

Seating

Seating is almost always good in Cleveland Stadium for a simple reason: if you don't like where you've been put, it's pretty easy to get up and find someplace else to your liking. Generally speaking, if you try to move to empty boxes, the ushers will attempt to catch you. If you simply move to somewhere else in the price category you paid for, you will rarely be disturbed.

The best spots in the park are the Field boxes ($10.50), and they are very good indeed. Comfortable plastic chairs practically on top of the action (foul territory in this park is short), these have to be rated among the better

*Sold only on the day of game.

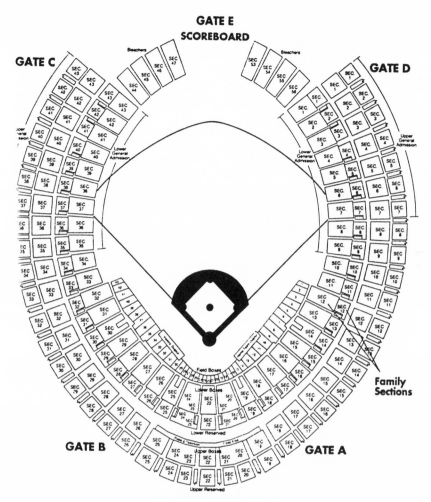

GATE E
SCOREBOARD

Seating chart, Cleveland Stadium.

seats in baseball at this price. Within the baselines in this area (sections 7–37, first to third) would be best, but any seat in this category is a good one.

Behind and an aisle past these are the Lower boxes ($10.50). Though not as good as the above, they're also pretty decent. The key here is to stay in the low rows (AA–DD are best) and within the baselines, which are the same as above.

Upper boxes ($10.50) are probably as good as the Lower box seats. You'll have a bit better view of the action, but you'll also be a level higher. Baselines here run from 15 (first) to 31 (third). Generally speaking, you'll want the lowest row possible, but you might want to avoid rows 1 and 2: the guard rail here is set at about eye level and can be a bit of a pain.

Reserved seats ($8) both upper and lower, decline in quality and cost. These hard yellow wood-and-metal chairs are set behind the boxes in both the lower and upper areas and are fairly far from the field. They also have many seats that are seriously obstructed by poles; that would be a problem in most parks, but in Cleveland, you can simply move to someplace where the view is better. On the whole, we'd suggest you favor the Lower reserved; it's a deck closer to the action, and to the food. The Upper reserved is serious nose-bleed country. Also make sure you stay within the baselines, which are set at the same sections as the boxes.

There's good news in Cleveland for penny-pinchers. Though many of the General Admission ($4.50) spots are the usual dogs, some are not. Try to arrive at the stadium a little early (these seats are first come, first served) and you can find a spot in this category right along the right and left field baselines, with a close in view of the outfield action and of one of the bullpens. Such spots in just about any other park will cost you $8 to $10 or more. If right field/first base action is your style, seek out General Admission Lower sections 8 and 9. You'll be perched near the visitor's bullpen. If you want to go for left field third base, select lower sections 35 and 36. The Tribe's bullpen will be to your left.

The bleachers ($3) open for day games and during the rare, crowded night contest. Composed of hard wooden benches with no backs, the bleachers are far from the action in this huge facility. Although this may be the place to sit if you're coming to the game to party, the extra $1.50 spend for General Admission seats is worth it.

You should also know that Cleveland Stadium has a "family reserved" area, where alcohol consumption *and* smoking are prohibited. Located in Lower box and Lower reserved sections 12, these are OK but not great spots about midway between first base and the right field foul pole. Frankly, we don't think there's much of a drinking problem in this stadium, but if you'd like to avoid it altogether, this is the place to sit. We regard the smoking ban as a real plus. Cleveland is one of only a handful of open air stadiums that offers this service to their fans.

Special Needs

Parking. Handicapped parking is available in the stadium's west parking lot, which is near the main gate. Show your sticker or plate to the attendant as you enter and you'll be directed to the proper area. You are also allowed to drop physically disabled people off at the main entrance. Look for the yellow poles between Gates A and B and stop anywhere between them to disembark or load passengers.

Seating. Handicapped seating is provided in Field box sections 1 and 2, and Lower reserved section 14. These are all decent spots, just past first base and reasonably close to the action. Overflow space is also provided in the aisle behind the Lower reserved sections. These spots are not so good.

Food and Features

Food. Cleveland is not one of North America's better restaurant towns, and that fact is evident in Cleveland Stadium, too. You won't starve here, but you'll pay more than you should for food that is less than what it ought to be.

Poorly designed and coordinated food stands are located throughout the park, but the biggest selection by far is clustered behind home plate where you will find hot dogs, Polish sausage, bratwurst, and popcorn. Nachos, pretzels, hamburgers, and chicken wing dings are also sold. All of it is pretty uninspired.

There are some specialties. The *Pizza Hut* stand behind section 24 (to the left of home plate) seems popular with fans, though we haven't the foggiest notion why. An overpriced slice of "French bread" pepperoni pizza tastes like cardboard. An unmarked stand in section 23 sells such "Lite Bites" (i.e., health food) specialties as tuna salad, bottled water (in Cleveland!?), no-alcohol beer, and a "veggie platter with dip."

By far the best dining at the park is available at *Alvie's Stadium Cafe,* the elevator to which is located under a canopy at Gate A. One of the few stadium club restaurants open to the public, Alvie's offers a lunch or dinner menu for dining before and during the game. The food is decent, the service is friendly, and the prices are fairly reasonable. The lounge stays open after the contest. Alvie's big drawback is that it does not have a view of the field, though, of course, there are TV monitors. Still, this would be a good place to get a bite to eat before the game.

Drinks. The usual drinks are available, including a "kiddie" soda and an outrageously overpriced "Souvenir Cup." The alcohol selection includes beer and Seagram's wine coolers.

Features. Features aren't a big deal at Cleveland Stadium, but there are some. You'll find a "Speed Pitch" concession behind section 6. Further, if you look overhead while wandering the main concourse, you'll see hanging banners outlining some of the baseball greats who have played for the Tribe. Prepare to be amazed, for it's quite a list. Cy Young . . . Bob Feller . . . Bob Lemon . . . Early Wynn . . . Lou Boudreau . . . Satch Paige . . . Addie Joss . . . and Tris Speaker. Certainly among the pitchers, no other team—not the Dodgers, not even the Cards—can match that list of names. It reminds you what a great team the Indians once were.

The Indian's newest feature is "Slider," a mascot introduced during the 1990 season. A yellow, purplish creature (a bird, maybe?), "Slider" seems primarily intended to keep the kids entertained. He didn't do a heck of a lot when we saw him, but then the Indians were winning that night, so folks didn't need comic relief.

Assistance

The Customer Relations Office is located behind section 22. This is the place to find lost kids or to shed yourself of obnoxious fans. It's people, like nearly all the service folks at Cleveland Stadium, are friendly and helpful.

Safety and Security

Safety. There's no appreciable inside-the-stadium security problem. Occasionally there is some rowdyism in the bleachers, but it's rare. One Tribe observer put it, we thought, rather well. "It's so uncool to be an Indian fan that only the real baseball people go to the games. They never cause any trouble."

Outside the park, in Cleveland, it's a different matter. Though Cleveland has improved in recent years, this remains a fairly dangerous town for those who don't act sensibly. You should have no problems in the parking lot areas, but don't hang around all night, either. And while it is possible to walk from the stadium to the popular Mudflats nightlife area, unless you are going with a group it would probably be better to drive or take a cab.

Health. Given the short foul territories here, foul ball injuries are pretty common. If you are sitting near the lines, stay alert. Sun can be a problem, too, particularly in the bleacher area. Bring lotion and shades if it looks like a sunny day.

Don't discount the cold here, either. Cleveland Stadium is located on Lake Erie, and damp, chilly winds off the lake can quickly drop nighttime temperatures. Bring a jacket or sweater with you for evening games. You may not need it, but then again maybe you will.

The Stadium's first aid office is located behind section 22. It offers the usual services.

Mementos

Souvenirs. Souvenir stands are located throughout the park, with the biggest selection being behind home plate.

Foul Balls. Cleveland Stadium is a great park to catch foul balls, or to get nailed by them.

The Upper Deck boxes wrapped around home plate seem to get a large share of the fouls. Sections 19 through 25 would be good places to sit. Lower box sections 28 to 30 are also good.

Although the Tribe doesn't make as big a deal of it as they do in Baltimore, this is another park where you may be handed an "honorary contract" if you make a spectacular catch. Since the Tribe is also one of the few teams that still holds open tryouts for the squad, this may be your chance to show the Indians that you're the next Cory Snyder.

Autographs. This is a fine place to get signatures. The Tribe's members enter and exit the stadium from Gate M, which you'll find between Gates A and D. Though there are security people to hold back the crowds, players often stop for autographs before going to their cars.

The situation is even better regarding the visitors. You'll see their bus parked outside the security gate, which is located between gates B and C. In order for the visitors to get to the bus, they need to stroll past you. Generally speaking, if fans are courteous, many of the players will be willing to do an autograph or two before boarding the bus.

DETROIT TIGERS
Tiger Stadium

Bands of people stand on streetcorners handing out literature and demanding that you sign petitions, men walk around carrying placards, and, when a helicopter bearing the owner departs from the roof of the building, dozens of people stop on the sidewalk to peer upward, curl their fists, and shout curses at the sky.

A union picketing action, perhaps? A rally of yuppie–Marxist assistant professors pronouncing their contempt for the bosses before snacking on white wine and brie? Nope. It's just the typical postgame scene these days at Tiger Stadium.

Who are these petitioners and protesters? Tiger fans, mostly. What is their complaint? Are they mad about the substandard Tiger performances over the past few years? Do they want Sparky Anderson dismissed? Not at all. What they are livid about is the impending replacement of Tiger Stadium with a modern, full-featured park. What the fans would like to see is a redesign of the facility, similar to the remodeling of Yankee Stadium, that would preserve its present location and its essential character.

Tiger Stadium, after the destruction of Comiskey Park, shares with Fenway the distinction of being the oldest stadium in baseball—both were opened on the same day in 1912. Throw in Wrigley (1916) and possibly Cleveland Stadium (1934), and you have all that remains of the classic old parks in anything that truly resembles their original forms: though it must be said that if Yankee Stadium had to be remodeled, it was done in a tasteful and effective way. These are the only parks left wherein was heard the swing of the bats of Gehrig and Ruth, where mounds exist that felt the treads of Bob Feller and Christy Mathewson, and where people got to see Ty Cobb's spike-first slides into base.

It was not always so. Up until the 1960s, over a dozen classic parks remained. Some were admittedly deficient places for playing the game. We know of few people, for example, who have a good word to say about the Phillies' "Baker Bowl." But others are remembered as being as fine, or possibly finer, than any park that exists today. Cincinnati's Crosley Field and especially Pittsburgh's Forbes Field seem to have been wonderful neighborhood parks, resonant with history and truly designed with the nature and dimensions of the game in mind. Did their replacements—Riverfront Stadium in Cincinnati and Three Rivers Stadium in Pittsburgh, two of baseball's most impersonal sports palaces—really benefit the fans? Yet those old parks were destroyed with little more than a peep of protest and a nostalgic newspaper article or two.

Now fans are making their feelings known. The proposal to replace Comiskey Park created a monumental row as fans resisted the destruction of one of baseball's most historic (and beautiful) facilities, while Illinois taxpayers wondered why they should foot the bill for a new home for the White Sox. Both the fans and the taxpayers lost that contest, but at least they inspired people with the idea that if the wheels of "progress" couldn't quite be stopped, they could at least be slowed down.

Now the battle has moved to Detroit, and it promises to be a real donneybrook. On one side is a motley collection of most Tiger fans (a minority favors a new stadium), taxpayer groups, Detroit politicians who fear that a move for the Tigers really means a move out of Motown, and baseball "purists" nationwide. Leagued against them are local boosters who feel a new stadium would add another prestigious feature to Detroit's skyline; the Tigers' employees, who are tired or working out of rathole offices; and the area's executive elite. Fans claim the legitimate needs of all three groups can be met be an extensive remodeling and have hired two architects to design changes. The resulting effort is called "the Cochrane Plan." The Tigers say that nothing less than a new stadium will get the job done.

Banker J. P. Morgan used to say that behind everything there were two rationales: "the right reason, and the *real* reason." Behind all of the Tigers' hoopla about how a new park would better serve the fans (the right reason) are two largely unspoken rationales for a new facility. First, the Tigers—and everyone else—knows that Detroit's decline has depressed attendance over the past decade or so, particularly during night games. The Tigers get a mostly suburban crowd these days (Detroiters seem to prefer the Pistons), and many people from the surrounding communities are reluctant to attend games in a town that has one of the highest crime rates in the country. The fact that the Tigers have no secured parking doesn't help the situation. A new stadium could mean a move to the suburbs, where the fans mostly are. At worst, it could at least result in an improved security picture for the park.

The second real reason is based on economics. Fans like to think that the game exists for them, but it just isn't so. The TV market became more important than the fans at the park some time ago. Increasingly, stadiums exist to rent out suites and catering services to companies that want to provide sports entertainment to their customers and clients. Baseball fans may sneer at this, but the fact is that corporate customers subsidize the ticket prices of average attendees. Accordingly, setting aside a reasonable amount of ballpark space for this audience is in everyone's interest. The question is, what is reasonable? Will the "Cochrane Plan"—or something like it—bring Lee Iacocca and his friends to Tigers games (actually, Iacocca does show from time to time) with regularity? Or is a new stadium the only way to snag the three-piece suit crowd?

The man who will ultimately have to decide is the guy up in the helicopter, The Tigers' owner, Tom Monahan. An American success story, Monahan was brought up in an orphanage, opened his own small business while in his early twenties, and built it into Domino's Pizza. Like many a successful businessman before him (a Ford, for example, owns the Lions), Monahan bought the Tigers more out of civic pride than as an investment. It was his way, he's said, of showing his love of the Tigers and of his community. Suffice it to say, Monahan has been getting anything but love in return. We'd imagine that by now he must be wondering why he ever got himself into this mess.

The stadium they are fighting over is, indeed, one of the classic ballparks, and it houses one of the most celebrated of sports franchises, the Detroit Tigers. In truth, however, though Tiger Stadium is old, it's not the baseball museum that Fenway and Wrigley are. Tiger Stadium has been remodeled so many times that it really is a kind of cornucopia of baseball park designs of all periods.

Whatever its deficiencies, though,

Tiger Stadium has character, and its design is highly suitable to the sport. Moreover, it has that undefinable old baseball park feel—something that never can be replicated. If you go to Tiger Stadium, you will not find it a totally satisfactory experience. The neighborhood isn't all that great, the food selection could be better, and the parking situation is bad. You could also end up seated behind a post. But beyond all this, you'll find yourself in a real ballpark with real grass, surrounded by real baseball people. Moreover, you'll be watching the game played where Williams, Gehrig, DiMaggio, and Greenberg and the "Georgia Peach" sweated, strove, and scored. It's an experience you shouldn't miss.

The Team

One of baseball's best known teams, the Detroit Tigers have been around a long time. Through all its long history, Detroit has been known for one thing: consistency. Not often the best team in baseball, Detroit has even less frequently been the worst. Almost every year, Motown gets treated to an interesting pennant race.

The Tigers were one of the original teams that formed the American League in 1901. Before that, in the 1880s, the Tigers had played in the National League and succeeded in winning a pennant in 1887. They are the only franchise to have captured the flag in both Leagues.

The story of the Tigers in its first two decades is really the story of one player, Ty Cobb. Of course, the Tigers had other great players on the team such as outfielder and Hall of Famer Sam Crawford, but Cobb dominated the Tigers—and baseball—in a way that few other players have. For an incredible nine straight years Cobb copped the batting title (1907–15). He is still the all-time runs scored leader and is number two in hits. During most of those years, he also led or came close to leading in the steal category as well: the thought of Cobb's spikes (which he sharpened to a knife's edge) slamming into their shanks was enough to encourage many an infielder to step aside and let the "Georgia Peach" have his base.

Of course, Cobb was anything but a "Peach." He was, in fact, one of the hardest characters ever to play the game. Ty was a driven man, driven to best others, to show his contempt for all around him, and to win. He once referred to himself as "a snarling wildcat," and it was no overstatement. A hard-core racist, Cobb once refused to share a hunting cabin with Babe Ruth because Ruth was rumored to be part black. He was incredibly violent, too. Once, when a handicapped New York fan shouted an insult at Cobb, the Georgian climbed into the stands and started jumping on the fellow with his spikes. When horrified spectators shouted to Cobb that his victim had no hands, Cobb yelled out, "I don't care if he's got no feet!" and pounced harder. After police dragged Cobb off the man, he was suspended for a while from baseball.

Whatever his deficiencies of character, though, nobody could deny that Cobb's incredible on-the-field performance produced victories. During his first three years on the club (1907–09) the Tigers went to the Series each year, though they lost each time. The 1909 battle against the Pirates, though, was of particular interest because it pitted Cobb for the first and only time against the only other player of his era who may have been "the greatest ever": "The Flying Dutchman," Honus Wagner. They were a study in contrasts: Cobb was violent, vindictive, and hated by many of his teammates; Wagner was kindly, humble, and uni-

versally loved. Wagner won the contest, outslugging Cobb .333 to .231, though Ty did have the satisfaction of winning game 2 with a dramatic steal of home plate.

It would turn out to be the last Series for Cobb ever, and the last for the Tigers for twenty-five years. Yet if the teens and twenties were not Detroit's salad years, the team continued to perform competently. It featured players like Hall of Famers Mickey Cochrane (catcher, manager), Heine Manush (outfield), and the laconic slugger Charlie Gehringer (second base), who was called "The Mechnical Man" because it was said that all you had to do was wind him up at the beginning of the season and he'd perform without flaw all summer long.

When four-time home run champ Hank Greenberg joined this talented squad in 1930, victory for the Tigers again seemed in sight. Detroit went to the series in 1934, but ended up getting "beaned and Deaned," courtesy of the Cardinal's "Gashouse Gang." This series was as much a street brawl as an athletic event: at one point, baseball commissioner Kenesaw Mountain Landis had to step in to stop the fighting. Thanks to two "Dizzy" Dean victories, and two more supplied by "Daffy," the Cards won, 4–3.

The next year Detroit was back, this time battling the Cubs, and finally Detroit took the prize, beating Chicago 4–2. After falling unexpectedly to the Reds in the exciting fall classic of 1940 (4–3), Detroit was again on top in 1945, again against the Cubs, and again winning 4–3, thanks in large part to the stellar performance of Hank Greenberg, who'd just returned from combat a few weeks before the contest.

Since World War II, the Tigers have, like Charlie Gehringer, performed according to expectations. There have been World Series victories (over the Cards in 1968, over the Padres in 1984).

close pennant races, and League division championships (1972, 1984, and 1987). The Tigers have continued to attract top talent such as pitcher Jim Bunning, and sluggers George Kell and Al Kaline.

Hall of Famer Kaline was a fine outfielder too, with a habit of snatching victory from the jaws of defeat. During a game against the Yankees, radio broadcaster Mel Allen, spotting a sure home run, announced "the Yankees win it, 5–4!" only to watch Kaline run up the outfield wall and pick the homer out of the sky for an out.

Today the Tigers have a solid squad, though perhaps not one of their best teams. Attracting the most attention during 1990, of course, was Cecil Fielder. Unable to find baseball work in the U.S., this hard hitting slugger had ended up playing in Japan when he was finally—and reluctantly—recruited by the Tigers. It proved one of the biggest recent coups in the game as Fielder took home run and runs-batted-in honors and became the first American Leaguer to hit over fifty homers in a season since 1961. The question is, was Fielder's performance a happy fluke, or is it the beginning of a great baseball career?

Yet Fielder is far from the only outstanding Tiger. Other solid players include hurler Mike Henneman and veteran infielders Alan Trammel and Lou Whitaker.

As exciting as Fielder's homers were last year, the season wasn't a great one for Detroit. Still, as it became obvious that Fielder was going for the distance, the squad pulled together and started to win. If Fielder and a few others can show similar fire, the Tigers might surprise people and again be contenders.

The Stadium

With this year's destruction of Comiskey Park, Tiger Stadium has become the oldest of the baseball parks, an honor it shares with Boston's Fenway: both were opened on April 20, 1912. Yet in a way, Tiger Stadium is older—and younger—than the Red Sox's home. Though 1912 is Tiger Stadium's official date, the team has actually been playing on the present site since 1901. On the other hand, the place has been renovated so many times that it's hard to figure out just what period in baseball park design it belongs to. It is a little bit of everything.

Tiger Stadium is about a mile west of downtown Detroit, at the junction of Michigan Avenue and Trumbull in Motown's "Corktown" neighborhood. It isn't much of an area. Around the stadium are some dilapidated stores and bars, as well as a variety of parking lots. Aside from an empty lot where souvenir vendors set up along Cochrane Street to the west of the stadium, there is little to detain you outside. Still, you might want to take a stroll to the Tiger's offices, located just past the advance ticket office on the Trumbull side of the park. On the outside you'll see a plaque memorializing "the greatest Tiger of them all," Tyrus Raymond Cobb. He was, the sign declares, "a genius in spikes."

Inside, Tiger Stadium is similar to many of the old ball parks: its interior aisles are wide but somewhat dark and dreary, its restrooms are OK, but archaic. As is the case in several of the older parks, the women's rooms have attendants. Concession stands are fairly evenly distributed, but have no special appeal.

Once you move into the stands, however, you are in a different world. Royal blue plastic-and-metal seats surround you on all sides. They are comfortable, have decent legroom, and at least in the box areas the rows are reasonably short. Two things about the seating strike you immediately. First, particularly in the box sections, you are exceptionally close to the action. That's because foul territories at Tiger Stadium are unusually short and because the upper deck has a very long porch. The distance from the top level to home plate, in fact, is only 85′ — the lowest in the majors. Next, you are struck by the huge number of bleacher seats. Indeed, Tiger Stadium has more than any other park in the game.

It's the natural grass field that catches your eye, though. Here you find yourself in the midst of one of the oddest playing areas in all baseball. What appears as a "U" shaped park in the Tigers' literature reveals itself as very nearly a rectangle when you see it in person. This effect is created by an unusually distant center field wall (at 440′ it's the deepest in baseball) which creates in turn a mammoth center field area; only an incredible athlete can cover this particular patch of grass. The rectangle is completed by left and right field foul poles that are set at, respectively, 325′ (right field) and 340′(left field). All of this would seem to make Tiger Stadium a hard place to get a home run, but players have nevertheless frequently risen to the challenge. Over the years, 22 balls have gone soaring out of the park, driven by a "Who's Who" of such great American League sluggers as Ted Williams, Mickey Mantle, Norm Cash, Frank Howard, Harmon Killebrew, Reggie Jackson, and George Brett. Probably the greatest blast of all, however, came off the bat of (who else?) Babe Ruth. No one quite measured it, but the ball clearly struck the pavement at at least 600′ and then rolled for 225′ more. Now that's hitting!

There are other oddities about the field, too. On the negative side, the electronic scoreboard hangs over the stadium in such a way as to be invisible to many fans. If it's important for you to see it, try to stay within the baselines when you book your seats. Another oddity is the flagpole which sits *in* center field, *in* fair territory! Though it doesn't happen too often, the occasional fly that hits the pole adds excitement to the game, because balls bouncing off below the yellow line painted on the pole are counted fair, while those striking above are home runs. The upper deck adds individuality, too because the third deck on the right hand side slightly overhangs the right field line; balls that hit here are fair, too.

It all leaves you licking your lips in anticipation. You lean back, a Coke in one hand and (because there are few other choices) a dog in the other, and you stifle the urge to stand up and yell "Play Ball!"

Highlights

"Time honored" Tiger Stadium has had many magic moments.

There have, for example, been plenty of no-hitters. Three of the most notable included one by Bob Lemon (June 30, 1948), another by Nolan Ryan (July 15, 1973), and Charley Robertson's "perfect" of April 30, 1922.

This park has seen more than its share of World Series highlights, too. It was in Detroit during the seventh game of the 1934 series that Commissioner Landis had to interrupt a fans versus Cards ruckus that threatened the game. It was here too that Mickey Cochrane scored his Series winning run in the 1935 contest. During the 1984 fall classic, Alan Trammel tore up the park, hitting .450 in five games.

The biggest highlights, though, have been wrapped around classic baseball careers. It was here, for example, that Ty Cobb achieved most of his landmark .420 1911 season and here that Hank Greenberg hit the majority of his 58 homers in 1938. Of course, it was mostly in Tiger Stadium, too, that Cecil Fielder achieved his 51 home run mark of 1990. Altogether, Tiger Stadium is a park where baseball history has been made — and continues to be made.

Fans

In many baseball parks, as soon as you pass through the turnstile someone will stick a souvenir in your face and demand that you buy it.

At Tiger Stadium, by contrast, the first item you're hit with is a program . . . though there's no hard sell whatsoever. Buy it and you'll notice that a scorecard is enclosed, as well as a sharpened pencil. No one asks you whether you'd like the pencil, and there is no extra charge. It's just presumed that you'll want to keep score. After all, everyone else does.

Having visited 26 baseball parks, we've concluded that fans, like fine wines, take some time to age. However many positive things can be said about the fans at the expansion parks (and there is much good that can be said of them), they rarely show the kind of sophisticated understanding of the game that you'll find in most of the old baseball cities. Nor do they often exhibit that kind of intensity of interest that you'll see, for example, in Boston, New York, or Baltimore. Just as it takes time to create a winning baseball tradition, years must also pass to create an audience that's really in synch with the nuances of baseball, and which shares with the players that competitive edge that helps to make the sport a transforming experience. This spirit by no means exists everywhere, but it certainly is there in Detroit. This is an audience that watches, that cheers, and that understands.

Who are these people? They are suburbanites, mostly, drawn from the areas around Detroit and from the Windsor, Ontario, region. Surprisingly, given Detroit's industrial roots, many Tiger fans seem white-collar types, rather than blue. During day games, families dominate. Nights are favored by a younger and, perhaps, a bit wilder crowd.

Like most real baseball fans, these people are partisan. They love the Tigers, dislike the officials, and are rarely willing to give the opposition the benefit of the doubt on close calls. Tiger fans rarely boo opponents. On the other hand, they don't fall all over themselves to make the visitors feel welcome. While a spectacular play on the part of the opponents will occasionally get an appreciative clap or two from Tiger fans, they'll mostly sit on their hands when the enemy does something right. Why, after all, encourage them?

All of this is not to say that Tiger fans are uncritical of the home team — they're not. Though fans will tolerate a slump for a while, their patience is not unending. Sooner or later, poor performers will hear about the fan's disappointment. Tiger admirers also have a streak of sarcasm. During a recent contest in which the Red Sox pounded out hit after hit, the Tigers' bleacher crowd started chanting "Double! Double!" People in the broadcasting booth wondered just what was going on until they realized that Boston was, indeed, threatening to surpass the all-time doubles in a game record . . . a fact that the bleacher crew picked up before the experts did. Despite the crowd's attempt to needle the Tigers into a stronger defense, Boston went on to set the mark. Still, in how many baseball cities would the audience have understood what was at stake in such a contest? And where else but Detroit would the fans have responded in a way more calculated to inspire performance than that?

It is said that teams enjoy playing before the Detroit fans. If that's so, it's easy to understand. Who doesn't enjoy performing before an audience that's appreciative, and that knows what it's about?

Getting There

More than any other city, Detroit — "Motown" — is home to the auto. Car or cab are not only the best way to get to the game. They are just about the only way.

By car. Tiger Stadium is located near the intersections of the three major interstates (I-75, I-94, and I-96), at a point about ½ mile directly west of downtown Detroit. The best routes are as follows:

From such *northwest* locations as Grand Rapids and Muskegon, take I-96 southeast to Detroit. Leave highway at Exit 50, and follow signs to the stadium.

From *Detroit Airport*, Ann Arbor, Jackson, and other points *west*, take I-94 east to I-96 south, and follow the above directions to Tiger Stadium.

Those coming from Toledo, Dayton, and other *south* areas should follow I-75 north to Exit 49 Tiger Stadium/Rosa Parks Boulevard. Follow Rosa Parks to the park.

From Windsor, Canada, and points *east*, take the Detroit-Windsor tunnel (there's a toll), and then follow the Lodge Freeway (US 10) to the Fisher Freeway, (I-75) going west. Take your first exit off I-75 and start looking for parking.

By cab. Cab is a great way to get to the park from the downtown hotels. The charge runs about $3.

The price is much stiffer if you are going into the stadium from the airport area; expect to pay abut $22.

Parking

Parking is a problem at Tiger Stadium for a simple reason: the Tigers don't have any parking lots.

That means that you have to check around the area for neighborhood spots. Actually, this isn't that difficult to do: on all the major approach roads you'll see guys and gals standing on the side of the street, trying to wave you into an abandoned lot or some spaces behind a tavern. As is usual in this situation, you'll pay more money the closer you get to the stadium. Far out lots can

go for as little as $2, while you may even find some free spaces, if you don't mind a considerable walk. You'll pay $6 or more for something very close to the park. Happily, there seem to be enough spots to fill the needs of Tigers' fans; even if you arrive near game time, you should find something. If, however, you would like a space near Tiger Stadium, you would be well-advised to get to the park well before the game.

There is something you should be aware of here. These "lots" are seldom paved, are often not lighted, and are almost never secured. Therefore, you should be absolutely certain to lock your car before you leave it. Particularly if you are attending a night game, it might be a good idea to arrive early and get one of the close-in spots. Though the Corktown neighborhood that Tiger Stadium sits in has, despite appearances, one of the lowest crime rates in Detroit, this is still a dangerous city.

Tickets

You can get Tiger tickets the usual ways: by mail, by phone, or by picking them up in person.

Tickets are generally available for Tiger games, but if you want to assure yourself good seats for popular match-ups, you might want to order in advance by mail. To do that, send your check, money order, or MasterCard or Visa number, expiration date, and signature to: Ticket Department, Detroit Baseball Club, PO Box 77322, Detroit, MI 48277. Make sure you mark down the dates and numbers of tickets you want, and include the Tigers' $3 service charge.

The Tigers' Ticketline handles phone orders. Call them at (313) 963-7300 to get your seats and be prepared to pay with a major credit card. You might also want to have the enclosed seating chart handy to find out where the Tigers intend to put you. The Ticketline is open from 9 A.M. to 5 P.M. daily. You will, of course, be hit with a service charge here, too.

We like advance ticket offices because you can take a look at a seating chart and argue about spots in person. The Tigers' office is located at the southeastern corner of the facility at the corner of Michigan and Trumbull. It's open from 9 A.M. to 6 P.M. every day.

Availability. With 52,416 seats, Tiger Stadium is a large park. Its attendance figures, on the other hand, are somewhat below average: normally, it attracts under 2 million fans per season. Season ticket sales are somewhat anemic, too; generally they run below 12,000.

What all this means is that even if you arrive at the park only moments before a game, you will almost certainly find a seat — and it may well be a good one. If you intend to attend weekend contests against such Tiger rivals as the Yankees, the Red Sox, or Oakland, you'd do well to order your spots well in advance. For other games, a call to the Ticketline or a visit to the advance ticket office a few days before the contest should net you decent seats.

Costs. The Tigers like to brag that their ticket prices are "the best sports value in Detroit." While this is no doubt true, their charges are not the lowest in baseball. On the whole, prices at Tiger Stadium are moderate. Still, there are so many high quality seats in the park available at low rates that it can be fairly said that Tiger Stadium has some of the best bargain seats in baseball — the problem lies in finding where they are.

More than in most parks, you need a seating chart to figure this place out. The Tigers' policy of offering all seats at only four price levels simplifies things wonderfully, but it builds into the system some glaring incongruities. If, for example, you sit in Lower Deck Box 101, you'll pay the top price in the park ($10.50), and you will find yourself nearly 300' from home plate near the end of the left field line. Buy a spot in Grandstand Reserved 507, and you'll be only a few feet further out — but you'll pay only $6. A little study before you purchase seats can pay you big dividends in your enjoyment of the game.

During 1990, Tiger ticket prices were as follows: Box Seats ($10.50); Reserved Seats ($8.50); Grandstand Reserved ($6); Bleachers* ($4).

Rainouts. Detroit gets a fair amount of precipitation during the summer, so you have a chance of getting caught in a rainout. If it happens to you, the club will allow you to exchange your tickets for another game. Should you not be planning to return to town, write to the Tigers explaining this and your money will be refunded.

Seating

Tiger Stadium has many good seats, some very bad ones, and an enormous bleacher area that provides some of the best bargain spots in the game. Price is not always a reliable guide to the quality of the seat.

Lower and Upper boxes ($10.50) are the most expensive seats in the stadium, and, within the baselines, are certainly worth the money.

The Lower Boxes feature comfortable blue plastic-and-metal chairs. They have decent legroom and relatively short rows, particularly in the areas closest to the field. Since foul territories are quite small in this park, those chairs in rows 1–6 in particular are right on top of the action — you can hear the crack of Cecil Fielder's bat and see the triumphant glint in his eye. The best spots in this area extend from boxes 115 (third base) to 132 (first). However,

*Sold only on the day of the game.

Seating chart, Tiger Stadium.

even seats a section or two beyond these areas must still be rated pretty good since Tiger Stadium lacks the midfield bulge that you find in some of the modern, round parks.

Tiger Stadium's basically sound design also contributes to the excellence of many of the Upper Box seats. Featuring orange plastic chairs perched a level above the field, in-the-baseline spots in this area are outstandingly close to the action. From home plate to the first row of seats in the upper level is only 85′, less than half what that distance is in, for example, Cincinnati's Riverfront. You are, then, less than a base length away from the field.

The problem with Upper Boxes is that they extend way beyond the baselines—in fact, some of them even wrap themselves around the right field fence and sit *over* the bleachers. Thus, you could find yourself spending big bucks for seats in this area and pass your time in a section of the stadium where you'll have the same view as the "bleacher bum." If you are going to sit in this area you must insist on in-the-baselines spots, or, at any rate, seats close to them. The best box sections run from 332 (third) to 356 (first). Getting a low row is important, too; rows 1 to 4, have an excellent view and avoid an obstructing walkway.

Upper and Lower Reserved seats ($8.50) are next in price, but may not always be next in quality. Sloping back from the box seats on both decks, both of these sections have comfortable blue plastic chairs and both have reasonable legroom. As far as this sort of reserved seating goes, many seats are reasonably close to the action, too, particularly in the low rows (A–F).

So what's wrong with them? Poles. Tiger Stadium has many of the nice features of the old classic ball parks, but it also has an abundance of old-fashioned post obstructions, too. Unfortunately, they are almost impossible to avoid in the reserved areas. In this section, only one row, "A," does not have posts. In all the rest, you will have to deal with this obstacle to one degree or another.

Actually, the problem isn't as bad as we've made it sound. We have, from long experience, become something of post connoisseurs. We can say of the Tiger variety that they are not nearly so fat as the ones at Fenway Park, nor are they so cleverly placed to frustrate views as those in Wrigley Field. As posts go, these aren't so bad. However, if you are going to have to put up with this problem, you should at least try to secure seats in the baselines. Here, they run from 416 (third) to 426 (first) in uppers, and from 216 (third to 226 (first) down below. You should make every effort to avoid upper sections 402 to 406 and 435 to 440. These spots are far from the field over the outfield walls and are in most respects inferior to the cheaper Grandstand Reserved spaces.

Tiger Stadium offers two categories of inexpensive seats, and both represent decent value. Grandstand Reserved seats ($6) are located in two areas. A very large section of seats can be found behind the left field wall (501–507). A smaller group is behind the start of the right field fence (535–537). Overall, these are decent spots. On the left field side, you should try to stay in sections

507 to 505; the wall slants back deeply here, and sections past 505 are pretty far from the field. Also, left in particular gets quite a bit of sun. If this is a concern to you, you might prefer the seats in right, realizing, of course, that fewer balls are typically hit to this side of the field than the other. Another big concern in this area is the ugly blue chain link fence that tops the right field wall: to avoid having to look through it all game, you might consider seeking seats in rows J or higher.

It's said that Tiger Stadium has the most "Bleacher" seats ($4) in baseball, and we can well believe it. This enormous area is divided into two sections, one on each deck, both wrapped around the center field wall. It's a generalization, but we think it is fair to say that the two areas gather different crowds, too. The sun exposed upper bleachers tend to attract a younger, mostly male crowd that likes to drink, party, and get a tan while cheering the Tigers and booing the umps. The shaded lower deck seems to pull in the family crowd, along with some of the elderly. Both sections have the same seats: hard aluminum benches, with no backs. The spots are unmarked. You can sit wherever you like.

How good are the bleachers? The seating is uncomfortable, and the food selection in this area is pathetic. However, the view is surprisingly good from both sections, and the price is fair. If you are going with a big family or if you'd just like to save a buck, this would be a good place to be.

Special Needs

Parking. The older parks don't do a great job for the physically disabled, and Tiger Stadium is no exception to the rule. There is no handicapped parking, if only for the simple reason that there is no stadium parking, period. However, if you are physically disabled and make this fact known to any of the Detroit police you'll see standing around the stadium before the game, they'll find a spot for you in one of the "no parking" zones close to the stadium. You may not even have to pay.

Handicapped seating is available throughout the park—it consists of a yellow line with marked spaces sitting at the concourse at the top of the lower deck. Many of these spots are OK, but all have the problems of obstructing poles and an overhanging upper deck that cuts-off views of pop flies.

It can only be hoped that when the Tigers either rebuild or remodel this stadium, they'll do a better job for their physically disabled customers than this.

Food and Features

Food. No one could accuse the Detroit Tigers of going overboard to satisfy the fashions of the times. While other clubs have spent fortunes trying to cater to fan palates with sushi, bar-b-que, fish tacos, and other tasty treats, the Tigers serve essentially the same fare they offered when Babe Ruth and Hank Greenburg were pounding balls out of the park: hot dogs, pretzels, peanuts, knockwurst, and beer.

Food at Tiger Stadium consists of the baseball basics. Hot dogs, which some claim are the best in the game, aren't cheap; they're good, but we don't know if they're quite that good. Knockwurst is very reasonably priced, peanuts are overpriced, and popcorn seems about right. Other favorites include nachos, caramel corn, and an ice cream sandwich. The standout selection of all is probably the Italian sausage sandwich, which comes smothered with onions and peppers; it's high priced, but it's worth it.

The one specialty in the park is Domino's Pizza, which is not surprising since Domino's owner Tom Monahan

also owns the Tigers. You can order a medium sized, tasty pie—which, if you like, can be delivered to your seat. However, you should know that there is a Domino's store outside the park on Michigan that will sell you the same pie less expensively and provide a box suitable for carting it into the game. Note also that pizza is not available in the bleacher area.

Food stands are located throughout the park. However, the best selections can be found behind home plate on the lower level and near the left field foul pole (behind sections 406–409) on the top. The upper deck area has some of the shortest lines in the stadium.

Drinks. The drink situation is basic, too: reasonably priced Bud Light and Coke products are offered throughout the facility.

Features. In true old ball park fashion, the Tigers operate under the assumption that you came to Michigan and Trumbull to watch baseball, rather than to play computer trivia games, toss basketballs, or test your pitching skills. The diamond is the only feature in Tiger Stadium.

Assistance

Fan Assistance and Customer Relations offices are another concession to modernism that the Tigers want nothing to do with. That's too bad, as this is one "newfangled" innovation that's been a real improvement to the game.

If you have questions, need information, or are running into problem fans, try talking with an usher. Many of the service people at Tigers Stadium are "old-timers" who have been working in the place since before you were born. Most are extremely friendly and very knowledgeable. More than a couple can tell you from personal experience what Joe DiMaggio's batting stance looked like and how fast Bob Feller's fastball really was.

Safety and Security

Safety. Detroit doesn't have a good image in the minds of many people, who consider it a dangerous, crime-ridden city. Outsiders, too, have their doubts about Detroit sports fans. Reports of vandalism, rioting, and even murder after Detroit's recent basketball championship victories have soured many people on the idea of attending games in Motown. People want a good time, not problems.

How valid are these concerns? Regarding the fans, we have heard many of the same reports you may have heard of obnoxious fan behavior in Tiger Stadium. We *saw* absolutely none of it. During our time in the park, the attendees proved to be as well-behaved and polite as any fans you would find anywhere. We suspect, actually, that there is a diversity in fan behavior in Detroit. During day games and during regular season night sessions, the audience is probably little different than you would find in Kansas City or Toronto. It may well be that a rowdier element turns out for postseason or other more intense contests. Even then, though, we suspect you could avoid any potential problems by staying out of the upper level bleachers, which is where the drinkers would be most likely to congregate. Fear of fan behavior should on no account discourage you from attending Tiger games.

As for Detroit, it *is* dangerous . . . make no mistake about it. Some of the restaurants in town have TV monitors in their dining areas, giving you a view of the parking lot so that you can make sure no one is swiping your car while you dine. They aren't spending money on that equipment for the heck of it. Should you decide to wander about town after the contest, watch yourself.

Having said that, it's important to note that the Corktown neighborhood in which Tiger Stadium is located has one of the lowest crime rates in the city.

This area is heavily patrolled before and after games, and the Detroit police have a substation on Michigan Avenue only a hundred yards or so from the park. Accordingly, you should not be overly concerned about safety in the immediate vicinity of Tiger Stadium, so long as you make a point of leaving with the crowd after the contest and going directly to your car. Alternatively, if you are planning on staying in the area for a bite to eat or a drink after the contest, make sure you return to your auto with a couple of other people. If you use your head, there is no reason to be worried about security at Tiger Stadium.

Health. A few years ago, a prominent Detroit attorney, aged 40, decided to hike up the steps to the upper deck stands rather than ask to take the elevator. It turned out to be more of a climb than he'd expected. Nearly reaching his seat, he felt an intense pain in his chest and arm as he collapsed to the ground.

Fast action on the part of the Tiger's medical staff, and, in particular, of nurse Diane Krzystun saved the man's life. In gratitude, he established a lectureship in her name at a local medical school—making Krzystun probably the first RN so honored since Clara Barton.

Yet this incident, despite its happy ending, points out two facts of life about stadiums today. First, tragedies can and do happen in them. One of the surprising things we learned in checking out ballparks is that many have a fatality or two a year, despite the best efforts of the assorted nurse Krzystuns to prevent them.

Second, and most importantly, most park health threats take place when fans do not use their heads. While problems will occasionally be caused by poor stadium design or by such unfortunate but unavoidable occurrences as flying broken bats, the vast majority of difficulties happen when fans drink too much beer or too little water, when they insist on sitting in the sun for hours without a hat, and when they push themselves to climb stairs when their bodies are telling them to take a rest. Park health problems could probably be improved marginally if baseball spent more millions on fancy high-tech life saving equipment than they have already spent. Health could be greatly enhanced, and many tragedies could be avoided, if people would realize that, number one, bad things can happen at the ballpark, and two, using your own common sense is the best way to prevent them from happening to you.

As far as Tigers Stadium goes, the potential health problems are the usual ones. Those sensitive to the sun should avoid the upper level bleachers and should favor seats along the left field line. If you are attending games early or late in the season, on the other hand, dressing warmly is a good idea. Since foul territories are short at Tiger Stadium, those near the foul lines should stay alert or move elsewhere. Older people and those with heart problems should ask ushers to point them to the elevators if they are sitting upstairs. They should know that if they are having any difficulty getting to their seats, the ushers will be happy to provide wheelchair service.

Should you have any troubles, you will find the first aid office behind section 213, just past third base. Nursing mothers will also find that this is a comfortable place to go with their babies.

Mementos

Souvenirs. There are a variety of souvenir stands throughout the park, but you might be better served to do your buying outside the stadium. *Sportsland, USA*, at 1444 Michigan Avenue, Detroit ([313] 962-7452), likes to point out that it's a "pop fly east of Tiger Stadium," which is just about right. Here you'll find a wide selection of major league goods at reasonable prices. Sportsland is open from 10 A.M. to 5 P.M. Monday through Saturday year round, and is also open before and after all Tiger games.

You might also want to walk over to Cochrane (as in Mickey) Avenue, which is west of the stadium. Here, vendors usually set up tables before a game from which they sell pennants, shirts, and baseball cards. Prices in this area can be excellent; we, for example, picked up a nice Tiger shirt for $2.

Foul Balls. Tiger Stadium is a great place to catch a foul ball, or to be rapped in the noggin while trying to make a grab for one. Since Tiger Stadium's seats are exceptionally close to the field, balls lose little of their velocity before hitting the stands.

If you are willing to risk bumps and bruises in order to snag a ball, try sitting in Lower Deck Reserved sections 215 to 217 and 224 to 226 and keep your eyes open. If you somehow manage to barehand one, you will most likely be greeted with a round of applause.

Autographs. Tiger Stadium is an OK place to get Tiger autographs, and an excellent spot to hook signatures from visitors.

The Tigers enter and leave the stadium from their private parking lot, which is located to the right of the Tigers' offices, near the intersection of Michigan and Trumbull. Tigers will sometimes stop on their way in or out to sign a few.

You'll have much better luck with the visitors. Their bus stops at the visitors' gate, which is located on the south side of the park on Michigan Avenue, midway between Cochrane and Trumbull. In order to go back to their hotel, they have to cross the sidewalk through their fans to get into the bus. Many are willing to do a few autographs on the way, so long as fans don't get too pushy and remember to say "thank you."

HOUSTON ASTROS
The Astrodome

In 1960, John Kennedy was elected President, Elizabeth Taylor won the Academy Award for *Butterfield 8*, and local boosters in a rapidly growing sunbelt city submitted to the National League a request for a new expansion franchise—and plans for a baseball park that its sponsors boasted would revolutionize the game.

Houston got the team, making it the first city in the Old Confederacy to be represented in the majors. They named the squad the Colt .45s after "the gun that settled the west." And, in January 1963, the Colt .45s broke ground for a baseball park that, for better or worse, is without question one of the most influential sports facilities built in North America in this half century.

Houston had tried to get a baseball franchise for over two decades. In the past, objections had always centered around one indisputable fact: it gets unbearably hot and humid in Houston during the summer. Would people really be willing to fry outside for hours just to watch a ballgame? As anyone who has endured August in the Oil City will attest, not very likely.

The Houstonians didn't really have an answer for that one until key booster—indeed showman, visionary, and promoter extraordinaire—Judge Roy Hofheinz made a vacation trip to Rome. There, like millions before and since, he was awed by a visit to the Colosseum. But what really floored the Judge was something the guide told him. The ancient sports facility, built in A.D. 80, had originally had an awning over the top of it to protect patrons from the sun and rain!

That really got the wheels turning. If Romans could build a covered stadium nearly two thousand years ago, why couldn't Americans do it today? And who better among Americans to do such a thing than Texans? They, after all, were accustomed to "thinking big." Moreover, Americans had one thing the Romans lacked: air conditioning.

Thus, planning began on the self-proclaimed "Eighth Wonder of the World"—a building that not only would represent a turning point in baseball but also would symbolize that sense of expansiveness, excess, and optimism about the future that characterized America in the early sixties.

One thing that was determined early was that the place would be cooled and hang the cost. The new park, said the Judge, would represent "a Texan's refusal to be shoved around by mother nature." Consulting with architectural guru Buckminster Fuller, Hofheinz became convinced that a geodesic dome structure was the way to go. Fuller had further told the Judge that size wasn't the issue—money was. "You can build it as big as you can fund it," said Bucky. Houston's pockets were deep, and its faith in the future was deeper. Thus, the park was made big indeed—its dome is high enough to enclose an 18-story building, and to this day no one has ever hit it in regular play.

Houston, too, started the concept of encouraging the development of a separate "world" around the stadium, an "Astrodomaine" including hotels, huge parking areas, conference centers, restaurants, and even an amusement park. Finally, the Astrodome forwarded the idea of building "creature comforts" into the stadium: seating was (and is) deeply cushioned, aisles were pleasingly wide, concession stands offered, for the time, an unusual variety of treats, and luxury boxes were established to accommodate the corporate crowd, as well as such Hofheinz guests as Bob Hope, Robert Mitchum, Walt Disney, and Ann-Margret. What emerged from all of this is the modern baseball park that we know today, with its pluses and minuses.

As the new park neared completion in 1964 and as a new Texan president moved the headquarters of the U.S. space program to Houston, Judge Hofheinz became convinced that his new park was the wave of the future and that the team he would site in it ought to have a name to underline that. Accordingly, he renamed the team the "Astros"—as in Astronauts—and to make the point clearer, he dressed the park's groundskeepers in space suits! Over time, Houston's park came to be called the Astrodome, though that isn't its real name. The place is actually the "Harris County Domed Stadium," as a plaque outside the door rather huffily informs you.

All of the above was the result of Houston's conscious plan. Yet another major feature of contemporary baseball that the Astros pioneered came about by accident. Originally, the Astrodome's field was natural grass—like every other field in baseball. Since the panels that made up the dome were (and are) of glass, the grass was able to get enough sunlight to grow properly, even though the place was covered.

Unfortunately, there was a serious problem with glare from the glass when players tried to catch pop-ups. The players naturally complained, and management painted the panels. After that, the grass turned brown. As a stopgap, the Astros, in true *Alice in Wonderland* style, had the grass *painted* green. But it was clear that something more permanent had to be done about the landscaping.

As this was going on, Monsanto Chemical Company was experimenting with a carpeting product designed for outdoor playgrounds; using the stuff for sports facilities had never occurred to the firm. Still, some enterprising Monsanto people read about the Astros dilemma and wondered if they'd bumped into a new product line.

The rest, as they say, is history. "Astroturf," named after the stadium, was born. The Astros found the solution to their problem, Monsanto found a new market, and baseball fans throughout the country got a ballgame wherein rainouts were fewer, but the action was less real. It can be fairly argued that the Astros and the other domed parks had little choice in the matter. What the excuse of everyone else is, we don't pretend to know.

Today, the Astrodome still rears its magnificent bulge out of the Texas swamp wherein it was born. It is no longer the biggest of the domed parks; Minnesota's Metrodome and Seattle's King Dome seat more. Nor is it the most magnificent. Toronto's new park takes that category. It may still be the prettiest, but Montreal's Olympic Stadium might be, too.

So what makes the Astrodome so special? It's simple: it was the first park of its kind, and by being first, it became the model for all the others. Today, it remains what it has always been, an exceptionally comfortably and commodious place in which to play baseball.

The Team

The team that has labored for a quarter century within this famous park has been one of the more enigmatic squads in baseball. Neither terribly good nor among the truly bad teams in the sport, the Astros have simply been there. Yet while the squad only sporadically supplies excitement during the regular season, each of its three postseason appearances has been a classic of sorts. The 1986 contest against the Mets ranks among the finest playoffs ever.

Authorized in 1960, the Astros first began play in 1962 as the Colt .45s, in a temporary stadium that, with the construction of the Astrodome, was sold to the Mexican League and carted off. A fan suggested the team moniker, declaring that "the Colt .45 won the West, and will win the National League!" Well, it didn't quite work out that way. The Colts, and later the Astros, turned in the usual dismal expansion franchise performance during the 1960s, finishing in the upper division only once in the decade. Still, the team brought baseball to Houston, and there were good players, such as Joe Morgan and Mike Cuellar, and some fine moments, too. In 1966, Willie Mays tied the all-time National League home run record with blast number 511. In 1964, the Astro's Ken Johnson got the second of what would be an incredible eight no-hitters that have occurred in the Astrodome — almost predictably, given how it was for the Astros in the sixties, Johnson was the first pitcher to go the full nine with a no-hitter and still lose the game, in this case 1–0. In 1969 the weirdness continued as Cincinnati and Astros pitchers hurled back to back no-hitters in the Dome — the only time that has ever happened.

Things improved during the 1970s. The team recruited some solid pitchers, such as J. R. Richard, Joe Niekro, and Don Wilson, and sluggers like Jose Cruz. The team started to get involved in pennant races that were pennant races.

The 1980s were the Astros' best decade. Things started off with a bang when the Astros, powered by Morgan, Niekro, and new recruit Nolan Ryan, brought the team its first NL West title in 1980. That match-up was a real humdinger, a heart stopping contest that literally went down to the wire as the Phillies won in the 10th inning of the final game, 8–7.

1981 brought more excitement to the sunbelt. This time, the split season caused by the baseball strike resulted in a playoff for the Western Division title between the Dodgers and the Astros. Again the series went down to the wire, the Dodgers snatching the flag in the last contest.

For thrills, chill, and improbabilities, few series in history can match the 1986 NL West contest against the Mets. Coming off a division-clinching no-hitter, the Astros' Cy Young Award winner, Mike Scott, pitched brilliantly in game one, carrying the day. The next game matched up Nolan Ryan and Bobby Ojeda. The Mets got that one and the next as well. Things looked bad for the Astros until Scott came back, out of rotation, to win game four.

The drama intensified during the fifth game, which featured one of the greatest pitching duels conceivable: Nolan Ryan, limping on a sprained ankle, versus the Mets' Doc Gooden. The Mets won, although many observers gave the pitching laurels to Ryan.

After that, game six should have been anticlimactic — but it wasn't. In an emotional, seasawing contest that ran through five hours and sixteen innings, the Mets finally stumbled over the finish line, winning 7–6. The pennant went to New York.

Since the 1986 playoffs, the Astros have been only mediocre. Having lost Ryan and second baseman Bill Doran, the Astros find themselves with a discouraging lack of talent. Only time will tell if players like Jim Deshaies, Craig Biggio and Ken Caminiti can return the 'Stros to prominence.

The Stadium

Located a few miles directly south of downtown Houston, the Astrodome dominates the landscape for miles around. It looks big, and it is big. That's something most people know. What they may not be aware of is that the facility is also attractive. When Judge Hofheinz helped to design the park, he was not only inspired by the huge Colosseum. He was also impressed with the intricate structure of a spider's web. Accordingly, he dictated that the "Eighth Wonder of the World" be laced along a gridwork, both inside and out. As a result, whereas *all* the other domed parks have a certain heavy concrete stolidity to their appearance, the Astrodome has a look that's almost airy. It's an interesting architectural effect.

The stadium itself sits on top of what once was a swamp that is now paved over with parking; in fact, the Astrodome has more parking than just about anything you can think of. Beyond the parking lots is a mixed area of moderately priced hotels, restaurants, stores, and run-down homes.

When you pull into the parking lot, the immediate urge will be to get in the air conditioned building, particularly if you are arriving in the summer months. If the heat isn't too stifling, though, you might want to stroll around a bit. One thing you'll note is that the place has only four entryways—that's to help keep you from losing your car. You'll also see that the Astrodome has attached conference halls, the principle use of which is for livestock shows—sometimes the smell emitting from the Astrodomain has nothing to do with what's happening on the field! Between the west and south gates you'll note the only statue in the parks honoring a woman. The middle-aged lady holding the baseball is Mrs. Vivian Smith, "The First Lady of Houston Baseball." One of the early shareholders in the club, she and her husband Bob Smith were among the earliest proponents of bringing the national sport to Houston.

Inside the stadium you'll immediately be struck by how much the Astrodome looks like a shopping mall. The aisles are wide, the restrooms are spiffy, neat and color-coded concession stands and stores beckon to you as muzak plays. Yep . . . another one of the Judge's ideas. He studied shopping malls, too, in designing the dome. It's all very pleasing, and even relaxing; you feel neither rushed nor shoved, which is exactly how the Astro's management wanted it.

You have to walk down to get to your seats in the Astrodome. As for the seats themselves, all that can be said is that they're simply wonderful. Happily, too, the Judge was at least passingly aware that fans want to sit close to the action. Accordingly, foul territory in the park is short, and seats at the field level are right on top of the play. Unfortunately, however, the place also suffers from round ballpark disease, an illness characterized by an absurd bloating of baseball stadiums at the middle, resulting in pronounced vision problems for anyone who sits in the decks past the first and third base lines.

Something you'll immediately notice is that the dugouts reach halfway to Galveston. In fact, for years rumor has had it that it's a toll call between the dugouts and the bullpen! Actually, the Astro's dugouts are the longest in the sport and represent yet another of the Judge's innovations. Wanting to satisfy his fans, and believing that people love to brag that "I sat right behind the dugouts," the Judge simply built longer dugouts so fans would not be tempted to lie.

As far as the field goes, it's astroturfed and pitcher-park standard. The distance at both the foul poles is 330', while the center field wall is set at 400'. The lack of any wind at all has helped to make the Astrodome second only to Yankee Stadium in the number of no-hitters that have been recorded in a park.

The scoreboard sits over the left field wall, the visual display is over the right, and huge U.S. and Texas flags are in the middle. Between the two are the divisional pennants (1980, 1986). You can bet that there's a spot reserved on top of that for whenever the Astros land the big one and bring it home.

Highlights

The Astros may not have won a series yet, but the Astrodome has seen its share of magic moments. Appropriately, given that this is a pitcher's palace, most of them have to do with the art and science of hurling.

But let's give the batters their due. The first person to get a hit in the park (April 9, 1965) was Mickey Mantle. Later in the same game, the Mick hit the Astrodome's first home run. On September 15 of the same year, Willie Mays hit his 500th homer.

There have been no-hitters galore. The Astro's Don Wilson got one of his two in the Dome on June 18, 1967, Nolan Ryan racked one up on September 26, 1981, and Mike Scott clinched the Western Division with a no-hitter against San Francisco on September 25, 1986.

Nolan Ryan's eight years of service with the club supplied many milestones for the fastballer. He got, in addition to his fifth no-hitter, his 4,000th strikeout (July 11, 1985) and his 250th victory (April 27, 1986) while with the club.

Fans

"Americans like a winner," the movie *Patton* has the World War II general say, "and they will not tolerate a loser."

Actually, as Chicagoans will attest, there is quite a bit of tolerance for losers in some parts of North America. But there is none whatsoever in Texas.

That fact becomes immediately apparent when you attend Astros games. When the team is winning, the audiences are louder and larger, for this is a squad whose attendance fluctuates with the standings. Go to the Astrodome when the team is in a tight pennant race, and you'll find fans who can stamp their feet and holler with the best of them. On the other hand, when the team isn't doing so well, a kind of sullen resentment settles over the assembled Texans. Attempt to rouse this crowd when things are going badly are usually fruitless. "By God!" you can almost hear Astros fans saying, "that organist won't get us to yell 'Charge!' when we're losing six to zip. We're not gonna cheer a bunch of losers! Damned if we will!"

It's not that Astro fans are fickle. Though you could fairly say that about some of them, the team has a substantial contingent of folks who will go to the Astrodome no matter what. Nor, like some Atlantans, will they take to cheering the visitors if their own team consistently lets them down. It's just that Astro fans, like most Lone Star staters, set high standards for themselves and for the teams they watch. They insist on performance.

Who are these sagebrush perfectionists? The Astros, actually, get one of the more diverse audiences in the majors. Most people are middle and working class Anglo Texans, as you'd expect, and lots travel in families. But there are plenty of Yuppie singles, too, for Houston is a town full of unattached professionals. Houston has a dynamic dating scene, some of which carries into the park. There's a strong Hispanic contingent (Mexican-Americans, unlike most Texans, prefer baseball to football), some blacks, and even a fair selection of Orientals, which bespeaks the key role Houston is coming to play in the international marketplace. Economically, you'll find that the place attracts all-sorts; "rednecks" from the rural areas sit cheek-by-jowl with Yuppie executives of Houston oil firms. More than in some other places, the crowd at the Astrodome is a miniature of the community it sits in.

Some baseball teams have "famous fans," folks known for their exceptional devotion to the squad, and the Astros is one of them. Their fan's name is George Bush. Due to a job transfer, George isn't seen too often at the Astrodome these days, though he still wears an Astros cap while fishing and running. Still, if you hear that he's in town, try spotting the President in the field level seats in the 250s; that's where he usually sits.

Getting There

Located a few miles directly south of Houston's gleaming downtown, the Astrodome is easy to reach by car, provided you don't get caught in one of Houston's incredibly dense traffic jams. You can reach it by cab, too. There are no practical mass transit options for visitors.

By car. From Dallas and other points *north*, take I-45 south through Houston to I-59 south. Follow I-59 to Route 288 south (be careful here—the distance is short). Take 288 south and exit at the Old Spanish Trail (Route 90 west). Follow Old Spanish Trail to Fanning. Turn left onto Fanning. Astors parking is about ¼ mile on the right.

From Beaumont, Lake Charles, New Orleans, and *east* locales, take I-10 west to I-59 south, and follow above directions.

From San Antonio and other *west* areas, proceed along I-10 to I-45 south to I-288 south, and follow above directions.

From *Galveston and William Hobby Airport*, take I-45 north to I-610 west.

Follow I-610 west to the Astrodome exit.

From *Houston Intercontinental Airport* take Route 59 south through Houston to Route 288 south. Exit at Old Spanish Trail (Route 90) and follow west to Fanning. Turn left at Fanning and proceed to parking.

Please note that all of these directions except the one for Galveston and Hobby Airport take you into the stadium "the back way." Taking I-610 to the Astrodome exits appears, from looking at the maps, to be the easiest route to the park, but the intersection there is often subject to traffic jams and delays.

By cab. Taking a cab to the game isn't cheap. Plan on paying $30 to $35 each way from Intercontinental Airport, $20 from Hobby Airport, and $10 to $12 from the downtown hotels.

Parking

Rumors to the contrary, the parking lot at the astrodome is *not* larger than Rhode Island—it just looks that way.

Ample lighted and secured parking surrounds the park on all sides. It never runs out, and is bargain-priced at $3.

Two tips about parking at the Astrodome. First, try to enter the lots from the eastern (Fanning) side of the park: there's much less crowding in that area. Second mark down your location before you leave your vehicle: it's incredibly easy to lose track of your car here, and you could easily spend an hour trying to find it.

Tickets

You can get Astros tickets the usual way, by mail, phone, or you can pick them up in person. In keeping with the Astro's futuristic image, you can also get seats by FAX.

To get Astro seats by mail, write to:

Houston Astros Tickets, PO Box 1691, Houston, TX 77001.

Be sure to mark down how many spots you want, the dates, in what class, and where you'd like to be located; the Astros will try to accomodate you. Also include your payment in full, including the extra $4 the Astros extort for a service charge.

Phone orders are handled by Teletron ([800] 264-5780 outside the Houston area, [713] 526-1709 in town). Be sure to have your major credit card ready and a seating chart to refer to. You'll pay a service charge here, too.

The advance ticket office is a good place to pick up tickets. You'll find it on the West Gate side of the stadium (Kirby Street). It's open seven days a week from 9 A.M. to 5 P.M.

FAX service is available, too—this is one of only a few parks where you can get seats this way. Simply take the information you normally would include for a mail order and FAX it to (713) 799-9525, along with information on what credit card you'll be using, its number and expiration date. Your tickets will be mailed that day.

Availability. With 54,816 seats, the Astrodome is a medium sized stadium—even though it *looks* king-sized, both outside and in. More than in most parks, ticket availability is subject to a single factor: how well the team is doing.

In recent years, both the Astros and attendance have been a bit disappointing; last year's total of 1.3 million was one of the lower totals in the majors. Accordingly, you are likely to find good seats for just about any game, although box seats may be limited during contests against such longstanding rivals as the Dodgers, the Giants, Cincinnati, and St. Louis.

All of this, of course, will change dramatically if the Astros start winning. Still, even during their best years,

the Astros rarely sell out their Dome. Thus, if you arrive in town at the last minute and decide you want to go to a game, you should simply get a car and head on down—they'll find a spot for you.

Costs. Ticket prices are pretty fair: the top spot in the park goes for $10, while kids can get into the Pavilion section for $1. Unfortunately, as is the case in most of the round stadiums, ticket prices are of little help as a guide to the quality of the seats you are buying. Without consulting a seating chart before you buy, you could end up pleasantly surprised—or really ticked off.

In 1990, the Astros ticket prices were as follows: Field Box ($10); Club Box ($10); Mezzanine ($8); Loge ($7); Upper Box ($6); Upper Reserved ($5); Pavilion* (Adults [$4]); (Children under 14 [$1]).

Rainouts. Rainouts never occur at the Astrodome. However, the park did once have a "rain in." Just before game time, Houston was hit by a horrendous downpour, which dropped ten inches of water on the city. Amidst the chaos, the Astros, the Pirates, and a handful of determined fans sloshed their way to the Dome—only to be trapped in it by flooding.

Determined to make the best of the situation, the Astros' management dragged tables and grills out to center field and put on an impromptu steak fry for the players and fans while the waters receded. Don't you wish you'd been there?

Seating

Before going into the specifics of the particular seating areas, we have a rose to toss to the Astrodome: it has, bar none, the most comfortable chairs in baseball. In all but the Pavilion areas, seat bottoms are deeply cushioned

*Sold only on the day of game.

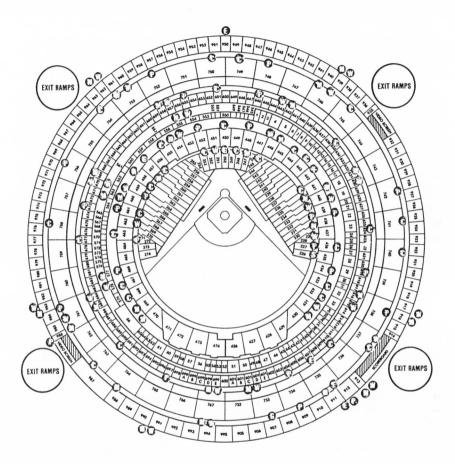

Seating chart, the Astrodome.

while backs are lightly padded and nicely rounded. All seats have handsome, polished wood armrests big enough to place a cup on, and legroom in all sections is decent. Even in the Pavilion area, the seats are well above the ballpark norm: they have backs (which is more than we can say about a lot of general admission seats), aren't too cramped, and also have some padding.

The most expensive seats in the park can be found at the Field and Club Box levels ($10).

Field Boxes are red chairs wrapped around and just back from the baselines, extending a bit more than halfway to the foul poles. Since Judge Hofheinz, the presiding genius behind the Astrodome, thought that fans like to be close to the action, this area runs exceptionally near to the foul lines, so a good seat here is very good indeed. Unfortunately, though, this area is also very deep; depending on the caprice of the ticket center, you could end up on top of the action, or frustratingly far away. Accordingly, in purchasing tickets, you should not only try to stay within the baselines, which are from 237 (third) to 262 (first) but also seek out a low row. Anything with a single letter (as in "B") should be fine. Double letters ("FF") will put you further from the field than you want to be. This area is also where the Astro's most famous fan, George Bush, likes to sit. He favors the high 250s, on the first base line.

Club Boxes sit at the press box level. The seating is nice, and the view is good within the baselines, but the aisle pattern is one of the most confused in baseball. Worse yet, seats in the club section wrap totally around the stadium — you can easily end up paying fairly big bucks for seats high over the outfield wall. If you want to sit here, try to stay within aisles 1 to 15 on the right field side, and 560 to 545 on the left.

Mezzanine seats ($8) might represent a better deal. This is a fairly low deck that sits on top of the back level of the field seats. As with all the round stadiums, this deck is set far too far from the field for our taste. Still, within the baselines, the spots are pretty good — but their quality deteriorates rapidly after that. Baseline seats here run from aisle 442 (third base) to aisle 458 (first base).

You are yet a level higher in the Loge spots ($7). These are handsome grey chairs in which the rows are pleasingly short and the legroom is ample, but you are pretty far from the field here. If you can get a seat behind the batter's box (aisles 645–649), you'll still have a good view at an excellent price. Otherwise, these seats are so-so. You should also be aware that the overhanding deck above the Loge section is something of an obstruction if you're trying to see pop-ups. If you get into rows A to F, you won't have a problem with this.

Upper Box seats ($6) and Upper Reserve ($5) are both ensconced on the same, wildly painted multicolored deck. The box seats occupy the first few rows, and are fairly good spots in the batter's box area, while the reserved chairs start after an intervening aisle and slope back from there into cloud-cuckoo land. For both of these, you pretty much need to stay within the baseline areas to have a seat that's really decent. Try to stay in aisles 747 (mid-third baseline) to 753 (mid-first baseline).

Pavilion seats are the cheapest in the park ($4), and many are better than at least some of the more distant seats on the decks above. Located in the traditional "bleacher" area behind the outfield wall, the section is composed of comfortable seats in inconveniently long rows, packed in fairly tight. Legroom is surprisingly decent. At row 15, serious pole obstructions come into play. The keys to this area are to stay in low rows and avoid entirely aisles 471 and 429, which do not have a full view of the field. If you are able to accomplish the above, you'll have some of the best low-priced seats in the majors.

Special Needs

Parking. As you'd expect in this ultramodern facility, the Astrodome has good facilities for the physically disabled. Handicapped parking is located next to the stadium, on its southwest side. Show your plate or sticker when you pull into the park and you'll be directed to it.

Seating. The handicapped seating may be the best in baseball. On the field level, aisles 249 to 251 are handicapped reserved, and are among the best seats in the park. Sitting on a raised podium directly behind home plate, these spots are convenient to restroom facilities and to food stands. The park organist also sits in this area. Located a deck above, the mezzanine has two reserved areas, too, 430 and 470, that are located at the extreme ends of right and left field. Though the view isn't great, the raised, separated areas provide both convenience and comfort.

Food and Features

Food. Dining opportunities at the Astrodome are not the best thing about the park and they aren't the worst. The food variety is good, quality is OK, and the prices are not particularly attractive—though there are lots of parks where prices are worse.

You'll find the usual standard ballpark stuff in stands spread throughout the facility. Included on the bill of fare are hot dogs, chili dogs, nachos, popcorn, and soft-serve cones. You can also get churros and a bar-b-que beef sandwich. It's all pretty undistinguished.

Happily, there are some specialty spots. *Bigger Better Burger* sells what you'd expect from the name: you'll find the stand behind aisle 455 (home plate) at the Mezzanine level. Pepperoni pizza is available at a stand behind 445 (third base), either as a whole pie or by the slice. *Domewich Deli*, behind 252 at the field level, sells roast beef, ham, corned beef, pastrami, and turkey sandwiches.

There's a restaurant, too. The *Trailblazer* Club, behind 661, is a cafeteria-style place that offers such treats as grilled chicken breast sandwiches, sliced brisket, baked potato, and salads. There a nice eating area next to the place, which, however, lacks a view of the field.

Drinks. Miller seems to be the park's beer, while Coke products are the soft drink choice. You can also get Inglenook wine at many stands.

Those preferring a better liquor selection should repair to the bar next to the Trailblazer Club where mixed drinks are available. Keep in mind that, unless you are seated at the Loge level, you will not be allowed to return to your chair with the drink.

Features. Probably the Astros' best known feature is "Orbit," the club's furry, spacey mascot. Recently called up from the minors ("Orbit" spent 1989 with the Tuscon Torros), the mascot seems principally intended to keep the little kids amused. Frankly, we weren't bowled over by this particular fuzzball, but if the younger crowd likes him, we suppose the Astros will keep him around.

The Astrodome is also one of only two parks in baseball (the other is Comiskey Park) that puts the organist out in the audience where people can see him—an excellent idea. John Steen plays a variety of favorites from behind aisle 250 (home plate) of the field level.

Assistance

The Astros have a Customer Service office located behind aisle 226 (left field foul pole) on the field level. Here you can look for lost kids, complain about or praise the food, or find out more about the park. There's also a Customer Service booth on the field level behind home plate.

Safety and Security

Safety. Generally speaking, the Astros get one of the quieter crowds in baseball. Rowdyism, drunkenness, and obnoxious behavior are pretty minimal. If you do have any difficulties with unpleasant fans, speak to one of the ushers and they'll take care of the problem.

Outside the Astrodome, in the parking lots, you should likewise encounter no difficulties: it's lighted and well secured. The surrounding neighborhood is more problematical. Those areas adjacent to the Astrodome—the hotels and nearby restaurants—are reasonably safe. The area beyond that, particularly to the north and east of the park, really isn't. If you decide that you'd like to check out the fast food spots along the Old Spanish Trail after a night game, you should drive rather than walk.

Health. Air conditioned and well-designed, the only real threats to your health in the Astrodome are your own overindulgences and fast flying foul balls. If you ate too fast or ducked too slow, report to the first aid office, which is behind aisle 442 (third base) of the Mezzanine level. In truth, we didn't find its staff very helpful when we asked what services they provide to fans, but maybe they're better at bandaging scratches than supplying information.

Mementos

Souvenirs. No one would dispute that the Astros have just about the most colorful uniforms in baseball — whether they're in the best taste is another question. Whether in good taste or bad, though, if your taste runs to the Astro look, you'll find an ample selection of club shirts, jackets, autographed balls, and the like at the *Houston Sports Exchange* shop, which is located behind first base at the Mezzanine level. Probably their most popular item of late is a T-shirt that simply says "Nolan Was Stolen!"

Foul Balls. Foul territories in the Astrodome are pretty short, so there are some fine foul ball snatching territories here. Aisles 237 to 240 (left field) and 261 to 263 (right field) seem to get the most balls.

Though they don't make as big a deal of it this is another stadium where, if you make a spectacular catch, you may well see an usher rushing down to present you with an honorary Astros contract.

Autographs. You have a reasonable shot at collecting autographs at the Astrodome. The Astros enter and leave from the TV entrance on the southwest side of the stadium, and they walk to their cars from there. Visitors go to their bus from the Harry Steven's loading dock at Gate 3, which is just to the right of the north gate.

KANSAS CITY ROYALS
Royals Stadium

Beauty is not a concept associated with baseball parks. Victory is not a term applied to expansion teams. Yet Kansas City, Missouri — the smallest population center currently represented in the major leagues — has shown since the inception of its current American League franchise that it has the "right stuff" when it comes to managing a winning, profitable, and fan-friendly sports enterprise. Its team has been singularly successful, its games have been well-attended, and its stadium is regarded as among the best designed, indeed among the most beautiful, in baseball.

Consider the following:

•In most major league towns, a team is thought to have accomplished something if the annual attendance breaks

2,000,000. The Royals have surpassed this figure for the past five years.

•It's accepted that expansion teams will have to endure years of humiliation before getting "good." Not in Kansas City. Since the franchise began in 1969, the Royals have maintained the best overall record in the American League's Western Division.

•Over the past two decades, the Royals have finished first or second in their division fourteen times, giving Kansas City fans something to cheer about nearly every year.

The Kansas City success story is a tale not of luck and demographics (actually, the demographics run against the club), but of sound planning, solid, no-frills management, and a commitment by the team to get the community involved in the franchise right from the start—indeed, a volunteer committee of local businessmen, the "Royal Lancers," provides much of the oomph behind the Royals' marketing efforts to this day. What the Royals experience means to baseball is that when the Leagues decide to expand (as the National League recently has), they should look not to cities with impressive population stats and deep-pocketed millionaire would-be owners. Rather, they should seek out towns that really, really want a club (Buffalo?), and management groups with baseball smarts and business savvy. For fans, Kansas City provides a baseball experience that is nearly unrivaled for convenience and comfort. If Kansas City lacks something of the baseball "tradition," moreover, it's rapidly on the way to acquiring one.

The Team

Though the Royals may be one of the newer teams, Kansas City itself has a long baseball heritage.

For decades, the Kansas City Blues, one of the Yankees' principal farm clubs, played host to some of the game's greatest players on their way up—and down—the baseball ladder. Mickey Mantle and Roger Maris are just a few of the Yankee greats that started their careers in K.C. The Negro League's Monarchs were also headquartered here; this was the team that Jackie Robinson was playing for when he got the call from the Brooklyn Dodgers.

One of baseball's best stories is told about Mantle's stay in the "Fountain City." A hot player from the nearby mining country of eastern Oklahoma, the Mick (who was named after baseball great Mickey Cochrane) learned most of his skills from his dad, a lead miner and baseball enthusiast. Moving up to the Yankee organization, Mantle muffed his first assignments, and was sent by Casey Stengel to Kansas City. Mantle expected to cut a mighty swath through the minors. Instead, he went 0-22 in his first starts. Discouraged, he called his father and told him, "I don't think I can play baseball any more."

The next morning Mantle was astounded when his dad (who had driven up from Oklahoma) barged through his hotel room door. Seizing a suitcase, the senior Mantle began grabbing the Mick's things and throwing them in. "What are you doing?" Mickey wanted to know.

"You don't want to play baseball anymore," his father declared, "so I'm taking you home. You can get a job in the mines."

Mantle got the message. He hit .360 for the rest of the season and was soon moved back to New York.

In 1955, major league ball finally came to Kansas City when the Philadelphia Athletics began the first of their moves west. Playing in Municipal Stadium, a colorful old place in one of Kansas City's tougher neighborhoods, the Kansas City A's were, to be generous, mediocre. Their sixth place finish in their first year was their best ever, while in their thirteen years in Kansas City they never had a winning season.

Yet if the A's weren't known for the quality of their ballplay, they were recognized for the eccentricities of their owner (from 1960), Charles O. Finley. Finley, for one thing, used an ass called "Charley O" as the team's mascot; some fans claimed that they couldn't tell the difference between the animal and the owner. He favored orange baseballs and color-coded bases (blue for first, red for second, etc.) Charley O also installed a mechanical rabbit under home plate that would come out of the ground and hand the umpire balls as required!

Finley was equally famed for his disputes with his players. During one controversy, he hired private investigators to "get the dirt" on team members, uncovering such damaging gems as the time one player smashed up a golf cart in frustration with his game.

Finally, Finley got tired of Kansas City and, after several false starts, managed to get the A's moved to Oakland. Normally, the loss of a major league squad is viewed by any city as a tragedy, but one of Missouri's U.S. senator's probably summed up the feelings of many when he declared the move a wash, in that although they had lost the team they had at least gotten Finley out of the state.

Major league ball returned to Kansas City with a vengeance in 1969 when, in its first expansion, the American League created the Royals. Playing initially at Municipal Stadium the new franchise had a respectable start, placing no worse than fourth in its first several years. With the introduction of Royals Stadium in 1973, the squad got hot. In 1976, the Royals won the first of three consecutive American League Western Division titles. They swept the West again in 1980 and took the pennant as well, only to bow to the Philadelphia Phillies 4–2 in the fall classic. 1984 brought another divisional title. Finally, in 1985, the Royals rallied to overcome a 3 to 1 deficit against the Cardinals to take their first World Series.

Some of the game's most outstanding players of the past two decades have donned the Royal blue. Included on this list are slugger and 1980 MVP George Brett (first base), double Cy Young award winning pitcher Bret Saberhagen, expert base stealer Willie Wilson (center field), all around first class players Amos Otis (center), and Frank White (second base), all-time "games caught" leader Bob Boone and, until recently, the multitalented outfielder, Bo Jackson.

The Royals currently have their most talented team ever. It's also their most expensive. The combination of Brett, Cy Young winner Mark Davis, pitcher Storm Davis, third baseman Kevin Seitzer, and Saberhagen makes for one of the most impressive line-ups in the majors. Thus, it was confidently predicted that the Royals would be a serious Series contender in 1990.

Actually, things didn't work out that way. Despite all the talent, the Royals only barely avoided a last place finish. The ability of this organization, composed as it is of strong individual players, to create a sense of team seems to be the key. If the Royals can get everyone on this fabulously talented squad to pull together, they're in a position to scoop up all the marbles once again.

The Stadium

In the 1960s and the 1970s, metropolitan areas throughout the U.S. and Canada went on a spree of stadium building. During this period, three quarters of the major league got new and supposedly better parks. At the same time, classic old stadiums like Crosley Field (Cincinnati), Sportsmans Park (St. Louis), and Forbes Field (Pittsburgh) were torn down.

Most of the new stadiums were impressive, full-service, multipurpose sport palaces, designed as much (or more) for the needs of football and rock concerts as for baseball. They made worthy additions to city skylines. Whether they really are an improvement on the stadiums they replaced, however, is debatable.

Some architects resisted the "cookie cutter" ballpark movement. In New York, faced with the physical deterioration of Yankee Stadium, planners ignored the call for a move and instead rebuilt the original, adding convenience but maintaining the baseball "feel" of the place. Stung, perhaps, by traditionalist criticism of their move from Brooklyn to Los Angeles, the Dodgers, too, built a ballpark of classic — and human — dimension. Possibly reflecting that commitment to good public art and architecture that is to outsiders the most surprising aspect of Kansas City, the Royals organization also decided to replace Municipal Stadium with a park in the traditional form.

Built in time for opening day 1973 (Royals' second baseman Frank White, a Kansas City native, was one of the construction workers) Royals Stadium is part of the Harry S Truman Sports Complex. It's a vast expanse of land that, in addition to Royals Stadium, also includes Arrowhead Stadium, home of the Kansas City Chiefs. Located about eight miles east of downtown Kansas City, the place is extremely well situated, resting as it does at the intersection of two major east-west and north-south routes (I-70 and I-435, respectively) and within an easy drive, and in some cases walk, of excellent hotels and restaurants.

The northern-most of the two parks, Royals stadium is an open-air, open-ended, three tiered park in the classic baseball modified "U" form. From the *outside*, the place seems to front on busy Interstate 70. However, within the park, creative landscaping (and

fountainscaping) has insured that the highway is all but invisible and inaudible. Outside, too, the basic simplicity of the place is apparent; there are only four entry gates, instead of the ten or so that can be found in some of the multipurpose stadiums. Nevertheless, the relatively small scale of the park insures that wherever you enter, you'll not be very far from your seat.

Inside, the place is a paradox, for it conveys a sense both of intimacy and spaciousness. The intimacy comes from the human scope: Royals Stadium is among the smallest in the majors, seating only 40,625. The spaciousness is due to the wide corridors and aisles as well as the open-air seating plan.

The concourses are a model of unobtrusive design. Food stands are color coordinated, well-spaced, and numerous enough that concession-lines are fairly short. Souvenir stands are placed in such a way that people gathered around them do not clog up the passages. Phones and restrooms are easy to find, while behind home plate on the plaza level, there's an interesting and tasteful "Royals Hall of Fame" display honoring great Royals from the past.

Much of Royals stadium fame rests on its field arrangements, and deservedly so. The field itself is strictly standard issue. It's a simple, straightforward diamond with a fanning field. Right and left field at the foul posts are set at 330', while the center field wall is a fairly-longish 410'. Since the surface is astroturf and the park is exposed to the wind, this can be a hitter's palace — not necessarily a disadvantage to a team enlisting George Brett.

The real interest focuses on what's behind the outfield wall. To the rear, atop a landscaped hillside, is a handsome stand of pines that separates you from the highway and, it seems, the non-baseball world. In front of these, on the left, is a circle of flags, celebrating each of the Royals divisional and pennant victories. At the center is the most famous symbol of Royal's Stadium, a 12-story electronic scoreboard built in the shape of an enormous crown (need we tell you that the crown lights up when the Royals hit a home run?) To top this, the scoreboard is framed on both sides by 322' of spectacular waterfalls and fountains, put there to remind you that Kansas City is "the Fountain City." As if all this weren't enough, if you were able to look down on the fountains and the scoreboard from the air, you'd see that they are designed to form an enormous number "1."

As we've said before, it's really all quite beautiful. Just how beautiful? On the night we attended, fans were invited to watch the Royal's "water spectacular" (a standard practice) after a long evening contest. At least half the crowd stood for ten minutes to see the show . . . and most stayed until the last drop fell.

Currently, a half-dozen teams are contemplating new stadiums. Their officials are visiting Toronto's fabulous SkyDome, which may not prove a good model for all clubs. Others are pouring over the drawings for the new park the Orioles are building, which does look like a winner. They would be well advised, in their studies, to steer their corporate jets toward Kansas City to get a close look at how good a stadium can be.

Highlights

As befits the success of the Kansas City franchise, the Royals have recorded a sizeable number of baseball milestones in Royals Stadium's brief existence.

For both Royals and Cardinals fans, October 27, 1985, is a day that will always be etched in memory—though Redbird admirers would love to scrub that particular recollection out. That was the day the Royals won the crucial seventh game in their come-from behind 1985 World Series quest in a crushing 11–0 romp. Few who saw this particular game will ever forget either its crucial 5th inning, when the Cards went through five pitchers, or Joaquin Andujar's maddened charge for the umpire after a series of what were, in truth, questionable calls.

The sixth game of the same Series (October 26, 1985) was equally memorable, and it was a better contest. Here the standout play was a timely 9th inning hit from the bat of the Royal's Dane Iorg that put the Royals up 2–1.

Sluggers have done fairly well in the park. Much of George Brett's 1980 30-game hitting streak was pounded out here. Bo Jackson slammed his first major league home run at Royals Stadium on September 14, 1986. Traveling a mammouth 475' to the embankment in left center field, the blast holds the record as the park's longest ball.

Jim Colborn threw the only no-hitter in the stadium hurled by a Royal pitcher on May 14, 1977. Four years earlier, on May 15, 1973, the California Angles' Nolan Ryan hurled the only no-hitter ever recorded by a visiting pitcher.

Fans

Ask anyone who travels extensively in the area what they think of plains staters—the inhabitants of that vast, flat, empty prairie that stretches from St. Louis to Denver—and you will hear a variety of superlatives. These people, you will be told, are "honest," "hard-working," "dependable," "courteous," and "down-to-earth." They will eventually admit, however, that plains staters are also somewhat boring.

The audience at any Royals game gives you a portrait of the plains. Indeed, due to the Royals' very effective marketing program, many of the people in the audience will be from Kansas, Nebraska, and Iowa. The Royals probably have the greatest geographic draw of any team in baseball. Given where they hail from, the Royal's crowd is white, middle-class, and dominated by families.

These are decent, well-dressed folk, who are friendly and have good manners. In fact, this audience's basic instincts and sentiments are very like those portrayed in the products of the Fountain City's largest employer, the Hallmark Card Company. Perhaps fittingly, Royals Stadium is the only place in the majors where the "Star Spangled Banner" has been replaced (thankfully, only on Sunday nights) by the syrupy and vacuous "God Bless America."

Whereas at some parks questionable calls by officials are greeted with shouts of derision, or even by "cuss words," you will see little of that behavior in Kansas City. After all, the umpires are doing the best they can. Similarly, while in other towns the entrance of the visitors can be the cue for a crescendo of boos, that doesn't happen here . . . it's not right. (But you won't hear much cheering for them, either. Plains staters aren't *that* nice). Nor are Royals fans particularly keen on ragging poorly performing players (though Mark Davis has been trying their patience). That isn't their style. When the Royals go south the fans don't moan about it. They simply stop coming. For make no mistake, however laid-back Royal fans may seem, they love a winner, and will not long tolerate (as the Kansas City A's found out) teams that always lose.

This is not an audience of baseball purists. Scorekeepers are rare, and few fans seem as "on top" of the game as people in some of the east coast cities. Nor is this a particularly sports crazy town. Mostly, plains staters seem to enjoy being out in the fresh air sharing a baseball experience with people very much like themselves. More than in most places, being a Royals fan is an expression of solidarity not just with a

team, but with a community and, indeed, with a way of life.

This is expressed dramatically in how K.C. fans react to the players. To put it bluntly, the performance of players out of the park is just as important to the typical Royals fan as his performance in it. "Jose Canseco," admits a Royals representative, "wouldn't make it here. He's too fast-track. We like our people wholesome." A lady fan put it to us even more bluntly when she told us that George Brett was her favorite Royal. What was it, we wondered, that she liked about him? His home runs? His batting average? Possibly his single status? "Well," she declared, "he's never embarrassed us." As might be imagined, Brett is universally admired in Kansas City, though if you took a poll, local boy Frank White might be the most loved Royal of all.

There are probably those, particularly from some of the more dog-eat-dog coastal cities, who would not feel at home with the Royals fans. "They're a bunch of conformists," they'd say. "There's nothing spontaneous or fervent about them!" And their criticisms would not be totally off base.

Yet at the same time, this is an audience that, in an age of rampant "me first" individualism, sees the connectedness between people, that in a time in which values are "relative," feels, however unfashionably, that there are some standards worth holding to. There's a place for such fans.

Getting There

The Plains States are vast, fairly flat and seem designed by God with the auto in mind. While you can get to Royals Stadium by bus and cab from many locales, in most situations car will be the best way to go.

By car. The Harry S Truman Sports Complex was put at the very center of the major north-south and east-west auto routes. There probably isn't another stadium in the majors that's easier to get to.

If you are arriving at *Kansas City International Airport*, take the airport service road to I-435 east and follow to Exit 63C Sports Complex/Raytown Road. From there, follow signs to parking. This is a fairly long ride, perhaps thirty miles, and should take you forty minutes or so.

From Oklahoma and other *south* locations take I-435 north to Exit 63C Sports Complex/Raytown Road and follow sign to parking.

From Jefferson City, St. Louis, and other areas to the *east*, take I-70 west to Exit 9 Sports Complex and follow signs to parking.

From Kansas City, Kansas, Topeka, and other destinations *west*, take I-70 east to Exit 9 Blue Ridge Cutoff/Sports Complex and follow signs to parking.

By cab. Cab is a practical option from the downtown hotels. It costs approximately $15 one way from most locations.

Taking a cab from the airport is another matter. To put the matter directly, Kansas City cabbies will sometimes try to cheat you on the fare, which would be large in any case given the park's distance from the airport— and the airport's distance from anything at all. You could easily spend more roundtrip than it would cost you to rent a car.

By bus. Bus is a perfectly sensible option if you are staying in the downtown hotels or in the Country Club Plaza area. Kansas City's *Metro* system runs a "Royals Express" service to and from all home games. The *downtown* route starts at the Crowne Center Hotel, and then proceeds to pick up passengers at the Hyatt Regency, the Americana, the Travelodge, and other downtown locales before heading out to the game. The *Country Club Plaza* route originates at the Best Western Seville Plaza and then stops at the Hilton Plaza

Inn, the Ritz Carlton, the Bellerive Hotel, the Ambassador Hotel, and the Hyde Park Hotel before moving on to the contest. The Royals Express service starts operating 1 hour and 50 minutes before the first pitch, and the last buses leave Royal's Stadium 50 minutes after the game. Fares are $2.50 roundtrip for adults, $1.25 for kids 6 to 11. The Metro at (816) 221-0660 would be happy to supply further details.

Parking

One of the advantages of the Truman Sports Complex's suburban location is that it has plenty of parking. Specifically, 18,000 spots surround the stadium, all uniformly priced at $4. In the extremely unlikely event that this should not prove enough, there are additional lots in the vicinity that parking officials will direct you to.

Royals Stadium, unlike most other baseball parks, will allow you to tailgate. It isn't a big deal here, but before most games you'll see a few people sunning themselves on lounge chairs or grilling hot dogs. You are, however, not allowed to bring liquor, or, indeed, any bottles or cans whatever, into the park.

Tickets

Royals tickets can be ordered by mail or phone, picked up in advance at the stadium, or bought just before the game—if any are left.

As the Royals are a fairly hot ticket, your best option is to order in advance. Write to: Mail Department, Kansas City Royals, PO Box 419969, Kansas City, MO 64141-6969. Be sure to specify dates, number of tickets sought, and the location you'd like. You can pay by check or by credit card, if you include your credit card's number, type, and expiration date. The Royals assess a $2 postage and handling charge on mail orders, so enclose that too.

You can get tickets by phone as well. Locally, call (816) 921-4400 or from outside Kansas City (800) 422-1969. Charge Line hours are 9 A.M. to 9 P.M. Monday through Saturday, and 9 A.M. to 6 P.M. Sundays. Have your credit card ready.

The advance ticket window is a good place to get tickets, because you get to see a seating chart. The Royal's office is located on the south side of the stadium, between gates A and B. Hours are from 9 A.M. to 6 P.M. daily. Terms are cash or plastic.

Important note: While you can buy tickets directly before a game, sales are operated strictly on a cash basis.

Availability. The Royals are a team that consistently draws over 2 million fans a year in a stadium that seats only 40,000. What that means as a practical matter is that tickets are tight.

Actually, even if you show up at the last minute, it's likely that you will get into most games. Sellouts are rare. However, you may find yourself sitting in the last row of the upper reserved or in the bleachers. Even if you do order several days before the contest, you may have difficulty getting really good seats. Currently, the Royals sell 16,000 season tickets, a figure that represents about 80 percent of the total number of box seats. The remaining 20 percent goes fairly quickly, particularly if the Royals are matched up gainst the Yankees, the A's, or the Angels.

Yet do not despair. Unlike some of the other parks, where a "bad seat" really is a bad seat, a bad seat at well-designed, close-to-the-action Royals Stadium is usually quite acceptable. In particular, the bleacher spots are fairly good, and a bargain at $4.

Costs. Royals tickets are uniformly priced based on the level you are sitting at. As in other parks where this scheme is used, the system trades the convenient uniformity of pricing for precision regarding which spots are really best. Royals Stadium is one of those places where the most expensive seats are not necessarily the best, while cheaper tickets can be surprisingly good.

In 1990, Royals ticket prices were as follows: Club Box ($11); Field Box ($10); View Level Box ($8); Plaza Reserved ($8); View Level Reserved ($7); General Admission ($4).

Rainouts. Though we are not fond of astroturf, we will admit that it is effective in preventing rainouts.

Royals Stadium's version of the stuff is said to be able to drain twenty inches of rain an hour. That, as a practical matter, means that rainouts occur here only about once a year. Should you happen to be so unlucky as to catch the annual drenching, you can exchange your tickets for replacement seats at any other game during the year. If a return trip to Kansas City is not in your plans, write to the ticket office explaining this. They will send a refund.

Seating

While there are few really poor seats in Royals Stadium, there are fairly wide discrepancies between the best seats and the worst ones, and price is not always your truest guide to quality. Checking out a seating chart (see chart) is always a wise idea.

Royals Stadium is a U-shaped, cantilevered place with three tiers leaning back from the action.

The 100 plaza level, at the bottom, contains both the Field boxes ($10), and the Plaza Reserved ($8). These seats are fairly comfortable, handsome red plastic chairs, with the railings done tastefully in royal blue. The boxes run from the field to an aisle, from which corridors lead down to a cavernous area with restrooms and a very limited food selection. Beyond this aisle is the Plaza Reserved section, which terminates at the lower concourse, where the best selection of food and features are. Within

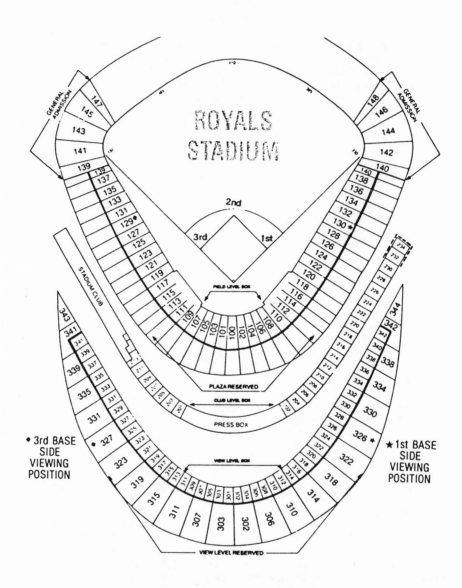

Seating chart, Royals Stadium.

the baselines (sections 118, first base, to 119, third, in both catagories), these are fine seats in either section, though the $8 Plaza Reserved seats, particularly in distant rows, are, in our opinion, not quite as good as the 300 level View

boxes, which sell for the same price.

Oddly, the most expensive seats at Royal's Stadium are not those next to the field. Rather, they are the Club boxes ($11), which share the 200 level with the corporate suites, the press box, and the pleasant (but restricted to season ticket holders only) "Stadium Club" restaurant. These are nice yellow plastic chairs with a great view of the proceedings, though they're located far from the best food selection, which is on the plaza concourse. Whether these seats are really worth more than a spot just behind the batter's box or across from first base is another matter, particularly since the press box at this level takes up the most desirable areas behind home plate. Anyhow, the best seats here can be found in even numbered sections 202 to 214 (the right field line from near the plate to first), and odd numbered sections 213 to 201 (third base to close to home). You might want to avoid the first row, A, as the railings will provide some view obstructions for many people. You should also try to stay out of sections 230, 232, and 234 (all in extreme right field), which have some pole obstructions. If you are sold tickets in seats in these sections, you are supposed to be informed if your chair has a limited view.

While your seats on the 300 level may not give you the closest look at the game possible, at least you'll get to see the skyline of Kansas City—if you sit on the right field side! In actuality, the 300 level consists of two sorts of chairs. View level box seats ($8), are located in the first several rows of the upper level. Particularly within the baselines (odd sections 325 to 301 is third to home, even sections 300 to 326 are home to third), these are good seats. They are superior in some ways to the Plaza Reserved spots on the 100 level and cost no more. Separated by an aisle from the boxes, View level reserved seats ($7) are alright, but are a bit too far from the action for our tastes. The best sections are numbered the same as the View boxes. As with the 200 level seats, the food selection in this section is somewhat limited. It's also quite a climb to this level. Ask an usher to show you to an elevator if you have heart problems or are getting up in years. Better yet, sit someplace else.

General Admission—the bleachers—is a good option for those who don't want to make the climb to the View level reserved seats, or who simply would prefer to save a buck. The bleachers are divided into two parts. Sections 139 to 147 are stretched out around the foul pole in left field. Sections 140 to 148 configure in the same way along the right field line. The seats are unusually comfortable for bleachers sections; all have backs and individual armrests. They also have good views; better, perhaps, than some of the more expensive view reserved seats. And while bleacher areas have a reputation for rowdiness in some parks, you are very unlikely to have a problem with that in Royals Stadium.

There are some things you should know if you decide to sit in General Admission. First, prefer the seats on the left field side; they get less sun. Second, try to find seats past the foul pole, which can obstruct your view. Third, have a meal before you come or be content with hot dogs. The food choice here is restricted. Finally, arrive early, as you can buy these seats only directly before the game and, at $4, these spots can fill up fast.

Special Needs

Parking. The physically disabled are treated well at Royals Stadium. Show either your handicapped plate or sticker to the parking attendant as you pull into the stadium and you'll be directed to parking lot M, which lies directly in front of the stadium's main gates (it's also where the players park). You are also welcome to drive handicapped people directly to the front door, where there are elevators that will whisk them to their spots.

Seating. Wheelchair seating is provided behind plaza reserved sections

101 and 102. Though a bit distant from the play, these are excellent spots located directly behind home plate.

Food and Features

Food. You won't starve at Royal's Stadium, but if you'd planned on a gourmet experience, you will probably be disappointed. Food variety at the park is good without being great, quality is decent, and the prices are reasonable, though they could be better.

Of course you'll find the standard ballpark fare: hot dogs, a "Colossal Dog with Kraut" (a somewhat bigger hot dog), polish sausage, peanuts, popcorn, and the usual hard nachos and tasteless "cheese sauce." Additionally, there are Royal waffle sundaes, frozen yogurt cups, and Gillette Malts.

There are a few specialty places. "Pazzelli's Pizza," which is behind section 111 on the plaza level, provides pepperoni and sausage slices or a "combo" slice. "Hot off the Grill," also behind plaza 111, offers such specialties as a grilled chicken sandwich, hamburger, cheeseburger, and bratwurst.

The standout choice, though, is "Casey's Bar-B-Q," which serves up a reasonably authentic version of Kansas City's regional food specialty, smothered in spicy-sweetish K.C. Masterpiece sauce. You can choose from beef brisket or ham for a single sandwich or a double. Fries and beans (the traditional choice) are available on the side, and both are good.

Drinks. Coke products are available at the usual high prices. You can also get lemonade and iced tea at some spots at the same prices. Beer drinkers will find a slight divergence of choices. Busch is what is generally offered by the concessionaires, while Coors Light is the choice of the vendors in the stands. Hard liquors, wines, and imported beers can be found only in the "Stadium Restaurant," and all liquor

sales stop in the 8th inning.

Features. Royals Stadium is not loaded with special features to keep you entertained. The idea here is that the game should keep you diverted. Even so, there are a few things you should look into.

Behind home plate on the plaza level is the Royals well-designed "Hall of Fame" display. Built to simulate players' lockers, each niche has the uniform and selected mementos of a well-known Royal of the past, as well as a general display case that includes the 1985 Series trophy and one of Bret Saberhagen's two Cy Young Awards. Specific players honored are Amos Otis, Steve Busby, Paul Splittorff, Cookie Rojas, manager Dick Howser, Dennis Leonard, and Hal McRae. It will escape few fans that, while these were all fine baseball people, none can be listed among the game's immortals. But maybe that's the point. The Royals got where they are today not because of superstars, but because of a decade of hard play by solid pitchers, fielders, and hitters. Maybe that's a point that needs reemphasizing today.

Those interested in Royals Stadium might want to take the park tour. Stadium tours leave from Gate A at 9:30, 10:30, 11:30, 1:30 and 2:30 Monday through Friday, except on home game days, when the 2:30 walkthrough is cancelled. Prices (which are not posted) are $2 for adults and $1 for kids 18 or younger.

What you get for your money is an informative, low-key trip through the park. You'll have the opportunity to see the view from the press box and the "Stadium Restaurant," will have the chance to tour the visitor's locker room (if the visitors are not in it), and will almost certainly be given the opportunity to check out the field in person. Two things may catch your attention. First, the astroturf is bouncy, a revelation that will come as no surprise to anyone familiar with this particular manifestation of man's perpetual desire to "improve" on nature. Especially if it's sunny, you'll also note that the field is damnably hot — in fact, the surface can heat up to 130 degrees! That's because there's a layer of asphalt under the astroturf, which, while providing drainage, also sucks up and retains the sun's rays. Keep that in mind the next time you see George Brett dancing on the balls of his feet while waiting for a hit. And you thought it was because he's such an athlete!

Assistance

If you're having problems finding your seat, locating a phone, getting shed of obnoxious fans, or with anything else whatsoever, you will find the folks in the Fan Accommodation Office behind plaza level 120 very willing to help you out. This is an inviting, walk-in style office, and it's open throughout the game.

Safety and Security

Safety. Royals Stadium is one of the safest parks in the major leagues. It is rare indeed for anyone to have any serious problem whatever in the park. Should you run into drunken, rowdy, or profane fans, a word or two to the security guards or ushers will quickly settle the matter. The parking lots are likewise virtually hassle free. Should you be staying at one of the neighboring hotels and decide you'd like to walk back to your accommodations, feel free to do so.

Health. The first aid office at Royals Stadium is located at the plaza level, behind section 101. We'd like to report what they have to offer, but no amount of persuasion, explanation, or showing of press passes could convince the personnel there to tell us what services they have available for fans. Still, given

the forethought that has gone into everything else in this stadium, we would be surprised if this office were unable to handle your cuts, scrapes, headaches, and overindulgences.

Big time worriers have probably already figured out what is the *one big health hazard* at Royals Stadium. And that's twisters, à la *The Wizard of Oz* (Kansas, after all, is only ten miles away). If this occurred to you, take heart. While a twister has never struck the park, there's a fully equipped tornado shelter in the basement.

Mementos

Souvenirs. Royals' fans are fairly fond of baseball paraphernalia. Reflecting that, there are souvenir stands throughout the park. The best selections can be found at the "Stadium Gift Shop" which has outlets behind plaza sections 117 and 102, and view section 307. Prices are moderate.

Foul Balls. It sometimes seems as if every kid in Kansas City has brought his mitt to the Royals game and is sitting on the edge of his chair, prepared for a blooper from the bat of George Brett. You can get the jump on these urchins by buying tickets in field box and plaza reserved sections, 113, 115, 119, 116, 118, and 120 and looking alive.

Autographs. Royal Stadium is a good place to get autographs. The visiting team's bus enters and leaves the stadium from the home plate area, between Gates A and B. Generally speaking, the visitors must walk past their fans to get to their bus, and they often will stop for signatures.

The Royals share parking lot M with the handicapped. It's located between Royals and Arrowhead Stadiums. Security is somewhat tighter in this area than around the visitor's bus, but some of the Royals will usually walk up to the barricades to sign a few for their admirers.

LOS ANGELES DODGERS
Dodger Stadium

Tradition is a concept that's easier to feel than to define. It is more than just "the way things have always been done." Rather, tradition is our emotional and psychological tie to those who have gone before us; it is the way the past links arms with the present and future. Tradition is how we cope with the transitory nature of our own existence.

Baseball is a sport more tightly bound to tradition than any other. Few are the baseball enthusiasts who don't know that the Yankees' pinstriped uniform has remained unchanged since the days of Gehrig and Ruth. Fewer still are those whose hearts don't beat a little faster when they gaze for the first time at those beautiful brick and ivy walls in Wrigley Field or at Fenway's imposing "Green Monster." Indeed, for most of us, as novelist Bernard Malamud once put it, "The whole history of baseball has the quality of mythology."

Of today's twenty-six major league franchises, perhaps a baker's dozen have a legitimate claim to being around long enough to be part of the baseball tradition. Of these, several are more noted for age than honors, while others have done little to preserve their link with the past. Of the remaining historic clubs, managements have labored to preserve their heritage to varying degrees, either through maintaining attractive "halls of fame," erecting statues of noted players, or preserving walls or chairs from ballparks of long ago. Only a few clubs, though, have consciously striven in how they run their daily operations to truly keep faith with the past. One of these, the Yankees, are

without serious question the greatest franchise in the history of the game. Another, the Dodgers, is certainly among the best loved.

When you go to a Dodgers game— and we strongly recommend that you do go—you'll see the club's commitment to maintaining baseball tradition reflected throughout your stay in the park. You'll see it in a stadium that, though modern and convenient, maintains the classic baseball configuration of the great parks of the past and features a beautifully maintained field of natural grass. You'll see it too in the "bleachers," which, thanks to a sensible alcohol policy, are still principally inhabited by kids and families—as they were meant to be. You'll notice this commitment also in the smaller details. The music played at the park is strictly (and beautifully) organ—no blaring rock. The food served is simple baseball fare, circa 1930: hot dogs, fries, soft drinks, and beer. This is one southern California park that most definitely will not offer sushi. The idea at Dodger Stadium is to give you a complete baseball experience—not just a game. Of course, it helps that the Dodgers themselves are one of the oldest, most successful, and most interesting organizations in the history of sports.

Two Teams

The tale of the Dodgers is really the tale of two clubs.

The first of these is the many-storied Dodgers of Brooklyn, a team that probably has had more sports writer's ink spilled over its fascinating, checkered past than any other team in the history of the game—save the Yankees. Starting out as the "Bridegrooms" in the last decade of the last century, this organization became, at least in the popular imagination, the "bums" by the 1930s, only to emerge, like the ugly duckling who became a swan, into the celebrated "Boys of Summer" during their last decade in the Big Apple.

The second club is the Dodgers of Los Angeles. Not as colorful a team as its predecessor, it nevertheless has been a more successful, popular, and profitable one. Taken together, these two clubs symbolize the way baseball has changed over the past half century, from a sport featuring idiosyncratic players, fervent fans, and penny-pinching owners to today's "big money" game, dominated by superstar players, professional management, big time TV contracts, and trendy, "In Search of Excellence"–inspired approaches to "customer satisfaction." Yet this could be said to be true only with the proviso that the Dodgers have, mostly, represented only the positive sides of both trends.

The Brooklyn Dodgers

Brooklyn never intended that its team should be called Dodgers. Instead, when the team entered the National League in 1890, it termed itself the "Bridegrooms," allegedly because most of the team members had gotten married shortly after the squad was formed. The record says nothing about the players' feelings about the married state, but it must have been good for their game, for the Bridegrooms won the pennant in their first year in the league, and won two more before the decade was out.

Brooklyn fans were delighted with this performance, but the Bridegrooms name didn't catch. In succession, therefore, management tried out such monikers as "Wonders," "Fillies," and "Superbas." None clicked. Instead, people persisted in terming the team the "Trolley Dodgers," a handle that referred to the life-threatening acrobatics necessary to get out to the game, Brooklyn then being, from the perspective of most gaslight-era New Yorkers, a distant suburb made up of crisscrossing trolley-car tracks. Finally, in the early 1900s, the team bowed to the popular will, and a shortened version of the original nickname came to represent the club.

After an initially strong start, the Dodgers played mediocre ball. Though they reached the series in 1916 and 1920, they bowed both times, respectively, to the Red Sox and the Indians. After the 1920 appearance, it would be a long time before the Dodgers would see the fall classic again.

Even if the results were not stellar during these years, though, Brooklyn could at least boast some outstanding players. These included the diminutive (5′4″) precision slugger "Wee" Willie Keeler, famous for his saying "I hit 'em where they ain't," and pitchers Joe "Iron Man" McGinnity (so-called because of his habit of pitching in — and usually winning—both games in doubleheaders), and Burleigh "Ol' Stubblebeard" Grimes, so-termed for his reluctance to shave before a game.

By the 1920s, the Dodgers seemed to reach the conclusion that if they couldn't be the best team in baseball, they could at least be the most entertaining. The twenties and thirties were the decades of the "Daffy Dodgers," the "Bums" who, if they couldn't play great ball, at least were able to keep you laughing. The line-up consisted of some of the greatest "characters" in the history of the game—people like Frenchy Bordagaray (when fined $50 for spitting at an ump, he said, "That's more than I expectorated"), Babe Herman, and pitcher Clyde Day (who used to celebrate his

his wins by flapping his arms and emitting a piercing hog call).

Probably both the oddest character and the Dodgers' greatest player of that time was pitcher Dazzy Vance. A career minor leaguer who professed to be a farm boy "hick" (he was actually a Des Moines city slicker), Dazzy got his start in the big leagues at age 31—and seemed determined to enjoy himself both on the field and off. Rarely on time for training, often to be found carousing with a group of players he termed the "O-for-Four" club (as in four at bats, no hits), Vance was nevertheless awesome on the mound. For seven straight years he copped the strikeout title, a Dodgers record. In 1924, he won 28 games and the MVP award as well—a rare feat for a pitcher.

Yet it was Vance's base-running that involved him in what was probably the most controversial play of the era. This happened in 1926 during a game against the Braves. When slugger Babe Herman stepped up to the plate, the bases were loaded, with Vance on second and Chick Fewster on first. Herman, strong and fast if not too bright, hit an enormous blast to center field and started off. The runner on third had scored and Vance was headed for home when the third base coach saw disaster in the making—the fleet-footed Herman was about to pass Fewster between second and third!

"Back! Back!" the coach yelled to Herman. The Babe, thinking he could make it, slid for a base, Fewster stopped in his tracks, and Vance—believing the warning had been meant for *him*—did a retreating dive. When the dust cleared, three Dodgers were hugging third while a perplexed Brave wondered just whom he ought to tag.

Of course, an enormous argument ensued. Vance, flat on his back, stayed where he was and asked for everyone's attention. "Mr. Umpire, fellow teammates, and members of the opposition," he declared, "if you will carefully peruse the rules of our national pastime, you will find that there is one and only one protagonist in rightful occupancy of this hassock—namely yours truly, Arthur C. Vance."

Vance, actually, was right, but that didn't stop the jokes about this particular episode of Dodger "daffiness." After that, whenever anyone in Brooklyn announced that "three Dodgers are on base," the standard response was "Which one?"

By the forties, thanks to new and capable management, the Dodgers once again got good. They went to the series three times (1941, 1947, and 1949) but lost each time to their uptown—and upscale—rivals, the Yankees. But at least the Dodgers were now contenders. In this same period, the Dodgers initiated two events that would change the sport forever. In 1939, they helped to arrange for the first-ever televising of a baseball game, a contest against the Cincinnati Reds. In 1947, baseball's color barrier came down when, despite resistance from other teams, the Dodgers persisted in sending Jackie Robinson to the plate.

The fifties were a golden time for baseball and the Dodgers. This was the period when the celebrated "boys of summer"—Jackie Robinson, Pee Wee Reese, Roy Campanella, Preacher Roe, and Duke Snider, among others—dazzled the sports world with their 105 wins in the miracle season of 1954. The next year proved probably the sweetest in the franchise's history as the Dodgers, on their sixth try, finally succeeded in taking the hated Yankees in the World Series.

Yet if the fifties marked the Dodgers' best years in Brooklyn, they were also the last. In 1957, in a move that's still controversial, owner Walter O'Malley announced that his team was moving to Los Angeles. With that move, an era in baseball ended as well.

The Los Angeles Dodgers

New Yorkers, stung by what they had regarded as the Dodgers' betrayal, confidently predicted that the relocated team would wilt in the California sunshine. Without Brooklyn's fervent fans to cheer them on, it would be impossible for the team to succeed.

Actually, the Dodgers, if anything, have performed better in Los Angeles than they did in Brooklyn. But they've also performed differently.

The Brooklyn Dodgers had featured famed sluggers and charismatic base runners; it was a team that ran on a lot of heart. The L.A. Dodgers, on the other hand, emerged as a squad driven by awesome pitching, solid but unspectacular batting, and overall professionalism. During the 1960s—possibly the finest decade in the franchise's history—two of the greatest pitchers of all time, Sandy Koufax and Don Drysdale, led the "Boys in Blue" to three pennants and two World Series victories—including a 4–0 sweep against the Yankees in their first contest since the club left New York. The seventies were only marginally less successful. Again there were three trips to the Series (1974, 1977, and 1978), though the Dodgers came up short each time.

The Dodgers over the past decade have been largely shaped by manager Tommy Lasorda's commitment to continuing excellence. Exciting and (in the case of pitcher Fernando Valenzuela, charismatic) new players were recruited, emphasis has been placed on training, and an admirable record of victory has been achieved: four Western Division titles (1981, 1983, 1985, and 1988) and two winning Series appearances (1981, 1988) capped by the Dodgers' 1988 "against the odds" 4–1 victory over the Oakland A's.

In 1990, the Dodgers placed second in their division, and prospects for the coming years look even more promising. The acquisition of outfielders Brett Butler and Darryl Strawberry adds two key players to a team already endowed with superstars like first baseman Eddie Murray, and pitchers Ramon Martinez and Orel Hershiser.

The Stadium

Describing its facility, the Dodgers 1990 Media Guide pulls no punches. "It all adds up to baseball's finest—and most beautiful—stadium."

Quite a statement, that—particularly in view of the charms of some of the competition. Yet while fans in Chicago, New York, Toronto, Boston, and Kansas City might disagree that the Dodgers' home is the standard to which all the other major league parks must aspire, few who have attended a game in it would dispute that Dodger Stadium sits near the pinnacle of achievement in terms of comfort, convenience, attractiveness, and that undefinable but so important baseball "feel." Indeed, the authors of this book are themselves divided on the place. One, a die-hard Red Sox fan, merely regards it as very, very good. The other flat out says it *is* the best.

The Dodgers, of course, were one of two teams that moved west in 1958. The other was the Giants. Seduced by the city of San Francisco, the Giants allowed their hosts to build them a shiny new stadium that opened only two seasons after their arrival. The team has had cold, incommodious Candlestick Park like an albatross around its neck ever since.

The Dodgers, by contrast, took their time. For several years they played in the quirky, highly unsuitable Los Angeles Coliseum while they scouted sites for a new stadium. Determined to have the new park represent their priorities rather than those of politicians and "urban planners," they— alone of the major league teams—

eschewed public support in building their stadium. The Dodgers' new home would be built by "private enterprise."

O'Malley and his crew found the place they were looking for adjoining Elysian Park, a forested, mountainous outcropping just to the north of downtown L.A. It was a tough spot to build on; initial elevations on the stadium site ranged from 400' to 700', and virtually the whole south side of the mountain on which the park sits had to be "reconstructed." Yet when the park was finished in 1962, it was clear to just about everyone that the work and the wait had been worth it.

The physical location of Dodger Stadium is among the very best in baseball. Situated high on a forested hill adjoining an urban park, the stadium is nevertheless within minutes of freeways, hotels, and some of Los Angeles' most interesting restaurant areas.

Yet it doesn't seem so. Despite the fact that you are only a mile or two from downtown Los Angeles, with its crime, traffic, and smog, Dodger Stadium is built in such a way as to give you the feeling that you are in your own baseball world. You're barely aware that the outside megapolis exitst. To the north of the park, visible to everyone except those in the bleachers, can be seen pines and eucalyptus trees, forested hills, and—on smogfree days—the majestic San Gabriel Mountains. To the south, from parking, there's a simply incredible view of downtown Los Angeles. During night games this area is transformed into a fantastic carpet of lights, and few are the occasions when lovers don't tarry a while here after everyone else has left the lots. It's hard to conceive of a better setting for a game.

The stadium itself is a thing of beauty. Mixing the best of the old (the park is designed in the classic "fluted" champagne glass configuration) with the

conveniences that we've come to expect in the new, Dodgers Stadium, on the outside, is a blue and white building of classic and understated dimensions, deeply indented around home plate into beautifully landscaped grounds. Neither immensely big nor a "Fenway"-style minipark, Dodger Stadium, at 56,000 seats, is just a touch above the mid-range in size. One of the things that could be said in criticism is that it has, perhaps, a few too many seats. On the other hand, it has never had any trouble filling them.

Inside, the aisles are wide and open, the bathrooms are modern, and the concession stands are color-coded, conveniently placed, and attractive. The whole stadium, in fact, is spanking clean; though it's thirty years old, it looks as if it could have been opened yesterday. This "fresh" appearance is maintained by a wet-mop crew that works silently—and efficiently—cleaning up spills that occur during the game.

The way seating and acoustical arrangments have been laid out shows that considerable thought went into planning this park. There is, for one thing, hardly an obstructed seat in the place. This is, of course, a statement that virtually every stadium built after 1960 has made, but in this case, it's true. Just as important for fans, rows in Dodger Stadium are unusually short in most sections: you won't have the game constantly interrupted by people getting up and down. All the seats are color coded by price, and there's at least some shade in all sections, even the bleachers.

The acoustics are just outstanding. From almost all sections of the park, you'll hear the crack of the bat. In some, you'll also pick up the whizz of the ball.

The field is a classic baseball "fan," featuring natural grass and moderate field lines: 330' at both right and left, and 395' in center field. As befits the tenor of the place, the grass is freshly clipped and neatly watered, providing a pleasing contrast to the surrounding arid hills. Standing behind center field is a first class "Diamond Vision" color scoreboard, the first in the majors. You will notice (or, hopefully, not notice) that this "Diamond Vision" features few, if any, advertisements. Current owner Peter O'Malley is adamant about keeping overt commercialism out of the park. He's said to leave over $1 million in ad offers "on the table" every year.

Altogether, it's a long way from home plate to the bleachers, which are directly behind the outfield wall. In fact, in twenty-eight years, only one player, Willie Stargell (who else?), has ever hit the ball out of the park. On August 5, 1969, Stargell sent a mammoth 506' blast over the right field bleachers. In 1973, Big Will did it again, sending a 470-footer out of the stadium by the same route.

Perhaps surprisingly, Dodger Stadium is not one of those parks filled with mementos of the accomplishments of the past. There is no "hall of fame" of great players here, nor any statues of the sluggers of days long gone. If there is a display of retired numbers, we were unable to find it. To the extent that a feeling of the baseball "tradition" is conveyed—and it is very much conveyed in Dodger Stadium—it's done through such things as the shape of the stadium, the hot dog-and-peanuts menu, and Nancy Hefley's effective and evocative organ music.

For awhile, this lack of celebration puzzled us. Then we understood. Other stadiums like to bronze their great moments, freezing them in time and place. The Dodgers, apparently, feel that theirs is a stadium where history is still being made.

Highlights

The Dodgers have been one of the most successful franchises in profes-

sional sports in recent decades. Accordingly, lots of recent baseball history has taken place within the confines of Dodger Stadium.

Pitching has provided many of the thrills. Most of Don Drysdale's 58 scoreless innings streak of 1968 occurred in Dodger Stadium, as did the most of Orel Hershiser's 1988 major league record-breaking 59-inning feat. Three of Sandy Koufax's four no hitters, including his "perfect game" of September 9, 1965, happened here, as did the one Bill Singer pitched in 1970. In 1990, Fernando Valenzuela electrified the game with his first no hitter in a long and distinguished career.

Thus far, Dodger Stadium has seen eight World Series, and the highlights of these games have been many. There was the 1963 contest, where potent Dodger pitching held the hard-slugging Yankees to 4 runs; the 1978 race, which featured rookie Bob Welch's dramatic strikeout of Reggie Jackson; and the 1988 contest, with Kirk Gibson's game winning ninth-inning home run off Dennis Eckersley in game one.

There have been moments of pain that have happened here, too—at least for the Dodgers. The 1966 Series ranks high among these. Nearly everyone that year anticipated a four game sweep as the mighty Dodgers faced the hapless, unhearalded Orioles, then in their first Series appearance. And that's what they got, except that it was the O's that did the sweeping. The key contest was probably game two, in which Sandy Koufax, in what would turn out to be his last appearance, faced an unknown Oriole rookie. Jim Palmer won with a four-hit shutout in what would be the end of one great "Hall of Fame" career and the start of another.

Oddly, the most famous Dodger Stadium moment had little to do with baseball. On April 25, 1976, during a Cubs-Dodgers contest, two demonstrator-types jumped onto the warning track, carrying a gas can and an American flag and heading for center field. Cubs left fielder Rick Monday, perceiving what was afoot, ran after them, rescuing "Old Glory" to the relief of the fans, who gave him a standing ovation.

Fans

Fans usually mirror the teams they extol. During the Brooklyn days, Dodger fans were a mercurial bunch, loud, raucus, fond of beer, and equally willing to cheer and or harass their beloved "bums." Like the team they backed, they didn't have a lot of class, but they had a lot of heart.

"Characters" were as common in the stands as on the field. One celebrated Depression-era Dodger fan (or maybe we should say "attendee") was Abe Rettan, who showed at every game to cheer the opposition. Desperate to do something about this guy who was tearing down the Dodgers' already low morale, management offered Rettan a season ticket if he'd knock it off. Abe accepted, but after a few games turned the seat back. "I'd rather pay," he said, "and boo."

It's safe to say that L.A. Dodgers fans are nothing like that crowd. For one thing, they're a good deal more laid back—perhaps even a little too laid back. But they are not uninterested in what is going on.

It's a fact that Los Angeles fans are among the most routinely attacked in baseball. In part it's because of their regrettable (indeed, deplorable) habit of leaving the game in the middle of the eighth inning, almost no matter what is happening on the field, a habit that's played up on the tube every time a Dodgers game is broadcast. And, let's face it, folks, another reason that we non–Golden Staters do not like Los Angeles fans is because they look so damned happy and relaxed. Don't they realize that life is serious, even grim? Why aren't they miserable, like the rest

of us? By God, it's immoral!

Three accusations are leveled against L.A. fans. Count 1: that they are lackadaisical and are uninterested in the game; Count 2: that they don't know anything about baseball; and Count 3: that they are a boring audience of middle-class conformists. Is there enough evidence to return an indictment?

First, item three ought to be dropped. While, tragically, major league teams in such mostly black cities as Detroit and Atlanta still pull in almost exlusively white suburban audience, this is not the case in Los Angeles. Indeed, of all the major league teams, the Dodgers seemed to us to attract the greatest diversity of races, classes, and types. Though families predominate here, you'll also find yuppies, hispanics, blacks, blue collar beer drinkers, corporate executives, and little old ladies in tennis shoes. There are "characters" (if that's what you call them) too, such as Betsy Chatsworth ("the Dodger Momma"), who's been voted the Dodger's #1 fan (generally, you'll see Betsy behind the Dodgers dugout. Of course, she wears blue and white), and vendor Bob Owens, celebrated for his weird and accurate peanut bag throws. That all of these diverse people demonstrate good manners while in the park is something that we regard as a plus.

The argument that they know nothing about baseball is more valid. You won't see many scorecards in Dodger stadium, though you will run into some radios tuned in to the play-by-play, thanks to the popularity of announcer Vin Scully. Both complaints and plaudits coming from fans are mostly generalized. A fan here is more likely to say "Boy, they really stink tonight!" than "Why did they put in Slobotnik? He can't throw against the Cubs. They should go with Meathead!"

Do they care? That's the big question. Our considered opinion is that they do. While L.A. fans won't hesitate to do "the wave" or break out the beach balls when things get boring (a not uncommon occurrence with strong-pitching teams), when the action starts you'll see people scurrying to their seats and kids primed at the edge of their chairs, waiting for that foul ball that Eddie Murray is about to send their way. L.A. fans may not be baseball's most fervent enthusiasts. But they're far from the most indifferent, either.

Getting There

Los Angeles is the land of the auto. If you are going to the game, you have two choices: drive yourself or be driven.

By car. Dodger Stadium is easy to get to, provided you have the patience of Job and the driving nerves of Mario Andretti. If you lack either of these qualities, carefully study a map before you go or be prepared to take a cab.

It's not that getting to the stadium is difficult. It isn't. The problem is that you may well find yourself tied up in bumper to bumper traffic, or, alternatively, caught between cars that think it's their job to prove that surface vehicles can break the sound barrier. Accordingly, even if you see what exit to take, you might not be able to get over to it unless you carefully plan your note.

Here are the best approaches: From San Francisco and the *north*, take I-5 south to Stadium Way and follow signs to Dodger Stadium.

From San Diego, Orange County, and the *south*, take I-5 north to Pasadena Freeway (110) west. Exit, and follow Pasadena Freeway to Academy Road. Exit and follow signs to stadium.

From San Bernardino, Las Vegas, and *east* areas, follow San Bernardino Freeway west (I – 10), to I-5 north. Proceed to Pasadena Freeway (110) west. Exit, and follow Pasadena Freeway to

Academy Road. Exit, and follow signs to the stadium.

From *LAX Airport*, follow I-405 to I-10 east. Proceed on I-10 east until you hit the Pasadena Freeway going north. Follow until you hit Stadium Way. Exit, and follow signs to park.

If you are leaving for the game around rush hour, allow lots of extra time. As a general rule, traffic into Dodger Stadium flows a bit faster on Academy Road than it does on Stadium Way.

By cab. Cab is a practical means of getting to the game if you're staying at the downtown hotels or are dining in either Chinatown or the Olvera Street area. The fee from any of these should be about $5 one way. You can get to the stadium by cab from LAX, too, but it's not recommended unless you have money to burn. The hit here is $40 to $45 each way.

Parking

Despite its urban location, Dodger Stadium has ample parking.

Altogether, there are 18,000 secure, well-lit Dodger-owned parking spots wrapped around the stadium, uniformly priced at $3 and area-identified by attractive lighted baseballs! This is enough spaces for most games, but sellouts can be a bit tight: if you're attending a weekend contest or a popular matchup, you might want to come early. It can also be something of a nuisance getting in – and especially out – of the lots. This, not apathy, is why fans leave early. We suggest that you consider sticking around for a few minutes after the contest and enjoy Nancy Hefley's organ while everyone else is fighting his or her way back to the freeways.

Should you have car trouble or simply need gas, don't panic. There's a service station located *in* the parking lot.

Tickets

Dodgers tickets can be ordered by mail, phoned for, picked up in person, or bought at the game.

Given their limited availability, mailing for tickets is probably your best option, though the $3 service fee the Dodgers charge on each order is pretty steep. To get tickets by mail, write down the area you'd like and send a check or money order for both the tickets and the service charge to: Los Angeles Dodgers, PO Box 51100, Los Angeles, CA 51100. You can get tickets on the phone, too. Call Ticketron at (213) 410-1062, and be prepared with a seating chart and your major credit card. You'll pay a servce fee here, too.

Particularly if you live in the L.A. area, going to the advance ticket office is a good idea. It's open Monday through Saturday from March to October from 8:30 A.M. to 5:30 P.M., and its address is 1750 Stadium Way, Los Angeles. Be careful to note that the advance ticket office *is not at the stadium.* It's about a half-mile away, near the Naval-Marine Center.

You can also buy tickets at the game. Here, you are strictly on your own. You may find good seats, you may find *a* seat, and you might end up with nothing at all.

Availability. The Los Angeles Dodgers have, for most of the past three decades, been the best attended team in baseball. They were the first team to cross the 3,000,000 attendance threshold, and currently they hold four of the top five all-time gate receipt records. Sellouts occur about once a week.

What this means is that if you want one of the better seats at a game, you should plan well in advance. Currently, the Dodgers cut off season ticket sales at 27,000 — about 80 percent of all the box seats available. The rest, offered at

the bargain price of $9, go fast. Even the cheaper seats at popular match-ups against such teams as the Giants, the Mets, and the Cubs have a tendency to disappear.

There's a saving grace in all this. Almost every spot in the park — including those in the bleachers — offers an acceptable view. However, if you'd prefer not to be enscounced among the cotton-candy crowd, you should take the precaution of ordering ahead.

Costs. Dodger tickets are among the most reasonably priced in the majors. Within each area of seating, however, there are considerable variations in view (see "Seating"). Still, while we wouldn't want to say that you can't go wrong in buying a seat at Dodger Stadium, you'll find it tough to locate a nook or cranny in this park where the view is really bad.

In 1990, Dodgers tickets were as follows: Box Seats ($9); Reserved Seats ($7); General Admission ($5); Children's General Admission* ($3).

Rainouts. As you'd expect in southern California, rainouts are rare — the Dodgers once went for eight years without one.

Still, it can happen. Should it occur, your ticket will be exchanged for one at another game of your choice — if available. Should a return trip to Los Angeles not be in your plans, write to the ticket office explaining this, and you'll be issued a refund.

Seating

Seating in Dodger Stadium is quite good in all sections. More than in most stadiums, price is a fair guide to value. If you pay for a good seat, generally you'll get it. If you pay at a reduced rate, though, you'll find the view is still pretty decent.

*Day of game only. Limited to 12 and under.

You won't get a crack at the best seats in the park. These spots, called the "Dugout" level, are wrapped around the baselines and provide a "players' level" view of the action. Featuring old fashioned big wooden chairs with comfortable cushions, these seats are truly special. Unfortunately, they are available on a season-ticket basis only.

Nine dollar box seats can be found in three different areas.

Field level boxes slope back from the diamond, providing an outstandingly close view of the proceedings. Featuring comfortable yellow seats, these should be your first choice—especially within the baselines, which are set at odd aisles 1 to 27 (third) through even aisles 2 to 26 (first).

If you don't mind a little altitude, though, maybe you'd prefer the 200 level Club boxes. Perched over the field at the press box level, these aisles feature short rows, shade, and the most comfortable chairs in the park—big wooden seats with cushions. Here too, staying within the baselines is the key. On this level, you want to ask for tickets in either odd aisles 201 to 221 (the third base line, this has the least sun distractions) or even aisles 202 to 220 (first base line).

A definite third choice in boxes is the 100 Loge level. These spots sweep back a fair ways behind the Field boxes, though they generally feature good views, particularly in the lower rows, A through J. Stay in the baselines, which are from 101 to 121 on the third base side and 102 to 114 along first, and you'll be in a fine spot to catch all the action.

By contrast with the box seats, the $7 Reserved chairs are in one very large area, a cantilevered upper deck that's set quite high over the action. Still, the view is decent enough, and besides, you get a great view of the mountains and sunset! In this area, the lower you stay, the better: A through J is best, while double letters (like BB) will put

you in birdland. Baselines here run from odd 1 to 11 (third) to even 2 to 12 (first). If you sit here, try to park directly behind the stadium's main entrance, where it's indented into the ground. You'll find that you'll be able to walk directly to your chair. If you enter along the sides, you may have to walk up as many as ten flights of stairs to get to upper reserved.

Dodger Stadium has two $5 General Admission areas. One, the "Top Deck," is high up indeed—it seems a perfect place for hang gliding. However, since the Dodgers management resisted the temptation to build this level all the way to the foul poles, and, instead, limited the deck to the baselines, we'd rate these seats pretty good for the price, particularly in the low rows—many seats here are superior to out of the baseline spots on the more expensive "upper reserved" level below.

Beyond the outfield wall are two "Pavillion" areas (right and left field)—spots that would be called "bleachers" in the east. Thanks to the Dodgers' no alcohol policy in these sections, this is very much the province of kids and young families. The youngsters chase each other, talk with the players in the bullpens, cheer on the home team, and often show by their comments that they know more about the game than their parents. Some will find this scene distracting. We rather liked it. The view from these seats, given the Dodgers short field lines, is quite good, though you sacrifice something in not being able to clearly see the Diamond Vision display scoreboard. If you sit here, consider sitting in the left field pavillion; it gets more shade.

Important seating note. Seating patterns are confusing in Dodger Stadium. Show your ticket to an usher and ask to be directed or you'll waste a lot of time wandering around.

Seat jumping is pretty common here, too, despite attempts to police it. Seat jumpers, actually, are easy to identify:

they're the only fans who seem to know where they are going.

Special Needs

Parking. Handicapped parking is available close to the stadium in lots 2, 3, and 4. Access to the park is quite easy from these points.

Seating. Most of the wheelchair seating in the park is located in the row behind the Loge boxes, at odd aisles 143 to 157 and even aisles 142 to 156. These are spots just past first and third on both sides of the park. They're good but not great.

Food and Features

Food. "We don't go crazy on food variety at the stadium," a Dodgers representative told us; "you won't find any sushi. But what we do have is good."

We found the spokesman right on both scores. Food choices in the park are limited, but the quality is excellent and the prices are reasonable. If you're the sort who enjoys hot dogs, fries, and beer, you'll like the food at Dodger Stadium. If you want a little something more, there's at least one other option.

The item the park is most noted for is the "Dodger Dog." A 12″ grilled weiner, the dog is darn tasty, and the price is right. There's a caution here, though: a few of the concessionaires will try to palm off a steamed hot on you and call it a "Dodger Dog." That's an atrocity. Real "Dodger Dogs" are grilled or broiled. In addition to the dogs, you'll find french fries (also good), popcorn, spicy dogs, peanuts (a bargain), and soft serve cones. Dodger Stadium's sole bow to the exotic (sort of) is the *Mama Mia* pizza store behind home plate on the 100 level featuring stiffly priced whole pies or a decent sized slice.

Those wanting a sit-down meal will find something approaching it at the *Cafeteria/Public Bar* located just past first base on the 200 Club level. Here, in a cafeteria setting, you'll find such specialities as fajitas, burritos, and tacos along with stews, deli sandwiches, and the like. There's also a full service bar. If you're coming, though, come early. Hot food service closes during the 4th inning while sandwiches become unavailable between the 5th and 7th, depending on business.

Drinks. The drink selection is limited to Coke products and beer (generally Bud). The only place for fans to get anything other than a beer is the *Public Bar*.

Features. You will find no videogames, "halls of fame," or other features at Dodger Stadium. "We try," says the team spokesman, "to let the game be our star attraction."

Assistance

In keeping with its goal of catching the "feel" of the baseball parks of old, the Dodgers have passed on many of today's newfangled ideas — including the customer service office. Therefore, if you need help, try talking with an usher. These folks seem well trained, and they should be able to provide assistance.

Safety and Security

Safety. Set off in its own self-contained world, Dodgers Stadium has no particular security problems either inside the park or in the parking areas. While there's no absolute guarantee of safety anywhere, you're about as safe at Dodger Stadium as you're going to be anyplace in the L.A. area.

Elysian Park is another matter. Though safe during the day, you probably shouldn't go for a stroll into it after a night game, though there's absolutely no reason for you to want or need to do so.

Drinking is the biggest security issue in most of the parks. At Dodgers Stadium, such controls as a two beer per person sales limit, a cut-off on all alcohol sales in the 7th inning, the elimination of vendor beer sales in the stands, and the banning of alcohol from the bleachers has insured that this problem in minimal. It's not impossible that you'll run into an obnoxious drunk at a Dodgers game, or even a fight (particularly during Giant-Dodgers contests), but it's pretty unlikely. In either case, the stadium's vigilant security people will quickly hustle the offending person out of the park.

Health. The biggest health threat at Dodger Stadium is getting too much sun. It's not a big issue. Much of the stadium is shaded, and temperatures in L.A. rarely get over 90. Still, if you are sun-sensitive, try to sit on the third base side of the park and avoid all but the last few rows of the bleachers.

Climbing can be a problem for older fans, particularly in view of the height of the upper reserved areas. You might enjoy the game more if you sit downstairs or in the bleachers. Should you wish to sit in this part of the stadium, though, elevators are available. The ushers will be happy to point them out, and, if necessary, can bring you to your place in a wheelchair.

Getting access to first aid is a problem. There's a first aid office, but it's located at the 8th level lobby area, way above home plate, a place that can be reached only by elevator or a very long walk up stairs. While walk-in visits are allowed, it's plain that the staff would prefer it if you talked to an usher about your difficulties before dropping by. Still, should you need to go, the office is there, and it is well-staffed with a doctor and nurses. There are two ambulances on site.

Mementos

Souvenirs. Dodger fans like to wear Dodger paraphernalia. And while you'll find the usual souvenir stands on all levels, the best selection by far can be found at "Top of the Park," the Dodgers gift shop, which is located behind home plate on the Top Deck level. It's open just before, during, and after games, and it is also open from 10 A.M. to 4 P.M. Monday through Friday during the off season and when the Dodgers are playing elsewhere.

Should you be seated in another part of the staidum and decide you want to visit "Top of the Park" during the game, it's a good idea to arrive around sunset. The view can be spectacular.

Foul Balls. Dodger Stadium is a good place to catch foul balls. Because it has an unusually low net, sitting behind the batter's box in field level aisles 1 to 5 is an especially choice catching zone. Other good areas are field level aisles 21, 23, 22, and 24.

Autographs. Signatures, on the other hand, are not easy to obtain. Hanging around the dugouts during batting practice (an hour or so before the game) sometimes works. Usually a player or two will drop by and sign. You could also wait outside the player's parking lot after the game, which is located just outside the left field pavilion. Though the lot is surrounded by a high fence, Dodgers will sometimes walk over to talk with fans and sign autographs — Eddie Murray in particular is generous about this.

Visitor signatures are the toughest to snag. After the game, their bus rolls into the park and picks up the visitors at their dugout. You are kept about fifty feet away in the stands. In order for the visitors to sign for you, they have to climb the wall from the field into the seats and walk up to your row. It happens every once in awhile, but don't count on it.

MILWAUKEE BREWERS
County Stadium

In October 1982, following a season in which the Brewers had won the American League pennant but had bowed in a close fall classic to the Cardinals, the Milwaukee city fathers decided to hold a ticker tape parade to honor their almot conquering heroes.

True to form, tens of thousands of Milwaukeans shrugged off the Series loss to turn out to celebrate their team. Thousands more flooded into County Stadium to listen to a formal presentation outlining the squad's accomplishments in the just completed season.

As the crowd watched the ceremonies, they noticed that someone was missing from the rostrum. People began to whisper to each other, "Where's Robin?" — referring to Robin Yount, the star shortstop who had done as much as anyone to put the Brewers into postseason play. Soon enough, players on the podium realized, too, that one of their buddies was missing. All of County Stadium was soon buzzing with the question: "Where's Robin?"

As if in answer, a roar came from the basement of the park, and a leather-jacketed Yount burst onto the field astride an enormous Harley. Revving up the machine, Rockin' Robin did a wheely around the full length of the warning track while the audience went wild. For anyone who was there, it was an unforgettable experience.

While not every game at County Stadium offers moments quite that dramatic, it's a fact that Brewers contests are frequently "experiences" in a sense they are not at other ball parks. The reason is simple. Far more than in many other areas, people in Milwaukee — indeed throughout Wisconsin — identify with their team in an emotional, visceral way. When things are going right for the Brewers, the smile quotient rises perceptibly. When things sour, as they have too often of late, you notice that, too.

It is one of the great myths about America that we are a "classless" society. As anyone who has thought about this country for more than five minutes knows, there's not the slightest bit of truth to that. We are not just Americans, we are also poor or rich or in between; some of us work exclusively with our minds, others work with our hands. What we are, and where we "belong," profoundly affects how we approach politics, life — and sports.

America has sports that are largely upper class (polo), those that are working class (bowling), and those that appeal primarily to folks in the middle (tennis). Baseball, happily, seems to turn just about everyone on. Even so, there are profound differences in the way the classes support the Great Game.

Take teams like the Angels or the Blue Jays. Both draw middle-class audiences, and both get a lot of support: their attendance records are among the best in baseball. Go to the games of either team and you'll find the fans polite, decent, well-dressed, and, well, frankly somewhat boring. Middle-class fans seem to pay attention, but, often, not all that many could really tell you in any depth what was going on.

Not so in those parks that attract a mostly working-class crowd. In places like Baltimore and Oakland, people dress less well, drink and smoke more, and are much more willing to yell expletives at the umps than fans are at the middle-class parks. All of that is to the negative. On the other hand, working people follow the game more closely, know more about it, and take it more seriously than the other crowd. To most middle-class people (there are exceptions) baseball is a game. To working-class folks, it is a good deal more than that. It is the dramatic expression of the values—teamwork, perseverance, individual excellence—that they believe are the keys to family success.

More than at any other ballpark, a game at County Stadium brings you in contact with the beliefs, customs, and aspirations of working-class America, if only for a few hours. County is not one of the prettiest parks in the sport; indeed, it is one of the ugliest. And while the food is pretty good at the stadium, there is surely better to be found elsewhere. As far as the Brew Crew goes, unless things change dramatically, they seem destined to remain what they have long been; a decent also-ran.

In truth, County Stadium does not excel in facilities, food, or its team's performance. Where it is outstanding, though, is in the quality of its crowd. Sure, Brewers fans can be loud, vociferous, and even on occasion profane. They can also demonstrate surprising kindness to outsiders, great enthusiasm, and a real understanding and love of the game of baseball. Overall, these are folks with whom it is a pleasure to spend a few hours.

The Team

When people think of Milwaukee baseball, the visions that come to their minds derive mostly from the 1950s. They are fleeting images of such hard-slugging hitters as Hank Aaron and Eddie Mathews, the steady pitching of Warren Spahn, and the 1957 World Series victory. While such conceptions certainly occupy a central place in the

heart of any Milwaukee baseball fan, these accomplishments have absolutely nothing to do with the current squad. All of these Milwaukee greats of the past played for the Braves, a team now ensconced, none too contentedly, in Atlanta.

The Brewers ancestry is of more recent, and humble, descent. In the late 1960s, in one of its periodic expansions, the American League placed a team in Seattle, Washington. Calling itself the "Pilots," the Seattle squad played a single campaign at that city's Sicks Stadium—and a sick season it was, too. Attendance was dismal. So was the team's performance. Early in 1970, the team beat a hasty retreat to Milwaukee where, seeking a name for itself at the last moment, it landed upon the moniker "Brewers," supposedly to honor its new home's largest industry.

Initially, the Brewers did little better in Milwaukee than they had done Seattle. Second division finishes were standard through most of the 1970s. Even so, the team accomplished one thing early on that not even the current Seattle squad has ever managed: it built a hard core of Brewer loyalists. By the middle of the team's first year, a group of vociferous fans had come together in the left field bleachers. Calling themselves "the Brew Crew," they announced that they were determined to cheer the team on to victory, no matter what. Today, of course, the whole team now goes by a nickname that orginally designated a small pack of fans. The fanaticism of Milwaukee baseball enthusiasts was shown during that same opening year when Brewer fan Milt Mason, a 69-year-old depressed at the squad's mediocre attendance, placed himself in a trailer which he had hoisted to the top of the Brewers' scoreboard and swore he would not come down until gate receipts topped 40,000. Although Mason had to wait seven weeks, Milwaukeans finally gave in and gave the fan the results he had requested.

During its first decade, the Brewers ran the usual expansion team formation. They suited veterans such as Tommy Harper and George Scott and fine players just starting out, like Gorman Thomas, and they lost. At one point, competing manager Billy Martin said of the squad's prospects, "If the Brewers can win with what they've got, I'm a Chinese aviator!" That year (1973) Billy, after a sudden Brewers pennant rush, was spared a trip to the orient after an equally sudden Milwaukee collapse.

In 1978, the devotion of Milwaukee fans started to pay off as the Brewers began to get good. During that year, the Brew Crew finished third, and fans nationwide got excited by such outstanding new players as Thomas (1979 home run champ) and shortstop Robin Yount (1982 MVP). By the early 1980s, such first class Cy Young award winning pitchers as Pete Vuckovich and Rollie Fingers had signed on, and by then the Brewers were contenders indeed. In 1981, the Brew Crew entered postseason play for the first time, bowing to the Yankees in the Eastern Division championship. In 1982, the team was back again, and this time they went just about all the way, taking the AL pennant, but failing 4–3 in a close and exciting fall classic to the always tough St. Louis Cardinals.

Since then, the team has done well enough, but it has not truly returned to winning ways. Many of the squad's older players have retired or moved on, while some exciting new team members, like infielder Gary Sheffield, have signed with the squad. Currently, Robin Yount is the hero of Milwaukee. *USA Today's* AL "player of the decade," Yount, at 35, still has at least an outside shot at topping Pete Rose's all-time hits record. A solid second place in the hearts of Milwaukeans would probably go to slugger Paul Molitor, a fine player who excited the baseball world with a 39-game hitting streak in 1987. Currently, however, the Brewers do not seem to have the players necessary to return them to the Series unless the squad can stay remarkably healthy. Even so, they have enough first-class people on board to keep their fans interested and seated at the edge of their chairs.

The Stadium

When people are asked to name baseball parks, the term "County Stadium" rarely comes up. In fact, if you were to ask many baseball fans who it is that plays in County Stadium, you might well get blank looks. That's because the Brewers' facility is one of the most obscure in the sport, though it is far from contemptible. Neither a classic ballpark of the 1910s or '20s like Wrigley or Fenway, nor one of the behemoth sports palaces of the 1970s, County Stadium occupies that twilight zone of parks built between the two great periods of stadium construction. It has neither the quaintness of the old parks nor the convenience of the new. It is just there.

Built in the early 1950s to accommodate the move of the Boston Braves to Milwaukee, County Stadium was constructed in a pleasant working-class neighborhood to the west of downtown, in a spot convenient to both buses and highway traffic. With the completion of the Braves' move, the first ball was thrown out at County Stadium on opening day, 1953. Milwaukee's teams have been playing in the place ever since.

Its construction was an odd combination of old ideas and fairly new ones. On the plus side, the place maintained the classic "U" baseball configuration of the older ballparks, and also laid out a field of natural grass. Its seating arrangements were also kept within humane dimensions; with 53,000 spots, the place is neither too small nor too large. Thus, although County Stadium may not be perfect, it is a baseball park. On the minus side, its decks were supported by poles; as a result, many seats have some obstructions.

From the outside, the place looks ungainly. An odd mixture of institutional bricks, dirty windows, metal girders, and corrugated metal panels, County shares, alone with Arlington Stadium, a look of the temporary. You wonder if they threw it up last night.

Inside, the oddness continues. Aisles in the concession areas are wide but dark. The lower seating areas are all right, but old-fashioned. Moreover, they are topped by a crazy patchwork of catwalks and stairs that rise up over the crowd to the mezzanine and the upper levels — County Stadium is no place to wear a skirt. On the top levels, there is more peculiarity. The most expensive seats, in the mezzanine, look for all the world like pressbox spots out of some 1930s Hollywood baseball epic. Chairs in the grandstand areas have the feel of something out of "Pride of the Yankees" or "Angels in the Outfield." Even the bullpen setup is strange. Pitchers are spread out under the center field scoreboard in an area where, alone in the majors, they cannot see the action on the field. It's little wonder that, when Tinseltown wanted to make a movie about a team that always lost, while they named the squad in *Major League* the Cleveland Indians, they filmed the flick at the outrageously idiosyncratic County Stadium.

The best thing about the park is the field. It's a pleasant expanse of green with fairly short lines. Right and left field are set at 315', while center field is 402'. Above the center field wall is the park's scoreboard and its visual display, which, unlike most others in baseball, shows replays only in black and white. Like most things in County Stadium, even the diamond vision is a step or two behind the times. Whether that's good or bad is, of course, a matter of personal judgement.

New Stadium

In recent years, the Brewers have become concerned about the obvious deficiencies of its current park and have hired architects to draw up plans for a new facility. While some suburban locations have been scouted, as of this writing it seems as if any new park will most likely be sited where the current one is. At present, plans call for a new facility that will recall some of the design features of the old Ebbets Fields. Supposedly, it will be constructed in time for opening day, 1994.

Although the designer of a new stadium could improve on County Stadium in many ways, keeping faith with the park's strong points could prove more difficult. Whatever may be wrong with County Stadium, what is very right with it is that it was built with the fan's need to feel close to the action very much in mind. Whatever a new park can add in terms of new conveniences, if it loses this, it has lost what really matters. On the other hand, if the new park can maintain intimacy while improving facilities, the Brewers' managers will have really done something positive for their loyal and long-suffering followers.

Highlights

Although Brewers fans will not like to read this, the Braves, in their brief stay in County Stadium, probably supplied more true baseball highlights to Milwaukee than the Brew Crew has yet delivered. In a brief period of five years, the Braves gave midwestern baseball some of the best moments it has ever seen.

For Milwaukee fans, the biggest date of all could be April 15, 1954. That was when Hank Aaron, a little heralded minor leaguer called up at the last minute, strode to the batter's box for the first time. September 23, 1957, was another important Aaron date. On that day the slugger belted out an 11th inning homer that captured the 1957 American League pennant. Game 4 of the 1957 Series set the scene for the famous Nippy Jones shoe incident in which Nippy, claiming that he'd been hit by a pitch, proved his case to the umpire by matching an incriminating streak on the ball to his shoe polish!

The Brewers have scored some highlights as well. On July 20, 1976, Hank Aaron hit his final home run in the park to cap one of the most outstanding careers in baseball history. Cecil Cooper singled in the tieing and winning runs in the 7th inning of the 5th and final game of the 1982 American League championship series versus the California Angels to give the Brewers their only pennant. On July 31, 1990, Nolan Ryan of the Texas Rangers won his 300th game in County Stadium in a contest watched throughout the Americas.

Fans

At most parks, going to a ball game is a simple affair. You drive in, walk to the park, watch the game, and then drive away. The whole business is cut and dried.

Not so at County Stadium. It can be that way if you like, but for everyone else, Brewers games are more than just an athletic contest. They're a moveable feast.

The partying usually begins about two hours before game time. If you come early, you'll notice people arriving in pickup trucks, campers, station wagons, and buses long before the contest starts. Indeed, to judge by the buses, it seems that every bar and nursing home in Wisconsin sends at least one delegation to every Brewers game.

Once the fans pile out of whatever conveyance brought them, they immediately begin setting up. Barbeque grills are lit, beer tops are popped,

picnic tables appear on all sides, and volleyball nets are strung. Soon frisbies and balls are whizzing about, cards are being shuffled, people are dancing to boom boxes, and fans are trying their luck at a speed pitch concession, which, alone in the majors, is set outside the stadium.

Overall, a festive air predominates. People are good spirited and outstandingly friendly. As you walk through the crowd, you may be offered a lawn chair, an Old Style, and a bratwurst by some welcoming family of fans. Our suggestion is that you accept the hospitality and discuss the Brewers' prospects with folks who, as it will almost certainly turn out, will know a good deal more about the subject than you will.

Once game time nears, the implements of play are put away, and fans flock to their seats. Eating, drinking, and general good spirits continue in the stadium, but the banter mostly ceases, for Brewers fans take their baseball seriously. Umpires and opponents are booed, veterans like Molitor and Yount are cheered almost regardless of how they perform, and whippersnappers like Gary Sheffield are viewed with suspicion, for it is characteristic of Brewers fans to be very tough to win over initially but to be unshakeably loyal once won. You may find fickleness in Los Angeles or Philly; you will see none of it in Milwaukee. Win or lose, Milwaukee loves the Brew Crew.

You might think that after all the drinking, eating, and partying before the game, the festivities would end after the contest. In truth, for many fans it does; but still others are happy to march out to the parking lot and set up their grills and picnic tables for more fun before heading home. How late does this continue? You've got us. We got tired and went back to our hotel.

Who are these party animals? Generally speaking this is a working-class crowd. Among the fans, young males, Poles, Germans, and families are well represented. Oldsters come out in force as well, and some seem no more adverse to punching a volleyball than many of the young people. Everyone is friendly, everyone likes beer, and everyone is out to have a good time. If you approach these folks in the same down-to-earth manner with which they will almost certainly approach you, you're almost certain to have a great time at the ball game.

Getting There

Located in a pleasant, mixed commercial and residential neighborhood three miles west of downtown Milwaukee, County Stadium is pretty easy to get to. If you are coming from outside of town, car is probably your best option. If you are in the city on business, both cab and bus present other good choices.

By car. County Stadium is directly off I-94, the major superhighway running through town.

If you're traveling from such *north* locations as Green Bay, take I-43 south to I-94 west. Follow I-94 to the route 41 south exit (308B). Then take the first exit left to County Stadium and follow to parking.

Those coming from Racine, Chicago, Milwaukee's *Mitchell Airport*, and other points *south* should proceed along I-94 north and take it through Milwaukee to the point where it then heads west toward Madison. From there, take the Route 41 south (exit 308B) and follow 41 to the first exit, which will take to County Stadium's parking.

People driving in from Minneapolis, Madison, and other *west* locales should follow I-94 *east* to exit 308A VA Center/County Stadium, and then follow signs to parking. Past experience shows that the right lane to parking often moves faster than the others.

By cab. If you're staying in the down-town hotels or even if you are coming in from the airport, cab is a good choice. The one way fare from downtown will run about $10; expect to pay $20 from Mitchell.

By bus. Though few outsiders use it, getting to the game by Milwaukee's County Transit System is easy enough if you are downtown. From there, take any #10 bus or any bus marked "Stadium" and ask to get off at the park. The charge will be $1, and you'll need exact change. You'll find bus stops for the #10 along Wisconsin Avenue and West Wells.

You can take the bus from the airport, too, though it is a bit more complex. From the airport, take the #80 bus to Milwaukee, being sure to get a transfer. Get off at Wisconsin Avenue and, from there, catch the #10 to the park. The charge is only a buck, which makes this option a real bargain. The Milwaukee County Transit's number is (414) 344-6741.

Parking

County Stadium has 11,000 parking spaces wrapped around the park, all uniformly priced at $4. That's enough spots to handle nearly any crowd. On the rare occasions when spaces in the major parking lot runs out, guards will direct you to overflow lots.

Traffic moves reasonably well into the facility. By contrast, getting out of the park is a real nightmare, particularly if you leave going west after a weekday game and hit Milwaukee's rush hour traffic. You'll note on leaving the park that many fans decide to make the best of a bad situation by continuing to tailgate after the contest. Sausages will be fried, people will play poker and cribbage, and a group somewhere in the lot will often get a game of volleyball going. We suggest that you bring along a lawn chair or two and join in the fun, at least until the traffic backs off.

Tickets

You can get Brewers' tickets the usual ways. By mail, by phone, or by stopping at County Stadium to pick them up.

Mail order tickets are available by writing to: Milwaukee Brewers Ticket Office, Milwaukee County Stadium, Milwaukee, WI 532143. When you order by mail, be sure to include the number of tickets you want, the locations and type, and enclose your money order or check for payment in full or your major credit card number and expiration date. The Brewers do not have a service charge for mail orders.

Phone orders are also accepted. Call (414) 933-9000 to place yours. When you call for tickets, be ready to give your credit card number and expiration date, the section you'd like seats in, and the number of tickets you want. The Brewers assess a very stiff $4 service charge for phone orders.

The Brewers' advance ticket office is located at the north side of the stadium. It's open 9 A.M. to 5 P.M. Monday through Saturday and 11 A.M. to 3 P.M. on Sunday.

Availability. With 53,142 seats, County Stadium is in the middle of American League parks in size, while Milwaukee is one of the smaller major league cities. The team as a whole has had only a fair performance record in recent seasons. The result of all of these things is that tickets to Brewers games are generally available.

Spots at night games and at contests against unpopular teams are the easiest to procure. Weekend day game seats are the hardest to come by. Milwaukee's rivals are the White Sox and the Twins, and these games are both the most crowded and (given the proximity of the cities) the rowdiest, as hordes of fans from the visitor's towns descend *en masse* on Milwaukee. If you want to attend one of these games, you should

order well in advance. For other contests, a visit to the advance ticket booth a day or two before the game should net you decent seats.

Costs. Brewers' tickets aren't the cheapest in the majors. While prices are below those charged by such popular squads as the Cubs and the Red Sox, they're also above the rates for most other teams.

There are plenty of good seats in County Stadium, but on the whole, ticket prices are not your best guide to where to find them. This is the sort of place where consulting a seating chart before you buy would be a good idea.

During 1990, Brewer ticket prices were as follows: Mezzanine ($12); Lower Box ($11); Upper Box ($11); Lower Grandstand ($10); Upper Grandstand ($7); Bleachers* ($4).

Rainouts. Milwaukee is not a city known for its balmy climate. Specifically, the place gets bitterly cold in the winter and it receives a fair amount of rain all summer long. Accordingly, while rainouts may not be as common as in, say, Boston, they happen often enough. Generally, you can count on about three to four Brewer rainouts per year. Snowouts, though rare, occur too.

Happily, the team is pretty fair about its cancelled game policies. If you are rained out, simply exchange your ticket for a future game, or, if you are not planning to come back to town, write for a refund explaining this.

A *caution*: make sure your game has been officially called before you leave the stadium! The Brewers are infamous for waiting hours, if necessary, for the clouds to clear so they can start play. If you leave and the game is resumed, you'll be out of luck.

Seating

County Stadium may not be one of baseball's most beautiful facilities, bu'

*Sold only on the day of the game.

we like it quite a bit. Why? Because when the place was constructed, the designers had the sense to put the park into the classic "U" baseball configuration. And while it is true that the place lacks many conveniences and that the quality of the seats themselves is not always what it ought to be, at least you'll be able to see the game from almost anywhere you choose to sit—that is, if you manage to avoid the poles!

The most expensive seats in County Stadium—and some of the oddest in baseball—are not next to the field. Rather, they are at the Mezzanine level ($12). To get to this area, you have to take metal catwalks over the lower deck crowds (kindly don't spill your beer here) and then follow guard rails out to the Mezzanine spots. Once there, you'll find yourself in a sort of wooden miniature press box, of the kind that teams used in the 1930s. You'll be seated behind a bench-like table, which is a good spot to dine from while you watch the contest.

In truth, despite the price, these are not the best seats in the park; you are closer to the action at the field level. Still, the view is very good, and the experience is certainly different, so you might want to give the Mezz a try. If you do, be sure to secure a spot within in the baselines, which here runs from 1 to 13 odd (first base) to 2 to 12 even (third base).

Lower boxes, and Upper boxes go for the same price ($11) and both offer many fine seats. Lower boxes run from the field wall back a dozen or so aisles and are composed of red plastic-and-metal chairs. These are reasonably comfortable spots with fine views throughout. You are best off here within the baselines, which run from sections 1 to 33 odd (first) to 2 to 34 even (third). Upstairs are the Upper boxes, which are also superior spots. Baselines here run from sections 1 to 13 odd and 2 to 12 even, as in the Mezzanine level. In either of these areas, if you are able to

snag a spot in any of the recommended sections, it is hard to see how you could go wrong.

Lower Grandstand seats ($10) are more problematical for one reason— poles. If you stay in the low rows in this area (1–18), there are no obstructions whatsoever; views are decent, though rows are inconveniently long, running to 26 places in most sections. Seats here are green plastic-and-metal chairs. Beyond 18, though, the story changes dramatically. The seating switches to old-fashioned wood-and-metal chairs, and pole obstructions become a problem in many spots. If you must buy a ticket in these sections, try to stay in the middle of the row, say from seats 6 to 20; these tend to have the best views. Also try to get in the baselines, which in this category run from sections 1 to 13 odd (third) to 2 to 12 even (first).

Upper Grandstand seats ($7) are cheaper and poorer, though it must be said that an upper seat in the first or second row might well be a better bargain than a downstairs spot in a high-numbered one. At any rate, the upstairs spots are all green wood-and-metal chairs, which are none too comfortable. Pole obstructions come in at row 3 and can be a problem, particularly in high- or low-numbered chairs. Thus, as was the case in the lowers, you are better off sitting in the middle seats if you can get them. The baseline sections here are the same as they were below.

All of the above makes the grandstand seats seem somewhat worse than most of them are. County Stadium's seating configuration is such that, if you avoid the posts and stay near the baselines, you will have a good view almost anywhere you sit.

County Stadium's cheapest seats are the bleachers ($4), which are located behind the outfield wall. These are very traditional bleacher spots: uncomfortable, backless aluminum benches where you'll bake under an unrelenting sun. Typical too is the crowd this area attracts; lots of kids who love to ram around, shirtless young adults, and oldsters out to save a buck. Still, if *you* want to save a buck, the bleachers might be OK for you, too. The crowd in this area is good natured, the view is decent, considering the price, and you can get a good look at the bullpens from most parts of sections L and K.

Special Needs

Parking. County Stadium has convenient handicapped parking, located in the two rows nearest the stadium entrance. Show your sticker or plate to the attendant as you drive in, and you will be directed to them.

Seating. The handicapped seating situation, on the other hand, could be better. Most of the spots are located at the back of the lower grandstand area. They're all right, but they are quite a way from the field. More spaces are located in the first row of the bleachers.

As the squad's name indicates, Milwaukee's fans are very partial to a cold brew. Sometimes, in fact, they are a bit too partial to one. If you want to avoid the whole alcohol scene and the bad language that often goes with it, you might want to order tickets in one of the park's "family sections," which are some of the most extensive in baseball. Current family reserved sections include, in Lower boxes, sections 56–58 (OK seats at the end of the left field line), Lower Grandstand section 3 (excellent spots just to the right of home plate), Upper box 4 and Upper Grandstand 4 (outstanding seats to the left of home plate), and bleacher areas L, M, N (right field side; has some shade).

Hint: if you want good seats at a night game but are ordering late and don't mind doing without a beer, try asking for a box seat in the family reserved area. These are often available long after the other box seats are sold, and some of them, particularly Upper box 4, are among the best spots in the park.

Food and Features

Food. Tailgating is so prevalent at County Stadium that you would think that the concessionaires would simply throw in the towel and not bother to serve any food at all—God knows, by the time the fans actually get into the park, most of them have eaten enough to last them through the game, and then some.

Happily for nontailgaters, the Brewers' people haven't taken that attitude at all. Food in the park is fairly priced, variety is decent, and the quality is often excellent.

Given Milwaukee's German heritage, you'd expect the Brewers to do a good job with sausages, and you would be right. Hot dogs in the park are fairly priced and are among the tastier weiners in the sport. But don't stop there. You'll also find Polish sausage, Italian sausage, "Barvarians," and bratwursts just about everyplace; we'd particularly encourage you to try the brats, which are delicious.

County Stadium, of course, also has the other usual baseball treats: popcorn, peanuts, and double-scoop cones.

There are specialty shops, too. The "Grand Slam" burger stand behind home plate on the lower concourse sells burgers and very acceptable cheese steak sandwiches. The "Back Shop" located in the same area has a first-class selection of bakery goods including brownies, "Brewers" cookies, and a pecan roll that is one of the best things to eat at any of the ball parks.

Drinks. Of course, the Brewers also provide plenty of drinks to wash all of this down, and at the top of everyone's list here is beer. Old Style is the brew of choice. Non-drinkers will find the usual Coke products, while some of the stands offer wine coolers, though no one seems to buy them.

Features. Since watching the game seems to be only a part of the Brewers fan's baseball experience, the team has thoughtfully provided some features in the park for those who are getting a bit restless. Behind Lower Grandstand section 20, you'll find a "Speed Pitch" and a "You're on the Air" radio broadcast booth concession. There's a "Speed Pitch" outside, too, behind the bleachers area.

Those interested more in edification than in entertainment will want to make two stops. At the lower level behind section 6, you'll find an attractive display of memorabilia concerning the career of the most famous Milwaukee player of them all, Hank Aaron. Behind section 11, Rawlings has an interesting display that shows step-by-step how baseballs and gloves are made.

Assistance

If you are having problems with drunken fans (certainly a possibility here), lost tickets, or simply want to know more about the park, you should seek out the Brewers Fan Assistance Office, which is located on the lower concourse behind section 18. You will find the staff friendly and helpful. In particular, many of the ushers at County Stadium are "old timers" who were guiding people to their seats back when Hank Aaron and Eddie Matthews were popping them out of the park. They love baseball, are exceptionally knowledgeable, and will usually be happy to tell you more about the stadium if you ask.

Safety and Security

Safety. Inside County Stadium, your biggest threats to life and limb come from your fellow fans.

We don't really know which baseball park has the most drinking, but County Stadium is certainly among those in the running for top honors. Beer consumption begins for a substantial part of the crowd before the game, continues through it, and proceeds after. Aside from having a "designated driver booth" and running ads against drunkenness, the team does little to control consumption. Beer is sold in the stands in vast quantities, and there appears to be no formal cut-off period.

Having said that, though, we should point out that there is fairly little drunkenness visible in the place when you consider the amounts that are being consumed. Accordingly, it is probable that you will have no problem with inebriated fans at the park. On the other hand, it's also possible that you will have a problem. As a general rule, the best way to dodge the drunks is to stay out of the left field bleachers, which is where they tend to congregate. You might also want to consider sitting in the family sections, particularly if you are attending a contest against the White Sox or the Twins, where rivalries are strong and tempers can sometimes run high. If you do find that you are having difficulties with obnoxious fans, a word to any usher will insure that the problem will be taken care of.

As far as other security concerns go, they are minimal. The parking area is secured and well lit, while the surrouding area is a pleasant and safe working-class neighborhood. You probably would want to drive if you intend to go to any of the bars or restaurants on Blue Mound Road after the game, but if you feel like walking there is really no reason why you shouldn't.

Health. The elements present the biggest health threat in the park. If you are planning on sitting in the bleachers on a sunny summer day, bring sun block. Make sure you have a sweater (or even a coat) handy if you are going to a game in April, May, or September. In short, use your head.

If you do find that you've had too much of either the sun or Old Style, you'll find the first aid room behind section 7 on the lower concourse. It offers basic first aid and Rolaids in quantity for whenever the Brewers start losing.

Mementos

Souvenirs. You'll find modest souvenir stands spread throughout the park. Prices are OK, but the selection is not what it ought to be. For a better choice of baseball goods, you might want to visit *Stadium Sports Stuff*, which is located a healthy hike north of the park at 5208 West Blue Mound Road, Milwaukee (414) 778-0007. The place is open from 10 A.M. to 5:30 P.M. Monday through Friday, from 10 A.M. to 5 P.M. on Saturday, and from 10:30 A.M.

to 5 P.M. on Sunday. The place also stays open before night games.

The team has a *Clubhouse Store*, too, which has a good selection but is not particularly convenient to the stadium. It's in the Brookfield Square Mall, which is located Off I-94. Call (414) 789-1148 for details.

Foul Balls. The Lower Grandstand seats behind the dugouts seem to be favored with the most fouls. To catch yours, try Lower Grand sections 12–16 (left field) and 13–17 (right field).

Autographs. County Stadium is a super place to snag signatures. After the game, the Brewers exit from Gate E. This is an excellent place for collection, as the players have to walk through their fans in order to get to their cars. The visitors' bus departs from just outside press gate X. Here, too, the players need to pass you to be on their way, and frequently will be willing to stop and sign a few before heading home.

MINNESOTA   TWINS
The Metrodome

With its vast, flat plains, trackless forests, and thousands upon thousands of pristine lakes, Minnesota is one of America's most northerly states — and one of its coldest.

This sometimes frigid land was settled slowly. Most pioneers heading west passed Minnesota by on their way to sunny California and fertile Oregon. Still, some folks saw opportunity where others saw only flat plains with soil so hard that a plow could barely crack it. German Americans from Wisconsin moved into Minnesota in search of new

dairy lands. They founded, on the banks of the Mississippi, the city of St. Paul Shortly after, Scandinavian immigrants began arriving in large numbers. Minnesota reminded them of home. They settled small farm towns throughout the state — places very like Garrison Keillor's Lake Wobegone. They also built in Minneapolis a great city, where even today, there is something distinctly Scandinavian about the state's largest town, while its capital, St. Paul, still maintains a German flavor.

It took a lot to wring a good living out of this hard land. You had to be willing to work hard, suffer privations without complaint, and pull together with others. In order to survive, people had to get along as members of a team, and quietly shine as individual performers.

These values are very much on display in Minnesotans today, in sports and elsewhere. One of America's most liberal states in politics (the Scandinavian influence), it has a population that is conservative in character to the point of stodginess. Home to supposedly antibusiness politicians, it nevertheless is the headquarters to some of America's best run companies. A place that likes to think of itself as being at the cutting-edge of "progressive" thinking, the state is nevertheless filled with a population that is homogeneous, and, it must be said, conformist. Minnesota is the part of America that is most like Canada.

Baseball has a long history in the "Land of Lakes." As early as 1884, St. Paul was a major league town, while Hall of Fame local boy Albert "Chief" Bender was one of the early stars of the game. Even after St. Paul lost its franchise, the Twin Cities, sometimes separately and sometimes together, continued to host popular and successful minor league squads. For decades the "Twins" dreamed of reentering the majors. Repeated efforts to procure a franchise, though, were frustrated by the refusal of the two towns to work together to achieve their goal.

Finally, when it became apparent that the Washington Senators, tired of poor turnouts and local indifference, were ready for a move, Minneapolis and St. Paul put aside their differences and labored to bring the Senators to town. Successful in their endeavors, the Senators—renamed, very diplomatically, the "Minnesota Twins"—moved to Minneapolis–St. Paul in 1961.

The Twins today have almost totally assumed the Minnesota character: indeed, their former connection with Washington is as forgotten as the fact that the Orioles were once the St. Louis Browns. Like Minnesotans, the Twins are always competent, sometimes excellent, and, frankly, a little bland. You rarely hear of Twins being arrested, knock down drag outs over pay are rare, and controversial managers who ruffle too many feathers (such as Billy Martin, who piloted the squad in 1969) soon find that they are looking for another job, even if, as in Martin's case, they leave after leading the team to a division championship. The great, and somewhat colorless, Harmon Killebrew showed the true spirit of the sponsoring towns when, asked by a reporter what his hobbies were, said, "Well, I like to wash dishes"—spoken like a true Minnesotan! In truth, other teams enjoy talking a lot about the great things they'll do. The Twins seem to prefer just going out and trying each day to do them.

The Team

Unlike their Milwaukee rival the Brewers, the Twins were never an expansion team. When the squad decamped from Washington to Minnesota, it had a full roster of players, an identifiable if lackluster record, and a few legitimate stars, including pitcher Jim Kaat and the man who is still probably the greatst Twin ever, Hall of Fame slugger Killebrew. As a result, the new team came out of the box with a running start, and had, during the 1960s, a successful first decade.

Powered by the team of Killebrew, Kaat, and three-time batting champ Tony Oliva, the Twins did well in the snow zone. 1965 was the most exciting year. During that season, the Twins went to the Series for the first time, and, surprising everyone, went the full count against the Dodgers, folding only in the seventh game of a thrilling fall classic against the hard to beat Sandy Koufax. For Minnesotans, 1969 and 1970 were almost as good: the Twins won the AL Western Championship each time, though on both occasions they lost the pennant to Earl Weaver's surging Baltimore Orioles. Despite these losses, though, the Twins could look back at their first decade in Minneapolis with satisfaction. They had finished in the first division seven out of ten times, their attendance was the highest in the American League, and their superstar Harmon Killebrew had hit more home runs during the decade than anyone since Jimmie Foxx in the 1930s.

If the 1960s had been years of glory for the Twins, the 1970s were a decade of the blahs. The team once more had an outstanding player in six-time batting champ and future Hall of Famer Rod Carew, who burned up the majors in 1977, hitting .388 and winning both the batting title and the Most Valuable Player award. But beyond that, little seemed to come together. Standings were, overall, OK but not great, and attendance sank dismally.

The 1980s, if anything, have combined the best and worst experiences of the club over its first two decades in Minnesota. There have been dismal showings, (1981, 1982, 1983, 1986), and fine ones (1987, 1988). In 1987, in another 4–3 heart stopper, the Twins finally took a Series, in this case against the St. Louis Cardinals. 1990, though, turned out to be another of the dismal seasons as the Twins could manage nothing more than a last place finish in a tough American League West division.

Currently, the Twins do have some talented individual players. Standouts include outfielder Kirby Puckett and veteran first baseman (and local boy) Kent Hrbek. These folks should be able to provide the Minnesotans much of the horsepower needed to get the job done. Whether the rest of the organi-

zation can supply the additional muscle required is a question only time can answer.

The Stadium

It's 1980, and we have just awarded you the task of building a brand new domed stadium for the Minnesota Twins in downtown Minneapolis. How will you proceed?

First, knowing that we are now well into the age of the automobile, you'd doubtless locate your park in an area where you could provide plenty of well-lighted and secured parking. You'd do that not only to please the fans, but also to help encourage people to come downtown in the first place, where, at least in the minds of suburbanites, fears of crime are real.

Next, to insure that you catered to real needs and Twin City sensitivities, you would be certain to provide plenty of parking and seats for the physically disabled. After all, it's the right thing to do.

Then, of course, you'd be careful about design. Learning from the admitted problems of the "classic" ballparks of the 1910s, you would banish obstructing posts. Learning from the disasters of the "bigger is better" stadium movement of the 1960s and '70s, you would plan a smaller park, and one in a more traditional baseball design than a dome or a rectangle: after all, there isn't a single rule of physics that declares that a domed stadium must resemble a hemisphere or a brick. You would certainly make sure that your stadium was in at least some semblance of a "U" form, and you'd be especially careful to guarantee that all the seats in the park have, at the minimum, a full view of the playing field.

That's what you would have done, and what we would have done, which, we suppose, is why neither of us got the order! Thrown up on a thin, publicly supported budget in 1982, the new and (according to the Twins' *Media Guide*) "beautiful Hubert H. Humphrey Metrodome" may well be the most unsuitable facility in baseball.

Set in a grimy commercial neighborhood to the east of downtown Minneapolis, the Metrodome is a nearly perfect retangle that resembles nothing so much as a tub of lard covered by a cloth. Beautiful? It is a veritable monument to ugliness. Around the park, there is no stadium parking whatsoever, for the disabled or anyone else. In fact, the whole feel of the area could be summed up in a building sign about a block from this edifice that reads "Wanted: Radiators, new, old, or trade."

Once inside, things improve somewhat. Aisles are wide, concession stands are attractive, and, indeed, the whole of the public areas of the place give the appearance of a very pleasant shopping mall. If that's what it were, the Metrodome would be a fine place indeed. Unfortunately, it is supposed to be a baseball park.

The seating arrangements are bad. Though we have no scientific measurements, the Metrodome seems, to us, to have as high a proportion of bad seats as any park in the majors thanks to (1) a highly unsuitable rectangular design that has no relevance to baseball; (2) the fact that support poles (in 1982!?) obscure vision in the upper level; and (3) the fact that substantial areas of the field, thanks to this design, drop out of fans' view from many areas of the park.

Sound is a problem, too. Blasting from the stadium's speakers, noise reverberates around the stadium, and it becomes very difficult for attendees to pick individual words out. Even so, we have been told that, on the playing field, sound "dies" immediately, and players can't hear each other when shouting signals or calling for balls. The Twins do not help the sound problem

by blasting out a sound track of obnoxious rock music and commercials (tied into the video display) throughout the contest.

Lighting causes difficulties as well. The lights in the Dome are bright, and during most evening games you'll see players struggling to contend with the glare while trying to field balls. Even the roof, which has holes in it, has posed problems. Once Dave Kingman hit a pop-up that embedded itself in a Dome venting tube, causing quite a donnybrook among officials as they tried to figure out what to do. We suppose watching that must have been one of the fun days in the Metrodome.

In short, the Metrodome is, to our way of thinking, a species of disaster. We feel sorry for Twin Cityites. They've spent a lot of money, and they do not have the ballpark that they ought to have had. Moreover, the Dome is a turkey that they will probably be stuck with for many years to come; we can't imagine the citizens of Minnesota voting another multi-million dollar bond for a ballpark for quite a while. It all goes to show that not everything that bills itself as "progress" is necessarily a good thing.

Despite our negative reaction to the Dome, there is a baseball field in this place. Here are some details. Specifically, the Metrodome has an astroturf surface, with moderate lines. The left field foul pole is at 343', the right field one sits at 327' (the rectangle effect), while center field is 408'. Above the left field wall is a plaque marking retired number 3 — Harmon Killebrew. Rod Carew's number 29 is on the center field wall. To the left of it are posters commemorating the Twin's record seasons: the 1987 Series, the 1965 pennant, and the Divisional Championships of 1969 and 1970. It all reminds you of what a fine team Minnesota has been.

Highlights

One of baseball's newest parks, the Metrodome has seen few major baseball highlights. However, the one big event that the Twins have experienced in their newish stadium is one that at least a half dozen other teams dearly wish would someday happen in their park. On October 25, 1987, after six tumultuous games, the Twins won in the Metrodome their first World Series. For once, the reverberating sounds of the Dome were anything but irksome.

Fans

Fans usually constitute a portrait of the citizens of the team's sponsoring locale. Yankee admirers are brash and vociferous, San Diegans are laid back, while Dallas–Fort Worth residents will "yahoo!" and whoop it up with the best of them.

It is no different in the Twin Cities. Like Minnesotans generally, Twins fans are decent, sober, courteous (they clap for opponents and even umps), and, well, stoic. It takes a lot to get Twins fans motivated. And, World Series victories apart, even when they do get excited, they rarely get really involved.

Homogeneous would be a good word to describe this crowd. People are white, mostly (but not exclusively) middle-class, and, as in Boston and Toronto, there is a very high proportion of women in the audience—we'd say upwards of 50 percent. Overall, the crowd is a bit youngish. There are some families, some kids, lots of Yuppies, and a fair number of dating couples, which is a reminder that Minneapolis is very much a "young singles" kind of town.

Overall, Twins fans are not baseball nuts. You rarely see people listening to radios for the commentator's views, and very few fans keep score. Mostly, people come to the Metrodome to have a

good time. And, mostly, that's exactly what they do have.

Getting There

Located directly east of downtown Minneapolis, the Hubert Humphrey Metrodome is easily accessible by car. You can also reach the stadium by cab or, if you are staying in the downtown hotels, by foot.

By car. For most out-of-towners, driving to the park will probably be the most practical option. If you do decide to drive, though, keep a few things in mind: first, take a look at a map and plan out your route before you go. Downtown traffic can be a problem, and if you aren't really sure where you're going, you could easily miss your exit. Second, if you're going to a game that you suspect will be crowded, try to leave a little early. Although there are plenty of parking spaces within walking distance of the Metrodome, the more people that attend and the later you come, the longer your walk will be.

If you're coming to the Metrodome from Albert Lea, Des Moines, and other points *south*, take I-35 north to the point where the interstate separates, and then follow I-35 west. Proceed to Exit 17C Metrodome Stadium and then follow 3rd Street to parking.

Those coming from Duluth, Superior, and other *north* locales should take I-35 south to Exit 17C Metrodome Stadium. From there, follow Washington Avenue to the dome area and start to hunt for parking.

Wisconsinites and those traveling from the *east* should proceed along I-94 west into the Twin Cities. Exit at 5th Street Metrodome and follow 5th Street to parking.

Prairie dwellers coming from such *west* locales as St. Cloud, Lake Wobegone, and Fargo should follow I-94 east to Minneapolis. Once there, take the 4th Street Metrodome Stadium exit and follow to parking.

From the *airport*, take I-494 west to 35W north, and then follow the traveling north directions given above.

By cab. Particularly if you are staying downtown, cab is a fine option. One way fares from any of the leading hotels should be $4 or less. From the airport, expect to pay $15.

By foot. Sited downtown, the Metrodome is an easy walk from many hotels. The Holiday Inn Metrodome, the Omni Northstar, and the Embassy Suites Hotel, in particular, are very convenient to the park.

Parking

Back in the 1910s, baseball parks such as Comiskey, Fenway, and Wrigley were built where most people lived, which is to say within cities. Little or no parking was provided for a simply reason: few people in 1912 owned cars.

Things have changed a lot since then. For one thing, these days nearly everyone has an auto, so you'd think that someone building a baseball stadium today would provide ample parking, right? Well, if you lived in the Twin Cities, you'd think wrong. The Metrodome, opened in 1982, not only doesn't have ample parking; it doesn't have a single space, not even a lot for the physically disabled. Incredible, but true.

The rationale for not providing parking is that since downtown Minneapolis has plenty of car lots, it would have been wasteful to build more. Well, we suppose so. However, we suspect that political pressure from owners of existing lots had a bit more to do with the lack of stadium parking at the Metrodome than any supposed excess of spaces, particularly when parking is a money maker for many facilities. Those who owned lots had a monopoly on the downtown parking business before the Metrodome was built, and they still have it, but with a lot more customers.

All of this means that if you want to bring your car to the Twins game, you'll have to do business with these folks. The way the system works is that, once you come off the interstate, you simply start tooling around the streets near the Dome, trying to find the cheapest lot close to the park. If you don't feel like walking far, plan on paying $6 to $8. If you're willing to hike a few blocks, you could find a spot as cheap as $3. Two pieces of advice: first, try to arrive early—you'll find a better parking selection and will avoid the traffic rush just before the game. Second, don't keep looking in hopes of finding a better bargain. As a rule, the longer you keep hunting, the more traffic there will be and the less spots will remain open. Find a reasonable spot, park, and start walking.

Tickets

You can get Twins tickets by mail, phone, or you can pick them up at the advance ticket office.

Those ordering by mail should write to the Twins at: Minnesota Twins, N1 8187, PO Box 66117, St. Paul, MN 55166-8187.

Be sure to include the dates, locations, and number of tickets you want. Also enclose your check or money order for payment in full, being sure to include the $3 service charge the Twins assess on your order.

Those wishing to purchase tickets by phone should call the Twins charge line at (612) 375-1116 in the Twin Cities, or (800) THE-TWINS outside them. Phone lines are open from 9 A.M. to 5 P.M. central time. If you are planning to order by phone, be prepared with your major credit card and the ticket locations you'd like to have.

Given the dearth of really good seats in the Metrodome, you might want to consider buying your tickets at the advance ticket office if it is at all possible. There, you'll be able to see a seating chart before you put your money down. The Twins' ticket office is located on the Chicago Avenue side of the park, and is open from 9 A.M. to 5 P.M., Monday through Friday (if there's a home game it stays open until the 7th inning). During the baseball season, the office is also open from 9 A.M. to 4 P.M. on Saturday and 9 A.M. to 5 P.M. Sunday (or until the 7th inning during a night game).

Availability. Ticket availability at the Metrodome varies wildly. During years when the Twins are doing well, tickets can be tight. Coming off their Series-winning 1987 season, for example, the Twins had the highest attendance in the American League, with over three million fans passing through the turnstiles. When the team is not doing so well, turnout drops precipitously. Declines of 30 percent between good and poor seasons are not uncommon. Accordingly, if you want to know how likely you are to get Twins tickets, the first thing you should do is check the standings.

After you've gotten the picture on how the Twins are doing generally, the next step is to find out who they are playing. The Twins' traditional rivals are the Brewers; tickets for games versus the "Crew" usually sell fast. Other popular matchups include Oakland, New York, and Boston. If you were planning on attending a game against one of these teams, you should probably order well in advance.

The final thing to keep in mind about availability is that although the Twins will almost certainly have some sort of seat available for your even if you show at the last minute, the number of really good spots in the park is fairly small. Accordingly, booking in advance here is pretty good policy almost no matter who the Twins are playing.

Costs. Twins ticket prices are reasonable — or terrible. It all depends on where you end up sitting, for this park has some of the best and worst chairs in the majors. In actuality, there is probably no other park in baseball where consulting a seating chart is as essential to insuring that you will be satisfied with the seats you buy.

In 1990, ticket charges for the Twins were: Lower Deck Reserved ($11); Upper Deck Reserved ($8); Lower Left Field General Admission ($6); Upper Deck Outfield General Admission ($3).

Rainouts. Neither rainouts nor snowouts ever happen at the Metrodome, which is a big switch from the way things used to be at the old Metropolitan Stadium.

Seating

Rectangles are a very fine geometric form for a football stadium. They do not, however, do much for baseball. Thus, while the Metrodome has some excellent seats, a shockingly high percentage of chairs in the park provide a second rate view, while some spots are just plain terrible.

Lower Deck Reserved seats ($11) are the most expensive ones in the park, and they constitute all the truly good spots, as well as some of the poor ones. They are comfortable blue plastic chairs with decent legroom; the lower deck seats wrap around the field lines, from foul pole to foul pole. As a result, those spots within the baselines (aisles 118–133) are quite good, particularly when you consider that foul territory in this park is very short. Indeed, if you are fortunate enough to end up in a low row close to the batter's box (say in sections 121–130) you will have a great view, and you'll wonder just what the heck it was that we were griping about. On the other hand, if the ticket gods put you in a place outside the baselines (which is very likely, as the best spots go to season ticket holders), you'll note that the view deteriorates rapidly the farther you are from home plate. If you end up seated in 139, for example, you'll be paying top dollar for a chair that is in the bleachers in some of the other stadiums.

Thus, if you are unable to get within or close to the baselines seats in the lower area, you might want to shop in the Upper Deck Reserved ($8). If you can procure spots in, say, rows 1 to 6 in sections 221 to 229 (the baselines), you probably should go for it: these are perfectly acceptable spots. Beyond these areas, though, the choices aren't so good. Altogether, the upper deck contains 31 rows — the top several are a good deal closer to St. Paul than they are to the field. After row 26, post obstructions appear, which can be a problem. Accordingly, if you are unable to find a baseline chair in this area, insist on a seat in a low row or consider going elsewhere.

One acceptable alternative is the Lower Left Field General Admission ($6), which in other parks is called the bleachers. This area sits behind the left outfield wall. In this section, the seating is comfortable, the view is OK, and the crowd is young and surprisingly lackadaisical. In truth, lower left has little to recommend it, other than the fact that some of its spots are better than some of the most costly upper deck ones.

Uper Deck Outfield General Admission ($3) seats have one thing going for them: they're cheap. That, literally, is about the only good thing that can be said for these seats, which run along the upper deck behind the outfield walls. From the best sections of this area (201–205), the players look like ants. From all the others, large areas of the right and center field literally drop out of view, particularly if you are seated in the higher rows. If you are sitting here, bring your binoculars — and your patience.

Chairs in the Metrodome are uniformly attractive and comfortable. They also come equipped with neat rings for holding drinks — a very good idea. If the designers of the park had just though to put these good seats somewhere near the action, the Dome would be a very fine ballpark.

Special Needs

Parking. The Metrodome has no officially designated handicapped parking. The way the system works for those who need this service is that, before each game, the police put up blockades sealing off Chicago Avenue (just west of the Dome) between 4th and 6th Streets. Then, if you need to be close to the stadium entrance, you simply pull up, show your plate or sticker to any officer, and you'll be directed to an on-street parking space appropriate to your needs. It's an awkward way of managing things, but it seems to work.

Seating. There's plenty of handicapped seating in the Metrodome. Specifically, two spots are located just inside the portals at every section entrance on the upper deck. While many of these spots are decent (see the description of the upper deck in "Seating" to locate the best ones), foul ball injuries are a threat in some of the closer sections. If you sit in, say, 221 to 229, pay attention to what's going on.

The Metrodome is also one of those parks that offers a "no alcohol" family seating area. Taking up section 229 of the upper deck, the family area here is situated right over third base and offers good views of the proceedings.

Food and Features

Food. The Twin Cities have many fine restaurants. That's good because, in truth, if you are hungry before the ballgame, you might be advised to dine before you arrive at the Dome. Sure, there's plenty of food to be had in the park for those who care to indulge. However, while the selection at the Dome is decent, the prices are high, and the quality's undistinguished.

You'll spot the usual ballpark choices everywhere: hot dogs, (not very good), a stiffly priced pretzel, soft serve cones, and caramel corn. Other choices include popcorn, nachos, and peanuts.

There are specialities, too. *Brats and Beyond*, located behind section 135 in the lower concourse and at other places, has a good selection of sausages at stiff prices. Choices include "Cheddar 'n Brat," "Beer 'n Brat," and "Louisiana Hot Polish"(!?). *International Specialties*, behind 119 sounds more interesting than it is. Among the exotic goodies you will find here are pizza, French bread ham-and-cheese, and a chicken breast sandwich. *All American Burger*, behind section 122, offers bar-b-que beef (not very good), bacon cheeseburgers, and the "All American Burger."

Drinks. If you want something to wash all this down, expect to pay through the nose for it. Coke products are overpriced, although beer is slightly more reasonable; Special Export Light seems to be the favored brew.

Features. The only feature in the park is the "Minnesota Sports Hall of Fame," a series of plaques that are placed on the walls throughout the upper and lower level corridors. You'll quickly note that most Minnesota sportsmen and women have been football players, golfers, hockey players, or bowlers. Still, there are a few baseball heroes. Hitter Pedro "Tony" Oliva can be found behind section 122 (near home), Charles "The Chief" Bender, one of the few Indian players and a Hall of Fame pitcher is behind 133, and probably Minnesota's most famous slugger, Harmon Killebrew, can be found behind upper level 203.

Assistance

The Metrodome isn't the kind of place where you are likely to run into problems with obnoxious fans or seat jumpers, but if you do, or if you have comments or complaints, the Twins' Fan Accommodation Office can be found behind section 119 on the lower concourse.

Safety and Security

Safety. There is no safety problem to speak of in the Metrodome. Obnoxious fan behavior is rare, and crime in the park is just about unknown. Games with Milwaukee can sometimes get tense, and a fight will break out once in a while when the "Brew Crew" is in town, but even that is something that only rarely happens.

The area outside the Dome is a run-down commercial and industrial district with little appeal. It's fairly safe, but not completely so. Once the game ends, therefore, you'd be wise to move with the crowd back to your car or your hotel.

A caution: the public preception is that Minneapolis is a "safe" city. That's not completely accurate. In particular, if you are staying at the Holiday Inn Metrodome or decide to go to the West Bank Theatre District for a drink after the game, keep clear of the neighborhood to the east of this area; it's a high crime district.

Health. Climate isn't a problem at the Dome. Foul ball injuries are. The Metrodome's design, with its rectangle shape and short foul territories, insures that if you are sitting in the baselines at the lower level, foul balls are likely to come spinning at you at a terrific clip. Accordingly, you have a better chance of being nailed than at most other stadiums.

Stay alert, particularly if you are seated in the infield areas. You will note that, practically alone in the major leagues, health personnel at the Dome are stationed in the stands. They are waiting to serve you. Disappoint them.

If you have health needs other than bandages, you will find the Twins first aid office behind 117 on the lower concourse. As a general rule, the Twins would prefer you talk with an usher before going to first aid, but walk-ins are treated.

Mementos

Souvenirs. Although the Dome has the usual assortment of souvenir stands, you'll find a much better (and cheaper) selection of fan goods across the street at *Dome Souvenirs*, 406 Chicago Avenue, (612) 375-9707. The place stays open all year from 9 A.M. to 5 P.M. and is also open during all Twins games. In addition, the place has a nice display of Twins memorabilia and sells ballpark foods "to go" at prices significantly lower than the ones you'll find in the park.

Foul Balls. Foul balls come in fast and furiously at the Metrodome. If you want to try your luck at snagging one, sit anywhere within the baselines at the lower level and keep your eyes open and your head up. If you can barehand one of these babies, you'll have done something.

Autographs. Domed stadiums are hard on autograph hunters. Players have too many good ways of sneaking out of them and avoiding you. If it's the Twins' signatures you are seeking, you are probably best off showing up early and standing near the Twins dugout during batting practice; team members are fairly generous about signing. The best place to hunt visitor signatures is in the small parking lot to the east of the Dome where you'll see the visitors' bus. Security keeps you pretty far from the players, but every once in a while someone will walk over to sign.

MONTREAL EXPOS
Olympic Stadium

We residents of the United States like to think of baseball as a uniquely American sport.

It's not that we're unaware that the game is played elsewhere. Sure, we'll admit, baseball is popular in Japan — but that's only because U.S. GIs taught the Japanese how to play it after the war. And while we know that Dominicans and other Latins can often tell the difference between a bat and a broomstick, our suspicion is that Latin enthusiasm for baseball is based on the hope (fairly realistic) that good play can win you a ticket to the States. It is, after all, an article of faith in the U.S. that, if everyone else in the world had their choice, they would really rather be Americans. Finally, we Americans feel that we have the right to ownership of the sport for a simpler reason: we invented it. Baseball, in our view, like the automobile, the camera, and the radio, is a product of "Yankee ingenuity."

Actually, the above beliefs are half-truths, at best. GIs did not bring baseball to Japan. The game took hold there in the early 1920s, and leagues were active well before Pearl Harbor. In fact, during the war, the worst insult Japanese soldiers could think to throw over the trenches at their American counterparts was "To hell with Babe Ruth!" Nor is Latin baseball simply a reflection of American scouting activity. Baseball is a well-organized phenomena throughout Central and South America. Games attract millions of fans who are only vaguely aware of what the "Norteamericanos" are doing in the sport. As far as the U.S. inventing baseball goes . . . well, if we invented baseball, then how come Jane Austen has characters playing a version of the game in her 1817 novel *Northanger Abbey*? As with the car (German), the camera (French), and the radio (Italian), Americans didn't invent baseball. What we did was take someone else's basic idea and perfect and popularize it.

Baseball is more international than we realize. Aside from Japan, the game is also popular in Taiwan and Korea — nor is it unknown in the People's Republic of China. It hasn't really caught on in Europe, but it's still played there. Even the cricket-loving English abandon their flat bats to play with rounded ones sometimes.

Canada has been involved with baseball as long as the United States. Farmers on both sides of Lake Ontario played the game well before the Civil War. Early in the history of professional baseball, Canadian teams arose across that nation's vast prairies and mountains.

Nevertheless, it was in neither English Canada nor in the Spanish-speaking world that "major league" play was first extended beyond the borders of the U.S. Rather, that honor fell to Montreal, Quebec. Thus the newly created Montreal Expos became, at one time, the pioneer major league team located outside of the United States, the first to broadcast its games in a primary language other than English,

and the first to begin its contests with two national anthems. Moreover, the Montreal Expos later became the first team in baseball to play in a stadium with a retractable roof — and you probably thought the initial club to have one of those was the Toronto Blue Jays!

Yet Montreal is also known for a baseball first that is more important than any of the above. For it was in Montreal — not Brooklyn — that Jackie Robinson first walked to the batter's box, thus reintegrating baseball after fifty years of effective segregation.

The Expos are one of those teams that baseball fans tend to neglect. Maybe it's because they're located in a town that's far from the baseball mainstream or maybe it's because the club has never been to the World Series. For whatever reason, the Expos are the Rodney Dangerfields of baseball . . . they get no respect. And that's too bad. For the Expos have a better record than many baseball admirers realize, they do more to make their fans "at home" in their stadium than just about anyone else in the majors, and they play in one of the most vibrant, exciting, and welcoming cities on the continent.

The Team

Though the Expos are a relatively new (1969) expansion franchise, they are the emotional descendants of one of the most distinguished teams in minor league history — the Montreal Royales.

The Brooklyn Dodgers' principal farm club, the Royales played against such teams as Toronto, Louisville, and Rochester in the International League. Many soon-to-be Dodger greats traipsed through Montreal on their way up, among them Duke Snider and a pitcher called Tommy Lasorda. But the greatest of all the Dodger farm club boys was undoubtedly Jackie Robinson.

In the mid–1940s, Dodgers owner

Branch Rickey decided to break baseball's color line. Realizing the delicacy of the operation and what rested on its success, Rickey took his time in selecting the player to initiate the great experiment. What Rickey wanted was a black man who would not only play great ball, but who would also set such an example of dignity and discretion as to shame anyone who would object to baseball's integration. The man he slected was Jackie Robinson.

Sent to Montreal to get some training in preparation for joining Brooklyn (ironically, the Royales manager was a Mississippian), Robinson broke baseball's color barrier on opening day, 1946. Of course, just as he would in the majors, Robinson had to put up with a lot of abuse during his year in the International League, particularly when the Royales fought a hotly contested "Little World Series" against the Louisville Colonels. Yet Robinson was also the beneficiary of much fan support and many gratuitous acts of kindness. Years later, he would say of his experience that "Montreal was a kind of heaven to me."

With the expansion of the National League in 1969, Montreal went "major league," selecting the name "Expos" for their new franchise to honor Montreal's recently concluded World's Fair, which was called "Expo '67."

In their first decade, the Expos were awful. They finished in last place four times and never made it out of the second division. Attendance declined, and disgruntled fans called for a return of the old Royales—who, the public claimed, could easily whip Montreal's misbegotten new club.

In the 1980s, though, things got better, fast. Powerhouse players like Gary Carter, Tim Raines (1986 batting champ), Tim Wallach, and Andre Dawson joined the squad. In 1979, Montreal placed second, finally moving into the first division. They did it again in 1980, and in 1981 they won the National League Eastern Division title. Only a run difference in the fifth and final game of the championship series against, ironically, the Dodgers, kept the Expos from winning the pennant.

Since then, the Expos have done consistently well (often placing third), but not well enough. There have been no more divisional titles. On the other hand, there haven't been any more last place finishes, either. In a pattern that's familiar to anyone from Boston, the Expos have developed the habit of coming frustratingly close to winning by midseason, only to fade in September. Free agency has not been kind to the club: unable to afford the fat salaries other squads can provide. Montreal has had difficulty over the past few years hanging on to its stars.

Currently, the Expos have a good club, if not a great one. It's a team that often runs more on heart and what the French call *élan* than on muscle or sheer ability. Infielders Tim Wallach and Andres "The Cat" Galarraga and pitchers Dennis Martinez and Dennis ("Oil Can") Boyd provide plenty of excitment.

Currently, the future of baseball in Montreal is unclear. Owner Charles Bronfman (of the Seagram liquor empire) has put the club on the block. At this writing, a move out of Montreal is possible. That would be a shame. Montreal is not the greatest baseball town, but it is one of the most appealing and exciting cities that baseball is played in.

The Stadium

Many stadiums where baseball is played were designed principally for football. Montreal's Olympic Stadium, known to everyone as the "Big O," is one of only two parks (Cleveland is the other) that was set up specifically to accommodate track and field events.

Olympic Stadium, though, does not resemble Cleveland Stadium—nor any other sports facility for that matter. Indeed, the question you'll probably ask yourself upon first seeing the "Big O" is, "When does it take off?" For the fact is that Olympic Stadium looks like a Steven Speilberg spaceship, straight out of "Close Encounters of the Third Kind." Some people think that Olympic Stadium is one of the ugliest parks in baseball; others regard it as one of the most beautiful. No one would dispute that it is the most unusual. We like it.

Olympic Stadium rests in east Montreal and is part of a complex of buildings that were set up for the 1976 summer Olympics. This is a beautiful, perfectly safe area, about three miles from downtown.

Directly to the north of the Stadium is the "Jardin Botanique"—Quebec's Botanical Garden, which is one of the best in North America. It's a perfect place for a before-the-game stroll. Just to the east of the garden is Park Maisonneuve, a big, attractive urban park that's ideal for a pregame picnic.

The Olympic facility itself has a variety attractions. There's an open-to-the public running track to the east of the facility, should you want to get in a few miles before the contest. Should swimming be more down your line, that's available too—Olympic Stadium has a huge public pool (this one really is "Olympic-sized") located at the northeast corner of the building; just follow the signs that say "Piscines." It's open from 9:30 A.M. until 9 P.M., Monday through Friday, and from 9:30 A.M. to 3 P.M. on Sunday. The price ("Prix") is $2.50 Canadian for adults (all prices, henceforth, will be quoted in Canadian currency, which was valued at about 15 percent less than American money at the time this is being written), $1.50 for kids. As if the above weren't enough, the Stadium also has an observation tower, which is also to the northeast of the facility. For a fairly high $5 adults,

$4 teens, and $3.50 kids, you can ride a kind of funicular car to the top for a spectacular view of downtown Montreal.

Outside the Stadium proper, Olympic Park looks like, well, a flying saucer. It's a massive, rounded building, topped by the observation tower, which rises like some sort of giant arm over the structure. From the tower come huge cables attached to the top of the "Big O." When the sun shines, the cables are retracted, thus raising the roof. When rain (or snow; this *is* Montreal) comes, the cables slide down and the roof snaps into place.

On the exterior of the park there's little to detain you, unless you were planning on a swim or a run. Still, if you have any interest in the 1976 Olympics, you might want to stop by the modest display that commemorates the event. Underneath a circle of flags to the south of the tower, you'll see listed plaques honoring the gold medal winners of these games. Below that of France, you'll find the Olympic boxing gold medalists: Leon Spinks, Mike Spinks, and Sugar Ray Leonard. The American flag flies over the name of basketball medalist Adrian Dantley; decathelon champ Bruce Jenner is also honored. Yet the person who really captured the imagination of the world during this Olympiad was from none of the major nations. Rather, it was Romanian gymnast Nadia Comanci. You'll find Nadia below the flag of Japan.

Once inside the "Big O," you feel like you've wandered into a shopping mall. Muzak, often of the "spacey" New Age sort, fills the air. Just as you come into the main concourse, along with a variety of office and shops, you'll find a coat room, just in case you brought your mink and don't want to bring it into the game. Montreal is the only park that has a coat room, and the only one that needs it (see "Fans").

The public areas are wide, immaculately clean, and well-organized—if your

French is up to par. Otherwise, you may be a bit confused. If so, never fear: ask directions of any usher. All are bilingual and extremely helpful.

The inside of Olympic Stadium is an impressive sight, particularly if the roof is up. The "Big O" is a big place indeed. Shaped into an enormous enclosed oval, Olympic Stadium seats 58,150 people for baseball, making it the fifth largest park in the leagues. Unfortunately, however, baseball is a game played around a diamond—it is not a road race. As a result, a substantial number of seats in the "Big O" are located very far from the action. Worse, the chairs are pointed in directions that have little or nothing to do with bats and balls. The track-and-field design has other limitations as well. The lights in the roof make it difficult for players to see foul balls; "errors" in the outfield happen here with some regularity. Moreover, the oval shape distorts sounds terribly. As a result, if you can't understand the announcements that are given in French, don't worry; soon you'll have the opportunity not to understand them in English, too.

The astroturf field itself is unexceptional. Right and left foul poles are set at 325' and slant steeply back to center field at 410'. Behind the field wall is more astroturf, as well as some seats that might as well be in Toronto or Quebec City for the view they have. The Expos have been known to move their field fence back and forth depending on who they have on their team.

Altogether, it must be said; Olympic Stadium is a wonderful facility, but it isn't a baseball park. With a team in which so much is right, this is one factor that needs fixing.

Highlights

Olympic Stadium is a park not especially rich in baseball highlights. For Expos fans, certainly the most memorable event was the 1981 National League Championship Series. It was one of those series where the losing team could truthfully say, "We came so close!" The Expos' pennant hopes were crushed in the fifth and final game when Dodger Rick Monday hit a game-winning home run. The Dodgers went on to win the Series.

A happier memory occurred in 1982. That year, for the first and only time, the All-Star game came to Montreal. Former Royales pitcher Tommy Lasorda led the National League to victory over Billy Martin, 5–1.

People who go to Olympic Stadium often ask, "Has anyone hit the roof?" The answer is "no." Both Dave Kingman and Darryl Strawberry have hit the roof's rim, however, so the day when the roof will be hit may yet come.

Fans

If truth be told, baseball is not the favorite sport of Canadians. By far and away, the national obsession is hockey, that wild game of flashing sticks, fervent play, and oafish players. However, it does not snow year round—not even in Montreal. So, though they're doubtless dreaming of puck triumphs to come, the Quebecois are willing to "do" baseball during the summer months "pour l'amour du baseball"—for the love of the game—as Expos literature likes to put it.

Who goes to the contests? Middle-class folks, mostly. Typically, the Expos attract a lot of males, some kids (many attracted by "Youppi!" the Expos' popular mascot), and a fair sprinkling of executives from Montreal's corporations. Most of the audience, like most of Montreal, is Francophone. There is, however, a strong contingent of English Montrealers, and more than a sprinkling of Americans. The Expos have a sizeable following in northern New York and Vermont.

Altogether, this is an exceptionally well-dressed audience. Expos fans would easily win the "best dressed" contest in baseball. While leisure clothes are common enough (though with collars; T-shirts will identify you as being from "the States"), sports coats and dresses are also seen. Moreover, should you be rushing from a business meeting in a three-piece suit, don't feel that you have to stop at your hotel to change; you will not at all look out of place in Olympic Stadium.

Montreal fans have some things in common with other Canadian baseball enthusiasts. They are unfailingly polite to outsiders, generally sober, and they will rarely boo opposing players or the umps (they will not necessarily extend such courtesies to the Expos). Nevertheless, Montreal is not Toronto, and the Quebecois have a different approach to life than their English-descended countrymen. To be blunt, English Canadians will tell you that the Quebecois are flamboyant, boisterous, and prone to exaggeration. They are the sort of people who might be tempted to run a red light if they didn't see the police around. (This never happens in English Canada). In fact, it's alleged, the Montrealer is disturbingly like an American. By contrast, Quebecois see other Canadians as decent sorts, really, but fairly boring, lacking in "joie de vivre."

In baseball terms, this translates into the fact that Expos fans are a fun audience. You'll notice it as soon as the game begins. People don't sing National Anthems in most stadiums, or, if they do, they mumble it. At Olympic, "O Canada!" gets a lusty, two-languaged chorus, despite the secession talk. Good sports, many in the audience will join in singing the "Star Spangled Banner," too. After all, it's a heck of a song.

During the contest, the good spirits continue. Trips to the food areas (and the food here is delicious) are frequent, a fair amount of tasty Canadian beer is consumed, and the audience spends almost as much time socializing as watching the Expos. During one game, for example, two young men sat next to us, and promptly announced that they had been construction workers on the stadium. "You must be very proud of it," we said.

"Proud!" they snorted. "This place could fall down any second. Believe me, Monsieur, this Stadium is a disaster in the making! A bomb about to explode! Why, half the construction workers in Montreal won't come anywhere near it."

Somewhat nonplussed, we wondered just what were they doing at the game?

"You have to die sometime," one shrugged. "Meanwhile, why miss the fun?" With its flamboyance, fatalism, and basic good spirits, the conversation was pure Quebecois.

In truth, Expos fans are not baseball purists. They certainly know their statistics; any fan can tell you absolutely everything about Wayne Gretsky or about the prospects for this year's *Canadians*. But remembering such things about baseball seems, to the Montrealer, hardly worth the time.

However, Expos admirers are anything but lackadaisical. Let a rally start and the black and white electronic scoreboard will call for "Bruit! Bruit!"—raucous noise. And, boy, does the crowd respond. Thunderous cheers rise from the audience. Soon ushers march into the stands, bearing real trumpets (we love this idea) and blowing the "Charge!!!" The audience just about goes wild. Soon, nearly everyone is on his feet, slapping the seat of his chair against its back, creating the most infernal racket you have ever heard in your life, while laughing, and craning his neck to see if "the Can" (Dennis Boyd) will throw that final strike.

It makes you feel, as the Quebecois instinctively does, that it's a good thing to be alive.

Baseball in French

Is it necessary to know French to go to Expo games? Absolutely not. All annoucements are in both English and French, as is the program (times, however, are given in the European system: a 7:30 night game starts, in Quebec, at 19:30). All ushers, security guards, and assistance personnel are bilingual. Some of the concessionaires, however, speak only French—so learn a few words of French to allow you to order ("Je voudrais" is "I'd like") or just point, smile, and say "s'il vous plaît" ("please") when making your request, and "merci" ("thank you") after you get what you were after.

Nor is it necessary for you to understand French baseball terminology—English translations are usually provided. Still, your enjoyment of the game will be enhanced if you know a few of them. Here are several: pitcher (lanceur); catcher (receveur); infielder (intérieur); outfielder (voltigeur); manager (gérant); shortstop (arrêt-court); left field (champ gauche); center field (champ centre); right field (champ droit). Occasionally, the electronic screen will demand that the crowd "Vague." That means that you're supposed to do "the wave."

Getting There

Mass transportation in all of Canada's major cities is excellent, and Montreal is no exception. Thus, the city's Metro is by far the best way to reach the game, even for those traveling from out of town. Olympic Stadium can also be reached by car and taxi.

By car. If you insist on driving to the game, reaching it presents no problems, although it is not located near any major highways.

From such *western* destinations as Hamilton and Toronto, take Canadian Route 401 (the Macdonald-Cartier highway) east to the point where it merges into Quebec Route 20 east. From there follow 20 east to the Avenue de Lorimer, where you will turn left. Follow the Avenue de Lorimer to the Rue Sherbrooke. Turn right on Sherbrooke. Olympic Stadium is a few miles down on the right.

From Plattsburgh, Albany, and other *south* New York destinations, take the Adirondack Northway north (I-87), to where it joins Canadian Route 15. Follow 15 north to Route 20 east. Take Route 20 east to the Pont Jacques Cartier. From the Montreal side of the Pont, follow the Avenue de Lorimer to the Rue Sherbrooke. Turn right and follow about two miles to stadium.

From Burlington and other *south* Vermont areas, take I-89 nroth to the Canadian border. Then follow Route 133 to Quebec Route 10, heading west toward Montreal. When you hit Route 20 east follow it to the Jacques Cartier Bridge and then follow the above directions.

From Quebec City and points *east*, follow Canadian Route 20 west to the Pont Jacques Cartier. Follow above directions to the stadium.

By cab. Given the excellence of public transit, we regard cab as a second-rate option. Still, if you want to go, a cab from most of the downtown hotels will run you $10 to $15, while one from Dorval Airport runs around $20. Plan on paying about $50 or more if you're coming from Mirabeau Airport, which is sited far from town.

By subway. The Metro is simply the best way to get around Montreal. Clean, safe, and efficient, this line is one of the best around. Despite the language problem, the Metro is easy to negotiate: its four lines are color-marked on maps in all the stations and transit points between lines are few in number and well marked.

Two stations on the Green line, Pie IX and Viau, provide on-site access to Olympic Stadium. Since the Green line runs through downtown Montreal, you may well not have to change trains to get between key shopping and tourist areas and the "Big O."

Many American Expos fans have learned that one of the best ways to get to the game is to park your car at the Longueuil Metro Station on the south side of the Saint Laurence along Route 20 and take the train into the game. To do this, take the Yellow line north to Berri-UQAM and transfer to the Green train headed toward Honore-Beaugrand. Subway fees from most locations are $1 for adults, and $.55 for children.

Parking

With the Metro available, not many people drive to Expo games. Those who do drive find ample parking. Covered spots under the stadium (not a bad idea in April or September — it sometimes snows) are $5. You can find neighborhood lots in the area that are cheaper if you drive around a bit.

Tickets

Expo tickets can be ordered by phone or picked up in person. By phone, call (514) 522-1245. Be prepared with your major credit card and the location of the area you'd like to sit in. There is a $2.50 service charge on phone orders. (Though it depends on whom you get, the operator will usually answer the phone in French. Just respond in English and he or she will switch over.) Your credit card company will bill you in American dollars based on the exchange rate on the day of the transaction. You can also purchase tickets by mail but the ticket office asks you to call to find the exchange rate if your check will be in U.S. dollars. The mailing address is: Montreal Expos, PO Box 500, Station M, Montreal,

Quebec H1V 3P2, Canada. To buy in person, simply show up at the Expos advance ticket office, which is located at the south east side of the "Big O" near the Pie IX.

You can also purchase tickets at the game. Since sellouts at the enormous "Big O" are just about unheard of, you will certainly get a seat, and probably a good one.

Availability. Never one of baseball's best attended franchises, your chances of getting good tickets for a game, even at the last minute, are excellent; crowds of 20,000 or so are typical in the "O," which seats nearly three times that. Altogether, the squad sells about 12,000 season tickets, which means, as a practical matter, that there are still some fine box seats left for many games.

Because of the Royales' heritage, contests against the Dodgers draw the biggest crowds. People in Montreal, as everywhere else, like to see the Mets and the Cubs, too.

Costs. Tickets for the better seats at Expos games are fairly expensive, as is just about everything else in Canada. On the other hand, if you are willing to sit in quite bad seats, prices are simply the best in baseball.

Unlike many of the other parks, the Expos do a pretty good job of delineating good seats from bad, and charging accordingly. Thus, you pretty much get what you pay for, with the proviso that you have to pay quite a bit for anything really good.

In 1990, Expo prices were as follows: VIP Box Seats ($20); Box Seats ($13.50); Terrace ($10); Promenade (adults [$8]); (kids and seniors [$6]); General Admission (adults [$5]); (kids and seniors [$3]); Bleachers ($1).

Rainouts. With its retractable roof, there are no rainouts in the "Big O." When the roof is open, though, it can get chilly. On a clear cool day you might want to bring a sweater just in case the roof is open.

How cold does it get in Montreal? Hard to say; but the park's biggest promotion has, for years, been "torque" day, when the team gives out free snow caps.

Seating

Just about everything about the Montreal Expos is right. It's a good team, playing in a safe, beautiful city, with a management that really cares about the fans. But the whole operation has one problem: the admittedly attractive stadium that the Expos play in is just not a baseball park. This isn't a fatal flaw — you can, and almost certainly will, have a great time at an Expos game in spite of this. But the problem nettles.

The "Big O," of course, was not built for baseball. It was designed for track and field events. As a result, all the chairs are focused straight ahead — where, presumably, the runners will pass by — rather than toward home plate. Moreover, since tracks are generally oval, so is the "Big O." As a result, seats past the outfield wall are often so far out that they might as well be in Ottawa for all you can see of the game, while even some of the close-in box seats do not have a full view of the field. We saw that dramatically in compiling these notes. Innocently, we wrote down that 375' was the distance at the left field foul post. Actually, it's 325'. The problem was that we were unable to see that part of the field from where we were sitting, which were expensive box seats over third base.

On the whole, the Expos give you a lot. But if the team were suddenly to announce that they were building another baseball park, I don't think this would be one of those places where marchers would fill the streets, demanding that the old not be replaced with the new.

Specifically, the VIP Boxes are just great: for $20 each, they ought to be. These are a thin row of yellow plastic-and-metal seats that rest just over the field wall and a few rows beyond. Mostly, they cover the baselines here, though in a few sections they go a bit beyond them. Still, it's hard to go wrong in this area, if you don't mind spending the money.

Box seats ($13.50) are significantly cheaper and nearly as good. These blue seats stretch back from just beyond the baselines into the stadium in a long, slanting row. Rows are comfortably short, legroom is decent, and the chairs are comfortable. The best boxes are found in the 100s, preferably from Sections 122 (third) to 121 (first). However, the corresponding sections at the 300 level are also fine.

With the Terrace spots ($10) you save $3.50, but at the cost of being significantly further from the field. This section is divided into two areas. The first is set high above the baselines, while the second is at the end of the field, near the foul poles. We much prefer the first, and regard seats in the baseline areas, sections 424 (third) to 421 (first) as being the best.

All the seats beyond these are inferior to varying degrees. Promenade seats ($8) are wrapped high over the action at a variety of levels. Those directly around the plate, sections 620 to 617, are the best. General Admission seats ($5) have the virtue of being cheap; there is little else to recommend them. If you have to go for these, try sections 736 to 735. You'll still be a ways from the action, but you should be able to read the numbers on the uniforms. The bleacher seats are the worst of a uninspired lot . . . very distant spots far beyond the outfield wall. Still, at $1 (about $.85 American) they have to be rated a bargain. Where else can you get live major league action for under a buck?

Special Needs

Parking. Handicapped parking is available in the lots under the stadium. Show the parking attendant your plat and or sticker, and you'll be pointed to the appropriate area. Olympic Stadium is very wheelchair accessible.

Seating. Seating for the physically disabled can be found wrapped around home plate, behind the terrace level (sections 401, 404, 405, 408, 409). These are good spots, very nearly the best of their class. Though people in this area will find it hard to see really high pop flies, the view of the action is otherwise very decent.

Food and Features

Food. We will stick out our necks and say it. The Expos have the best food in baseball.

This statement will outrage admirers of Fenway Franks and Dodgers Dogs. How can choice or quality be matched against tradition, after all? It will also drive to distraction those park managers in such cities as Anaheim, Baltimore, and Philadelphia who've really gone out of their way to provide fans with a cornucopia of tasty treats. And it's not that these parks (and perhaps a half dozen others) haven't done a good job—they have. It's just that the Expos have gone a step beyond what anyone else has achieved.

Most of the food of interest can be found in the main concourse, behind home plate. And what a selection you will find there!

There is, of course, the standard ballpark fare . . . but with variations. Unless you stop them, your hot dog will be served to you Quebecois style, with mustard, relish, onions, and vinegary cole slaw. We suggest you try it their way; it's delicious. Available too are pretzels, popcorn, ice cream, and "Screaming Yellow Zonkers."

Beyond that, there is simply incredible variety. "*Le Poulet Frit Kentucky*" is—you guessed it—"Kentucky Fried Chicken," the only outlet of this popular franchise in the majors, although priced fairly stiff. *Burger King* is represented as well, with the usual selections at inflated prices. Italian fans will fined decent pizza at *Place Trevere*.

Had enough? Ah, the feast has just begun! Fans of oriental food will want to stop at *Win Wah*, where you can get surprisingly generous plates of Chinese food. *Kojak* serves up Greek food, and it is just delicious. Don't say the souvlaki is overpriced until you've tried it. Possibly best of all is *Briskets*, which carves up all manner of smoked meat sandwiches. Note, this is not the "luncheon meats" you bought at A&P; rather these are quality cuts, served "thick."

Still hungry? Then perhaps you'll want to reserve a spot at the *Double Jeu* (double play) restaurant, which is located just past third on the left field line. There, for a stiff price over thirty dollars you'll get a good all-you-can eat buffet dinner before the game, and an excellent seat with a nice view during the contest. Moreover, the "Double Jeu" bar stays open throughout. Theoretically, you should reserve a spot here well in advance, but, if you show at the ticket office ninety minutes or so before the game, a seat will often be found for you.

Drinks. Coke products can be found throughout the park, and juice is also available.

Though France itself may be a wine-drinking country, Quebec has always preferred "biere." A fine selection of mostly Canadian brew can be found throughout the park. Vendors do not sell beer in the stands.

Mixed drinks and wine can be found in only two areas, namely at *Double Jeu* and at *Salon 76*, a kind of after-the-game bar.

College students may be glad to know that Quebec is one of the few places left where they can legally get a beer. The provincial drinking age is 18. If you do decide to indulge, do us all a favor and take the Metro home, or have someone else drive.

Features. Recognizing that baseball is not Montreal's sport, the Expos knock themselves out thinking of ways to keep the fans amused.

Probably the Expos most famous feature is "Youppi!" (it means, say, "Wahoo!" in English), the team's highly popular mascot. A green fuzzy "thing" in a uniform marked with a exclamation mark, "Youppi!" is the "Big Bird" of baseball, a friendly, comforting creature who seems intended mainly to keep the kids amused. However limited his (?) purpose, though, it would be hard to deny that the creature has appeal. "Youppi's" autographs are as much sought after as any of the current crowd of Expos.

Before and after many games, entertainment groups are often posted in the lobbies. Sometimes the fare will be jazz (Montreal is a great jazz town), other times rock, while occasionally a magician or an accordionist will be on hand. Dancing in the main lobby after the game, with a French D.J. no less, is not uncommon. There is simply no way for you to predict what the Expos will have in store for you on any given night. Go and find out.

Traditional amusements are also available. The main concourse has a "Speed Pitch" concession behind section 331. In the same area, there's also a free computer trivia quiz machine. Americans trying to operate it, though, will find it a bit of a problem: you have to tell the device where you live before it will deal with you, and it doesn't like American zip codes. Our advice: copy the Canadian zip given on the sample and play away.

There's also one spot devoted to edification. Just behind home plate, near the food emporiums, you'll find a plaque dedicated to Jackie Robinson, who, like many another visitor to Montreal, found the place a paradise.

Assistance

The Expos' fan assistance office is located at the main concourse level, well past the food areas and out near the subterranean entrance, on the right just as you are about to pass out the main doors. Its staff is quite helpful in either language.

Safety and Security

Safety. Montreal isn't crime free, but it is as close to it as any major city in North America. There is no security threat whatever in the stadium, in parking, or in the surrounding neighborhoods. It isn't impossible, of course, to get mugged even here, but it is highly unlikely.

Health. Since drinking too much is rarely a problem in Olympic Stadium, and since the roof controls climate, the biggest health threat comes from foul balls. All we can say is, look alive.

The first aid office is located near the "Kentucky Fried Chicken" stand, which is on the main concourse behind home plate. It has the usual services and facilities.

Mementos

Souvenirs. The Expos run an attractive souvenir shop, just outside the main gate behind home plate. Prices are not especially cheap.

Foul Balls. With its open, slanting main tier, Olympic Stadium is a good place to catch them. Try sitting in the 200 level box seats, in sections 222 to 226 (left field), and 221 to 227 (right field); a lot seem to land in these areas.

Autographs. The Expos provide

enough formal opportunities to get signatures that it makes little sense chasing
players through parking lots here, which,
in any case, are underground at Olympic Stadium and difficult to get to.

Standing outside the dugouts during
batting practice seems to work better
in Montreal than elsewhere; maybe it's

because crowds are smaller and fans
are more polite than in some other
places. Also, two players and "Youppi"
are generally made available for signatures on the team's many "autograph
days," which occur on most home game
weekends. You might want to ask about
this when you call for tickets.

NEW YORK METS
Shea Stadium

New York is really two cities.

The first of these towns is the one
that everyone loves—or hates. That's
Manhattan, that magical land of soaring
skyscrapers, famous celebrities, great
restaurants and museums, tony urban
neighborhoods, and dangerous "mean
street" slums. This is the New York of
Donald Trump and Leona Helmsley,
Cardinal O'Conner, David Dinkins,
and, in part, of Woody Allen. This is a
world that the New York Yankees are
very much a part of.

But past the Brooklyn and the 59th
Street bridges, there's another "Big Apple" that outsiders are only vaguely
aware of and rarely visit. In fact, if they
see this New York at all, they usually
only catch glimpses of it through
smudged cab windows on the way into
town from Kennedy or LaGuardia. This
is the New York of the "Outer
Boroughs"—Brooklyn, Queens, and
Staten Island—where there are few
great restaurants, no really important
museums, and where the lion's share of
New Yorkers actually live. Whereas the
emblem of Manhattan might well be
the skyscraper, that of Queens or
Brooklyn could be a row of townhouses
of the sort that Archie Bunker lived in.

In point of fact, the Bunkers, residents
of Queens, lived less than a mile from
Shea Stadium. Overall, the "Outer
Boroughs" are a land of single-story
homes and modest apartment houses,
inexpensive ethnic restaurants, and
close-knit communities. It's the world
of the New York Mets.

If New York is two towns, New
York's baseball history has had two
chapters. The more familiar story concerns the Yankees, the team that has
represented, and continues to represent, the public face of the "Big Apple"
to the world. It's the story of the Babe,
Lou Gehrig, "Joltin' Joe" DiMaggio, and
a legion of other "Bronx Bombers" who
made much baseball history. Beyond
this tale, however, is the epic of those
other teams that once, long ago, represented the other New York: the Giants
and the Dodgers. Though both played
a rougher sort of ball than their more
elegant uptown brethren, both also
made important contributions to the
game. If the Yankees were usually better than the Dodgers and the Giants,
both of New York's National League
squads nevertheless supplied the game
with some of its most magical moments
and some of its most memorable players.

What would baseball be like without Christy Mathewson, Mel Ott, Sandy Koufax, Jackie Robinson, Dazzy Vance, Duke Snider, or Gil Hodges?

In 1957, the hearts of outer borough dwellers were broken when both the Giants and the Dodgers decamped for sunny California. Indeed, to this day, the name "O'Malley" (he's the guy who changed the "Brooklyn" to "Los Angeles") is still a kind of curseword in some Brooklyn bars. Yet after a five-year period of moaning, depression, and protests, New Yorkers were rewarded when the National League, in its first reluctant expansion, awarded new franchises to Houston (now the Astros) and New York. To recognize the special audience that it was playing to, the new squad called itself the "Mets" — as in "Metropolitans" — and announced that, though it would start play in the Polo Grounds, the old home of the Giants, it would build a stadium in Flushing Meadows, a location far from downtown, but smack in the heartland of its new constituency. The outer boroughs had baseball again.

Most teams can't become "legends" in a short period of time. Some old teams, such as the Braves and the Phillies, still haven't achieved "legendary" status. Nevertheless, the Mets, only twenty-eight years old, have already achieved mythic statute. One of the most popular and recognizable teams in the sport, the Mets, with the possible exception of the Blue Jays and the Royals, have been the most successful expansion franchise in history. They are without question the most popular.

What's behind the Mets incredible popularity? For one thing, the team is in New York, North America's leading media market and the place where the three leading newspapers and the five leading magazines in the nation are published. That certainly helps. Second, the Mets have recruited over the years a series of spectacularly talented players, from Tom Seaver to Darryl Strawberry to "Doc" Gooden. Finally, there has been the spectacle of the Mets' incredible rise from being one of the worst teams ever to take the field in major league baseball — a squad once called "a bunch of frauds" by its own manager — to the Mets we've come to know today, who are capable of fighting it out for the pennant nearly every season, right down to the wire.

If you are one of those Mets fans who has decided to make the pilgrimage to Shea Stadium, be prepared to endure some inconveniences in order to see your heroes. Shea isn't in the nicest area of New York, nor is it the nicest stadium in the league. The food prices are a bit high, the charges for local accommodations are absolutely too high, and you will perhaps be disappointed, as we were, with the lack of any real pre- or post-game fan dining activity within the vicinity of the park. On the positive side, though, you will get to see the Mets in action, in their native habitat and amongst some of the most loyal, partisan, and loud fans in the game. You will also find yourself vacationing in North America's largest, most exciting, and most complex city. The "Big Apple," whatever else could be said about it, is an experience. And it is something that should be experienced by everyone at least once.

The Team

Today easily one of the five most popular teams in the sport, the New York Mets had one of the worst starts of any baseball team in history.

The Mets began play in 1962 and set standards of incompetence that few teams had ever achieved before, and none has achieved since. By the end of its first campaign at the Polo Grounds, the Mets had won 40 games and lost 120. That left them no only in last place in the National League, but over 60 games — or two solid months — out of first place. The only category the team led in the majors during that first dispiriting season was "errors."

The stories of that first, horrible season have contributed to the Mets legend. Many concern "Marvelous Marv" — Marvin Eugene Thorneberry, an indifferent slugger whose initials just happened to spell "MET." Once, after a solid hit, Thorneberry charged into third on what he thought was a triple, only to be called out for not having touched second. An enraged Casey Stengel, who was managing the sorry squad, charged out of the dugout, intent on a confrontation with the umpire. Stengel was intercepted by the first base coach, who gently suggested to Casey that he should not make too big a stink, as Thorneberry hadn't bothered to tag first, either! Later in the season, Thorneberry was to tell the New York press that he was a real asset to the team, in that the desire of fans to come to the park to boo him had had a very positive effect on ticket sales. Possibly the Mets reached their nadir when, during a contest against the Giants, a fight broke out in which the New Yorkers came up short. The headlines the next day read: METS CAN'T FIGHT, EITHER.

It woud have been bad enough for the Mets if they had endured their first humiliating season and then had made some improvement, but that didn't happen. Throughout the early and mid-sixties the team occupied last place — or, in good seasons, second to last. People began to think that they were a team that was born to fail, and the pathetic Mets became standard joke lines on the borscht belt circuit.

Yet while Johnny Carson was having fun with the Mets on the "Tonight Show," and as most Mets had seemed to accept that defeat was their cross to bear in life, one young player refused to believe that things had to be that way. Pitcher Tom Seaver, brought on the

team in the late sixties, endured one of the team's awful finishes in 1968 and decided he didn't like losing one bit. He started building a contingent of young Met players who believed things could be different. Seaver also recognized something about the Mets that had escaped most observers: they now had a talented team. In addition to Seaver, the pitching staff included Nolan Ryan, Jerry Koosman, and Tug McGraw. Backstopping the team was Jerry Grote, a man that Johnny Bench had once said was a better catcher than he was, while the shortstop was the always admirable Bud Harrelson. By God! thought Seaver, this was a squad that could win!

Seaver was able to infect the other Mets with his enthusiasm in 1969. Still, the transfusion didn't seem to be enough; by the middle of August the team was nearly 10 games behind, and it looked like the old Mets were back.

But "Tom Terrific" and his friends refused to give up. In one of the greatest drives in baseball history, the Mets proceeded to win 38 of the next 49 games, seizing the National League East title. After a three-game playoff romp over the NL West champion Braves, the "Miracle Mets" went on to beat the Orioles in one of the most exciting, hard-fought Series ever. The long-suffering fans at Shea went wild with delight, detaching pieces of turf and the back of chairs for souvenirs. Though it wasn't the right thing to do, you could hardly blame them. Seaver's contribution to the total effort netted him the first of his three Cy Young awards.

Though the 1970s were certainly an improvement for the Mets over what they had endured through most of the sixties, the decade produced results that were both positive and negative. To the bad, the team did not win a single Series, while its standings during some years was less than great. On the positive side, fine new players like sluggers

Rusty Staub and Dave Kingman joined the squad and Seaver racked up two more Cy Young awards. In 1973, moreover, the team made a successful pennant rush that was, in its way, as spectacular as the 1969 effort, although it ended in a narrow defeat in the fall classic by the Oakland A's.

During the late 1980s, the Mets returned fully to glory. A spectacular new pitcher, Dwight "Doc" Gooden, became the second Met in history to capture the Cy Young award (1985). The year before that, he also snagged "Rookie of the Year" honors. Great new players such as outfielder Darryl Strawberry, third baseman Howard Johnson, catcher Gary Carter, and first baseman Keith Hernandez joined the squad.

These elements all came together in 1986, a year that saw in both leagues some of the greatest baseball ever. Winning the National League East, the Mets faced Houston in a championship series that, for thrills, chills, and spectacular baseball, was one of the greatest divisional series ever. In the sixth game the Mets won the contest by one run in a gut-wrenching sixteen-inning knockdown-drag-out that left most North Americans biting their nails for over five hours.

The 1986 Series against long-suffering Boston was, if anything, more dramatic. The crucial game, fought at Shea, was again the sixth, and Boston went into the tenth inning with a seemingly insurmountable two-run lead with two outs and two strikes. Below, in the Boston dressing room, the champagne was uncorked while, in the broadcasting booth, Beantown hurler Bruce Hurst had been tabbed as the Series MVP. Then Boston, through an incredible series of mistakes, proceeded to blow it. They gave up three singles and a wild pitch, and in what was probably the worst error in the history of the sport, Boston's first baseman Bill Buckner watched a ball go through his legs to give the game to the Mets. Two days later, after their win in the seventh game, the Mets had won their second Series.

Since 1986, Series play has eluded the Mets, although they have done well. Pitchers Gooden, Frank Viola, and Dave Cone, and infielders Gregg Jeffries, Howard Johnson, and Dave Magidan currently lead a Mets team that is very good, but perhaps not the best in the squad's history. Still, this team placed a close second in 1990, so, with good management, they certainly have the potential to go all the way in the years to come.

The Stadium

Named after the lawyer who brought baseball back to the outer boroughs, Shea Stadium is, because of the popularity of the team that plays in it, probably one of the best known baseball parks. Whether it's one of the best loved is another matter.

Shea is located in the Flushing Meadows section of Queens, about six miles east of downtown Manhattan and three or so miles from LaGuadia airport. Millions of Americans, in fact, who have never gone to a Mets game have seen the park from the air on their landing approach into New York. In fact, the planes sometimes come so close to Shea that flyers can actually see players running the bases. While watching this scene may be pretty for sky travelers, it can present serious problems for fans and players down below; the roaring of jet engines is a frequent distraction at any Mets contest.

The area around the stadium isn't very attractive. To one side of the park, to be sure, is Flushing Meadows Park, site of the 1968 World's Fair and of the U.S. Tennis Open. It's a pleasant place and would be suitable for a pregame picnic or stroll. On the other side, though, is a grimy neighborhood composed of junkyards, auto parts dealerships, burned out cars, dilapidated houses, and stores.

It doesn't look very safe, and it isn't. Stay out of this area.

Shea itself, from the outside, looks like a sort of huge blue hockey puck with a notch taken out of one side. Along the outside of the facility are enormous neon figures that represent ballplayers. Otherwise, the place is featureless and, it must be said, pretty unappealing.

If the outside of the park is unappealing, the public areas inside are just downright ugly. With dark corridors, metal girders, and rusty pipes all around, the place looks like nothing as much as a chemical plant, though most chemical plants we've been in have been a good deal cleaner. Even at the beginning of the game a fair amount of litter can be seen in the halls; as the contest proceeds, everything gets much worse. Large areas of the plant look as if they could use a new coat of paint.

The seating areas are much better. Though many of the levels have steep pitches, and though legroom is pretty limited, all spots in the park are composed of comfortable plastic-and-metal chairs that are attractively color coordinated. Moreover, except at the extremes of the stadium and in the highest rows (N and beyond from the Mezzanine level up), there are no obstructions. With few exceptions, you will at least have an acceptable view of the game at Shea no matter where you sit.

The field is, thankfully, natural grass and appears to be well-maintained. Overall, the dimensions of the park are moderate. Both foul poles are set at 338', while the deepest part of center field is 410'. Thus, Shea is neither a "hitter's park" nor a "pitcher's park," and the team has had, over the years, great players in both categories.

On the left field wall you will see plaques commemorating the Mets' three retired numbers. These are #14, former manager Gil Hodges; #37, former manager Casey Stengel; and #41, future Hall of Fame pitcher Tom Seaver. Just past the center field wall you'll see the Mets' celebrated cap. Whenever the Mets hit a home run, the cap lifts amidst flashing lights to reveal a giant apple—it's kind of neat, and it's very popular with the fans. Over the cap you will find the Mets' scoreboard with the electronic display to its left.

While Shea has its strengths, we don't regard it as one of the better ballparks. On the other hand, we know of absolutely no one who has ever traveled to a Mets game because they really wanted to see Shea. One good thing about less-than-great stadiums is that they put the weight of the fan's baseball experience squarely on the team, which is really where it belongs. The Mets have shown over the past two decades that they have more than the shoulders required to bear the burden.

Highlights

Though Shea has been around for only a bit more than a quarter century, baseball history has been made in its confines more than once.

Pitching has supplied some of the thrills. The great Tom Seaver matched an all-time strike out per game record in the park on April 22, 1970, when he fanned 19 Padres, a feat that was not bettered until the Red Sox's Roger Clemens struck out 20 in 1986. The Phillies' Jim Bunning threw one of baseball's few "perfects" in the stadium on June 21, 1964—an event that occurred only two months after Shea opened.

In 1964 Shea hosted its first and only All-Star game. The Nationals won 7–4, thanks to a dramatic ninth inning homer off the bat of the Phillies' Johnny Callison.

New York fans like winners, so dates associated with World Series triumphs hold a special place in their hearts.

October 16, 1969, was the day the "Miracle Mets" captured their first Series. October 25, 1986, is a day that will live in infamy — in Boston. That was the date of the celebrated, and decisive, sixth game of the 1986 Series. Two days later, on October 27, the Mets put the wraps on their second fall classic win.

Fans

Mets fans are like many people in the city they inhabit; they are smart, loud, driven to succeed, and sometimes abrasive.

Mets fans know the game. Listen to any radio talk show in the area and you'll hear Mets admirers holding forth, usually in a very informed way, on just what the team's management should do to insure victory. They can cite statistics the way some fundamentalist preachers can cite the Bible, and they are usually just as insistent that theirs is the *one right way* to do things.

Nor do Mets fans mind letting other people know exactly how they feel about these issues. Any contest at Shea will be enlivened by fans standing up and giving management the full benefit of their vast experience, shouted at the top of their lungs. And if a Mets fan finds other fans giving the wrong advice, or, even worse, cheering the visitors he is liable to give them a piece of his mind, too, usually enlivened by a few expletives.

This general willingness to be extremely vocal about just about everything carries into every aspect of the game. If the Mets do something right, you will hear a stupendous howl of delight. Let an umpire make a wrong call — which is to say any call against the Mets — and the Catskills will reverberate with the anguished cries of rage. Visiting teams are treated with the greatest contempt, no matter where they come from.

If Mets fans like to get their two cents

in, they also love to see their team win, while they hate to lose. When the Mets are playing well, you'd think they descended to the stadium on clouds the way they are treated when they take the field. But let a Met fail to produce and God help him. Met fans have zero tolerance for substandard performance, a fact pointedly established by the slogan for a popular after-the-game radio talk show: "Tune in and see who's on the bus to Tidewater [the Mets' AAA club] tonight." And while other towns may prefer squeaky clean baseball heroes of the Dale Murphy or Orel Hershiser type, Met fans frankly admire people who are willing to fight, spit, and claw their way to victory if they must. Ty Cobb would have probably been a big hit at Shea, and would have felt very much at home with this audience. "We like," one fan told us, "players who are willing to get dirty."

Who goes to the game? The Mets get a pretty mixed audience in terms of ages: there are lots kids, lots of young males, and a pretty fair number of oldsters, many of whom used to go to Dodgers games. As you would expect given the population in Queens and Brooklyn, the Mets have many Jewish fans. There are some blacks, some hispanics, and a large assortment of others, too.

To be frank, this is an audience that can get on one's nerves. While the vast majority of fans at Shea are fine sorts who come to the stadium just to enjoy a ballgame, the percentage of people who seem to be there just to annoy everyone else is unusually large here. Drunkenness, gross behavior, and, especially, bad language are all too common in the park, and there seems to be little you can do to keep from being exposed to some of it. While we think "family reserved" areas are a nice idea, there are only a few parks where behavior problems are such that they are really necessary. Shea is one of them. If you are coming to the stadium with your kids, you might want to keep this in mind.

Putting this negative note aside though, you are liable to find attending a Mets game an exciting experience, for the enthusiasm of the fans can be highly infectious. To some fans, and especially those on the west coast, baseball is a game. At Shea, baseball, like life in New York, is a constant struggle in which some win, some lose, and everyone is very much alive.

Getting There

Located in the Flushing Meadows Park in the borough of Queens, Shea Stadium is located about six miles east of downtown Manhattan. If you are arriving at the park from outside of town, car is probably your best option. Those staying in New York should probably take the subway to the stadium, while those arriving at New York's LaGuardia airport will find that Shea is a short cab or bus ride away.

By car. If you are traveling to Shea by car, keep in mind that you are in New York. The traffic is fierce, the rush hour jams can be terrible, and there's a real possibility that you'll miss the facility if you don't stay alert and keep your eyes open.

Those traveling to Shea from such *west* locations as New Jersey and eastern Pennsylvania should follow I-80 over the George Washington bridge into New York. From there, take the Major Deegan Expressway (I-87) south to the Triborough Bridge. Cross the Triborough Bridge and take the Grand Central Parkway east to Exit 9 Whitestone Bridge/Northern Boulevard. From there, follow the ramp towards Northern Boulevard and follow the signs to Shea Stadium parking.

If you are coming from such *north* points as Kingston or Albany, follow the New York Thruway (I-87) to the Triborough Bridge and then follow the above instructions.

Those driving from New Haven, Bridgeport, Boston and other *northeast* locales should take I-95 south or west to the Hutchinson Expressway (I-678) south. Proceed on the Hutchinson over the Whitestone Bridge and then follow the Whitestone Expressway south to the Grand Central west. Follow the Grand Central west to the exit for Shea Stadium and proceed from there to parking.

People coming from *east* areas of Long Island should take the Long Island Expressway west to the Grand Central Expressway north (Exit 21) and then proceed from there to the Shea Stadium exit and parking.

If you are going to the game directly from *LaGuardia Airport*, take the Grand Central west to Exit 9 and follow Northern Boulevard and the signs to the park. Those flying into *Kennedy Airport* should take the Van Wyck Expressway (I-678) north to the Grand Central north and then follow that to the Shea Stadium exit.

By cab. Cab is a fine option if you are arriving at LaGuardia. The cost is a reasonable $4 or so, and you'll be at the game in about ten minutes, depending on traffic. From downtown Manhattan expect to pay about $23.

If you travel by cab in New York, be aware that cabbies in this city have been known to take out-of-towners by the "scenic" route and charge them far more than the going rates. Therefore, be sure that you agree with your driver on an approximate price in advance and that it at least roughly corresponds with what we've given you above.

By bus. Though you can reach Shea by bus from downtown, subway is a better alternative. On the other hand, it is a fine option from LaGuardia if you want to save a buck or two. Simply pick up bus #48 Flushing from outside the baggage area of the terminal, and ask the driver to let you off at Shea Stadium. You'll pay $1.15 for the service, and you must have exact change.

By subway. If you are staying in downtown Manhattan, subway is probably your best option. To get to the park, take any #7 Flushing Line train to the Willet's Point/Shea Stadium exit and walk from there to the park. You can pick this train up at Times Square and Grand Central Station, among other locations. The ride to the park takes about a half hour and costs $1.15.

Parking

Shea Stadium is surrounded with ample lighted and secured parking. Though 6,000 spaces may not seem like an enormous amount, team officials claim that spaces have never run out. Give that this is New York City, the price is a fair $4.50.

Tickets

Mets tickets are available by mail, by phone, and at the stadium.

To purchase tickets by mail, write to the team at: Mets Ticket Department, Shea Stadium, Flushing, NY 11368.

Include the dates you want, the number of tickets, and the general locations. Enclose your payment in full or give the Mets your MasterCard or Visa card number and your expiration date. Be sure to include the Mets' $2 service charge.

Ticketron (212) 947-5850 handles Mets phone orders. If you call, have your credit card and the seating chart included in this book ready.

The Mets' advance ticket office is located at Shea (the address is 126 Street and Roosevelt) near Gate D. This is the place to go if you want to see a seating chart before you buy and argue a bit about where the Mets intend to seat you. The ticket office is open from 10 to 7 on Monday through Friday, from 10 to 6 on Saturday, and from 12 to 5 on Sunday.

Availability. With 55,601 seats, Shea Stadium is in the midrange of baseball facilities in size, and its team is quite popular. In fact, the club currently holds three of the twenty all-time best yearly attendance records. As a result, ticket availability is somewhat restricted. Generally speaking, Shea sells out two or three times a year, with contests against the Giants, the Dodgers, and the Cubs being the most likely candidates for those sell-outs. During most other engagements, you will almost certainly find a spot, even if you show up at the last minute.

The question is, what kind of spot? Presently, the club sells about 24,000 season tickets, one of the highest totals in the majors. As a practical matter, that means that most of the good seats are sold before you even have a shot at them. If you wait until the last minute to order yours, your chances of getting, say, a field level box seat are just about nil. Therefore, though it usually isn't absolutely necessary, this is one park where it would probably be a good idea to order your seats well in advance.

Costs. Though Mets tickets aren't the cheapest in baseball by a long-shot, they are not the most expensive, either. Given what prices are for just about everything in New York, that makes them almost a bargain. Thus, while $12 for a Mets box seat may not seem like a great deal, it compares pretty favorably to the Red Sox's top price, which is $16.

Unfortunately, ticket quality at Shea has only a passing relationship to ticket price. There are many fine seats in the park, and not all of them go for the top rates. There are also some pricier spots that are no great shakes. If you do your homework you'll likely end up with a far better seat than those fans will who just accept what they are given.

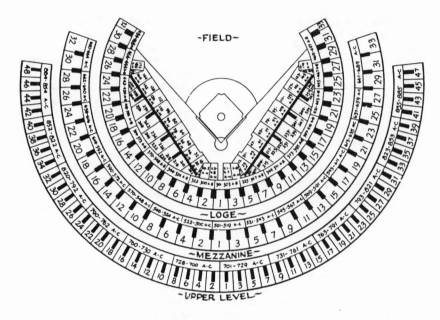

Seating chart, Shea Stadium.

The Mets' 1990 fees were as follows: Box Seats ($12); Loge and Mezzanine Reserved ($10); Upper Level Box ($10); Upper Level Reserved ($6); Senior Citizen* ($1).

Rainouts. Rainouts happen with some frequency at Shea Stadium. In point of fact, we got rained out of two Mets games trying to write this book! If the weather looks threatening outside as you are about to head out to the park, you should consider calling the team's postponement information line at (718) 507-RAIN. They'll give you the latest scoop on whether the contest is likely to take place. If you are involved in a cancelled contest, your ticket will be exchanged for a future game. If you are from outside New York and have no plans to return to the "Big Apple," write the team a short note explaining the situation and enclosing your stubs, and your money will be refunded.

Seating

Shea is one of those stadiums where you would be wise to consult a seating chart before picking your spots. Though you stand a fair chance of getting decent seats here, there is also a potential for getting burned.

The most expensive in the park are the Field boxes ($12), and all of them are pretty good. Wrapping the playing area from foul pole to foul pole, these constitution most the really fine spots in the park, as well as a fair selection of seats that are good but not great. If you can somehow wrangle seats in the baselines here, which run up to 78 and 232 (third base side, even numbers) or up to 93 and 239 (first base side, odd numbers), you'll have super spots. Anything in this area outside these sections will not be quite up to par, but, given Shea's ticket availability problem should probably be snapped up.

*Designated days only. Ask about them at the ticket office.

Loge and Mezzanine Reserved seats ($10) sit on two higher decks and are all that much farther from the action. Getting baseline spots would be a good idea here. Ask for Loge sections between 300 and 394 or 2 through 14 (third base) or on the first base side between 1 and 13 or 301 to 395. Try to obtain Mezzanine seats in sections 500 to 590 or 2 to 14 (third base) or sectins 1 through 13 and 501 to 591 (first base).

Upper level box seats ($10) are higher yet, and are pretty pricy for what you get—you are quite far from the action here no matter where you sit. If you must buy here, try to stay in the batter's box area, which runs from 760 even to 761 odd. The Upper level reserved spots ($6) are more distant from the action yet, and, really, they have only price to recommend them. If you find yourself stuck here, try to get the Mets to let you sit in even sections 2, 4, 6, and 8 and odd sections 1, 3, 5, and 7.

Special Needs

Parking. The Mets provide plenty of parking for the physically disabled outside Gate A of the stadium. Show your sticker or plate to the attendant as you pull into parking and you will be directed to this lot.

Seating. Handicapped seating spots are located directly behind home plate ($14) and behind right and left field ($6.50). In all sections, the seating is designed for one handicapped person and one accompanying person. In the outfield sections, the accompanying person should be sure to bring a folding chair.

The Mets also offer a special "family reserved" no-alcohol area which, in this park, might be something you'd wish to take advantage of if you are bringing youngsters to the game. Upper reserved sections 8 to 14 and 24 to 30 allow "no beer vending," while sections 16 to 22

forbid alcohol consumption entirely. Overall, these are OK spots along the left field line from home to a bit past third.

Food and Features

Food. Food prices at Shea are too high. Other than that, though, the dining situation in the park is pretty acceptable. The park offers a reasonable number of food choices, and the quality is respectable, if not exactly great.

A "regular frank" in the park is stiffly priced, while a "kosher" will set you back even further. Soft serve cones are available, as are "helmet sundaes," Dove Bars, and a knish (a Jewish potato and cheese pastry). You can also find at most stands such standard ballpark fare as pretzels, peanuts, and popcorn at inflated prices.

The two *Fielder's Choice* areas, one of which is located between the Field and Loge levels at the right field foul pole and the other of which sits behind upper section 4, both offer a selection of goodies at a variety of stands. At the places marked *Chef's Corner* you'll find decent sausage and pepper heros, onion rings (a good buy), and cottage fries (excellent). *Franks to Fries* offers, among other things, fried chicken, while *Sweet Stuff* has tasty New York cheesecake. Those fans who like pizza should repair to *Casey's*, which is located behind Loge level 9. The place also has hero sandwiches and corned beef.

Drinks. The big drink at Shea is beer, which isn't, however, the only drink. Royal Crown products are sold throughout the park, and many stands sell lemonade and orange juice.

Those wanting something a bit stronger will also find their thirst slaked. The *Bullpen Lounge*, on the field level behind third base, offers full bar service, as does *Casey's*, behind section nine at the Loge level. Both places offer wine, mixed drinks, and bottled beer.

Features. The Mets only feature is nine innings, and occasionally more, of great baseball.

Assistance

The Mets operate several mobile "Fan Relations" offices. They are usually located behind home plate on the Loge or Mezzanine levels, but they also may be found on the field level.

The folks who staff these offices will be glad to help you with any problems you are having with obnoxious fans, seat jumpers, lost tickets, and the like.

Safety and Security

Safety. Shea Stadium is not the safest facility in the leagues. Although it's not by any means a common problem, drunkenness in the park can lead to occasional fights in the stands. Though security moves in fast to break these things up when they occur, there's at least a potential that you, as a bystander, could be involved in some unpleasantness.

As far as the parking situation goes, the Mets take every reasonable precaution to insure that you and your car are safe in their lots. The place is lighted, secured, and policed. Nevertheless, we were told by some fans that crime problems sometimes happen in the area. Our advice is that when you leave the stadium, go with the crowd, get in your car, and drive home. As for the neighborhood around the park, it is, after dark, dangerous. Stay out of it.

People always ask about how safe the New York subways are. We have traveled on them dozens of times and have never had any problems whatsoever. Even so, a public transit system that averages one murdered patron a month cannot be said to be really secure, however much New York City officials would like outsiders to believe that all is well in the "Big Apple." By all means take the subway to the game, but use your head and stay in cars that are well-populated with other fans.

Mementos

Souvenirs. Shea Stadium is one of those ballparks where people just love to dress up in team paraphernalia. At times, in fact, the stands look like a sea of Mets hats, shirts, and banners. You'll find a reasonable selection of all these things at the souvenir shop behind section 9 of the Mezzanine level. There you'll find handsome Mets caps for $8 and up and shirts for $18.

Foul Balls. People at Shea take pride in their ability to catch fouls, so if you want one, you'd better be prepared to tussle a bit for it. If you feel up to the task, try sitting in Field boxes 80 to 110 and 63 to 109.

Autographs. Shea is a fine place to get signatures. The visitors' bus leaves from behind their bullpen, which is located at center field. Though you'll find it hard to get close to the visitors here, some wander over to the fans for signatures. The Mets walk to their parking lot from outside the Diamond Club offices and must pass you to get to their cars. During the games we attended, we were pleasantly surprised with the willingness of many Mets, after a hard night, to stop and sign for their admirers.

NEW YORK YANKEES

Yankee Stadium

Tradition is a word much abused in the world of sports. Teams that have indifferent records extol their "winning tradition," sports organizations that have existed for a few decades boast of their distinguished history, and teams that, in truth, have suited up few outstanding performers nevertheless retire numbers with abandon and set up attractive little stadium museums honoring players whose contributions have added but little to their respective games. All of this is done in the name of preserving the link with the past, of protecting "tradition."

Those who want to find out what a sports tradition is really all about would do well to travel to New York City. There in the borough of the Bronx stands Yankee Stadium, a building that is without question the most famed sports edifice constructed since the Colosseum. It is a stadium associated worldwide with excellence. Within that building for all but two of the past sixty-seven years has played a team that is not only the most successful baseball squad of all time but also the most recognizable franchise of any sports team ever.

Just how good have the Yankees been? Altogether, the squad has copped 33 pennants. The Cardinals are second, with 15. The New Yorkers have taken home the fall classic trophy 22 times now. The Cards, second in this category, too, have walked away with the laurels 9 times.

Next take a look at the honors. Most teams are happy if a handful of their stars manage to win the Most Valuable Player award. Yankees have won the MVP twenty times, while three players

(Joe DiMaggio, Mickey Mantle, and Yogi Berra) have swept the honors three times each. The Yanks are, if anything, even stronger in the category of home runs. Babe Ruth alone won the title ten times while with New York (he also won twice in Boston—when he was a pitcher!), while the team has, altogether, copped 26 home run titles, far more than anyone else. The Yankees win, place, or show in almost every statistic. Even the squad's pitching, always its weakest link, has still been marked with outstanding performances from some of the games best hurlers: Whitey Ford, Catfish Hunter, Lefty Gomez, Herb Pennock, Red Ruffing, and Waite Hoyt.

Then there are the players. Other teams—the Cardinals, the Dodgers, the Giants, the Red Sox, and one or two others—have certainly supplied the game with some of its most legendary figures. One, in fact—the Giants—has more people in the Hall of Fame than the Bronx Bombers. But who can match a line-up that includes Ruth, Gehrig, DiMaggio, Dickey, Berra, Mantle, Maris, Jackson, Winfield, Mattingly? The answer: nobody.

Even today, with the Yankees turning in during the 1980s one of their worst performances ever, both the team and the stadium it plays in continues its hold on the imagination of the public, both in North America and across the world. George Steinbrenner's problems, Don Mattingly's injury, and Andy Hawkins' frustrating no-hitter, which the pinstripers still managed to lose, all captured the national spotlight in 1990, even though the team remained stuck in last place.

As for Yankee Stadium, thousands of fans each year brave the rigors of The Bronx's "mean streets" simply to drive up to the park, walk around, and take a few pictures of "the House that Ruth Built." Groundskeepers and security men in the facility are sometimes offered bribes by fans who are willing to spend more than a ticket costs just to get a chance to look around and, perhaps, walk out a bit on that almost mythic field on which Ruth, Gehrig, DiMaggio, and the other legends played. If baseball has a temple, Yankee Stadium is it.

Surprisingly, in this world in which so few things live up to their billing, Yankee Stadium is one sight that rarely disappoints. Stuck as it is in an unappealing neighborhood, far from the glittering lights and fabled sights of downtown Manhattan, the place nevertheless remains one of the best designed ballparks. It is almost impossible to buy a really bad seat in the park. And if the food in Yankee Stadium isn't all that great, and if the prices for it are on the steep side, Yankee's immaculate housekeeping and fresh-painted look is very impressive, particularly when the park's neat appearance is contrasted with the somewhat run-down look of nearby Shea Stadium.

For sixty years now, attending a game at Yankee has been one of the greatest experiences the sport can offer. As far as we are concerned, it still is.

The Team

In 1900, responding to the near monopoly that the powerful National League had established over the sport, a group of baseball enthusiasts centered around Ban Johnson and Charles Comiskey created the American League. Composed of new teams created out of whole-cloth, such as the Boston Puritans (later the Red Sox), as well as a few squads lifted from

the Nationals, the new and untested league took the field in 1901, beginning a season that was to prove a surprising success.

Many major cities were represented in the new league. Initial franchises went to such important towns as Chicago (today's White Sox), Detroit (now the Tigers), and Cleveland (currently the Indians). One city that was left out was New York. For one thing, the new league had a midwestern base, which prejudiced it against the east coast metropolis. For another, the city already had not one but *two* National League franchises (now the Dodgers and the Giants). Could any town support three baseball teams?

The New Yorkers were determined to find out. One of the squads that had crossed out to the Americans was the Baltimore Orioles, one of the strongest and most innovative squads of the 1890s. Under the new league, though, the Orioles had fallen on hard times. Was it possible that their franchise was available?

As it turned out, it was—for $18,000. Thus, under circumstances that remain disputed to this day, the Orioles moved to the "Big Apple," beginning play there in 1903. Over time, they became the New York Yankees. (The current Orioles, by the way, are actually descended from the St. Louis Browns.)

For their first two decades in New York, the team was known first as "the Highlanders" and then as "the Americans." The "Yankees" term, though it was first suggested in 1909, did not become official until 1913. The squad also did not play in The Bronx. The initial home was Hilltop Stadium in Manhattan, which was located around where Columbia Presbyterian Hospital sits today. After that, they were situated in the Polo Grounds, which was also home to the Giants and, later, even to the Mets for a while.

In their first twenty years in New York the Yankees were not all that good. They didn't win a single pennant, though they did manage to challenge for one on several occasions, most notably in 1904 when they lost the flag to Boston on the last game of the season.

During these years, the Yankees fielded few outstanding players. One incredible exception was pitcher "Happy Jack" Chesbro, who in 1904 won 41 games for the new squad and, in time, won himself a place in the Hall of Fame. Chesbro's mark remains the modern era major league record. In 1915, the Yankees made an important move; they first began issuing the pinstriped uniforms that continue to be worn to this day. The idea that the pinstripes came in as a means of disguising Babe Ruth's girth is a great story, but it is nothing more than that.

In 1918, the diminutive Miller Huggins became manager of the club and things began to get better. In 1920, Babe Ruth and pitcher Carl Mays came down from Boston, and, suddenly, the Yankees were hot. In 1921, the team clinched its first pennant, though it lost the series to its Polo Grounds companions the Giants. The next year they took the flag again, but with the same result against the same team.

In 1923, Yankee Stadium opened, with an appropriate home run blast off the bat of Ruth. In that year, too, the Yankees, in their new home, got their revenge on their fellow New Yorkers as they bested the Giants 4–2 in a Series dominated by Ruth's powerful slugging and Herb Pennock's fine pitching performance.

The next twenty years were heaven for Yankee fans, and hell for the fans of just about every other squad in the sport. First under Huggins and then under the equally talented Joe McCarthy, the Yankees built what may have been the finest baseball team ever to take a field. Dominated by a list of hitters whose power was, collectively, so awesome that they were simply called "Murderer's Row," the Yankees reigned over the sport in the 1920s and 1930s. The club made eleven trips to the Series during those years, and they came back with the prize eight times. In 1927, the team set a mark that has been exceeded but once, winning 110 regular season games.

During these two decades, giants strode the field of Yankee Stadium. Principal among these, of course, was Ruth, a man of enormous power and enormous appetites, but also an individual of great humanitarianism; he really did go out of his way to help kids, whatever his other faults may have been. Nearly equal to Ruth in talent but very different in demeanor was Lou Gehrig, a man who carried books by Socrates and Schopenhauer into the locker room and who, learning that he was dying of an incurable disease, nevertheless stood up at Yankee Stadium before thousands of New York fans at his farewell party and told them that he considered himself "the luckiest man in the world."

The team also had characters during those years, one of whom was pitching great Waite Hoyt. A man who once seriously considered a career as a mortician, Hoyt is supposed to have, as a favor to a relative in the business, once picked up a corpse in the Bronx, put it in the trunk of his car, and driven to Yankee Stadium. There he got out, pitched a game (a shutout, in fact) and then drove the body to the funeral home, where it belonged!

If the 1920s and 1930s were spectacular for the "Bronx Bombers," the next two decades only served to confirm the Yankees absolute suzeraignty over the sport. Great new players such as Joe DiMaggio, Bill Dickey, Mickey Mantle, Yogi Berra, and Elston Howard joined the team. So did a new manager, the inimitable Casey Stengel.

The unassuming DiMaggio started the 1940s off with a blast by starting in Yankee Stadium in 1941 a hitting streak that ran an incredible fifty-six games before finally coming to an end in Cleveland. Over the course of the forties, the Yanks made five trips to the fall classic and captured the trophy four times. Perhaps the most exciting year of all was 1949, when the Yanks, in an exciting pennant race with the equally talented Red Sox, captured the flag and showed anyone who had any doubts after the war that baseball was indeed back. The Series performance in the 1950s was even more awe-inspiring. During the decade, the Yanks went to the classic nine times, winning five trophies.

All of this threw baseball fans in the rest of the country into the most profound despair; a phenomenon that inspired one of the most popular Broadway musicals of the era, "Damn Yankees"—based on the book *The Year the Yankees Lost the Pennant*. An amusing concoction, the show was based on the premise that the only way the Yankees could ever be kept from the flag was by one of the other team's (in the musical's case, the Washington Senators) willingness to make a deal with the Devil. It was all very flattering to New York.

As in the past, as the Yanks swept to victory after victory, team members assumed legendary proportions. The talkative, aggressive Mickey Mantle and his withdrawn roommate and friend Roger Maris became a national phenomena in the late 1950s as both pounded out homer after homer. In 1961, the pair set out to smash Babe Ruth's all-time 60 home runs in a season record. Mantle fell a bit short at 54 while Maris, with 61, went all the way, albeit in a few more games than it had taken Ruth to set the mark. Probably just as much a legend as any of the players, though, was the team's oddball manager, Casey Stengel.

Casey would do anything to win. He would also go to any lengths necessary to get an umpire to change a call, in-

cluding faking a fainting spell while out on the field in order to gain sympathy. Stengel tried this for the last time during a conflict with umpire Beans Reardon. Normally, an ump would come to his assistance as soon as Stengel faked his collapse, but on this occasion the Yankee manager found himself flat on the field with no aid. "Then," recalled Casey, "I peeked out of one eye and saw Reardon on the ground, too. I knew I was licked."

No one, not even the Yankees, could keep up the pace the team set in the 1920s and continued through the 1950s. Starting in the early sixties, the Yankees stopped being supermen and became mortals again, who, on occasion, lost. They made five trips to the Series in the sixties, three in the seventies, and only one journey in the 1980s—their worst decade performance since the 1910s.

Yet if the Yankees weren't as commanding a squad during these years as they had once been, they were just as colorful as ever. Reggie Jackson, the flamboyant "Mr. October," thrilled Yankee fans with tons of homers and his famed late season pennant drive performances, just as he drove Yankee managers to distraction with his chest-thumping press statements boasting of his accomplishments. 1970s pitcher Sparky Lyle, who termed the squad "the Bronx Zoo," seemed to be a reincarnation of the 1920s hurler Dazzy Vance as he mingled great on-the-mound performances with off-field antics. Once, after a coffin had been delivered to a Yankee Stadium office (don't ask why), Sparky learned that Bill Virdon, the manager, had scheduled a meeting in the room to discuss an upcoming battle with the Orioles. About half-way through the session, Lyle, dressed like the Mummy, popped out of the coffin and asked in his best Bela Lugosi voice: "How do you pe-itch to Brou-ks Rob-in-son?"

The most celebrated pair of Yankees during this era, though, were the team's owner, the driven George Steinbrenner (known as "George III" to the press), and his on-again off-again manager, Billy Martin. Altogether, the gifted but troublesome Martin was hired and fired five times by Steinbrenner, who apparently couldn't live with the man, or live without him.

In 1990, the Yankees moved into a new and uncertain era as these two men, who had dominated the team for more than a decade, moved out of the picture. Martin perished tragically in a car accident in December 1989, while Steinbrenner, who had long worn out his welcome, was driven out of baseball by the commissioner during the 1990 season, in part as the result of allegations that he had set a spy on one of his former players.

Currently rudderless and coming off their worst season in years, the Yankees have one of their poorest squads ever. Don Mattingly, the team's star and a man who reminds many long-time fans of the young Lou Gehrig, was suffering from serious injury-related problems. Happily, in 1991, he was able to return to baseball. Beyond Mattingly, the Yankees have only a few top players: second baseman Steve Sax and oufielder Jesse Barfield. There are some talented new players wearing pinstripes, too, among them Kevin Maas. Whether they'll be the Mantles and Marises of the 1990s remains to be seen.

Can the Yankees make it to the top of the heap again? It's hard to say. One thing is clear. From where they presently are, they can only go up.

The Stadium

Yankee Stadium may not be perfect, but, as ballparks go, the place is about as close to that ideal as you can get. The facility has an incredible history, rich in associations with the great baseball legends of the past. It is also extremely well-designed. Virtually every seat in the place has an unobstructed view of the game.

One of the classic ballparks, Yankee Stadium was built in 1923 to allow the team to handle the huge crowds that were flocking to the park to see "the Sultan of Swat." Thus, Yankee Stadium came to be called "the House that Ruth built," a term that is still used today.

For the next few decades Yankee Stadium, with its vast decks and its celebrated short right field porch, was the very model of the modern ballpark. By the 1960s though, the place had become dilapidated, as had the neighborhood around it. The Yanks could do nothing about The Bronx, and the thought of moving away from that sacred ground where Gehrig, Mantle, Maris, and DiMaggio had played was, of course, unthinkable. However, they could do something about the ballpark. Accordingly, the team moved to Shea Stadium for two full seasons (1974 and 1975) while Yankee was remodeled from top to bottom. The changes, alas, cost the place some of its "old ball park" feel. Still, though, Yankee's wonderful shape was maintained and its field was kept intact. In truth, if the classic stadium had to be remodeled, the job could hardly have been done with more sensitivity and taste. As a result of these changes, the Yankee Stadium we know today was born.

Yankee is located in the South Bronx, smack in the center of an urban neighborhood that has few attractions. On the plus side, the area is very accessible to the major highways passing through New York. Though going to Yankee by car may not be the best opton for everyone, you'll encounter few difficulties if you do decide to drive to the game. To the negative, the area around the park is only a step up from a slum. The run-down stores, decaying apartment buildings, and broken-glass litered streets that frame Yankee Stadium look unsafe for a good reason: they are. However, the area is so well policed during and after contests that security, so long as you don't wander too far from the crowd, is no real concern.

The stadium itself sits next to "Lou Gehrig Plaza," a pleasant, cobblestoned area where, before and after each game, you'll find a variety of vendors selling pretzels, hot dogs, souvenirs, and the like. If you are yearning for one of the Yankee's celebrated "dirty water dogs," this is the place to buy it. You'll find that the weiners outside the park are cheaper and tastier than the ones within. Other than a fairly interesting street scene of vendors, scalpers, and fans, there's only one thing to detain you in this area, and that's the enormous smokestack you'll see rising from the base of the plaza. If you step away from it a bit and think about it, you'll note that the stack is in the shape of a bat. Today it serves as a well-known gathering place for youth groups and dating couples. "Meet me at the bat" is a phrase whose meaning is understood throughout the metropolitan area.

On stepping inside Yankee Stadium, you'll note almost immediately that the place has a fresh-painted look about it; concession stands are color-coordinated and nicely spaced, corridors are wide, and all the bathroom facilities are in top working order. Indeed, it seems almost as though the park opened yesterday, instead of 1923. You will also be impressed with Yankee Stadium's absolute cleanliness. George Steinbrenner, whatever his faults, was something of a bear about neatness and making sure that everything looked right when the gates swung wide. This, at least, is one area in which the man is liable to be missed.

We cover the seating arrangements elsewhere, so we won't belabor the subject here except to point out that the percentage of seats with good views as opposed to those with poor ones is outstandingly high in Yankee Stadium.

Appointments in the stands, as well as throughout the park, are a pleasing blue and white. Chairs in all areas of the stadium except the bleachers are quite comfortable.

It's the field that people come to Yankee Stadium to see, and it is a sight to behold. A vast expanse of green open to the sunshine behind the bleachers but otherwise cradled within Yankee's in-close stands, the area features a natural grass playing surface. The field's dimensions are famous. The left field foul pole is set at 318', center field is a long 408', while right field is the area of the "short porch," an effect only suggested by the 310' marking at the right field foul pole.

There are a number of things of interest behind the outfield wall. Above everything you'll see an attractive arched façade—a remnant of the old Yankee Stadium. Near the middle of this area are the scoreboards and also the park's creative video display area.

Below the façade and behind the left field wall is Yankee Stadium's evocative "Monument Park" (see Features), the touring of which will add much to your enjoyment of a visit to the stadium. To the left of the park is the visitors' bullpen, while to the right is the Yankee bullpen. There are baseball legends connected with this locale, too. During his career with the team, the brash and confident Whitey Ford would often see to it that a table with a checked cloth, a full dinner service, and candles was set up in the pen during his starts. He'd also order hero sandwiches for all, saying to the squad's relievers, "Since you guys won't be working tonight, I though you ought to at least enjoy yourselves."

Like Whitey's relievers, you won't be working either during your trip to Yankee Stadium. Instead, you'll be feasting, too; but with eyes and ears as you take in one of the most perfect settings for a game of baseball that has ever existed, or is likely to exist.

Highlights

So much baseball history has happened in Yankee Stadium we could easily devote pages to this category alone, and still not cover the topic fully. Instead, we will simply supply a list hitting a few but far from all of the top moments.

The 1920s saw the opening of Yankee Stadium on April 18, 1923, an event highlighted by the park's first homer, which came off the bat of the Bambino himself. June 1, 1925, marked the date of Lou Gehrig's first appearance in the line-up while September 30, 1927, was the day Ruth hit his celebrated 60th home run.

The 1930s saw Lou Gehrig's consecutive games streak of 2,130 come to an end. That, however, occurred in Tiger Stadium on May 2, 1939. July 4 of the same year was "Lou Gehrig" day, when the dying hero gave his famous speech saying he was "the luckiest man in the world."

DiMaggio's hitting streak, which began at Yankee on May 15, 1941, started the club off on another successful decade. It also saw that Yankee great of a previous generation, Babe Ruth, make his final appearance at the park on June 13, 1948.

The Yankees' star of the 1950s, Mickey Mantle, suited up and headed out on April 17, 1951. That same year saw the retirement of DiMaggio. Don Larsen, not one of the game's greatest pitchers, nevertheless immortalized himself in the park on October 8, 1956, when he hurled not only the sole "no-hitter" in Series history, but also the only "perfect."

Roger Maris got the sixties off to a fine start, topping Ruth's old home record by banging out number 61 on October 1, 1961. The 1970s saw the first of Billy Martin's many appearances as manager on August 1, 1975. On October 18, 1977, the boisterous Reggie Jackson proved that he was "Mr. October"

indeed by smashing out three homers to lead the Yanks to their twenty-first World Championship.

Though the 1980s have not been the New Yorker's finest decade, there have been some magic moments. In 1983, the club celebrated the Fourth of July with a Dave Righetti "no-hitter" thrown against the team's great rivals, the Red Sox. On September 29, 1987 Don Mattingly got his turn to tuck it to the Sox, smashing a homer that set the all-time record (six) for the number of grand slams hit in a season.

Fans

In the seats behind us a woman old enough to be a mother — indeed, possibly old enough to be a grandmother — stands up every inning or so to do a bump and grind in time with the music, which seems to be blaring everywhere. Seeing Toronto's famed outfielder nearby, she starts shouting endearments out to the field. "Mookie! Mookie!" she cries, "I love your buns!" Some of the surrounding fans applaud and others laugh. The woman's husband just slaps his palms to his forehead, shakes his head, and says nothing.

Meanwhile, below us, another "character" strolls by. This one wears cymbals and carries a stick holding, on the bottom, a tiny drum, and on the top a sign that declares that "MATT (Don Mattingly) NEEDS A FAT BAT!" The crowd seems to like him, too, and they applaud whenever he passes. He, for his part, gives all a benediction, similar to those the Pope offers. Possibly he thinks he is the Pope.

Finally, next to us is a rather rotund fan who, but for his rather wild eyes, looks for all the world like a Manhattan executive — which, for all we know, is exactly what he might be. Throughout the contest he keeps popping up and turning to the audience, waving his arms manically and leading cheers. For awhile the audience gleefully follows along until they (and we) realize that the man is under the impression that he's at Shea Stadium. (His yelling "Go Mets!" was the tip-off). Then the approbation turns to boos, and, after awhile, he sits down, shuts up, and probably starts to wonder just where the heck he is.

You, however, should have no doubts, for the scenes above could occur in only one of two places; Yankee Stadium or Bellvue. We *think* we were at Yankee Stadium.

Go to any Yankee game and you'll see two shows, one on the field and one in the stands. Which one provides more entertainment is something we wouldn't care to comment on!

What makes a Yankee fan? Aside from a slight touch of insanity, which probably comes staring too long at such mythic figures as Mantle, Ruth, Gehrig, and Martin (after all, the ancients believed the insane had been "touched by the gods"), Yankee fans have certain attributes in common which separate them from all others.

One that is clearly evident is knowledge. Yankee people know their sport in a way that fans in only a handful of other cities do. But unlike fans in, say, Baltimore, they are rarely scholars of the game. Rather, they make a point of learning enough to show that the Yankees are the greatest team ever, in every category. Facts that conflict with the above theory are blithely disregarded — unless they illustrate what a terrible owner George Steinbrenner was.

Partisanship is another key to the Yankee fan psyche, and it manifests itself in both positive and negative ways. On the plus side, you haven't heard anything in your life until you've been in Yankee Stadium when a rally is going. Fans cheer till the rafters shake, stamp their feet until pictures fall off the wall in the club offices and yell a "Charge!" that seems like it could be heard in Cleveland. It's an unforgettable experience.

The negative side of partisanship relates to the way Yankee fans respond to the other team. Be polite to the opposition? Treat umpires with respect, for they are only doing their job? Yankee fans have one catch all phrase for those ideas, which they like to shout towards the field after questionable calls: "YOU HAVE GOT TO BE KIDDING!!" Yankee fans delight in putting opposing players and all umps through hell from the moment they set foot in the stadium. As far as Yankee fans are concerned, visitors and umps are the enemy, deserving no quarter.

Fans of the visiting team receive only slightly more consideration, and, indeed, slightly less if they are from Boston! Indeed, fights between Yankee fans and those who are too enthusiastic in their praise of the opposition are not unheard of.

We had regarded this as one of the bad things about the place, so we talked with some security people about the issue. They patiently explained that while disputes did occur every once in a while, it was all the fault of the visiting fans. "The people from Boston come and are treated well," one officer said, "but then the Sox begin to lose, and they start picking fights." We found the thought of a few hundred Red Sox fans throwing themselves on 30,000 peace-loving New Yorkers pretty funny until we saw a contingent of Toronto enthusiasts do exactly what the officer had alleged during a visit to the park. So maybe it isn't all the Yankee fans' fault.

If Yankee fans are partisans, they are also obsessed with tradition. They love "Monument Park," and delight in taking out-of-towners to the stadium to see it. They also are big respecters of the National Anthem. You won't see a cap on in the park when it's sung, often beautifully, by a popular entertainer or by stars from the Metropolitan or City

Operas. They also each make a point of knowing all the details about the stadium, the club's history, and the biographies of its many great players. At the drop of a hat, any of them will be happy to tell you all about it.

Finally, Yankee fans are uninhibited. Life in the "Big Apple" can get pretty hectic. Yankee Stadium, set far from the bustle of Manhattan, is a place where, by contrast, uptight metropolitans can have a beer or two, cheer a team, and let their true selves come out, knowing that so long as they confine their wildness to the stadium it won't be held against them. Thus people dance in the aisles, do "high fives" with strangers, shout endearments to players, and, in short, let it all hang out. Some of this behavior, it's true, can be vulgar and occasionally offensive. The lion's share of it is entertaining, good-spirited, and fun. Yankee Stadium is a kind of permanent Mardi Gras for New Yorker's minds, bodies, and souls.

It's a tradition in this crazy park that at the end of every game, win or lose, "New York, New York" is played. Invariably, a very substantial portion of the fans will stick around to dance it out. After a night at Yankee Stadium, we bet you'll feel like boogying, too.

Getting There

One of the surprising things about Yankee Stadium is that, nearly alone of the classic old parks, it is pretty easy to get to by car. Particularly if you are traveling from Manhattan, though, going to Yankee Stadium by subway or cab is your best option.

By car. Located in the borough of the Bronx, just across the Harlem River from Manhattan, Yankee Stadium is conveniently situated near the intersections of I-80, I-95, and I-87 (the New York Thruway/Major Deegan Expressway). And to think it wasn't even planned that way!

To get to Yankee from such *north* points as Kingston, Albany, and Buffalo, take the New York Thruway (I-87) to New York City, where it becomes the Major Deegan Expressway. From there, proceed to the 161 Street exit, and follow the signs to Yankee Stadium parking.

Those driving from such *southwest* locales as Philadelphia should take the New Jersey Turnpike (I-95) north to the point where it crosses the George Washington Bridge into the "Big Apple." From there, follow I-95, which will now be turned the "Cross Bronx Expressway," to the Major Deegan Expressway (I-87) going south. Proceed along the Major Deegan to the 161 Street exit, and follow the signs to Yankee parking.

If you are going to the game from *northeast* areas like New Yaven and Boston, take I-95 south to the Major Deegan Expressway (I-87) south, and then follow the Deegan to the 161 Street exit.

Long Islanders, who live to the *east*, and those coming from *LaGuardia Airport* should take the Grand Central Parkway west over the Triboro Bridge and then follow the Major Deegan Expressway (I-87) north to the 149 Street exit. From there, follow signs to Yankee Stadium parking.

If you are driving up to the park from Manhattan to the *south*, take the Henry Hudson Parkway north to the Cross Bronx Expressway (I-95) going east. Proceed on I-95 to the Major Deegan (I-87) headed south, and then follow the Major Deegan to the 161 Street exit.

By cab. Cab is a decent alternative if you are going to the game from Manhattan or LaGuardia. Expect to pay about $12 from downtown and about $10 from the airport. Agree on an approximate price before you get in the cab though, as New York cabbies are infamous for taking visitors on the "scenic route" and then charging accordingly.

By subway. Particularly if you are coming from Manhattan, subway is the best way to get to the game. From downtown, take any IND 6th Avenue D or CC train northbound to the 161 Street/River Avenue Station. It's an easy walk from there to Yankee Stadium. The charge for the subway is $1.15.

Parking

The parking situation at Yankee Stadium is OK, but it isn't any better than that. The Kinney Company runs a variety of lots around the park, all priced at a fair $4. Some are very close to the stadium, others are a block or two away. Overall, there are enough spaces to take care of most games, but at very crowded contests parking can and does run out.

We suggest that you try to arrive at the park early, say at least an hour before the game. That way you'll be able to find an in close parking spot and you'll also have time to enjoy batting practice and to tour "Monument Park" (see *Features*). If you arrive just before the first pitch, you probably will find a parking space. However, if you end up in one of the more distant lots, you'll find yourself walking past the Bronx House of Correction on the way into the Stadium. Not a pleasant thought when you contemplate that, if you are at a night game, you'll be walking back past the House at 11 P.M.

Tickets

You can get Yankee tickets by mail or phone, or you can pick them up in person at the stadium's advance ticket office.

To get tickets by mail, send your order to the club at: New York Yankees, Mail Order Department, Yankee Stadium, Bronx, NY 10451.

Include the number of seats, the locations, and the dates you want along with your payment in full by check or money order. The Yankees also assess a fairly reasonable $1.75 service charge, which you should include as well.

Yankee phone ticket orders are handled by TicketMaster at (212) 307-7171. If you call, have your major credit card and a seating chart handy. You'll be assessed a service charge here, too.

The Yankees advance ticket office is located at the park, and it is open from 9 A.M. to 5 P.M. seven days a week throughout the season, as well as during and shortly after all home night games.

Availability. With 57,545 seats, Yankee Stadium is one of the bigger parks in the majors. In recent years, attendance at the facility has been very good without being fantastic. Unlike some of the other clubs, the Yankees have never surpassed the 3,000,000 mark. Generally, you can anticipate that about 2.7 million fans will pass through the turnstiles in a season.

All of this means that ticket availability is good. Games against such rivals as Toronto and, especially, Boston, can get pretty packed. Other than that, even if you show up at the park at the last minute you will almost certainly find a seat somewhere. Of course, the further you order in advance, the better that seat will likely be.

Costs. By the standards of New York City, where a seat at a Broadway play now goes for about $45, Yankees tickets are one of the town's better entertainment values. Twelve dollars, in fact, will buy you the best seat in the house—if, of course, it is available. Overall, Yankee spots aren't cheap, but they compare pretty favorably to prices at such other classic parks as Fenway and Wrigley.

Generally speaking, you get what you pay for with Yankee seats. In fact, if you limit yourself to the basic rule of trying to get spots in the lowest rows possible as near the baselines as can be arranged, you'll do fine. One of the best designed parks in the game, Yankee Stadium has lots of fine spots, and almost none that won't do in a pinch.

In 1990, Yankee ticket prices were as follows: Lower and Loge Box Seats ($12); Tier Box Seats ($11.50); Lower Reserved ($10); Tier Reserved ($8); Bleachers* ($4.50).

Rainouts. It rains quite a bit in New York during the summer. Accordingly, the Yankees end up cancelling three or four games a season due to bad weather. If you get caught in a downpour, your ticket will be exchanged for a future game. If a return trip to the "Big Apple" isn't in your plans, drop a note explaining this to the Yankee ticket office along with your stubs and your money will be refunded.

Seating

We have made the point several times in this book that the classic baseball shape is a "U." Actually, that's not strictly true. The true model for the perfect ballpark is the bell of a fluted champagne glass. Unfortunately, it's impossible on a typewriter keyboard to show exactly what *that* looks like, so we haven't used the term; instead we've substituted the "U." Now, though, we can show you what this ideal park looks like. Just take a gander at the following seating chart for Yankee Stadium.

You'll note three things about this design. First, it wraps the seats on every level of the infield right over the action, which is just where they belong. You don't find in this form the "midriff" bulge that you see in the round stadiums. Next, this design fans out with the outfield, as, of course, it must. But once again, seats in this area are about as close to the field as they could

possible be. Finally, seats at the very end of the stadium tail back in towards center field. This has the effect of focusing the eyes of those seated in this area, which is the furtherest from home plate, directly on the infield. This, in our view, is what a baseball park should be like. It is too bad that so few of them actually look this way.

Many ballparks boast that "every seat is a good seat." Yankee Stadium is one of only a handful of places where this is generally true. There are no obstructions in the park to speak of, and while those seated in the top rows of the upper deck are quite far from the action, they at least have a complete view of the field.

The most expensive seats in the park are Lower and Loge boxes ($12). Both sections are composed of comfortable blue plastic-and-metal chairs with decent legroom. Lower boxes run from foul post to foul post directly back from the field. Loge boxes cover the same ground from a level above.

There is really nothing terribly wrong with any of these spots. The Lower level is probably preferable, as it is a bit closer to the action. However, since most of the season ticket holders are seated here, your chances of getting into one of the really close rows probably isn't very great. Thus, the choice between these sections is probably a draw. If you order early, you stand a decent shot of snagging baseline seats in this area. In Lower boxes they run from about 240 even (left field) to 241 odd (right field). Upstairs in Loge they go from around even 440 (left field) to 441 odd (right field).

Tier level boxes ($11.50) are the next in price and in quality. Located a level higher than Loge, spots out of the baselines here are a bit too far from the action to justify the high price. On the other hand, those over the batter's box area have an ideal bird's eye view of the

---

*Sold on the day of the game only.

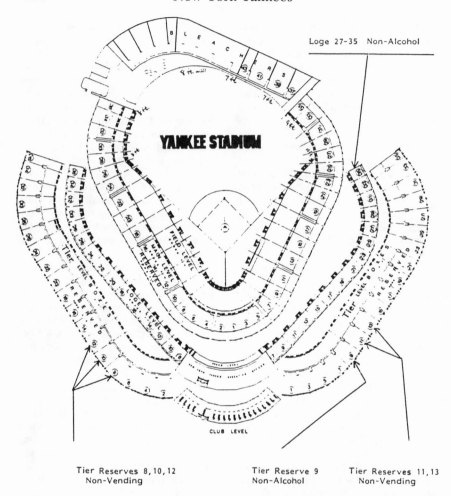

Loge 27-35 Non-Alcohol

Tier Reserves 8,10,12   Tier Reserve 9   Tier Reserves 11,13
Non-Vending   Non-Alcohol   Non-Vending

Seating chart, Yankee Stadium.

proceedings, and are better seats than many of the more expensive Lower and Loge boxes. If you stay in the baselines, which go from near even 640 (left field) to odd 641, you'll do very well here.

There is absolutely nothing wrong with Lower Reserve seats ($10), and the price is right. Located on the lower deck past the field seating areas, these spots are further from the action, have longer rows, and are a bit cramped for legroom. However, from any seat you'll have a full view of the field. You are

bestoff, as always, trying to stay in the baselines here, which go from even 16 (left field) to odd 15 (right field). We can be less positive about the Tier Reserve seats ($8). Like all upper deck nonbox seats, these spots are too far from the play for our liking. Still, the lively crowd that congregates in this area will make you feel like you are part of the game—you certainly shouldn't skip a Yankees contest if these are the only spots available. Baselines in this are run from 16 even (left field) to 15 odd (right field) and it would be unusual if you were not able to get a seat in these sections.

The Yankee bleachers, as we mention elsewhere, are something else. Still, if you don't mind (or prefer) being surrounded by a wild and crazy crowd, you'll find that the views in this area are perfectly acceptable, though the blue backless bench seats are fairly uncomfortable. If you do choose the bleacher seats, try to sit on the right field side. Yankee Stadium has a short right field "porch," so that if you select a space in this area you will be that much closer to the action.

Special Needs

Parking. Parking for the physically disabled is located near the stadium at the lot on 157 Street and 151 Street. Show your sticker or your plate to the attendant as you enter parking and you will be directed to this area.

Seating. Wheelchair seating is available in the park at Row K of the field box level. These are outstanding spots. Those located within the baselines (see chart) are among the best seats in the stadium.

The park also offers a "family reserved" no-alcohol seating section on the Loge level. These are neither the best nor worst spots in this admirable area. Thus, they represent a good option for those who wish to take advantage of this service.

Food and Features

Food. You won't go hungry, but food is not one if the principal strengths of Yankee Stadium. Although the selection is good, prices are pretty outrageous and lines at concession stands can be daunting.

Before covering the possibilities, we feel we should advise you of something that every New Yorker already knows; namely the fact that the hot dogs in Yankee Stadium aren't so hot! If you really relish one of New York baseball's celebrated "dirty water dogs," buy a couple from one of the horde of vendors outside the park and bring them in with you. You will find that they are cheaper and taste better.

As you would expect at a classic stadium such as Yankee, standard baseball fare tops the menu: popcorn, pretzels, jumbo hot dogs, and Steve's ice cream. Other popular items include French bread pizza, hamburgers, knishes (Jewish potato and cheese pasteries), and chicken fingers with fries.

The *Food Court* area, located at the field level behind section 20, has the best selection of specialities in the park. Items available here include deli sandwiches (roast beef, corned beef, ham), buffalo wings, tasty Italian sausages, and Louisiana red hots.

Drinks. Yankee fans, like baseball enthusiasts everywhere, have a taste for beer but it's a taste that can be expensive in this stadium. Talk about a stiff drink! Those who prefer more exotic brews will find them available too, at prices that are no worse than the domestics. The *Food Court* area has "Beers of the World" concession where you can get Corona, Fosters, Heineken, and others. Here, too, you will also find good spring water, though why it's necessary we don't know, for New York City has some of the world's purest and best tasting tap water. Soft drinks are also available in the stadium, of course, and they are a lot more resonable in price than the beer. Finally, those looking for mixed drinks or wine will also have their tastes satisfied. The *Pinstripe Pub*, on the field level behind Section 11 offers a full range of alchoholic beverage at the usual terrible prices.

Features. The Yankees have the most interesting and evocative in-park feature in baseball.

Called "Monument Park," it is a special area behind the left field wall in which there are bronze plaques honoring many of the Yankee greats of the past in a nicely landscaped setting. Each plaque has the name of the player or manager, his number, a bust, and a paragraph outlining his achievements in the game. Among the all-time greats profiled on this short walk through Yankee (and baseball) history are Lou Gehrig ("A man, a gentleman, and a great ballplayer"), Babe Ruth, Joe DiMaggio ("The Yankee Clipper"), Mickey Mantle ("The most popular player of his era"), Casey Stengel, Lawrence Peter ("It ain't over 'til it's over") "Yogi" Berra, Whitey Ford, Miller Huggins, Elston Howard ("A man of great gentleness and dignity"), and the most recent inductee, Billy Martin ("A Yankee forever").

It is simply impossible to stroll through this area without being deeply affected by the accomplishments of these players and by what the Yankees have meant to baseball. In truth, if you visit the stadium and don't stop by "Monument Park," you will have missed a vital part of the Yankees baseball experience. If you want to go, though, come to the stadium early. The Yankees close this area off to the public about a half hour before game time.

Assistance

The Yankees have a "Patron Service Office" in the park, located at the field level behind section 15. This is the place to go if you've lost your keys, are being bothered by seat jumpers, or have any questions about the stadium.

Safety and Security

Safety. Many fans from outside New York, who have heard about crime problems in the Bronx in general and at Yankee Stadium in particular, have been hesitant to attend Yankee games. That's too bad, because these folks are, by not going, depriving themselves of one of most rewarding experiences in baseball. In the next paragraph or two, we'd like to examine this issue as we've seen and experienced it.

First, there are security problems both inside and outside the park, although both are often overstated. Within the park, the principal area of difficulty is the bleachers. Though it's perfectly possible (and, indeed, likely) that you and your family could sit in this section without the slightest disturbance, incidents of drunkenness and fighting do happen from time to time. Illegal drug use in the bleachers is not unknown either; New York fans don't call this area the "Yankee reefers" without reason. As bad as all this may sound, though, you should also know that the Yankee's internal security force is extremely good at pouncing on trouble the moment it breaks out. If they need any help, the New York City police's precinct station happens to be in Yankee Stadium's basement. The stadium's policy on troublemakers is, moreover, pretty hard-nosed. Drunken fans and those involved in fights are hustled out of the facility pronto. Drug users are photographed, ejected, and, if they are in the park on either a corporate or their parent's season tickets, they get their boss or parents called. If they show up in the park and try it again (which is why the photo is kept) they get escorted down to the police station, where charges are filed. Thus, while we can't promise you that your visit to Yankee Stadium will be problem-free, we do believe that any difficulties you do run into are unlikely to keep you from being able to enjoy the game.

As far as the security situation outside the park goes, the neighborhood around Yankee Stadium is neither nice nor safe. Before and after the game you should experience no problems at all, as the district is heavily patrolled by both uniformed and undercover police. On the other hand, this is not a place to hang around in, either. After the contest is over, go back to your car or head to the subway with the crowd. If you do decide to, say, go over to Stan's Sports Bar for a drink after the game, do it with a group. If you act sensibly, there's no reason why you and your family shouldn't go to Yankee Stadium. Indeed, we'd suggest that you do go.

Health. The major health problems that you are likely to run into in Yankee Stadium are (1) getting too much sun in the bleachers or along the ends of the right field line; (2) getting hit with stray balls; and (3) (and most seriously) falling off the upper deck while reaching for a foul. If you bring sun tan lotion, keep your mind on the game, and resist the temptation to go that extra inch for a Don Mattingly ball, you'll have few difficulties. If you do have a problem, you'll find the Yankee's top-rate first aid staff located behind section 2 on the field level.

Mementos

Souvenirs. Yankee fans love to dress in pinstripes. Indeed, there are few parks in the Majors where participants are more intent on looking like the players. If you want to pretend your Steve Sax, you'll find an ample selection of pennants, shirts and the like at the "Yankees Gift Shop," which can be found behind section 14 at the main level, and in other locales as well. Particularly popular are shirts with #23—Don Mattingly's number.

Foul Balls. The best place to catch a foul ball at Yankee Stadium is at the field level, just past first base and third. You may, however, have difficulty in finding any seats in the area. A good alternative would be 601 and 601 in the upper boxes. The Yankees give would-be fielders a real incentive to perform in this area, as they often award handsome Wilson A3000 gloves to the fan who makes the most spectacular catch of the night.

Autographs. The best place to get an autograph is around the press gate, which is near Gate 4. This is where both the Yankees and the visitors leave the stadium.

OAKLAND ATHLETICS
The Coliseum

Baseball isn't just the history of great players and famous franchises. It is also the story of outstanding teams. Not franchises, but teams assembled in specific seasons within a franchise—a unique gifted group of players that comes together under a manager capable of forging their individual skills into a powerful, cohesive unit, capable,

for a while at least, of reigning over the sport.

This is something that doesn't happen very often, and it doesn't last long. Still, there have been teams that have dominated the game during their times. The most famous of these was the "Murderer's Row" Yankees of the late 1920s; indeed, their 1927 edition may well have been the finest squad ever to take the field. But there have been others too: Cincinnati's "Big Red Machine" of the mid-seventies, the Dodgers' 1950s "Boys of Summer," Casey Stengel's 1950s Yanks, the Card's 1930s "Gashouse Gang," and perhaps a few more.

This rare phenomenon may be happening today in Oakland, California. One thing that baseball play in the late 1980s made clear is that manager Tony LaRussa has assembled for the A's the most talented club in baseball. Outstanding members of the Athletics include base-stealing artist and Future Hall of Famer Rickey Henderson, sluggers Jose Canseco, Harold Baines, Mark McGwire, and Carney Lansford, and pitching aces Dave Stewart, Bob Welch, and the deadly Dennis Eckersley. This is a lineup that simply can't be matched.

But does it constitute one of the all-time great teams? By winning three staight pennants decisively, the Oaklanders clearly established their claim to baseball dominance. Had the A's, as expected, won the 1990 Series crown, few people would have disputed their contention—which they have never minded voiceing—that they deserve to be numbered among the few truly all-time outstanding organizations. The club's 4–0 defeat, though, at the hands of the unheralded Cincinnati Reds put the A's claim to that distinction just beyond their reach: if they stretch they can touch the laurels, but they cannot quite grasp them. Another Series victory, though, and they'll be entitled to seize the crown. If the A's by some misstep falter now, they will go down as the most awesome "almost greats" that the game has ever seen.

The betting in this corner is that the A's, despite their temporary set-back, will still manage to slug, tag, hurl, and boast their way into the halls of all-time baseball glory. Love the A's or hate them (the only choices, since no one is lukewarm about this team) the A's have the players, the manager, the support, and the will to just keep on winning.

The vast popularity of the Athletics is drawing fans from around the nation to Oakland. What do they find? The Coliseum is not one of the more attractive ballparks. Nor does it rate very high in terms of serving up great food for the fans and providing lots of nice amenities. Moreover, the area around the facility, which is a mixed industrial and commercial area in south Oakland, isn't all that appealing. Just as the Pittsburgh Pirates may have the prettiest external setting for a ballgame, the A's could well have the ugliest.

But these drawbacks are offset by other assets. The park is easy to reach by both car and subway. It is close to a wide range of restaurants and hotels. The Coliseum itself, while it may not be beautiful, is serviceable. As the A's like to point out, their stadium is painted in two primary colors: blue, as in sky, and green, as in natural grass. At the Coliseum you will see both colors in abundance.

Most out of town fans, however, don't come to Oakland to peer at a beautiful sports facility, or even to enjoy an expansive sky. They drive or fly hundreds of miles to see Rickey Henderson, Jose Canseco, and Dennis Eckersley play. They come because they understand that, at this moment in time, Oakland is where baseball history is being made.

Actually, the business of making history isn't anything new to the Athletics. It's a task that they've been about for many of the past ninety years.

The Team

In 1876, on a windy corner in what is now downtown Philadelphia, professional baseball in the U.S. had its beginning as the Philadelphia Athletics faced the Boston Red Stockings in what was the first National League game ever.

Boston won the contest, though it didn't cover itself with glory in the rest of that first season. The squad went on, though, to become the Boston (and now Atlanta) Braves. The A's folded before the season ended.

Still, though the team was gone, Quaker City residents remembered the name with fondness. Thus when, in 1901, the new American League decided to site a franchise in Philadelphia, they decided to recall the earlier moniker. The Philadelphia Athletics was born, a team destined to be owned and managed through all but a handful of the next fifty years by the great Connie Mack.

During most of its first two decades in the American League, the new organization performed well. It also assembled for a few years one of those outstanding teams the occasional appearance of which has been the principle distinguishing feature of the A's up to the present day.

In the first decade of the modern era, the Athletics performed creditably, copping pennants in 1902 and 1905 and doing well in the standings during the other years. During the 1905 Series, Christy Mathewson's stellar pitching for the Giants gave the New Yorkers the title. Still, it had been a good decade.

Certainly the outstanding player on the A's during this period was the great, and dissolute, Rube Waddell. A carouser and all-around pain in the neck, Waddell's antics had gotten him thrown off the Pirates in 1901. Mack decided that he had to have the pitcher for the A's. After a futile series of letters and telegrams fired off to the hurler's home town, to which Rube didn't bother to respond, Mack despaired of ever signing the man. Finally, though, Waddell sent Mack a one line wire: "Come and get me."

Mack did exactly that. Getting Waddell to agree to join the Athletics, Mack led Rube back to the train station.

There were a number of stops, though, as the pitcher hauled Mack into one shop after another to get his new manager to pay his debts. Finally, they had just about reached the platform when Mack and Waddell were met by a gang of seven men who slowly formed a semicircle around the pair. Connie braced for the worst when the leader of the group stuck out his hand. "We've been sent to thank you," the fellow declared, "for taking *him* out of town." Mack accepted their accolades and hurried off with his ace.

During the 1910s, Mack assembled the first of his two great teams. Boasting Hall of Fame pitching stars Charles "Chief" Bender (who really was an Indian), Eddie Plank, and pre–Ruth round-tripper king Frank "Home Run" Baker, the A's were awesome. They took four pennants (1910, 1911, 1913, 1914) and won the Series the first three times. The 1914 contest looked, on paper, to be the easiest, for their opponents were the hapless Boston Braves, who had been in last place (their usual position) as recently as July. Nevertheless, the Braves pulled off one of the greatest upsets in Series history, blanking the A's 4–0.

Mack was so infuriated at this poor performance that he broke up his team. That turned out to be a decision the A's would pay for as they quickly sank to the cellar — and stayed there for most of the next fifteen years.

In the late twenties, though, Connie got a second shot at glory. New stars signed on with the Athletics, and in short order the organization had a line-up that was the near equal of the New York Yankees. The star hurler of the squad was the terse and tempermental Lefty Grove, who would pound his locker in fury when he lost a game, but, as later teammate Ted Williams noted, would always be sure to pound things with his right hand. Backstopping Grove was Mickey Cochrane, possibly the greatest catcher of all time. Supplying power —

and ferocity—was the great Jimmy Foxx, whose fitting nickname was "the Beast." All three are now in the Hall of Fame.

This potent trio lead the A's to three pennants in three years (1929, 1930, and 1931). They won the first two Series, against the Cubs and the Cards, but then the "Gashouse Gang" from St. Louis got their revenge by coming back and beating Philly in the third.

The 1929 classic, though, was the source of one of baseball's great stories. During the regular season, Connie Mack had decided that it was time to let go of Howard Ehmke, an aging second rate hurler. He called Ehmke into his office to give him the bad news.

Realizing that the club was headed for the Series, Ehmke pleaded for his job. "Please let me stay, Mr. Mack. I just know there's one more great game left in this arm."

Mack paused and, as he later said, got a hunch. "OK," he agreed, "you stay. But I want you to keep an eye on the Cubs. I've decided that you're going to pitch the Series opener."

When, a few weeks later, Connie announced that the veteran had been picked to open the Series over Grove and over 24-game winner George "Moose" Earnshaw, Philadelphian—never the most trusting fans—howled with outrage. Ehmke silenced the complaints, though, by trotting out to the mound and shutting the Cubs down, setting in the process what, at that time, was the one-game World Series strikeout record.

The Athletics' record was too good to last, and it didn't last. After their defeat to the Cardinals, the team headed back to the cellar and stayed there for a long, long time.

The fans eventually began to blame the A's poor performance on Mack's alleged senility, until in the early 1950s, the "Grand Old Man" of baseball was nudged aside. Still, things didn't get better.

Facing dismal attendance, the club decamped for Kansas City in 1955. During their first campaign there they placed sixth in what would turn out to be the best season in their dismal twelve year sojourn in the Midwest. They also acquired a new owner, the innovative, irascible Charles Finley. Anxious to get out of Kansas City where, in truth, he had overstayed his welcome, Finley successively tried to move his club to Dallas and then to Atlanta. Finally, he succeeded in taking the A's to Oakland. There they have matched the greatest accomplishments of their Philadelphia glory days.

Charles Finley, as most baseball fans know, was something of a character. A tinkerer who was constitutionally incapable of leaving well-enough alone, Charlie O. brought to the game such novelties as orange baseballs and color coded bases, innovations that didn't exactly catch on. He also came up with the desingated hitter, the idea of staging World Series games at night, and the "pinch base runner."

Most of Finley's players over the years despised the man, who was so tight-fisted that he once passed out World Series rings with artificial emeralds. In fact, feelings against the owner ran so deep that, on a plane to the east coast after a World Series game in which Finley tried to fire a second baseman for making an error, the A's met and held a vote on whether to toss the owner out of the emergency door. The plan was reportedly derailed only when someone pointed out the negative effect depressurization would have on the A's card games!

Liked or disliked though, Finley has to be given credit for one thing; he was a wizard at assembling talented baseball teams. Shortly after arriving in Oakland, Finley began signing such standout players as sluggers Gene Tenace and Reggie Jackson and pitching aces Rollie Fingers and Vida Blue. He also kept Kansas City star Bert

Campaneris, who was so multitalented that during one game in K.C. he played all nine positions!

This group, known as the "Mustache Crew" because of the team's fondness for facial hair, became the first of Oakland's two great baseball dynasties. Three times in the 1970s this squad took the AL pennant (1972, 1973, 1974). On each occasion the Athletics went on to win the trophy, becoming the only team other than the Yankees to win three fall classics in a row.

The "Mustache Crew's" combustible mixture of egos and resentments, though, couldn't be expected to hold together forever, and it didn't. Following a spectacular series of contract disputes with the parsimonious Finley, the team began to fall apart. By the late 1970s, the recently unbeatable Athletics were back in the cellar.

The recruitment of Tony LaRussa as manager in 1986 marks the beginning of Oakland's second dynasty. LaRussa sought out talented people and helped to convince the team's owners that outstanding players were worth the millions that were often required to get them to sign with the team. He also helped the squad develop the aggressive, no-holds barred style of play that the A's are famous for. Probably LaRussa's greatest accomplishment, though, has been in getting his wildly talented team to pool their skills and work together. There are probably a dozen or so baseball players who know in their hearts that they are the greatest player in the game. At least half of them wear the green and gold. Anyone who can get Jose Canseco, Rickey Henderson, and Dennis Eckersley to subsume their own egos and pull toward a common goal deserves to be manager of this or any other year.

LaRussa's work first yielded results in 1988, when the A's took the pennant and walked into the Series against the Dodgers as heavy favorites. L.A. stunned just about everyone by winning the

Series 4–1. In 1989, under similar circumstances, San Franciscans hoped their Giants would pull an upset. It was not to be. Despite earthquake delays, the A's proved unstoppable, winning the contest 4–0 in a result that left many wondering if the Giants had forgotten to bring their bats to the ballpark.

In 1990, it was Oakland's turn to be swept. Still, they have the players, they have the fans, and they have that psychological edge essential for victory. Can their dynasty continue? At this point, there is no reason to believe that they won't do at least as well in the future as they have in the past.

The Stadium

The Oakland Coliseum is named after its somewhat older namesake in Rome. We feel it is only fair to warn you though that any other resemblance stops there.

It's not that the Oakland facility is a terrible place to play ball. It isn't. It is just that the place is undistinguished, with a capital "U."

The Coliseum is located in south Oakland, near the airport and within a mile of San Leandro Bay. The area around it is fairly grim: warehouses, some stores, and a few restaurants along Hegenberger road, telephone poles, factories, and BART tracks. It's not that the area is particularly unsafe; it isn't. The place just isn't all that appealing.

Your first good look at the Coliseum will come when you pull into the parking lot, for the stadium is recessed into the ground and, in any case, doesn't stand particularly high. We regard this as something of an advantage, actually, because a low height in a park usually means that the seats in the top decks are closer to the action than they are in some of the taller facilities. In point of fact, the most impressive looking stadiums—

Riverfront, Three Rivers, and Olympic—often have some of the worst seats. Some of the unprepossessing ones, like the Coliseum, treat their customers better.

As we point out elsewhere, the Coliseum from the outside looks like a bowl buried in the pavement. To its right, you'll see another building, one that resembles a hockey puck. That's the Oakland Arena, home of the NBA Golden State Warriors. For at least a few weeks during the year, it's possible to attend Athletics baseball on one night and go to professional basketball on the next, all of which makes the area around the Coliseum something of a mecca for the sports obsessed.

Unless you are into tailgating (see *Fans*) there is really nothing to detain you outside the park. Once you're inside, you first notice the absence of light at the lowest level. Happily, once you move upstairs you see that most of the decks face the open air outside the facility, giving the place a spacious feel that's kind of nice, particularly if the weather is fine. In fact, from the northwest side of the top deck concourse it's entirely possible, on a clear day, to see over the bay to downtown San Francisco, about fifteen miles away. If you are really eagle-eyed, or if you have binoculars, you should be able to pick out Candlestick, which is slightly to the left of San Francisco's skyscrapers.

On the top deck, too, you almost certainly notice something else: the place is pretty darned windy and, frequently, cold. While the Coliseum isn't the coldest park in baseball—that's its brother across the bay—anyone who travels to Oakland from elsewhere in order to attend a few games would do well to keep in mind Mark Twain's statement that the coldest winter he had ever spent "was July in San Francisco." Dress accordingly.

The interior of the Coliseum bowl looks, well, like the interior of a bowl. The three main decks of the Coliseum

start at just past the left field foul pole and then wrap back to just past the right field foul pole. In the gap between the decks are the stadium's humble, cheap, and raucous bleachers. This area makes you truly sense the recessed nature of the facility, for at the top of the back row of the bleachers is a nicely landscaped hill, complete with a series of attractive green and gold flower pots. No hitter has yet sent a ball over this area, though slugger Rick Monday did once manage to nip the bud off one of the flowers.

Although there are some problems with the seating areas of the Coliseum, we will detail those later. The one great strength of the park is its setting in a natural environment. In many of the newer round ballparks you are closed in, almost a captive in an artificial world of concrete walls, plastic seats, and phony, garish green "grass." This is certainly not the case at the Coliseum. Here the air is fresh, the sky is blue, the grass is green, and the sun is warm on your skin. There are some disadvantages to all of this, to be sure, for the Coliseum is an easy place to both freeze and get a bad sunburn—we know, because they both happened to us! Still, we wouldn't have it any other way.

The Coliseum's field is one of the more individual ones in baseball. Its dimensions *seem* normal enough. The foul poles are set at 330', while the back wall of center field is 408'. Beyond that, though, the Coliseum has attributes that make it a classic "pitcher's park." One aspect of this effect is the weather. During most games, and particularly during night contests, cool moist air drifts over from the nearby bay, which has the effect of almost "sitting" on the ball, keeping its loft down. Also, the wind, as it curves around the deck, has a tendency to blow in, pushing the ball back toward the gloves of Henderson and Canseco. Finally, there's the foul territory issue to consider. To put it simply, the Coliseum has, by far and away, the largest foul territories of any park in baseball. All of which means that if you hit a pop-up stray, God help you. You might just as well head back to the dugout because if it's not too deep, McGwire, Steinbach, or Lansford is going to have it as sure as you're standing there. All of this can lead to exciting play. However, the fat foul territories also have the effect of putting the fans all that much further from the action.

A's admirers are more serious baseball fans than most west coasters, so the team goes out of its way to supply the Coliseum's patrons with information. Past the flowers and over the left field wall is the A's electronic scoreboard, which supplies lots of details. In the same area on the right field side is another display tracking the out-of-town action, so you can stay right on top of the pennant race.

Finally, in center, is the Coliseum's "Diamond Vision" video display. It's impressive, but it runs far too many ads for our taste. About thirty years ago, most baseball parks made a big fuss about the need to remove those old-fashioned billboards ("Call for Phillip Morris!") that used to grace the outfield walls—and can still be seen in some of the minor league parks. The argument was that such displays represented crass commercialism and took away from the dignity of the game. So the baseball clubs got rid of the ugly old things—and replaced them with obnoxious electronic thirty-foot-high beer and soda ads, which blast unasked for images and rock music at you while you try to watch a game in peace. That's not crass commercialism? That doesn't take away from the dignity of the game? Like they say on the broadcasts, "you make the call!"

To summarize, the Coliseum is neither the best baseball park nor the worst. Unlike the Athletics, its strictly middle-of-the-road.

Highlights

Given the Athletics' outstanding record in Oakland, you'd expect the Coliseum to be what it is: a place filled with milestones of recent baseball history. On October 14, 1972, Oakland catcher Gene Tenace made World Series history when he blasted two homers in his first two at bats in the first game of the 1972 fall classic. Thanks, in part, to an outstanding Tenace performance in the rest of the contests, the Athletics went on to their first World Championship since 1931. A year later, on October 21, 1973, "Mr. October" himself, Reggie Jackson, joined Bert Campaneris in smashing out two homers that gave the A's their second trophy in as many years in the seventh game of the 1973 Classic.

Pitching feats have contributed much to getting the A's where they are today. On May 8, 1968, Catfish Hunter threw a rare "perfect" in the Coliseum. On September 28, 1975, in one of baseball's most bizarre moments, four Athletics pitchers (Vida Blue, Glenn Abbot, Paul Lindblad, and Rollie Fingers) combined to toss a single no-hitter.

Other players have accomplished things at the park besides those who wear the green and gold. The great Hank Aaron hit his 750th homer in the Coliseum on June 18, 1976. On June 11, 1990, forty-three-year-old Nolan Ryan delighted the baseball world by hurling his sixth no-hitter in the stadium against the always tough A's.

Fans

West coast transplants who were brought up in such eastern baseball towns as New York and Philadelphia who've had their fill of laid back California fans should close this book, climb into their cars, and head for Oakland. If you like the sorts of fans you saw at Yankee Stadium, Shea Stadium, and the Vet, chances are that you will love the crowd at the Coliseum.

No one could accuse A's fans of being disinterested. During any game their attention remains focused on what's happening on the field. Particularly outside the bleachers, many fans carry walkman radios, so they can keep in touch with the play by play. And Athletics' admirers are partisan to the point of being rabid. They boo opponents, officials, and the fans of opposing teams with mad abandon. Nor are they willing to concede much to the opposition. Let Cecil Fielder hit a home run, say, into the Sierra Nevadas, and you can bet that most Oakland fans will sit in sullen silence while some will boo. At least a dozen others will jump up and shout "Wait till McGwire gets up, you jerk! He'll hit it to the Rockies!" The bleachers fans will do anything in their power to distract visiting players.

Nor will you find sushi in the Coliseum. This is a park where the patrons like peanuts, hot dogs, and, especially, beer. You won't see too many beach bunnies sunning themselves here. Nor will you see too many executives trotting around in three piece suits. Well dressed at the Coliseum, especially in the bleachers, means a tattered old "Spuds McKenzie" T-shirt with cut-offs and sandals. However, some fans don't bother to come well-dressed.

Are you beginning to get the picture? A's fans resemble their team. They're brash, bold, and big-mouthed. Moreover, they don't give two hoots (they'd put it a bit stronger than that) what anyone thinks of them.

Who comes to the games? The Coliseum attracts a working class crowd. There are lots of young men, some kids, some minorities, some hispanics, and a fair number of hard-bitten oldsters who sit with plugs in their ears and scorecards in their laps. This last group, in particular, is composed of very savvy types who critique every decision in

vast detail, and will on occasion rise to join their younger brethren in giving Tony LaRussa, at the top of their lungs, the benefit of their ideas on exactly what he ought to do.

Hero worship is a big thing with this crowd. And their idea of what a hero is centers around one central concept: heroes win. Thus, while some of the A's players may not always exemplify the game's highest standards of modesty, sportsmanship, and decorum, that's a matter of little concern to the average Oaklander, as much as that detail might bother people in Kansas City. What people in Oakland want to know is, is Canseco or Henderson going to help them win? If the fans regard any player as an asset, they'll back him no matter what. If they feel, however, that someone isn't contributing to the effort, they get down on him with a vengeance.

As seriously as it may take the contest though, this is an audience that likes to party, and going to a game in Oakland is a kind of festive experience. Long before the contest starts, groups of fans are tailgating in the parking lot, frying hots on small hibachis, throwing frisbees, and playing poker. You are, of course, welcome to join in. When game time comes, the picnic goods are put away, but the "party attitude" is simply carried into the Coliseum with the fans.

Fans of this sort value their traditions. As at several other parks, fans in the Coliseum claim they invented "the wave." Whether they discovered it or not, they certainly enjoy doing it. During the seventh inning stretch, instead of singing "Take Me Out to the Ballgame" (which would be a bit out of character here), everyone rises to dance out "It Feels So Good," with, of course, special emphasis placed on the "A - A - A" chorus in the lyrics. Indeed, blasting rock and roll music is very much part of the scene here. Particularly popular with fans is the "Bash

Brothers" bash. This male bonding gesture, pioneered by Mark McGwire and Jose Canseco, involves two players smashing forearms together after someone has done something especially right. The A's do it, and, in imitation, so do the fans.

Truth in book writing compels us to tell you that some Oakland fans, particularly in the bleachers, can be pretty hard to take. Most, however, are vibrant, exciting, interesting, and alive. If you like your audiences tough, dogged, flamboyant and voluble, you'll probably like the Oakland fans.

Getting There

Though it isn't set in the world's nicest area, the Oakland Coliseum is pretty easy to get to. Located near many of the bay area's major interstates, getting to the game by car is easy. Travel to the Coliseum by BART, the bay area's subway system, will be an even better option for many. Additional means to get to the park include cab and bus.

By car. The Coliseum is located in an industrial district in south Oakland, only a short distance from San Leandro Bay. The Nimitz Highway (I-880) passes directly by the park.

If you are coming to the Coliseum from such *south* locales as San Jose and San Luis Obispo, take Route 101 north to the point where it joins the Nimitz Highway (I-880) north. Then follow the Nimitz to the 66th Street Exit. From there, follow signs to Coliseum parking.

Those traveing from Sacramento, Reno, and the *east* should take I-80 west to I-580 going toward Hayward. From there, take I-980, going toward downtown Oakland. From I-980, get on I-880 going south and follow to the 66th Street exit. From there, follow signs to parking.

If you are coming from the *west*, which is to say from San Francisco, take the Bay Bridge east to I-580 toward Hayward. From there, follow I-980 to downtown Oakland. In downtown, pick up I-880 going south and follow the above directions.

People driving to the game from such *north* points as Santa Rosa should take Route 101 south to the San Rafael Bridge going west. From there, proceed to I-80 going south. From there, take I-580 toward Hayward, and then pick up I-980 headed for downtown Oakland. Next pick up I-880 south and drive to the 66th Street exit, where you will follow signs to Coliseum parking.

Getting to the park from *Oakland Airport* is easy. Simply follow Airport Drive to the point where it turns into Hegenberger Road and follow signs from there to stadium parking.

Many fans from the Los Angeles and San Diego areas prefer to drive to the bay area via I-5 north. If you are traveling this way, take I-5 to I-580 headed west and then follow I-580 to the Nimitz Highway (I-880) going north. Exit the Nimitz at 66th Street and then proceed to parking.

By cab. Cab would be a good way to get to the game from Oakland Airport; the charge runs around $7.50. If you want to take a cab to the stadium from the San Francisco Airport, on the other hand, be prepared to spend $50.

By bus. If you are arriving at the Oakland airport, bus is a great way to get to the game. Simply pick up any Air-Bart bus from outside the baggage claim area and take it to the Coliseum Station. From there, the stadium is a short walk away. You will pay $1 for this service.

By BART. Taking the bay area's clean and efficient BART subway system to the game will be, for many, the best way to get to the park. Trains serve San Francisco, Berkeley, Oakland, Fremont, and a variety of other bay area locales. From downtown San Francisco, for example, take the Fremont/ Green Line train to the Coliseum

Station. You'll pay $1.90 from most SF locations. From downtown Oakland, take the same train; the charge is $.80. If you do take BART to a night game, though, keep in mind that the Coliseum Station closes down at midnight.

Parking

The Coliseum is surrounded by 9,200 parking spots, all priced at $4. This is enough spaces for most contests, but on occasion overflow lots in the area have to be used. When this happens, you'll be directed to the appropriates spots — which, by the way, are free.

Tickets

You can get Athletics tickets by mail, phone, or you can pick them up in person.

To get A's tickets by mail, simply write to the team at: A's Tickets, PO Box 2220, Oakland, CA 94621.

Indicate the number of tickets you want, the dates, and the locations. You can pay either by check, money order, or by including your Visa of Master-Card number and expiration date. Be sure to include the very high $4 service charge that the Athletics assess.

Phone orders are handled by BASS/TicketMaster at (415) 762-BASS. If you call, be sure to have your credit card ready. You will pay a service charge here, also.

The A's advance ticket office is the best place to purchase your seats, inasmuch as you can take a look at a seating chart and discuss things with the personnel before you buy. The A's ticket office is located at the stadium and is open Monday through Friday from 9 A.M. to 6 P.M., Saturday from 10 A.M. to 4 P.M. and Sundays from 12 P.M. to 4 P.M.

Availability. With 49,218 seats, the Coliseum is one of the smaller parks in baseball. The team that plays in it is wildly popular. This means that if you want seats to an A's game, and particularly if you want good seats, you had better order early.

Weekend contests and games against such long-standing rivals as New York and Boston tend to be most popular. Games against close Western Division rivals also get pretty packed. Particularly if you plan on going to any of these games, early reservations are highly advisable.

Having said that, though, we should point out that actual sellouts are fairly rare. Most of the time, if you show up at the ticket office on the morning of a game you will be able to get something — though it might well be a chunk of nosebleed territory in the upper rows of the third deck.

You could, of course, try to improve the quality of the seats you'll get by doing business with the horde of scalpers wandering the stadium parking lots before games. You might indeed get better seats, but you could also buy counterfeit ones. Worse yet, the person who sells your tickets could be an undercover cop.

Costs. Ticket prices at the Coliseum are pretty fair. Eleven dollars buys the best seats in the house. Moreover, since season ticket sales are only moderate (12,000) you have a chance of getting one of the better spots if you order early enough. On the other side, a modest $3.50 will give you a seat (or, rather, a spot on a bench) in the bleachers. If you find sections within the baselines, there is a fair match between what you pay for a ticket and what the view is worth. Outside the baselines that isn't always true.

A's ticket prices in 1990 were as follows: Mezzanine Loge Box ($11); Field Level ($11); Plaza Level ($10); Upper Reserved ($7); Bleachers ($3.50).

Rainouts. Rainouts are pretty rare in Oakland. Fog, on the other hand, is

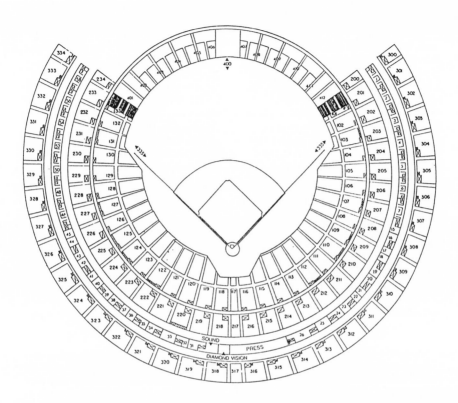

Seating chart, The Coliseum.

quite common. If, however, you should manage to get rained out, or even fogged out, your tickets will be exchanged for a future game.

The team has no policy regarding refunding the tickets of out-of-towners who have no plans to come back to the area. Even so, the organization is fan-oriented enough that we suspect that, if you turn your stubs in to the ticket office with a note explaining this, you will probably get your money back.

Seating

Take a bowl, recess it in the ground, and then cut a noche out of the back. What you will end up with will look very much like the Oakland Coliseum. No one would accuse the place of being beautiful. Still, it serves its purpose, which is to provide a space in which people can play and watch baseball.

Within the bowl are three tiers of seats, shaped in a bit more than a semicircle. Between the arms of the semicircle is a large bleacher area. As a basic rule in the park, the closer you are to the bottom of the bowl and the further your seat is from any of the bleacher areas, the better the chair you will have.

Mezzanine Loge boxes ($11) are rated the best in the park, but we don't know why. Located below the third deck, the Mezzanine seats have the advantage of privacy and a pretty good view, but they are further from the action than virtually all of the Field level spots and even some of those chairs in the cheaper Plaza area. If getting away from the hustle and bustle, though, is important to you, these spots might be fine. If you are going to sit here, try to secure spots in the baseline sections, which in this area run from 10 (right field) to 24 (left field). Consider refusing spots in sections 1 to 3 and 31 to 33, which are beyond the foul poles and are further from the field than many of the bleacher spots.

Field level ($11) seats are our favorites. Set on the 100 deck, which is the closest one to the field, many of the spots have outstanding views. Most of those that don't at least provide an acceptable peek at the action. In this area, if you can get baseline spots (110 to 124) they'll be very fine. Even if you are off the baselines most of the spots will be pretty good, though those in areas 101 to 105 and 133 to 129 are too far down the baselines for our liking.

Basically, everything we said about Field seats would also be true about Plaza level ($10) spots, so long as you keep in mind that the chairs in this area are a level higher and a bit further back from the action than those in Field are. Baseline spots here run from 210 to 224. Sections to be avoided include 200 to 205 and 234 to 229.

Totally exposed to the sun and wind, Upper Reserved ($7) seats are a fine location in which to freeze or fry. They are no sort of place to watch a ballgame, for you are far, far from the action: from the third deck the "Bash Brothers" look more like the "bug brothers." Still, if you want to save some money by sitting here, or if seat availability gives you little choice, try to wrangle spots in the batter's box area (314 to 320). Low row numbers would also be important here: from the top few aisles you can see the game at Candlestick about as well as you can see one happening in this stadium.

The "bleachers" have two things going for them. First, the price is right. Major league baseball for $3.50 would have to be a rated a good deal anywhere. When you consider who suits up with this team, though, it's (as Rickey Henderson would put it) a steal. Second, views in the bleachers, all things considered, are pretty good.

That's the positive side. To the negative, the area is crowded, it is terribly exposed to the sun (as one of the authors learned to his sorrow), and the fans in this area can be rambunctious and, on occasion, pretty foul mouthed. The seats are hard, backless wooden benches with no marking separating one spot from another. If you can put up with these problems, you still might want to sit here. Otherwise, you should consider going elsewhere.

Some comments should be made concerning the overall seating situation. In all sections except bleachers the seats are fairly comfortable metal-and-plastic chairs. Unfortunately, they are cramped together pretty much on the sardine principle, the idea being to fit as many fish — or fans — to a row possible. Legroom is minimal in nearly all sections.

The result of all this is that, throughout the game, you'll find your elbow in your neighbor's mustard, or his hair in your beer. If your neighbor happens to be, say, Madonna, these little difficulties could provide an opportunity to strike up a conversation. It's more likely, though, that the next fan will be a 300-pound construction worker in a "Party Naked" T-shirt, who will tell you precisely where he intends to put his hot dog should you make the mistake of touching it again.

The elements are a problem, too. It can, and does, get cold in the park, particularly during night games. Accordingly, you should always bring a sweater or a jacket to the Coliseum, even if you don't think you'll need it. More often than not, despite what you thought, it will turn out that you'll be glad you brought the coverings along. Sun is a big problem, also. Sun exposure isn't too bad along the right field line, it can be a problem in left field areas, and as for the bleachers — watch out! Particularly if you are sitting in this area on a sunny day, be sure to bring along a hat and sun block. If you are especially sensitive to the sun, try booking seats on the right hand side of the stadium.

Special Needs

Parking. The Athletics do a superior job of providing for the needs of the physically disabled. Indeed, they may do the best job in this area of any club in baseball. Handicapped parking spots are offered in all four stadium parking lots. When you drive in, show your disabled plate to the attendant and you will be directed to the area closest to your seats.

Seating. Handicapped seating, almost alone in the majors, is offered in nearly all parts of the park. At the Field level, designated areas include portions of 14 sections. Of these, baseline spots in sections 120, 122, 114, and 112 are the best: they're fine seats in every way. The reserved sections 216 and 213 are upstairs at the Plaza level. They're great spots, right on top of the action. In the bleachers, spaces are set aside near both foul poles. For the money, these are good locations, too.

In addition to the above, the A's also offer a special "Box 1" area at the park for the visually impaired. This is a special Loge box that offers piped in sound and special play-by-play sound coverage. If anyone else in baseball also offers this service, we don't know of it.

The A's are also good on the smoking issue. In 1990, they became the first open air park in the majors to ban smoking entirely.

The team does a poorer job serving their "no-alcohol" clients. There is not a single "family reserved" section in the park. The Athletics' official position on this issue is that no such place is needed, as the whole of the Coliseum is a "family reserved area." As one of the bleacher fans might put it, "B_____!!"

Food and Features

Food. Basically, A's fans' interests run to two things: baseball and beer. Food is clearly secondary to what goes on in the park. Accordingly, all that's really available at the Coliseum is the standard baseball fare. Personally, we doubt that any of the A's regular crowd wants or is looking for anything more.

Franks aren't very popular in most California parks, but they like them in Oakland. You can get a regular hot dog or a "Colossal"; also available are peanuts, very popular here, popcorn, and a decent slice of pizza. If the selection sounds uninspired, it is.

You'll find a better selection of foods by far in the *Coliseum Cafe*, which is located down a passageway behind section 120 of the Field level. Although there is no direct view of the game here (there are, however, television monitors), this is a plesant enough area with sit down tables and a variety of dishes served cafeteria style, including full meals (the menu changes daily) and a variety of sandwiches.

If you want to eat in the Cafe, though, come early. This cafeteria stops serving food at the top of the 5th inning.

Drinks. Beer is the beverage of choice at the Coliseum; Budweiser seems to be the park brand. Additionally, at various spots throughout the facility such specialty beers as Anchor Steam, Beck's, Bass, and Harp are sold. You can also find the usual Coke products throughout the park.

Those wanting wines or mixed drinks will find them at the *Coliseum Cafe*. There, wines, call drinks, and draft beer is available.

Whether you want food or drinks, though, we have one piece of advice for you: eat early, or eat late! Concession lines throughout the Coliseum are very long and more very slowly, particularly in the middle innings.

Features. The A's have a large features area at the Field level down a passageway behind section 120. Concessions in the area include a basketball toss ($.50 a shot) and a "speed pitch" (3 hurls for a buck). Here also you'll find the A's "Family Place," a pleasant "kids and parents only" cafe with picnic tables where you can take a breather while giving the children a chance to toss and pitch off some of their energies.

One thing that the A's do not have is a museum or any other display highlighting the great accomplishments of their close to 100-year history. Indeed, if you want to see such a thing, you have to travel to Philadelphia, where the Phillies have put together a modest memorial to their former American League rivals. Why don't the A's create an Athletics' "Hall of Fame" for the fans? We suppose it's because they are too busy continuing to make history.

Assistance

We are tempted to say that if you are being bothered by foul mouthed fans, the place to go is Los Angeles. Actually, that's not so. You should take this complaint, and any other concerns you have about lost tickets, stray kids, seat-jumpers or the like to the A's "Guest Accommodations" office, which is located at the Main Gate near the ticket office. You will find the people there uniformly helpful.

Safety and Security

Safety. Safety in the Coliseum isn't a big problem at all, but it is a slight con-

cern. The main difficulties are drunkenness, bad language, and lewd and rowdy behavior, particularly in the bleachers. If you want to avoid any possible problem, stay out of this area. If you do, nevertheless, run into fans who are giving you trouble, move, if possible, or take it up with on of the security guards.

If you feel that you are going to have to talk with an official about someone, do everyone a favor and do it sooner rather than later. Too often fans who are being bothered wait until things have gotten entirely out of hand before complaining, which, when the guards have to crack down, just makes everything more difficult for everyone.

All the main parking areas at the Coliseum are lighted and secured, which means that you should not have any problems. As for the area around the park, it doesn't look terribly safe, and, overall, it isn't, though it certainly is not a high crime district. Still, the area has little to offer fans. Accordingly, after the contest you would be well-advised to hop in your car, or head to the BART station, and go home.

Mementos

Souvenirs. Everyone loves a winner, and, accordingly, A's caps, shirts, pennants and posters are immensely popular — not just in Oakland, but throughout North America. Within the Coliseum, you'll find souvenir stands all over the place, although the one behind Field level section 129 has an especially large selection. Here you can find handsome A's hats for $10 while shirts start at the same price.

The A's also have a modest baseball card store behind section 232 of the Plaza level. We think this is a very good idea.

Foul balls. The Coliseum's huge foul territories mean that Terry Steinbach,

Carney Lansford, and Dave Stewart can be counted on to grab a fair proportion of the stray balls that you had your eyes on. Occasionally, though, even these titans let one get past them. You'll have at least a decent shot of snagging one of the ones that got away if you sit in Plaza level 209 to 214 (right field) and 218 to 224 (left field).

Autographs. The Coliseum is not, to say the least, signature hound heaven.

Visiting teams board their bus outside the north pass gate. Lots of luck in getting to them. The A's have a parking lot directly to the east of the stadium, behind the bleachers area. When you walk the overpass to the BART station, you can look directly down into their cars. Occasionally, a Jose Canseco or Carney Lansford will wave to fans as he gets into his auto. With considerably less frequency, he will stop on the way out to sign a few.

PHILADELPHIA PHILLIES
Veterans Stadium

A number of years ago, the Philadelphia Phillies third baseman (and future Hall of Famer) Mike Schmidt discovered that his daughter had left for school without her lunch box.

Racing to his car, Schmidt caught up with the school bus and got the driver to pull over so he could drop off the lunch. As soon as the kids saw who was stepping on board, they began chanting "Choke! Choke!" Schmidt is supposed to have smiled wanly and said "future Phillies fans!" under his breath.

Just about every baseball park, it seems, is famous for something. Fenway Park has the "green monster," the Toronto SkyDome has its retractable roof, and, of course, San Francisco's Candlestick has the worst weather this side of Fairbanks, Alaska. Philadelphia is known far and wide for having the sport world's most finicky fans. While fans on the west coast may express an attitude that in effect says "entertain me," and while those in the Midwest insist that they be moved, the Phillies fan

preeminently wants to be impressed — and like a Broadway theatre critic, he isn't impressed easily.

Just how tough are the Philadelphia fans? Once, to celebrate the Christmas season, the Philadelphia Eagles (who, like the Phillies, also play in Veteran's Stadium) dressed someone up as Saint Nick for the half-time show. When Old Kris Kringle missed a step, the fans booed. "If they'll boo Santa," says a long-time Philly fan observer, "they'll boo anyone."

It's not as though Philadelphia fans are brutal to their opponents. Actually, it's not that way at all. The entrance of opposing teams (unless it's the Mets) is greeted with polite applause, while good plays handled by the visitors will often elicit a stifled cheer. No, like the Mafia — an organization not totally unknown in the South Philadelphia neighborhoods near the stadium — Philly fans only kill their own. Schmidt is a case in point. Surely one of the greatest players of the past two decades, Schmidt was nevertheless frequently booed during his years in Philly. Yet, when he retired, the same fans turned around and voted him the best player in the team's history.

Irrational? Maybe. But a fan put it to me this way: "The rest of America knew how good Mike was. Only we knew how good he could be."

Actually, explains a Phillies representative, the players understand this about the fans. "Most of them," says one, "see the ragging as a kind of compliment." Right.

All of the above makes Philadelphia fans seem like an ill-tempered bunch. Nothing could be further from the truth. Attend a game at the Vet (no one calls it Veterans) and you'll be surrounded by courteous fans who know the game as few fans do. Moreover, you'll be seated in some of the most comfortable chairs in the majors in a stadium that is about as clean and convenient as you'll find anywhere. Should you need assistance in any way, you'll be helped by a stadium management that takes an interest in the audience and has really made an effort to create a fan-friendly environment. It's a sad fact that attending a game at some parks can be an ordeal. By the time you've slugged your way through traffic, searched endlessly for parking, and queued up under a hot sun for tickets, you're about ready to grab a bat and start swinging yourself. At Veterans these difficulties have been minimized. As a result, whether the Phillies win or lose, it's almost impossible not to have a good time at "the Vet."

The Team

The Phillies own the oldest name in the National League, though perhaps not the most distinguished.

On April 22, 1876, baseball history was made in the City of Brotherly Love when the Philadelphia Athletics played

Boston in the first game sponsored by the spanking new "National League of Professional Baseball Clubs." The Athletics lost that contest and folded that autumn when they were unable to come up with funds for a western road trip. (Their name, however, was revived when the American League located a team in Philly some time later.) In 1883, Alfred J. Reach bought the national league franchise of the Worcester, Massachusetts, "Brown Stockings" and moved the club to Philadelphia, picking the name "Phillies" to honor the new locale; Philadelphia was popularly known as "Philly" even then.

Over the next eighty years or so, the Phillies played what was, for the most part, mediocre ball. Like the Boston Braves, the Phillies played second fiddle for decades to the city's more dynamic — and successful — American League affiliate, in this case Connie Mack's Philadelphia Athletics. It wasn't that the Phillies totally lacked moments of glory or fine players; it was just that such moments were few and far between. After 32 years in the majors, for example, the Phillies finally managed to make it to the 1915 World Series, which they lost to Boston, 4–1. The Phillies waited another thirty-five years for their next Series (1950) and lost 4–0. During these decades, pre–Ruth home run king Gavvy Cravath, famed sluggers Napoleon Lajoie, Ed Delahanty, and Richie Ashburn, and Hall of Fame pitchers Grover Cleveland Alexander and Robin Roberts gave Philly fans something to cheer about.

Finally, in 1955, the Athletics began their trek westward, stopping for a while in Kansas City. And, miracle of miracles, the Phillies slowly began to get better. In 1964, the Phillies made a convincing run for the pennant, only to fold in the last few days of the season. By the seventies, now boasting such players as Mike Schmidt, pitchers Steve Carlton and Tug McGraw, and outfielder Greg Luzinski, the Phillies were consistent contenders. Finally, in 1980 — aided by new team recruit Pete Rose — the Phillies went over the top, beating the Royals 4–2 in the Series. In 1983, with the addition of veterans Joe Morgan and Tony Perez, the Phillies were again in the fall classic, this time bowing 4–1 to their Interstate 95 neighbors, the Baltimore Orioles.

Since then, the Phillies have been fairly cold. During their last couple of years on the club, Mike Schmidt and Steve Carlton were no longer able to lead the team the way they had always done in the past. Rose, Morgan, and Perez were traded, and young players did not live up to expectations. The standout newer players on the squad — outfielder Len Dykstra and first baseman Ricky Jordan — have, thus far, been unable to return the Phillies to their winning ways.

Yet that kind of statement can become quickly dated. The Phillies are one of those teams that is capable of getting very hot, very fast.

The Stadium

Starting with the construction of Candlestick Park in 1960 (a stadium that was lionized as the most beautiful baseball park ever built during its first season, and that has been criticized mercilessly ever since), architects and city officials succumbed to a "bigger is better" mentality in their approach to stadium design. Reflecting, perhaps, the confidence in America's seemingly limitless possibilities that many felt in the 1960s as well as the "keep up with the Joneses" mindset that said that if your neighbor's stadium held 58,000 fans, your had to hold 59,000, cities vied with each other to see who could build the largest baseball park, with the most superlatives attached to it.

Whereas the early baseball stadiums — Fenway Park, Forbes Field, and Crosley Field — had been small, intimate,

and an integral part of the neighborhoods in which they were situated, the "cookie cutter parks," as they've come to be called, would bring drama and prestige to their city's skylines. While the older parks had been built specifically for baseball, in a time when trolleys and buses were the principal means of transit, the new parks would keep the needs of the auto and football in mind — indeed, in many of these places, the needs of football would take precedence. Whereas the classic stadiums had accepted the inconstancies of nature and were built for fans who were willing to put up with the occasional rainout in order to enjoy sunlight and natural grass, builders of the new parks knew that nature could with today's technologies, be manipulated or even abolished. Grass was ripped up and sophisticated astroturf was installed, and, in some cases, domes were added.

Baseball fans today are living with the consequences of the "bigger is better" stadium movement, for both good and ill. On the positive side, all of these stadiums — and the Vet is one of them — have conveniences that the old parks never dreamed of. Most have restaurants of some sort, nearly all have convenient parking and virtually unobstructed seating — no poles between you and the action. On the other hand, these places are usually characterless, have seating that is surprisingly far from the action and do little to enhance that interaction between fan and player that is essential to exciting baseball. These parks are cold and impersonal.

Veterans is among the newer stadiums (it was opened in 1971) and is the third largest in size. With 62,383 seats, it is bested only by Anaheim (64,593) and Cleveland Stadium, which reflects the empire building dreams of another age at 74,483.

A massive concrete circle, the Vet sits in the middle of a field at the bottom of South Philly, near where the

Schuylkill River empties into the Delaware. This is a heavily industrial area, and it is not an especially safe one. Driving up to the park along I-95 from the Philly airport, you see the stacks, pipes, and containment vessels of enormous refineries and chemical plants. To the north and west of the Vet are neighborhoods that you would do well to avoid should you decide to take an after-the-game stroll.

The City of Philadelphia has taken the trouble to make the area directly around the park quite pleasant. The Sports Complex, as it's called (the Spectrum, home of the NBA 76ers, is directly south of the park), is a well-lit, nicely landscaped place with ample parking, good directional signs that lead you quickly from the lots to all the major highways, and a clean and convenient subway station that provides quick service to all the major downtown hotels. Gates into and out of the Vet are clearly marked, and there's a very good statue of Connie Mack, the man whose team overshadowed the Phillies for so many years, located outside the southwest gate.

Inside, the Vet is almost a catalog of the pluses and minuses of the "cookie cutter" parks. On the convenience side, the place features wide aisles with concession stands that are well-designed and rarely overcrowded, excellent plastic chair seating that is genuinely comfortable, modern, clean restrooms, and one of the few "Stadium Club" full-service restaurants in the majors that's open to the general public (see *Food and Features*). Stadium personnel are courteous and well-trained; in the field box sections your chair will often be dusted off by an usher before you sit down.

So what's wrong with it? For one thing, the place is just too big. This has two effects. First, since the Phillies generally attract only a moderate crowd, it's difficult for the team to generate all that much enthusiasm in

the park; you simply have to shout over too many empty chairs. Next, because of the large number of seats combined with the circular design, the inexpensive seats in the upper decks are simply too far from the action to see much. This doesn't matter all that greatly in football. However, in baseball, where stance, nuance, and the ability to get close to the action are essential to enjoying the game, it makes a big difference. The Vet is one of those parks where, if you can get and afford a good seat, you should buy it.

The dimensions of the astroturfed field are pretty standard. Distances at both the right and left field posts are 330', while the center field wall is 408'. Center field has a display of the Phillies' four retired numbers: #36 (Robin Roberts), #32 (Steve Carlton), #1 (Rich Ashburn), and #20 (Mike Schmidt). Above this same area is the Phillies "Phanavision," a Diamond Vision style visual display of players and plays, and an informative electronic scoreboard.

Beyond the field wall, it's a *long* way to the upper decks. Only a handful of shots has ever made it up to the 500 Loge box level, and only one blast, from the Pirates' Willie Stargell, has ever hit the 600 Reserved seat area. Supposedly, there is a star that marks the spot in section 601 (over right field), where the Stargell homer landed.

Highlights

Though it's a reasonably new park, the Vet has already seen its share of baseball history, some of which is commemorated in an attractive "Philadelphia Baseball Hall of Fame" area which can be visited during or before the game. It's located behind home plate at section 224 of the Field box level. For most Philly fans, the biggest highlight was their 1980 World Series victory, which was clinched on October 21 at the Vet. Also memorable were

Mike Schmidt's 500th career homer on April 18, 1987, and Pete Rose's National League record breaking 3,631st hit on August 10, 1981. Other landmarks that happened here have included Pascual Perez's 1988 no-hitter for Montreal, and much of Steve Carlton's 15-win 1972 pitching streak.

The Fans

Philadelphia's enthusiastic, outspoken, and censorious fans are an interesting bunch of folks to spend an evening with. In fact, what goes on in the stands is sometimes more exciting than what happens on the field.

The typical Phillies fan, if there is such a thing, is a white male in his early thirties. He's reasonably well-dressed, though no one would term him a fashion plate. He's reasonably fond of a cool brew, though he's rarely drunken. Most important, he's a sports enthusiast.

The Phillies fan is not the baseball expert that the Oriole admirer is. Scorecards, while some keep them, are not almost required, as they are in Baltimore. Nor do you see too many Phillies people with transitor radio plugs stuck in their ears, tuned in to the play-by-play. Mostly, Phillies fans watch the game, curse bad plays, and discuss the contest with anyone around them who's willing to listen. In just about every section, moreover, at least one fan will feel called upon to rise every inning or so to give the Phillies' management the full benefit of his or her vast experience—usually at top volume.

Lest you think that Philadelphia fans are too hard on the Phillies, take comfort in knowing that they are just as tough on themselves. In most stadiums, it's customary to give a round of applause to a fan who catches a foul ball. The Vet is the only place in the majors where you will usually be booed if you *do not* catch it.

Normally, the Phillies fans extend a good deal more tolerance to the visiting team than to their own. "Normally" breaks down whenever the Mets blow into town. While the Mets-Phillies rivalry may not be the most famed in baseball, it's certainly keenly felt. Moreover, the emnity is enhanced by the habit the Mets fans have of descending like a plague of locusts whenever their beloved outer borough bombers are playing Philly: it is, after all, just a short drive for them down I-95. Games between the Phillies and the Mets, therefore, are generally among the most popular, usually the wildest, and almost always the hardest fought. If you have a choice of Phillies contests to attend, those involving the Mets should be at the top of your list.

The most famous Phillies fan rivals only Len Dykstra in public recognition. He's green, furry, has bug eyes and a nose which looks like a cross between the bell of a trumpet and an elephant's snout. And, like most Phillies fans, he's a "Phanatic."

"The Philly Phanatic is the best mascot in baseball," a Phillies representative told us at the beginning of this trip, "and that includes the Chicken." Tough talk, we thought, coming from a team that was, at the time, running a race for last place. It was particularly tough considering the Chicken's universal fame (and he is good, as we found out along the way), as well as the claims of Baltimore's Oriole, the Mariner's Moose, and Montreal's beloved "Youppi." After visiting twenty-six teams we decided that the Phanatic *is* the best mascot—including the Chicken.

Why has the Phanatic, alone almost of the imitators who followed the San Diego Chicken, been so successful? It isn't enough to say that he's funny, though he is. The Moose can be funny, too. Nor is it the costume; the Oriole's is smarter, while that of Youppie is more imaginative and more comforting to little kids. No, the key to the Phanatic's success is that he realized something very basic about humor, a lesson that goes back to Laurel and Hardy and Warner Bros. What the Phanatic knows is that if you come up with something that's funny for kids, it's funny *only* for kids. But if you take a product that seems to be pitched at kids, and make it funny for adults, both groups just love it.

Take the Montreal Expos' Youppie. What is he really but the "Big Bird" of baseball? Little kids love Big Bird, and they love Youppie, too. He bores adults stiff. The Phanatic, on the other hand, is "Bugs Bunny." He's irreverent, sarcastic, boorish, and has a decided taste for blondes; and he's very capable, like his carrot-chewing counterpart, of keeping both sides of his audience in stitches.

In truth, the Philly Phanatic is really a satire on Philadelphia's demanding fans. That they respond to the Phanatic so well is a tribute to the Phillies fan's own basic good humor. In truth, Phillies fans are that rarest of audiences, critics with some class.

Getting There

If you want to attend games at the Vet, there are several practical options. You can drive, take a cab, grab a bus, or travel via Philadelphia's SEPTA subway system.

By car. Given the easy availability of parking at the Vet and the stadium's proximity to all the area's major highways, travel by auto is a good way to go.

If you're arriving at the *Philadelphia International Airport* and have rented a car, take the service road to I-95 north. Follow this for about five miles to Broad Street and exit going north. The Vet is ¼ mile away. Follow the same directions if you're coming from such *south* locations as Delaware of Maryland.

From New England, New York City, and the *north*, take I-95 south across the Delaware River. Exit at Broad Street North and proceed to the Vet.

People traveling east on the Pennsylvania Turnpike (I-76) from such *western* areas as Harrisburg and Pittsburgh will want to exit at Broad Street and head south.

By cab. Taking a cab to the game is practical, too, if you don't mind the cost. The trip from the airport should run you a pretty stiff $28 or so round trip. From the downtown hotels the price is more reasonable; expect on paying about $8 to $12 roundtrip, depending on where you are staying. Yellow Cab's number is (215) 922-9400.

By bus. We hesitate to recommend city bus lines to visitors because they are often confusing. However, from the airport the bus is certainly the best inexpensive means of reaching the Vet. On arrival, get your bags and head out to the bus stands outside the baggage area. From there, hop aboard bus #3 and ask the driver to let you off at the Sports Complex. The charge is $1.50 and the #3 buses run every ½ hour during busy periods and less frequently on Sundays and holidays.

By subway. Particularly if you are staying at the downtown hotels, Philadelphia's SEPTA subway may be your best option. From the downtown hotels, take SEPTA's Broad Street line south to the Pattison station—you'll find yourself right in front of the Vet when you exit. The charge is $1.50. While SEPTA is not the world's safest mass transit line, you should have no problems traveling between the stadium and downtown so long as you stay with the crowd going to and coming from the game.

It's also possible to take a combination of train and subway to reach the game from the airport. To do this, take train R1 from the airport to Penn Center/City Hall (this service is very regular). Then change to the Broad

Street line south to Pattison. The charge is $1.90.

Parking

Unlike some of its East Coast counterparts, the Vet is blessed with plenty of parking. Wrapped around the stadium, there are 5,000 parking spaces, well-lit and securely enclosed by a chain link fence. Should additional spaces be required (they rarely are), there are 5,000 more spots across the street at the Spectrum. Both are uniformly priced at $4.

Occasionally, people will park in the neighborhoods to the west of the park to avoid the charge. This can be done sometimes, but as this is a high crime area it's not recommended.

Tickets

Phillies tickets can be ordered by mail or phone, picked up in advance at the stadium, or bought just before the game.

As is the case with all the baseball parks, it's best to order well in advance by mail. To do this, write to: The Phillies, Advance Tickets, PO Box 7575, Philadelphia, PA 19101.

State the dates, seats, and sections you want, and make sure to enclose payment in full.

Phone orders can also be accepted if you have a major credit card. To place these, call (215) 463-1000.

Often, it's best to simply pick up your tickets at the Advance Ticket Office, where you can see a seating chart to make sure you're getting the best value for your money. The Phillies Advance Ticket office is under Gate B at the Vet, and is open from 9 A.M. until 8 P.M. weekdays and from 10 A.M. to 4 P.M. on weekends.

Availability. Given that the Phillies are a not particularly successful team and that they inhabit one of the largest stadiums in baseball, good tickets for nearly all games are available. The fireworks spectacular that the Phillies stage on or near Independence Day is the club's only consistent sellout, though opening day and Met's games can also get pretty packed. Therefore, should you decide at the last minute that you want to go to the game, just head out to the Vet—there will almost certainly be space for you.

Whether you'll get one of the best seats is another matter. Despite their problems in recent years, the Phillies sell a respectable 16,000 season tickets, almost all of them in box seats. If you want a box in the better sections, you should order well in advance.

Costs. Phillies ticket prices are uniform, based on the level of the stadium (field, terrace, etc.) you're sitting in. While this simplifies ordering tickets, it can also mean that some of the cheaper tickets are a lot better than some of the box seats (see *Seating*). Always consult a seating chart (see chart on p. 218) before you buy.

In 1990, Phillies ticket prices were as follows: Field Box (200 level [$10]); Terrace Box (300 level [$9]); Loge Box (500 level [$9]); Reserved (600 level [$6.50]); Reserved (700 level [$4]).

Rainouts. Postponements due to rain—and even snow—happen at the Vet around three times a year. If you are caught in one, your ticket can be exchanged for any other game during the season. If you're from out of town and are not planning another trip to Philly, write to the ticket office and explain your situation. You'll probably get your money back.

WCAU AM (1210) keeps track of the weather before and during Phillies games and is the first to announce postponements. If conditions look bad, you might want to tune in before you head to the stadium.

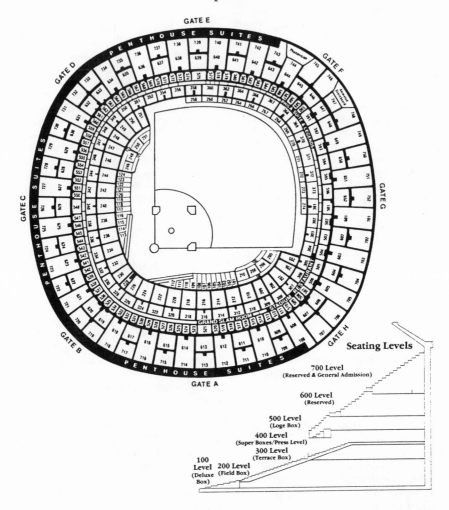

Seating chart, Veterans Stadium.

More than in most parks, this is a stadium where a glance at a seating chart is a *must* if you want a good view.

The Vet is a round stadium, designed more with the needs of football than baseball in mind. What that means as a practical matter is that there are large areas of the Vet where you are very far from the action indeed. There are also areas, mostly in the outfield, where you will be unable to see all the play.

The best seats are at the 100 Deluxe box level. Unfortunately, these spots, which run the baselines along the field wall, are all reserved for season ticket holders, who pay a premium for them.

Field box seats at the 200 level are the next best choice, but only in certain areas. Sections 216 through 238 cover the infield from first to third. These are excellent spots with great views. Whether the boxes from 214 to 205 (the right field line from first base to the foul post) and from 240 to 251 (the left field line from third to the foul post) are better than cheaper Loge box seats that are higher up but closer in is a judgment call we leave to you. The Vet also has "boxes" along the outfield wall (sections 258 to 274). Why anyone would pay $10 for what are bleacher seats in many other stadiums is a mystery to us.

Terrace boxes (300 level) slope back from the 200 level seats with only an aisle to separate them. These are perfectly fine seats, though at the back rows you are a bit far from the field. As in the field boxes, you are best to stay within baselines (Sections 316 to 340).

We like the 500 level Loge seats. Though a level higher, many seats in this section are closer to the action than the Terrace spots. At $9, these seats aren't cheap, but if you stay in the baselines (Sections 521 to 547) you'll have a fine view of the proceedings.

The remaining two levels, the 600 and 700 Reserved seats, are the cheapest spots, and are strictly for the birds— some of whom you may see flying around. This is serious nosebleed country, but if you want or need to save money, than make sure you sit in the sections wrapped around home plate (616 to 624; 716 to 724). As the 700 level is General Admission, choosing your section should present no problems. You can sit anywhere you want.

People who do choose to sit in the Reserved seat area should keep in mind two things. First, if you plan to head down to, say, the Loge or Terrace levels between innings to avail yourself of the better seats, forget it. The Phillies security force is vigilant about keeping Reserved seat people in the area (if not always the seat) they paid for. Also, keep in mind that the upper deck has a limited food selection, and you will not be able to get downstairs to avail yourselves of the wider choices available on the lower concourse. Finally, if you are getting up in years or have a heart condition, play it smart and ask an usher to point you to an elevator. Getting to the Reserved section represents a considerable climb.

Special Needs

Parking. Facilities for the physically disabled are available at the Vet. Reserved handicapped parking is situated near the entrance gates. If you show your handicapped plate or sticker to the attendant when you pay for parking, you'll be directed to the area closest to your seats.

Seating. Parts of five sections in the park are set aside for the handicapped. Box level sections 205 and 251 are near, respectively, the right and left field foul poles. That's pretty far from the action for $10 seats. On the Terrace level, sections 346 and 347 are similarly designated. These are along the end of the left field line and are neither better nor worse than the above.

The standout choice for the physically disabled is Terrace section 328. These $9 spots are directly behind home plate and are some of the best seats in the house.

Food and Features

Food. The food situation at the Vet is good. There's a wide variety of choices available, prices are no worse than in most other parks, and the quality of food and service is quite acceptable.

The Vet offers all the usual ballparks foods at stands throughout the park: generous "Phillie Phrank" (just a hot dog, folks), personal pizza, and pretzels. Other standard fare includes peanuts, soda, popcorn, cotton candy, ice cream cones, and nachos. Kids can get a "Phanatic Fun Meal," which includes a hot dog, potato chips, a small soda, and a plastic "Phanatic" figure.

Beyond these choices there are some more exotic selections. In the "Food Court" areas near home plate at both the 200 and 500 levels you'll find Funnel Cake (a Pennsylvania Dutch specialty), spicy Caribbean tarts, ice cream waffle (with real waffles—delicious!), sweet and sour chicken, and, of course, a Philly cheese steak sandwich.

If you feel like having a fullblown sit-down meal while enjoying the game, that can be arranged, too. While a majority of stadiums now have full-service restaurants, they're usually limited to season ticket holders. Not so at the Vet. The "Stadium Restaurant" (imaginative name) offers a buffet, starting about ninety minutes before the game and running through most of it, that consists of such items as chicken cacciatore, stuffed flounder, and rolled loin of pork, along with full bar service. The prices are high ($19 for adults, $14 for kids), but the food is surprisingly good, as is the view of the contest. You can get to the Stadium Restaurant by taking the elevator behind section 209 and getting off at the 4th floor.

Drinks. Drinkers will also find their thirsts slaked. Miller Lite is the standard brew, and it's a bit costly. In the Food Court area you can find a selection of imported beer, while the full service "Winners" lounge is located behind section 247. It offers wine and mixed drinks in addition to beer, the only problem being that you're not allowed to carry the mixed drinks out of the lounge.

Features. Features, on the other hand, are limited. There is a "speed pitch" concession behind Section 236. You get three balls for a buck. Alone in the majors, the Vet has two baseball-only "newstands." They are behind section 246 on the lower concourse and in back of home plate at the 500 level.

Assistance

One of the best things that has happened in the ballparks in recent years

has been the establishment of customer relations offices to assist fans who are having troubles finding their seats, kids, or tickets, or who wish to be moved away from obnoxious fans or cigars. The Fan Accommodations Office at the Vet is located behind section 226 (home plate), and its people are uniformly helpful.

Safety and Security

Safety. The Vet is a reasonably safe place to attend a ball game.

Inside the park, there is no security problem worth speaking of. The Vet's sensible alcohol policy (a two beer per purchase limit, a cut off on sales in the 8th inning, and the absence of beer vendors in the stands) has insured that alcohol problems are minimal. While you may occasionally be subjected to a drunk or to foul language, a trip to the Fan Accommodation office will generally net you new and often better seats, while a complaint to an usher or security guard will often result in the offender being escorted out of the stadium. Fights do break out every great once in a while, but security is trained to remove troublemakers quickly.

The parking areas are safe, too, with the proviso that you don't decide to hang around all night. Ditto the subway. Go with the crowd and you'll be all right.

The neighborhood around the Vet is another matter. While the landscaped area near the stadium is safe enough, if you feel like taking a walk in the neighborhoods around the park, either do it in daylight or travel in a group. Better yet, go home—there isn't that much to see in this part of Philly anyway.

Health. The biggest health hazard at the Vet and at most other parks is the consumption of too much alcohol. Drink moderately or not at all, and you'll probably have no problem. Those sensitive to sun might want to avoid seats in the outfield sections, particularly in the upper reserved area. If you are suffering from a heart condition, play it smart and sit downstairs.

If you do have a health problem, the Vet's First Aid office is located on the 200 level behind section 224. The staff includes a doctor and two nurses and can respond to most emergency situations. There's an ambulance on site, should it be needed. Here also you can find assistance with more mundane needs, such as aspirin for headaches, a cool place to sit when the heat is too much, bandages for cuts caused by that foul ball you just missed, and a place for mothers to nurse babies.

Mementos

Souvenirs. Though there are souvenir stands throughout the park, you'll find the best selection behind home plate (section 234) on the lower concourse. Here Phillies caps start at $9, while shirts are priced at $12 and up.

Foul Balls. Foul balls are free, if you can catch them! Many seem to land in sections 236 to 240 and 214 to 218.

Autographs. If you get to the game early, you have a reasonable shot of getting autographs by hanging around the dugouts during batting practice. Some of the players drop by to sign. After the game, visiting team buses depart from the press gate area, while Phillies head out of the main gate ramp.

PITTSBURGH PIRATES
Three Rivers Stadium

In 1990, during the National League Championship Series, baseball fans across the country tuned into an exciting battle between the NL West (and, later, world) champs the Cincinnati Reds and their Eastern Division rivals, the Pittsburgh Pirates. Both teams were regarded as pretty equally matched, though the Pirates had won more games during the regular season.

The first two games were fought at Cincinnati's Riverfront Stadium before an enthusiastic, standing room only sell-out crowd. The contenders split the contests. Next, the scene shifted to the Iron City. There, as the Pirates and Reds slugged it out on the field below, thousands watched — and thousands more didn't, for the game was not a sell-

out. To be sure, most of the seats were sold. Even so, had you arrived at Pittsburgh airport that day and decided that you wanted to go to the Championship Series, you could have driven up to the stadium, bought a ticket and a dog, and enjoyed a wonderful contest between two great teams.

Excuses were made for this poor turnout. It was claimed that, because the playoff was a day game, people could not get time off to see it. It was pointed out that, once the offices let out, the stadium would start to fill, which it did. Even so, we strongly doubt that there is another major league city where playoff seat tickets could be had on the opening day of a Championship Series.

Pittsburgh is a real anomaly in the

baseball world. There are towns out there that have great baseball traditions and hordes of passionate baseball fans — cities like New York, Boston, and Chicago. Other places have the enthusiasts but lack the traditions — Toronto, for example. Finally, there are even some cities that, while they have teams, have neither the traditions nor the fans! Seattle is one. But Pittsburgh is the only town we know of that has a great baseball legacy and a population that, from all appearances, couldn't care less about it. To give just one more awful example, last year, as the Pirates led the National League through most of the season, their employees could be seen on downtown streetcorners, trying to flog seats to passersby! Even doing that, they still could not fill the park for a pennant race that had the rest of the country enthralled. It is the damnedest thing we have ever seen.

Does anyone in Pittsburgh really care about baseball? Certainly the Pirates and the members of their families care. No doubt there are other Pittsburghers that care, too, though they certainly keep quiet about it. Beyond that, what most Pittsburghers seem to be interested in is when are those characters with their funny sticks going to clear out of Three Rivers so that the real game — football — can begin? We found it all pretty discouraging. You really have to ask yourselves, does Pittsburgh deserve the Pirates?

The authors would like to point out at this juncture that they are residents of Raleigh-Durham, North Carolina, an area that doesn't have major league baseball, but that does have a great minor league tradition. We'd also like the Pirates to know that "Blackbeard" — the most famous freebooter of all — was a native of our state, in case they are not aware of that fact. Bucs, we are ready whenever you are. Come on down!

The Team

Whether or not Pittsburgh deserves the Pirates, they've had them around for a long, long time.

Back in 1876, the Pittsburgh Alleghenies (named after the river) were one of the initial professional teams in baseball. In 1882, the squad joined the American Association, one of the precursors to today's major leagues. The team played, in those far off days, on the north bank of the Ohio River, right about where Three Rivers Stadium sits.

In 1887 the Alleghenies found a permanent home in the National League, where they were in combat against their Keystone State rivals, the Phillies. In the 1890s, the Alleghenies lifted several players from the Phillies' staff, an act that caused outrage throughout the larger metropolis. The Pittsburghers, one Philadelphia paper declared, were nothing more than a bunch of Pirates! The Pittsburghers gleefully agreed with this assessment, and the name stuck.

During the last century, the Pirates were an alright team, but they won few laurels. As the new century dawned, though, Pittsburgh became, for a decade, one of the most powerful organizations in the game.

Two players were in large part responsible for this development. One was the powerful, erratic pitcher Rube Waddell, who pointed the squad toward its first pennant in 1901. The other and more important one was the great shortstop Honus Wagner. An incredibly consistent hitter and a faster-than-the-wind base stealer, "the Flying Dutchman" was, to the National League, what Ty Cobb was to the Americans throughout this era — he was simply baseball excellence personified. There, however, the comparison stopped. Whereas Cobb was a mean-spirited, spiteful man, intensely disliked by his teammates, Wagner was a model hero, generous, moral, and kind.

Under Wagner's leadership, the Pirates won five pennants in the first decade of the 1900s. The team appeared in the first World Series ever (1903), and was expected to triumph easily over the new American Leaguers. Instead they fell to the Boston Red Sox in a defeat that so annoyed National League officials that they refused to allow a fall classic in 1904. The 1909 contest was, for Pittsburgh, a sweeter affair. On this occasion, the Pirates faced the Tigers in a Series that featured the only head-to-head matchup between Wagner and Cobb ever. Pittsburgh won the Series 4–3 behind a stellar Buc pitching performance by Babe Adams. Wagner showed his speed and power, too. His .333 batting average and six steals outposted Cobb's .231 and one purloined trip.

That was the Pirates' last trip to the classic for a while, but the squad stayed competitive, placing in the upper division in most years and staging close pennant races in more than a few. In 1925, sixteen years after their initial Series triumph, the Bucs went to the Series again. Once more they copped the laurels in a 4–3 battle over the Washington Senators, despite the heroic efforts of the Senator's star pitcher Walter Johnson to stem the tide. The Bucs, however, had no such luck when they went to the classic in 1927. On this occasion they ran into the buzzsaw of the Yankee's fabulous "Murderer's Row" and fell in four short games.

During these years the Buc's star players were sluggers Paul and Loyd Waner, the only brothers in the Hall of Fame. Known as "Big Poison" and "Little Poison," they were, in truth, pretty close to equal in talent, though Paul was the more intriguing character. A man who read classical (as in Greek and Roman) literature in the clubhouse between innings, Paul was also one of the game's principal drinkers: pitchers used to gauge how they would throw to the man depending on how much he had consumed before game time. Still, the guy was a fantastic player. Casey Stengel, who considered Waner the greatest right fielder of all time, once said of him, "He was a graceful player. After all, he could slide without breaking his hip bottle."

Until the early forties, the Bucs at least stayed in the race. By late in the decade, though, they had fallen to a perpetual dead last and became something of a national joke. In 1952, the team hit rock bottom, becoming the first National League squad in history to place dead last in all major statistical categories — quite an accomplishment when you consider that the Pirates played in the same league as the Phillies. After the Dodgers left New York for sunny L.A., former Dodger general manager Branch Rickey was given a shot at seeing what he could do with the Bucs, but he had little luck. Pretty soon local wits were referring to the Pirates as "the Rickeydinks." As for the high-spirited, diminutive gang that composed the Bucs' infield, they were known collectively as "the Singing Midgets.

As bad as the Pirates were during these years, though, they still had some good players, one of whom was Hall of Fame slugger Ralph Kiner, who collected during the late forties and early fifties more National League home run titles than any other player in history. Kiner, a practical man, was once asked why he focused on hitting out-of-the-park bombs as opposed to lots of little hits. He responded with his most famous quote. "Home run hitters drive Cadillacs," Ralph intoned. "Singles hitters drive Fords."

Kiner's interest in getting rewarded for his efforts can also be illustrated by another story. Once, having won back to back NL home run titles, Ralph went in to see his manager, intent on getting a raise. The manager heard him out, and then asked a question. "Kiner, what place did the Pirates come in last year?"

"Well, last," the slugger responded.

"Frankly, Ralph," said the manager, "I think we could have done it without you."

Despite these bad times, though, the Bucs started their crawl out of the cellar in the late 1950s. In 1960 they surprised just about everyone by winning the pennant. In their Series against the Yankees, just about everyone expected a repetition of their 1927 humiliation. The 1960 Yankees were a powerful squad. They had won 97 games in the regular season, and their lineup included Mickey Mantle, Roger Maris, Bill Skowron, Yogi Berra, Bobby Richardson, and Whitey Ford.

Sure enough, the pinstrippers performed to expectations. They set new all-time World Series records in team batting average (.338), runs scored (55), hits (91), total bases (142), and RBIs (54). It was an awesome performance, except for one thing — the Yankees lost. They had gotten the "most" of just about everything, but the Bucs got exactly the number of hits they needed to win — a process that, for the Bucs, was culminated when Bill Mazeroski put the Series away with a dramatic tie-breaking homer in the bottom of the ninth in the seventh game. For once, Pittsburgh went baseball crazy.

With the 1960s and especially the 1970s, things began to go the Bucs way. The team recruited outstanding new players, such as home run blaster Willie Stargell and ace slugger and all-around nice guy Roberto Clemente, whose lifetime .317 batting average still stands as the highest for a right hander since World War II. In these years, the Pirates returned to Series action, too. In both 1971 and 1979 they took on Earl Weaver's tough Baltimore Orioles. Both times they walked away with the prize by 4–3 margins.

The 1980s initiated another Pirate slump, one so severe, in fact, that it seemed for a while that this historic team would fail. As in the past, however, the Bucs somehow, from somewhere, found the inner resources to dramatically improve their performance. They surprised just about everyone by winning the National League East in 1990. Now no one will be surprised if they do well in the years to come.

At this point, the Pirates have a solid, talented squad. Key players include Cy Young award winning pitcher Doug Drabek and players Barry Bonds, Bobby Bonilla, and Andy Van Slyke, who together compose the strongest outfield in the game. The Bucs also have something more important yet: the will to win.

The Stadium

A Pittsburgh joke. Man #1: "Did you hear that the people in Cincinnati stole Three Rivers Stadium last night and left Riverfront in its place?" Man #2: "How could anyone tell?"

Cruel, perhaps, but the jest has more than a measure of truth. Though they are not really precisely alike, Riverfront and Three Rivers are not only just about the closest National League parks to each other physically, they are also nearest in shape, soul, spirit, and age — for Riverfront is only seventeen days older than Three Rivers, both parks having been opened in 1970. We do not know whether the pair were designed by the same architectural firm, but if they weren't, we think that whoever sketched out Riverfront has a very strong (and very big) prima facie case that his ideas were stolen.

Does it matter that the two stadiums look a lot alike? Probably not very much. We only wish that, if the denizens of Pittsburgh and Cincinnati had felt in a mood for imitation, they would have decided to copy Yankee or Dodger Stadium instead of each other.

At the outset, it must be said that,

whatever its limitations, Three Rivers Stadium has the most beautiful setting of any major league baseball park. Located just a bridge away from Pittsburgh's spectacular "Golden Triangle" downtown and set in Roberto Clemente Park, an attractive slice of greenery on the north bank of the Ohio River, Three Rivers rests at precisely the point where the Allegheny and the Monongahela join to form that massive stream. It is hard to imagine a more majestic site to place a ballpark. Particularly as you view the area from the Duquesne Heights neighborhood, Three Rivers looks spectacular.

In part, that's because the stadium is a pretty place. Like all the round ballparks build in the 1960s and 1970s, it cuts an attractive figure along a city's skyline, and, given the place's setting, that fact is particularly evident here. Pittsburgh's city leaders are no doubt proud of the place.

Outside the park, there is only one thing to detain you, and that's the handsome statue of Honus Wagner that you'll find outside Gate C. We liked the realism of this work very much. The artist doesn't really try to prettify the man. Rather, we see Wagner as he probably was; solid, a bit stocky, and dogged looking. You might also catch the fact that Wagner's arms are, here, a bit long—as they were in real life. One player claimed that "the Flying Dutchman" could tie his shoes without bending over—perhaps a slight exaggeration.

If you are turned on by cement, you will love the public areas inside, for the greyish stuff is everywhere. Corridors are resonably wide, but they could be wider. Many of the ceilings leading to the seats are fairly low. The whole place, in fact, has a closed in look that we found somewhat uncomfortable—a few holes knocked out of the walls to let in sunshine and air would have been very welcome.

Though neat, clean, and nicely color coordinated, the seating areas at Three Rivers have the same problems as Riverfront, Busch, Atlanta, and the other round parks: too many seats are just too far from the playing area. Given the low attendance figures that the Pirates often chalk up, getting a good seat at Three Rivers is something less of a problem than it is in Riverfront or Busch. However, if the Bucs keep playing as they have been playing recently, that could prove to be a temporary advantage.

Like many of the modern ballparks, Three Rivers has an astroturf surface. The advantages and the disadvantages of that particular manifestation of man's ingenuity have been hashed and rehashed enough by others to make it pointless for us to add anything on the score. It all comes down to the fact that some people like artificial surfaces while others believe they take away from the game. We are in the second category.

The field dimensions are fairly standard. The foul poles are set at 335′ while the furthest reach of center field is 408′. On the outfield wall you will see some attractive plaques outlining the team's World Series achievements. Above that is the scoreboard and visual display area.

Overall, Three Rivers is not a bad place to play ball. It's clean, convenient, and pretty. Many seats have fine views. It's very possible that you could come to the stadium and have a great time at the ballgame. You might even grow to like Three Rivers Stadium very much.

We don't dislike Three Rivers, but we were not enthralled with the park, either. There's little to interest you, there are few things to get excited about, and there is nothing to surprise you at all.

Highlights

Some important baseball highlights have happened at Three Rivers, most of them connected with the team's World Series victories.

One highlight that didn't happen at the park was Bill Mazeroski's incredible seventh-game, ninth-inning homer that gave the Pirates the 1960 baseball crown over a stunned Yankee team and an incredulous America. That happened at Three Rivers admirable predecessor park Forbes Field on October 13, 1960.

The first Series came to Three Rivers in 1971. Although the Bucs took the trophy in Baltimore, the crucial 5th game, in which the Pirates began to turn the tide their way, was won in Pittsburgh on October 14, 1971. Leading the drive towards the fall classic crown was the great Roberto Clemente, who hit .414 in the Series.

As it turned out, the 1971 Series would be the last Clemente would ever play in. In 1972 the Pirates, behind Clemente and Willie Stargel, made another pennant drive that ended with the Bucs emerging as the NL East champs, only to be defeated by Cincinnati in the playoffs. In that Series, Clemente made his last appearance at Three Rivers on October 8, 1972. Less than three months later, while on a mercy mission to aid earthquake victims in Nicaragua, Clemente was tragically killed in a plane crash. Shortly after that the 3,000-hit slugger became one of only two players in history (the other is Lou Gehrig) to be admitted to the Hall of Fame before the traditional five-year waiting period.

July 23, 1974, saw Three Rivers' only All-Star game. As usual during this period, the Nationals won behind the fabulous hitting of Los Angeles' Steve Garvey.

World Series action came back to Pittsburgh in 1979. Once again the Pirate's victims were the O's, once more the title fell to the Bucs in Baltimore, and yet again game five in Three Rivers was a key to the contest as Bill Madlock led the way for the Bucs,

piling up 4 hits to save the Pirates from elimination and propel them to victory. The date was October 14.

Fans

Pittsburghers overall like football more than they do baseball. The Pirates traditionally get lukewarm support in this town, while the Steelers pack 'em in to Three Rivers every season.

The blue collar nature of the Iron City may have something to do with this fact. There are, to be sure, blue collar towns that are absolutely sold on baseball: Milwaukee and Oakland are two. In many other burgs, though, working class audiences often opt for football. Perhaps they like the more physical nature of the conflict.

Whatever the reason, the crowds at Three Rivers tend to be a bit smallish and a tad subdued. Pirates fans are not, to be sure, as laid back as the audiences on the West Coast. On the other hand, you'll see here little of the hollering, foot stomping shenanigans that you typically run into a game in New York or Boston. Bucs admirers are willing enough to cheer the team on to victory, and they are quite partisan — you won't find anyone cheering for the visitors here. On the other hand, they aren't going to bust a gut over a ballgame, either.

Overall, the park draws an audience a bit heavier in males than most, with fair numbers of young adults and some kids. Basically, these people are mid–Americans. They are mostly white, reasonably well-dressed, and display few ethnic characteristics. They aren't scholars of the game. We saw few people keeping score, and no people tuned into the play-by-play on radios at all. On the other hand, most fans seem to pay attention to the contest, as opposed to socializing or wandering around. These folks aren't experts, but they are interested.

Overall, this is a crowd that goes to

the park for some fun. They enjoy shouting a bit, watching a bit, and downing a couple of beers — or perhaps more than a couple beers, for these fans are fonder of the stuff than most. They also like to see their team win. Given the Pirates' stellar performance in 1990, it is hard to believe that these people didn't have a fine time. Maybe in the years to come they will return, and bring their friends.

Getting There

Pittsburgh is one of the smaller and more compact cities in the major leagues. Traffic isn't all that bad, and the downtown area, where Three Rivers Stadium sits, is pretty accessible by car. Some fans also arrive by cab while some walk over from the downtown hotels. A third and very pleasant option is to arrive by riverboat.

By car. Three Rivers Stadium is located in downtown Pittsburgh on the north bank of the Ohio River, at the very point where it joins the Allegheny and the Monongahela; hence the name "Three Rivers" Stadium.

It's a pretty spot — and it's also easy to reach by car, as the stadium is quite close to the major interstates that pass through the area.

Those going to the park from such *east* locales as Harrisburg and Philadelphia should take the Pennsylvania Turnpike (I-76) west to I-376 west, headed toward Pittsburgh. Follow I-376 west through downtown Pittsburgh, and then cross the Fort Duquesne Bridge over the Allegheny River. From that point, exit to Three Rivers Stadium parking.

Those traveling from *north* cities like Erie will want to take I-79 south to I-279 east, headed toward Pittsburgh. Once you get into town, watch for the exit to Three Rivers Stadium and follow signs to parking.

People headed to Three Rivers from

such *west* towns as Youngstown and Cleveland should take I-76 (The Pennsylvania Turnpike) east to I-79 south, and then should follow I-79 south to I-279 east, headed toward Pittsburgh. From that point, follow the above directions.

Those going to the game from such *south* cities as Washington and Morganton should take I-79 north to I-279 north, headed toward Pittsburgh. Once you pass through downtown, follow the signs to Three Rivers Stadium parking. If you are coming in from the *Pittsburgh International Airport*, follow the Airport Parkway to I-279 north and then pick up the above directions.

By cab. Cab is a fine option if you are staying in the downtown hotels. A ride to the park from any one of them should run you no more than $5 or $6. Going to the game by cab from the airport, though, is an expensive propostion. Expect to pay $25 each way.

By riverboat. You can take a riverboat to and from Three Rivers Stadium! Special riverboats leave for the game from the Station Square Dock on the south side of the Monongahela River from about ninety minutes before the contest, and sail from there directly to Three Rivers past Pittsburgh's appealing skyline. After the contest, the boats pick up passengers at the Three Rivers dock and return them back to the Station Square area, which is the site of some of Pittsburgh's best nightlife. The charge for transportation is $1.25 each way.

We can think of few more pleasant ways to start and conclude an evening of baseball than to take advantage of this excellent service. To get current schedules, call the Gateway Clipper Fleet at (412) 355-7980.

By foot. From many of the downtown hotels, and especially from the Hilton, it is entirely possible to walk to the park. It's fine exercise, and downtown Pittsburgh is very appealing.

Parking

The parking situation at Three Rivers is pretty good. The stadium has five well-lighted lots situated around the park. If you arrive in the area early, you'll be put right next to the facility. If you get into the area late, you'll be directed to a spot where you'll have a short walk to the stadium. All spaces are a reasonable $4.

There are also some neighborhood lots around Three Rivers Stadium that charge a buck or so less. There's really no reason that you shouldn't patronize them if you don't mind the extra stroll.

Tickets

Pirates tickets can be obtained by mail, by phone, or you can pick them up in person at the stadium.

To get tickets by mail write to the team at: Ticket Manager, Pittsburgh Pirates, 600 Stadium Circle, Pittsburgh, PA 15212.

Include with your order the number of tickets you want, the dates, and locations. Enclose your check or money order plus the $2.50 additional service charge that the Pirates assess.

To purchase tickets over the phone, call Ticketmaster at (412) 321-BUCS. If you call for seats, be prepared with your credit card and some idea of the sorts of locations you want to buy. You'll get whacked with a service charge here, too.

You won't have to pay extra, on the other hand, if you visit the Pirates' advance ticket office, which is located at Gate A at Three Rivers Stadium. There also you'll be able to take a look at a seating chart and have some input into the seats you'll be getting. The advance ticket office is open Monday through Saturday from 9 A.M. to 6 P.M.

Availability. It seems that no matter what the Pirates do, they cannot get Pittsburghers to flock into their park. During 1990, for example, the Bucs had the best record in the National League. Was that enough to sell out Three Rivers for the playoffs? No way. As millions of fans from outside of town who would have loved to have been there watched, the cameras panned row after row of empty seats during one of the championship games.

Anyway, Pittsburgher's loss is your gain. As a point of fact, seats are always available at Three Rivers for every game. Unless you are attending one of the team's more popular match-ups, which is to say contests against the Mets and the team's principal rival, Cincinnati, you have a good chance of getting a fine seat even a day or two before the game.

Costs. Prices at Three Rivers are mid-range. They aren't especially cheap, but they could be worse, too. Overall, ticket prices pretty much match the view you'll get from the various area, as long as you realize that Three Rivers, one of the round parks, doesn't have all that many really great seats to begin with.

In 1990, the Pirates' ticket prices were as follows: Club Box ($11); Mezzanine Box ($8); Terrace Box ($7.50); Family Boxes ($6); Reserved ($6); Reserved General Admission ($5) General Admission (Adults [4$]); (12 and under [$2.50]).

Rainouts. Despite the astroturf, Pirates games still rain out from time to time; we know, as we were caught in a cancellation. If your game is scrapped, your tickets will be exchanged for spots at another contest. If you aren't planning a return to Pittsburgh, send your stubs in to the ticket office explaining this and your money will be refunded.

Seating

We've said enough about the drawbacks of round stadiums in this book to belabor the point in this chapter. The bad news about Three Rivers is that a lot of its seats are pretty far from the action. The good news is that the team is so neglected locally that you may still get a very good seat.

The most expensive spots are the Club boxes ($11), and if you don't mind spending the money, you should probably go for them — they are far and away the best seats in the park. Composed of attractive and comfortable plastic-and-metal chairs, those seats in the low numbers, which run 1 (right field) to 82 (left field) are all pretty close to the action, though the very low (1 to 18) and the very high (67 to 81) sections are past the baselines. Still, these spots are all pretty good. Those Club boxes with numbers between 218 and 268 are, on the other hand, pretty far from the field. Spots in this subsection within the baselines, which is to say from 230 (right field) to 256 (left field), are still decent. Those beyond these areas are less appealing.

Mezzanine boxes ($8) are second in price, but third (or fourth) in view; these are near the field seats wrapped around the foul poles. In many parks at least some of these spots would be called bleachers — at very few would they go for the second highest price in the facility. We don't think you will really be getting your money's worth if you sit here, though this category might be all right if you get into the very low rows.

On the whole, though, you'll be better off in the Terrace boxes ($7.50). Set at both the press box level and a tier above that, some of these seats, notably the ones behind the batter's box, are pretty good. Spots beyond these areas, though, as in all stadiums that have this design, deteriorate rapidly in quality. If you are going to sit here, see if you can book 437 to 439 at the press level or 529 to 541 above.

Family boxes ($6) are overpriced bleacher seats, with a no alcohol/no smoking policy. They have good enough views, but are no great shakes. In this area, rows A through E are best. Some of the seats past row F have some view obstructions. Reserved General Admission spots ($5) are worse — they are further back from the action than the Family spots are, and are only a buck better in price.

The top deck has two categories of inexpensive seats. Reserved ($6) seats are way up the yardarm; you'll be a lot close to the Jolly Roger than you will be to the deck where the Pirates are cavorting. Batter's box sections here (631 to 637) are the best of a sorry lot. General Admission spots ($4) are worse, though if you find something in the lower fourth level (seats in the 400s) as opposed to the truly distant sixth, it might not be too bad. Anyway, the price is right. A family of five can sit in this area for $15.50.

Special Needs

Parking. Parking for the physically disabled is available at the park under Gate C. Simply show your plate or your sticker to the parking attendant as you pull into parking and you will be directed to this area.

Be aware, though, that there are only fourteen spaces in this section. If you want one of them, it is imperative that you get to the stadium early. There are other spots, too, if these run out, but they are not nearly so close to the park.

Seating. Handicapped seating is available, too. Specifically, the park has 78 wheelchair spots located on the first level just past their right field foul post. The view here isn't so hot, but the price ($6) is right. Here you will have better spots, for example, than many of the folks in the more expensive Mezzanine boxes.

The park also offers a special "no-alcohol" and also "no smoking" family reserved area, located in the best sections of what in most parks would be the bleachers. These spots must be rated as good when their relatively low price ($6) is taken into consideration.

Food and Features

Food. Three Rivers Stadium is strictly a hot dot, beer, and fries sort of place. If you relish these standard ballpark items, you are liable to find the park's food pretty acceptable. If you were hoping for something a bit more exciting you will probably be disappointed.

The usual baseball favorites are on sale throughout the park at fairly reasonable prices: hot dogs, nachos, a smallish pizza slice, french fries, and soft serve cone.

Drinks. The drinks include beer and the usual selection of Coke products.

There are two nice places to consume all of the above, and a few other things as well. One is *The Bullpen Cafe*, a patio-like area over the Pirates' bullpen that has nice views, picnic tables, and a concession stand that sells "grilled jumbo hots," dogs that are significantly better than the steamed weiners sold elsewhere in the facility. The *Cafe* also sells an assortment of imported brews, such as Heineken, Beck's, and Foster's. The *Boardwalk Cafe*, located on the first level outer concourse between gates A and B, has decent Philly cheesesteak sandwiches plus other items.

Features. Like a number of other parks that have trouble bringing in the fans, the Pirates go out of their way to provide features to keep people amused. At Three Rivers, in fact, a whole area called the *Three Rivers Boardwalk* has been set aside for this purpose. Located on the first level outer concourse between gates A and B, the Boardwalk has a speed pitch, a batting cage, a Pirates photo booth, and a number of other features.

The team also has a mascot, the "Pirates Parrot." What little kids see in this fat green bird we don't know, but they seem to like him.

Assistance

The Pirates' "Guest Relations" office, located inside Gate B at the 100 level, is a genuinely welcoming place full of friendly, competent people who will be happy to provide assistance if you want to be seated away from smokers, if you can't find your child, or if you'd simply like to know more about the Pirates.

Safety and Security

Safety. Some Pirates fans drink a bit more than they ought to, so some of the problems that are associated with inebriation occur in the park from time to time. They are, however, fairly infrequent. If you simply avoid the Reserved seats and General Admissions during the tenser contests—say those against Cincinnati or the Mets—you will probably be able to avoid any problems.

The park itself is located in the downtown area of a big city. This should spell something of a security problem, but it doesn't seem to. Uniformly, everyone we talked with— fans, Pirate people, and police— insisted that there was really no reason why anyone should hesitate about walking back to his hotel from the park after a night game. In truth, the area looked safe and well-policed to us.

Health. The big health threats at Three Rivers derive from overindulgences and the failure to dress appropriately for the season. In the first category, all we can suggest is that you know your limits for beer and stay within them. In the second, dress lightly during the summer and bring sun block if you plan on sitting in the top deck. During the spring keep in mind that it can get pretty cold in Pittsburgh in April; carry with you a sweater or a jacket.

If you fail to heed these words of wisdom, you'll find the Pirates' first aid office behind home plate at Gate A. The people there are helpful and friendly, like all the other Pirates service folks.

Mementos

Souvenirs. You'll find the widest selection of Pirates goods in the park at their Gift Shop, which is located at Gate A on the first level outer concourse. The prices are a bit high.

Foul Balls. You'll have a decent chance of snagging a stray if you sit in the Club boxes sections, say in setions 61 to 67 along the left field line and in 15 to 23 on the right.

Autographs. The Pirates' relatively low attendance makes this a good place to get autographs at batting practice. Try to arrive at the stadium an hour or so before the game and join the crowd hanging around the team dugouts. Players often come over to sign a few.

ST. LOUIS CARDINALS
Busch Stadium

What is North America's greatest baseball town?

Talk to fans in Chicago, Boston, New York, or Cincinnati, and they will all claim that their home city deserves the laurels. In truth, you could make a solid case for the baseball preeminence of any of these towns; all have their place in the sport's annals, and in all four there are thousands of knowledgeable, devoted, and vociferous baseball enthusiasts.

Even so, if you really wanted to pick one city that exemplifies what baseball can really mean to a community, and what, in turn, a community can mean to the game, you might well single out St. Louis. As distinguished, for example, as are Chicago's claims to baseball dominance, the hard fact is that its teams have won relatively little over their long histories. And while the Cincinnati Reds may be baseball's oldest squad, it has in most years been far

from the best—although it has had some great moments, too. As for Boston, well, anybody who has ever gone to Fenway knows that Beantown denizens are as enthusiastic a baseball crowd as one could ask for. The only problem with the Red Sox is that they simply cannot seem to pull themselves together to win a Series.

St. Louis' real competitor for the honors is New York. On behalf of the Big Apple, it must be admitted that that town has suited up more great teams and more great players than any other place. St. Louis fans, though, would argue that if, overall, the Yankees have been the best team in the history of the sport, the Cardinals have at least been the second best (a contention the Dodgers would object to). Moreover, the Cardinals have been around a lot longer than the Yankees, and they played a far more formative role in the formation of the game than the New

Yorkers ever did. Besides, it would be said, while New Yorkers are fickle in their loyalties, sharing their favors with basketball and football, St. Louis fans have always put the Cardinals first, last, and always.

Who has the better side of the argument? We'll leave that for you to judge. We will say, though, that with the possible exception of Cincinnati, St. Louis is the most baseball-obsessed town we have ever seen. Drive into this midwestern metropolis during any summer day and you'll see red—specifically Cardinal red—just about every place you go. It's on the signs, it hangs from pennants over the streets, and it enlivens billboards throughout the community. Visit any conclave of St. Louis people—it doesn't matter whether they are executives, birdwatchers, or brewery workers—and sooner or later (and usually sooner) the conversation will come around to baseball. St. Louis is that kind of place.

A trip to St. Louis, for the baseball fan, will probably not be a completely positive experience. Busch Stadium, while beautiful, is not one of the better stadiums in the majors from the standpoint of allowing fans to see the game. Further, prices in the park could be better. Despite these minor problems, though, visitors to St. Louis will find themselves in the middle of one of America's most interesting and exciting towns; it's a city where the restaurants are good, where there is much to see and do, and where every second person you meet will likely share your interest in your favorite game. St. Louis, overall, is baseball city.

The Team

Few teams can say that they were there "at the beginning." The St. Louis Cardinals, at least to a degree, is one of them.

In 1876, when the National League was founded, St. Louis was represented with a club that was a predecessor of the current Cardinals team. It finished second that season, behind the granddaddy of all the continuous franchises, the Chicago White Stockings—now called the Cubs. St. Louis did pretty well in its second season, too, but then dropped out of the League.

By 1882, St. Louis was back with a new squad, this one an American Association franchise called the Browns, handled by player-manager Charles Comiskey, of later White Sox fame. This time the team performed superlatively, winning pennants in 1885, '86, '87, and '88. The team also was responsible for some innovations that would later greatly influence the game. It was in St. Louis during these years that "hot dogs" were first introduced to baseball. It was here, too, that the word "fan" was born. When someone asked the team's owner what he thought of his customers, he said they were a bunch of "fanatics"; part of the terminology stuck. Finally, play in St. Louis during these years was graced, if that's the word, by the antics of Walter Arlington Latham, an acrobatic player who was known to somersault over first basemen on the way to the bag and who was called "the freshest man on earth." Not content to simply wow the opposition with his gymnastic feats, Latham also seemed determined to talk them to death. "Chatter" was born.

In 1892, St. Louis rejoined the National League and changed their name to the "Perfectos." This new moniker proved no charm, and when, in 1899, a lady said of the team's new uniforms that they were "a lovely shade of cardinal," a local sportswriter seized on the term to dub the team with a new name that stuck. Thus the bird that graces the team's logo actually has no relation to the squad's name, just as the term "Braves" actually had nothing to do with Indians (see "Atlanta Braves").

Arguably, the Cardinals' first two

decades in the National League were the worst in their history. By the 1920s, though, powered by Rogers Hornsby's incredible hitting (he won seven batting titles and two "Triple Crowns") and the fine pitching of Hall of Famers Jesse Haines and Grover Cleveland Alexander, the Cards were at the top of their League.

The first of the Card's *fifteen* Series appearances, and the first of the ten down-to-the wire 4–3 classics that the Redbirds have participated in occurred in 1926. It was also the scene of one of the most dramatic moments in Series history.

The hero of the contest was Alexander, an aging (39 at the time) epileptic star with a big-time fondness for drink. Going up against the awesome power of Ruth and Gehrig, Alexander nevertheless managed to win the second and sixth games for the Cards. Then, thinking his work done, he went out on one of his legendary benders.

The next morning found the Cards in a horrible fix. They were leading by only one in the seventh inning and the Yankees had the bases loaded. Clearly, a pitching change was needed, and manager Rogers Hornsby's eyes fell upon the hung-over hero. "How do you feel?" Hornsby asked. "Okay," the still whoozy Alexander replied, lumbering out to the mound. "Just don't do any warm-ups. That would be the giveaway." In an awesome performance, Alexander proceeded to completely shut-down the Yanks, bringing St. Louis its first Series win. Asked later to explain his unusual choice of relievers, given the situation, Hornsby said, "Hell, I'd rather him pitch a crucial game for me drunk than anyone else sober."

Two years later, the Cards were back to the Series, but this time the Yanks got their revenge, winning 4–0 behind a torrid .625 Babe Ruth batting performance. Two years later, the Cards were back again, this time to take a beating courtesy of the Philadelphia A's, who

won 4–2. It was pennant time again in 1931, and this time the Cards, led by the hard-charging rookie Pepper Martin, were victorious over the A's, winning 4–3.

The decade of the thirties was probably the greatest in St. Louis baseball history. Led by some of the game's most colorful and talented players (Pepper Martin, Leo Durocher, Dizzy and Paul Dean, to name a few), a group known collectively as "the Gashouse Gang," the Cards achieved the impossible during these years: they got fans to pay attention to something other than the Yankees.

"Pepper" Martin, so called for his temper as well as his speed, was typical of the crew. He was a madcap of the bases. Once, during a game in blistering 100-plus heat, he and Dizzy Dean built a bonfire in the middle of foul territory, put on winter coats, and began warming themselves! Having a very short fuse, Martin also once tackled an umpire and had to be hauled off the man. He was later asked by the judge just what was going through his mind while pulling a stunt like that. "I was thinking," Pepper replied, "that I'd choke the son of a bitch to death."

But as far as "characters" go, few in the history of baseball could surpass the great pitcher Dizzy Dean. A self-proclaimed backwoods "hick" who specialized in murdering opposing batters and the English language, Dean seemed to enjoy nothing better than leading reporters astray regarding his background. When once challenged about his inconsistent stories, Dizzy declared "them ain't lies, them is scoops!" When criticized by the St. Louis Board of Education for his bad grammar, Dean responded with what, during these Depression years, became his most famous line: "A lot of folks that ain't sayin' ain't, ain't eatin'."

Statements like these made Dean notorious — or admired — nationwide. Once, when beaned during a Series game, Dean was carted off in a stretcher to the hospital. When the newspapers appeared the next morning, they carried what is probably the most famous headline in baseball history: X-RAY OF DEAN'S HEAD SHOWS NOTHING. Millions nodded in agreement.

Whatever one thinks of Dean's behavior off the mound, few could find fault with his performance on it. Probably the greatest season for both Dizzy and his only slightly less gifted brother, was 1934. That spring, reporters asked Dizzy just how well he was going to do. He predicted that he and Paul would win "between forty-five and fifty games." How many of those, the press wanted to know, would he, Dizzy, win? "Why, all the games that Paul don't," Diz replied. In the end the pair won forty-nine. At the fall classic that year, the Cards bested the Tigers 4–3; Paul winning two games, and Dizzy taking two.

Although the Cardinals in the 1940s were less colorful, they were equally successful. Altogether, the Cards made four trips to the fall classic, and came home with the trophy three times (1942, 1944, and 1946). Actually, in 1944, the Cards didn't even have to leave home to go to the Series, for their opponents were the hapless St. Louis Browns, who also played in Sportsman's Park and who were making their sole Series appearance. In a contest complicated by the fact that the managers of both teams shared an apartment, the Cards won 4–2.

During these years, "Red" Schoendienst and Enos Slaughter performed yeoman services for the squad. The key player on the team though, and one of the all-time greats of the game was slugger Stan Musial. There are relatively few stories about this star, for the simple reason that Musial, a modest and admirable man, let his bat do most of the talking for him. One of the most consistent hitters the game has ever seen (second in total bases, fifth in

RBIs), Musial was a hurler's nightmare. Once the Dodger's "Preacher Roe" was asked if he knew what the secret to pitching to Musial was. "Sure," the ace responded. "Throw him four wide ones and try to pick him off at first."

More modern times have also been kind to the Cards. Hall of Fame greats like Lou Brock (former all-time stealing champ) and pitcher Bob Gibson propelled the Redbirds to three pennants and two Series victories (1964 and 1967) in the sixties. New stars such as gold glove short stop Ozzie Smith, speedster Vince Coleman, 1985 MVP Willie McGee, pitchers John Tudor, Lonnie Smith, and the erratic but awesome "Cuckoo Jar" Joaquin Andujar made the Cardinals one of the strongest teams of the 1980s. Three trips to the Series (1982, 1985, and 1987) resulted in one victory (1982). Although the 1982 contest with the Brewers was the sweetest for the Redbirds, the 1985 battle against the Royals provided the most spectacle. This classic debacle started badly for the Cards when Busch Stadium's high-tech automatic tarp machine proceeded to run over Vince Coleman, knocking him out of the Series. Still, the Cards forged forward to win three games, only to lose a tight sixth game after a hotly disputed call at first base. In the seventh meeting, the Redbird's frustration showed as ace hurler John Tudor put his fist through a glass door after being pulled off the mound and Joaquin Andujar, frustrated over calls, charged the batter's box with such fury that it took a full bench of Birds to keep him off the umpire. At least the Series provided drama.

In 1990, the Cardinals turned in their worse performance in decades, finishing dead last in their division. Perhaps even more significantly, Whitey Herzog, long-time manager and mastermind of the Cardinals' success throughout the 1980s, quit. Now, the team seems to be in a state of limbo, trying to plot a way back to greatness.

The Cardinals have some fine fielders and pitchers. Unfortunately, the Redbirds, at this point, are almost totally lacking in the power hitting department. If they can correct this deficiency while continuing to improve the team as a whole, the Cardinals may find themselves in contention once again.

The Stadium

It must be admitted that Busch Stadium is beautiful. A perfect circle rising in downtown St. Louis just west of the Mississippi and the city's soaring landmark arch, it cuts an attractive figure along the St. Louis skyline as seen from the Illinois side of old Miss. Its open-sided, spacious design gives the place an airy look, avoiding the leaden appearance of many of the newer concrete sports palaces.

The park is not only attractive; it's convenient, too. Despite the facility's downtown location, planners wisely made provisions for plenty of parking. The stadium itself is clean, modern, and convenient. As for the downtown location, that was probably something of a negative in 1966, when Busch opened. Then, St. Louis was near the bottom of what had been an extended decline. Today, though, the stadium's location at the center of things is pure joy, within a easy stroll of the park are fine hotels, great restaurants, exciting shopping areas, nightlife, historic sights, the arch—you name it.

These are among the many good things about Busch Stadium. The only negative word that can be said about the stadium is that it is not a baseball park. If you can put that minor difficulty out of your mind, it's likely that you won't find a flaw in the Busch set-up at all.

Busch couldn't have a better location. Downtown St. Louis is one of the most exciting and interesting urban centers in the Midwest. As for the stadium area itself, there are a few stops you should make before moving inside. At the northeast corner of the park, at the corner of Broadway and Walnut, you'll find a wonderful statue of Stan Musial. Inscribed on the base are the words of baseball commissioner Ford Frick: "Here stand baseball's perfect warrior, here stands baseball's perfect knight." Perhaps the tribute is a bit overblown, but, on the other hand, it's hard to imagine any other major leaguer who would more epitomize those words than Stan the Man. To the right of the statue is the entrance for the "St. Louis Sports Hall of Fame," located within and under the park. This is a very worthwhile attraction (see *Features*). Finally, outside each of the stadium gates, you'll see a pennant describing the accomplishments of one of the Cardinal's retired number players, a list which includes Stan Musial (#6), third baseman Ken Boyer (#14), pitchers Dizzy Dean (#17) and Bob Gibson (#45), stolen-base champion Lou Brock (#20), and former owner August Busch, Jr. (#85).

Inside the park, the aisles are pleasingly open to the sun, the appearance is clean, and the concession stands are well-placed and color coordinated; though there may not be enough of them, as the lines can get pretty long.

One look at the seating area and you'll see what the problem with Busch is. A perfect circle inside, its deck are set far, far back from the field. In fact, its' a bragging point on the park's stadium tour that almost no one has ever hit Busch's upper deck. If the tour guides would think about that statement for a second, they'd realize that the fact is nothing to boast about. Would you want to watch a ballgame from a distance so far that, say, even Willie Stargell couldn't hit a ball to you?

How you'll feel about the field depends on how you feel about technology and its proper uses. The playing area is covered with astroturf, which in turn covers a surface of asphalt and limestone. There is indeed an automatic tarp machine that rests under the carpet; it pops out from time to time to protect the field and or devour players. If you look in the area of the first base lines, you may be able to see its outlines.

Busch has a bigger outfield than most stadium; indeed, it is a "pitcher's park" for reasons that become obvious whenever you consider who the Redbird greats have been. The foul poles in the facility are set at 330', while the farthest reach of center field is 414'. To the left of center field is the Cardinal's big and informative electronic scoreboard. To the right is a large and effective diamond vision display that runs fine playbacks during the game — and too many commercials.

Busch, overall, is such an attractive place, its location is so perfect, and the team that plays in the stadium is so central to the history of the sport that attending a game here has to be considered a near "must" for any fan. Still, when you see the inside of the stadium and realize that Sportsman's Park was torn down so that this facility could come into being, it makes you a little sad.

Highlights

With the Cardinals listed high among the most successful franchises in the sport, it isn't surprising that they've filled their stadium with baseball milestones.

For Cards fans, the biggest highlights would have to be their World Series victories. Altogether, Busch Stadium has seen the Cards in the classic five times and victorious twice (1967 and 1982). In both cases, though, the Cards clinched the title away from home.

Pitching has provided some thrills, too. Ace Cardinals hurler Bob Forsch

pitched two no-hitters in the park, one in 1978, the other in 1983. During 1968, Hall of Fame Cardinal Bob Gibson burned up the leagues with a pitching performance that included a 22-9 record, including 13 shutouts, and an incredible ERA of 1.12. Unsurprisingly, Gibson copped both Cy Young and MVP honors.

Batters have hit some milestones in Busch, too. On August 13, 1979, Hall of Famer Lou Brock recorded his 3,000th hit in the park.

Fans

St. Louis baseball admirers are the original "fans": the people the term was invented to describe. Yet if "fan" means what it meant originally, if it is just shorthand for "fanatic," then that doesn't really describe what the crowd that congregates at Busch is all about. If Cardinal fans were that way, they'd support their team right or wrong, they'd festoon themselves with Cardinals pennants and gear, and they would pile abuse on umpires, opposing players, and visiting baseball enthusiasts not smart enough to cheer for the home team — in short, if they were really fanatics, they'd behave like Mets or Giant admirers! If, on the other hand, to be a "fan" means to take a serious interest in the game as a whole while having a preference for your team in particular, *that* would describe Cardinal admirers to a "T."

Look around the audience the moment you sit down in Busch Stadium and you'll notice something a bit peculiar. A very large percentage of the patrons will be wearing red, specifically, "cardinal." Indeed, red suddenly becomes very popular in St. Louis every summer. Beyond this, the differences between Redbird admirers and fans in other parks will be a matter of shading rather than degree. You'll note that, while St. Louis people are polite to opponents, applause for their own team is louder and more sustained than in many other places. You'll also see that Cards fans pay a bit more attention to the game than most baseball enthusiasts, and that scorecards are in evidence in many rows, even if their use is far from universal. And as much as Cardinals fans love their team to win, they are baseball people before they are Cardinal people. A spectacular play by the opposition will get an appreciative acknowledgement.

John Wilkerson, a middle-aged man, is emblematic of the Cardinal fan. Known as "the Mayor of the Bleachers" (he wears a shirt to that effect, so if you're sitting in the bleachers you are likely to spot him), John has attended virtually every Cards game for the last ten years. He is unlike such other famous fans as Betsy Chatsworth ("the Dodger Momma") and the Indian's John Adams. They are basically cheerleaders, out to boost fan support for their team. John Wilkerson, by contrast, is more of a scholar. Sometimes he applauds, sometimes he looks down and shakes his head, and at all times he has a very sophisticated understanding of what is happening on the field. Ask Betsy or John Adams how their team will do, and they will both probably say "great"—though Adams may wink as he says it. Ask John Wilkerson about the Cards' prospects only if you really want to know.

What is the audience like? The Cards pull in a well-dressed, middle- and working-class crowd. There are quite a few women in the audience and, always, lots and lots of kids. The Cards invented the "knot hole gang" kids baseball marketing concept, and they draw a horde of youngsters to the park to this day. Overall, there is nothing extraordinary about this audience. They are simply real baseball fans.

Getting There

Located in downtown St. Louis just a few blocks west of the famed arch,

Busch Stadium could hardly be easier to get to. No matter what direction you are coming from, as soon as you get near the central business district you'll find cardinal red signs pointing the way to the park.

As a practical matter, most visitors to the stadium will want to go by car or cab, though for those arriving at the airport, van is also a good option. You can avoid the need to drive into the park at all by the simple expedient of staying at one of the downtown hotels; virtually all are within an easy stroll of the Cardinal's home.

By car. Those traveling to Busch Stadium from such *east* locales as Evansville and Louisville will want to take I-70 west to the point where it crosses the Mississippi River into downtown St. Louis. As soon as you turn into downtown, exit at the Stadium/9th Street and follow signs to parking.

If you are coming from such *west* areas as Jefferson City, Kansas City, and Lambert St. Louis airport, take I-70 east to Exit 250B Downtown Stadium going east. Follow signs from there to stadium parking.

Residents of Springfield, Chicago, and other *north* points who want to go to the game should proceed on I-55 south to where it crosses the Mississippi River, then take I-70 north to the Stadium/9th Street exit and then follow the signs to the park.

Those coming from Memphis, south Missouri, and west Tennessee should take I-55 north to downtown St. Louis and then should follow I-70 to the exit for Market Street west. From there, follow Market Street to stadium parking.

By cab. There really is no need to take a cab from most of the downtown hotels to go to the stadium. If you do decide to take a cab, it will cost you $3 or less.

Taking a cab to the park from the airport is a more expensive proposition. Plan on paying a minimum of $20 each way.

By van. Those coming to Busch Stadium from the airport might want to pass on taking a cab and instead utilize the shuttle service that runs from the aiport to the major downtown hotels. Simply get your bags and go to the bus. Once you buy your ticket ($6 one way), ask to be dropped off at the Marriott Pavilion Hotel. It's directly across the street from the park.

Parking

For a stadium located smack in the middle of the downtown section of a major city, Busch Stadium's parking arrangements are pretty acceptable. Covered, high rise parking lots sit across the street from the stadium on the east and west sides at Broadway and Stadium Plaza, and south of the park is a large uncovered lot. The uniform charge for all three facilities is $4.

While these three lots provide enough parking for nearly all games, if you are driving you might want to consider coming to Busch Stadium a little early. You'll get a closer parking spot, and you'll avoid the last minute rush that can clog this area up to a fare-thee-well just before game time. On your way out, too, you might want to dawdle a bit and give the lots and the traffic a chance to clear before going back to your car.

Tickets

Cardinals tickets are available by the usual means. You can order them by mail, purchase them over the phone, or pick them up at the park's advance ticket office.

To get tickets by mail, write to the Cardinals at: St. Louis Cardinals Ticket Office, PO Box 8787, St. Louis, MO 63102.

In writing, be sure to include information on the number of tickets you want, the dates, and the general locations. Also be sure to enclose your check or money order for payment in full, being sure to enclose an extra $3 for the Cardinal's service charge.

Phone orders are handled by the Cardinals at (314) 421-2400. When calling, be sure to have your credit card ready (Visa or MasterCard), and be prepared with the enclosed seating chart to make sure you get the best seats possible. You'll be assessed a $3 service charge here, too.

The Cards' advance ticket office is located at the west side of the stadium, and is open from 9 A.M. to 5:30 P.M. Monday through Saturday during the regular season, and from 8 A.M. to 5 P.M. Monday through Friday during the off-season. Buy your tickets here and you'll have a chance to check out a seating chart before you plunk your pennies down — a very good idea at Busch Stadium.

Availability. Over the years, the Cardinals have consistently been one of the hottest tickets in baseball. In 1989, for example, St. Louis lead the National League in attendance, and was one of only two teams that season to break the 3,000,000 mark. During most years, the club sells well over 20,000 season tickets, and sellouts, while rare, do happen.

What does this mean for the visiting fan? First, if you want good seats — and, in truth, there are not all that many good seats in Busch Stadium — you should order well in advance, particularly if you intend to go to games against such popular Redbird rivals as the Cubs or the Mets. Even if you don't mind sitting in seats that may not be the best, you should still think about calling in an order a week or so before you will be in town, just in case.

Having said all of this, it's still true that, even if you show up at the last minute, you will probably find a seat. It will then be a question of what kind of seat (see *Seating*).

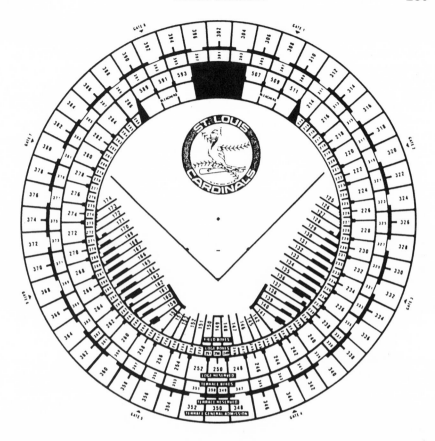

Seating chart, Busch Stadium.

Costs. Ticket prices at Busch Stadium are reasonable without being exceptionally low. In most cases (there are some important exceptions) what you pay for your seats will match the view of the game you'll get.

In 1990, Redbird ticket charges were as follows: Box Seats ($10.50); Reserved Seats ($8); General Admission ($5); Bleachers* ($4).

Rainouts. Though the Cardinals' astroturf minimizes their number, rainouts do occur at Busch Stadium a couple of times a year. If you get caught in one, the team will be happy to ex-change your ticket for a ticket for a future game.

Seating

Busch Stadium is impressive, beautiful—and perfectly round. Thus, like Riverfront, Three Rivers, and several other sports facilities, the Cardinal's home park is one that cuts a great figure on the city's skyline, but has a low percentage of truly good seats.

"Boxes" ($10.50) is the category of Busch's most expensive seats. But

*Sold 1½ hours before the game.

boxes come in different shapes and sizes.

The first grouping of box seats are the Field boxes, and they are indeed the best spots in the house. Forming an arc around the central playing areas of the field (see chart p. 239), these spots are nearly all closer to the action than just about any of the other types of boxes, and accordingly they should be snapped up. If you can get within the baselines here, which run from 134 (first) to 164 (third), so much the better.

Loge boxes are a level higher, and are supposedly hung over the field. Nonsense. They are all, without exception, set back a good ways from the action. If you can get within the baselines, from 236 (first) to 264 (third) you'll still have an alright view. If you get seats in Loge outside these sections, though, we don't feel you'll be getting your money's worth.

Terrace boxes are yet a level higher. Unlike the Loge boxes, at least all the seats in this area are within the baselines, and, therefore, have acceptable views. However, at the price, seats in the Terrace level, unless in the very lowest rows, can't be counted as being among the better buys in the game.

"Reserved" ($8) seats are next lowest in price, and they vary greatly in quality, as they wrap completely around the stadium. Thus, if you find yourself behind the batter's box, you'll have a pretty decent view, while if you get put out in center field the players will look like ants.

Loge reserved seats are set behind the Loge boxes. About the best that can be said for them is that, within the baselines, they are OK. If you plan on sitting here, try staying between sections 236 (first) and 264 (third). Ditto the Terrace reserved seats, which are yet a level higher. Baseline sections there correspond to the ones below, and run from 336 to 364.

General Admission ($5) seats in the park have only their price to recommend them. Set far from the action in the top rows of the top deck of the stadium, these spots are so far from the field that you hardly feel that you're part of the game. Still, from most of the G.A. spots along the right field line, you'll at least be able to see the arch; we suppose that's some compensation. If you are going to sit here, try to get into the sections behind the batter's box (346 to 352); these spots are less bad than the others. If you can't get into this area, at least think about going to the bleachers.

The bad thing about the bleachers ($4) is that the seating is uncomfortable: seats are old-style backless wooden benches. The area also gets a young crowd, with lots of kids. The plus of the category is the view. Set behind the outfield fences in the traditional "bleacher" area, these spots are closer to the action than many of the more expensive reserved seats on the levels above. Accordingly, you might want to consider sitting here if you want to save a buck and see the game. If you do go to bleachers, though, be aware that the concession stands in this area offer a minimal selection, and you will not be able to get to areas where the choices are better.

Some overall comments should be made about seating. Seats in all sections except bleachers are fairly comfortable metal-and-plastic chairs. Within the box areas, rows are reasonably short and there's decent legroom. Outside the boxes, though, rows are very long, legroom is constricted, and people trying to get in and out of their seats can present real problems in terms of trying to see the game with a minimum of interruptions.

The vending situation makes all of this worse. The stadium is simply over vended; people bearing large crates of peanuts, beer, and hot dogs seem to be in the aisles constantly, and they present frequent view obstructions. Some of the vendors, particularly the beer-sellers, are overly pushy in hawking their wares. Several times in the course of a game you may find yourself wanting to yell out to them to "sit down and shut up!"

Special Needs

Parking. Handicapped parking is available in the east and west stadium parking garages, but it is not available in the open south lot. When you drive into the parking garages, show your sticker or plate to the attendant, and you'll be directed to the appropriate area.

Seating. There's plenty of handicapped seating in the park. At the field level, spaces are set aside in sections 147 to 151. All are superior spots behind the batter's box. The Loge level offers spots in 252, 254, and 214. The first two are great batter's box locations, the third is far from the action. There are also a few spaces set aside in the left field bleachers, but they can only be purchased just before the game.

Busch Stadium has no special "family reserved" seating. However, there is an attractive family picnic area located behind center field at the main concourse level. The place has a snack bar, kid oriented foods, and tables. It will give you a place to watch the game for a while (you can stay here only two innings), while the children are free to move about a bit.

Food and Features

Food. Like most of the midwestern baseball parks, food at Busch stadium is mostly standard baseball fare, with a heavy emphasis on sausages. There are, however, some other choices available, too. Overall, Cardinals' food is neither

exceptionally good nor terribly bad; it's just there.

Stands throughout the park hawk the usual stuff: hot dogs, brats, jumbo hots, nachos, popcorn, Edy's ice cream, peanuts, and rope licorice are all sold throughout the park. Pizza Hut runs a *Pizza Express* concession behind 224. That sounds good, but in actuality the pizza sold isn't real pizza at all but rather the "French bread" pizza you'll find at several parks that tastes terrible and is overpriced.

There are some specialities, too. *Diamond Grill,* located behind sections 234 and 268, offers grilled burgers, chicken sandwiches, and fries. "Sweet Treats," behind 268 and 232, has such soft serve specialities as cones, sundaes, and no-fat frozen yogurt. Set behind 230, you'll find the *Mexican Cantina,* which has tacos, burritos, and taco salad. Probably the best of the bunch is *The Steer House,* which serves up a tasty though pricey sirloin steak sandwich. You'll find this stand to the left of home plate on the Plaza level.

Drinks. Need you ask? Budweiser owns the Cardinals, and, accordingly, Bud products are the drinks of choice in Busch Stadium. Should you not choose to join everyone else in hoisting a few, you'll find Coke products at good prices, lemonade, and even Seagrams wine coolers.

Features. St. Louis has one of baseball's richest heritages, and the Cardinals do a lot at their park to make you aware of it.

Outside the stadium gates, you'll see attractive banners (Cardinal red, of course) honoring the team's most celebrated players of the past. Also outside, of course, is the Stan Musial statue (see *The Stadium* p. 235).

Beneath the stadium is the St. Louis Sports Hall of Fame. Certainly the best in-park museum in the sport, the Hall has an outstanding collection of memorabilia saluting not just the Cardinals but also their hapless fellow townsmen the St. Louis Browns, that storied team that was "First in booze, first in shoes, and last in the American League." Among the things you'll see in the museum are the base Lou Brock stole when he broke Ty Cobb's record, a model of the classic old Sportsman's Park, where both the Browns and the Cards played, and a display honoring St. Louis' famed 1930s "Gashouse Gang" of players, which included such one-of-a-kind stars as Dizzy Dean, Frankie Frisch, Pepper Martin, and Leo Durocher. The most impressive display of all simply replicates the Hall of Fame plaques of the Cardinals and the Browns over the years; included in the area are such names as Dean, Stan Musial, Bob Gibson, John McGraw, Cy Young, Satch Paige, and a mighty host of others. It provides eloquent proof for the contention of many St. Louis fans that theirs is the greatest baseball town of them all.

You have to pay to get into the museum ($2 for adults, $1.50 for kids), but it is worth it. The place is open until 11 P.M. on game nights, and from 10 A.M. to 5 P.M. seven days a week throughout the season. During the off-season, you can visit the museum from 10 A.M. to 5 P.M. Monday through Friday.

The Hall of Fame also runs interesting tours of the stadium at fair prices. If you go you'll get a chance to visit the broadcasting booths, the dugouts, and the exclusive "Stadium Club" restaurant for sure. If the Cards aren't around, you'll also get to visit the dressing rooms, and you will see the basement playground where the players' kids amuse themselves while their dads work. The tarp machine that ate Vince Coleman will certainly be pointed out and you may even get to see it operating, but don't stand too close!

The tour charge is $2.50 for adults and $2 for kids. Tours depart daily at 10:15, 11:00, 1:00, 2:00, and (if there is no game) 3:00.

Assistance

The Cardinal's Guest Relations office can be located at the Plaza level, behind section 248. This is the place to go if you've lost your tickets, can't find your seats, or would just like a question or two answered about the stadium.

Safety and Security

Safety. While drinking-related problems are not overly common in Busch Stadium, the do exist. The bleacher and terrace areas can get a little rowdy from time to time, particularly during games against the Cubs. This isn't a big problem, but you should be aware of it. You will also on occasion run into inebriated fans on the streets directly after the game. Again, this isn't a regular occurrence, but it can happen.

In our view the stadium's and the team's owners (they are different) ought to share some of the responsibility for these difficulties. Liquor controls in the park are lax. There is no limit on the number of beers that are sold to an individual at one time, and the park's beer vendors are unrivaled when it comes to exhorting fans to drink more. While Budweiser, the team's sponsor, posts signs and runs ads encouraging fans to drink responsibly, the Busch crew also uses the stadium's video display for a seemingly endless barrage of beer commercials. Indeed, instead of playing "Take Me Out to the Ballgame" during the stretch, the park shows films of prancing Clydesdales and suggests that it would be a good time to have another. Nor is there any escape from the constant alcohol push. The park doesn't have a "family reserved" seating section, and even the children's picnic area sells beer.

We are not among those who feel that it is any team's responsibility to play nanny to adults and tell them whether or not they should have a drink. That's a matter of individual choice. And while we think controls are usually a good idea, we would be the first to admit that some stadiums that do little to limit alcohol consumption (Atlanta is one) nevertheless seem to have few problems. Even so, we do believe that fans ought to be allowed to enjoy a ball game in peace, without having beer thrust upon them constantly.

When you step outside the park after the game, you are in downtown St. Louis. If you've attended a day game, there will be no security problems to speak of. You might well want to stroll over to the arch or any of the other downtown tourist attractions after the contest. At night things are reasonably but not totally safe. Going to nearby hotels or over to such night spots as Mike Shannon's will present no problems if you stay with the crowd, but if you want to go down to, say, St. Louis' exciting Laclede's Landing nightlife district, you should probably hail a cab.

Health. Aside from alcohol related problems, Busch Stadium presents few serious health threats. If you are elderly or have heart problems, you should probably avoid sitting in General Admission—it's a long climb. If you are coming in April or September, pack a sweater; if you intend to sit in the top deck during the summer, wear a hat to keep the sun off you and drink plenty of water.

Should you have any health problems, the Cardinal's first aid office will be happy to provide assistance. You'll find First Aid offices behind home plate at both the Plaza and Terrace levels.

Mementos

Souvenirs. The Cardinals run an excellent souvenir shop in the lobby of the St. Louis Sport Hall of Fame, which is near Gate 4. In addition to the usual stuff, you'll find such hard to find items as authentic St. Louis Brown caps. Prices are a bit stiff, though. The souvenir shop keeps the same hours as the museum (see *Features*).

Foul Balls. Though you'll be in competition against a mighty horde of St. Louis kids, you'll have a decent shot of snagging a foul if you sit in sections 163 to 166 and 137 to 134 of the Field boxes.

Autographs. Busch Stadium isn't the best park for autograph hounds, but occasionally persistence nets fans a signature or two.

The bus for the visitors meets them near the ticket office on the west side of the park. You have a fair shot here. Getting Cards autographs is more problematic. Their parking lot is located on the south side of the stadium, east of the pedestrian walkway. You can't get into the area, and most Cardinals simply go whizzing by in their sports cars. Still, every once in a while one of the players will stop for a signature or two.

SAN DIEGO PADRES
Jack Murphy Stadium

Baseball may be the national sport, but it's also simply one of many entertainment choices confronting contemporary North Americans. No where is this fact more apparent that in San Diego.

In places such as St. Louis, Boston, and New York, baseball has been around long enough and has supplied enough tight pennant races that a bonding process has taken place between town and team, players and patrons. If baseball is one of many choices, it is, for Bostonians for example, the choice that is closest to their hearts.

Not so in San Diego. There, fun seekers can choose between one of the world's best zoos, a prominent aquatic showplace, a vibrant theatre scene, historic neighborhoods, hiking, sailing, surfing, or simply enjoying sunning themselves — for free — on some of the greatest beaches north of Mexico. Or they can go to the Padres game. Since the Padres have provided only one pennant in their history and only a handful of truly exciting seasons, there is, to be frank, only a small population of Padre die-hards in the community who can be counted on to show no matter what. Thus, every day throughout the season, the Padres find themselves battling San Diego's many other attractions for attention and attendance.

It is a battle that the team fights very, very well. Recognizing that they are competing in part against a free beach, the Padres have kept their prices pleasingly low; $9.50 will buy you the best seat in the house. Recognizing that San Diegans love to dine, the Padres have filled their stadium with some of the best food choices in the Majors. Realizing, alas, that southern Californians don't know a heck of a lot about baseball, San Diego has chosen to emphasize in its stadium the entertainment aspects of the game; promotions are common (including a wildly popular annual "Beach Boys" concert following a game), and people are encouraged to bring their bathing suits, lotion, and sunglasses and get a tan while enjoying "baseball under the sun."

All of this makes for a very pleasant experience. San Diego offers a fine stadium, good food, fair prices and,

pretty often, a great game of ball. What more could anyone want?

The Padres

The Padres are one of the newer major league teams, but they played AAA ball for decades with the Pacific Coast League before moving up. Without a doubt their most famous player then — or since — was local boy Ted Williams. Ted's mother was a Salvation Army activist known simply to San Diegans as "Salvation Mary." Despite the razzing he received from other kids because of the nature of his mother's work, though, Williams had a normal enough childhood. He attended school, played ball, and approached everything he did with that intensity that later made him, if not the greatest hitter that ever lived, without question the ball player who knew the most about hitting.

Receiving an offer from a Texas semi-pro team while still a minor, Williams asked his mom if he should take the job. She seemed favorably disposed until Ted told her the name of the team: the "Texas Liquor House." "If I had said Murder, Inc.," Williams later recalled, "I wouldn't have gotten a quicker refusal."

Ted ended up with the Padres, and, like Babe Ruth — that other contender for the title "greatest hitter ever" — started his career as a pitcher. Williams' career as a hurler was of a shorter duration than the Babe's; he pitched just three innings before management figured out that his natural baseball skills lay elsewhere.

After a short time with San Diego, Williams moved up to Boston. After a much longer time with the Pacific League, the Padres moved up to the National League in the 1969 expansion.

Their first years in the majors were pathetic. The new squad finished in the second division every single year and attendance sank accordingly; during 1971, only 549,000 fans passed through the turnstile. By 1974, the team was on the edge of collapse, and the franchise was scheduled to be sold to Washington. Only a last minute intervention by McDonald's owner Ray Kroc, who bought the team, kept baseball in San Diego. Yet while Kroc's intervention saved the team, it didn't, at least for awhile, turn the Padres around in the standings; the Padres remained in the doldrums throughout the seventies. Outstanding individual performances, however, by 1976 Cy Young winner Randy Jones, by 1978 winner Gaylord Perry, and by hard-hitting outfielder Dave Winfield at least gave the fans something to cheer about.

Things were better in the 1980s. Pitcher Goose Gossage provided some excitement for awhile, at least until he was released after indicating that hamburgers weren't his favorite food. Meanwhile, a third place finish in 1985 and a second in 1989 put the Padres in the middle of exciting pennant contests. The big year, though, was 1984. After winning the NL West championship, the Padres crushed the hopes of long-suffering Cub admirers worldwide by beating them for the pennant in a hotly contested series that put a national spotlight on the talents of Padres star player (and only retired number) Steve Garvey. During the series, Garvey hit a blistering .400 and popped a game winning homer into the stands during the ninth inning of Game 4. If the fall classic that followed was something of a letdown (the Tigers beat the Padres 4–1), at least San Diegans could cherish the memories of one of the more exciting playoffs of recent years.

Currently, San Diego suits up the most outstanding squad in its history. Key players include three time (1987, 1988, 1989) batting champ Tony Gwynn, star catcher Benito Santiago, and pitcher Bruce Hurst. Accordingly,

it was confidently predicted by many that 1990 was going to be the year when, at last, San Diego was going to go all the way.

Actually, that didn't happen. By year's end the team had finished a disappointing fourth. Still, with the kind of raw talent that the Padres have, and with such exciting players as slick fielding shortstop Tony Fernandez and slugger Fred McGriff now coming on board, they have to be considered in contention for 1991 and for the next several years to come.

The Stadium

In their years in the majors, the Padres have had only one home, Jack Murphy Stadium. And a pretty fine home it is. We've been critical of many of the ballparks built in the past few decades. Too often, we've felt, they sacrificed intimacy and good views in order to overawe and impress. By contrast, Jack Murphy, though big (it's the fourth largest park in baseball) and multipurpose (the Chargers play here, too) seems to have been built on a human scale, with the customer very much in mind. Maybe the Padres were influenced by the Dodger's also admirable park in Los Angeles, or maybe they just hired baseball-smart people to design the place; whatever the reason, San Diego has one of the better modern stadiums in baseball.

Named after a famed local sports reporter and set in the "Mission Valley" district of San Diego (it's within long walking distance of Father Junipero Sera's first California mission), Jack Murphy is located in a pleasant mixed commercial and residential neighborhood about eight miles east of the ocean. In the immediate vicinity of the park are five hotels in all price ranges, good restaurants, and vibrant nightspots.

The park itself is a fairly attractive

building, with a modified "wing" design and an attractive mural painted behind the scoreboard. Though built to serve the needs of football as well as baseball, it thankfully isn't round; rather, the shape is a close approximation of the "U" you see in most of the classic parks and a few of the modern ones.

Outside the gates, unless you're into tailgating (see *Fans*) there isn't much to detain you. Inside, this being San Diego, you are mostly outside as well; corridors in all areas of the park save one are spacious, immaculate, and open to San Diego's beautiful sunshine. The exception to this rule is one of the several quirks in this park: in order to get to the field seats, the best in the house, you have to walk an incredible ways down a long, dark corridor. In order to get out to get the better selection of food that's available behind the Plaza level, you have to hike all the way out again.

The seating areas are exceptionally well laid-out. All the chairs are located in attractive, brown-and-orange color coordinated sections, and all seating in the park is composed of comfortable plastic-and-metal chairs. Legroom throughout the facility is decent, although it could be better. Those located in the bleachers under the park's "Diamond Vision" will have difficulty seeing it, however, that represents the only significant field viewing restriction on any seat in the facility.

The field is natural grass, as you would expect in California. Its dimensions are regular, but a bit short. The field poles are set at 327', while the maximum expanse of center field is 405'. As a result of this slightly constrained field, views from the bleachers are pretty good, and home runs are reasonably common; the upper deck here has been hit seven times, a good deal more often than in similar facilities. Out in the field, there are two things that merit your attention. In right center field, you'll see a plaque marking the spot where Steve Garvey clouted a crucial home run in the 1984 National League playoffs. Note too the bullpens at the ends of the field; if you are eagle-eyed, you'll see that the long benches on both sides stick out so that there's at least a potential for balls to hit fair and bounce under the bullpens benches. Actually, this happens occasionally, and the spectacle of players diving under the benches and sending the opposing pitchers flying has enlivened a number of games. Of course, even if an outfielder in this situation *does* manage to snag a ball and throw it for an out, the question is then asked (usually heatedly by the opposing manager, with much kicking of sand) just which ball was it that the player grabbed, since there will usually be a dozen or so lying around in a bullpen. Benches have emptied over this issue on more than one occasion.

So, you might ask, why don't the Padres simply move the benches someplace else? Probably because they like them just where they are. Of both the bullpens and the ballpark, we too would say that there is very little that we would want to change.

Highlights

When you think of where the great moments of baseball history happened, Jack Murphy Stadium is not the first park that comes to your mind. Even so, the place has had at least a few of them.

Probably the biggest moment for the sport occurred in 1977 when Lou Brock broke Ty Cobb's all-time base stealing record. The 1978 All-Star game was fought in Jack Murphy, and during it Steve Garvey, then a Dodger, wowed San Diegans with his game-winning triple in the eighth inning. The Nationals won 7–3.

Steve Garvey was involved, too, in what for Padre fans was probably the most magic moments of all. On October 6, 1984, Garvey hit a game-winning ninth-inning homer in game 4 of the National League Championship Series that saved the Padres from elimination. On the next day, Garvey joined with his teammates to bring San Diego its first pennant.

Fans

Watch TV baseball over any period of time and you'll notice something a bit curious: no matter who is playing, a very high proportion of the game "lead-in" tapes will be coming to you from San Diego's Jack Murphy Stadium. Study those tapes a bit more closely and you'll understand why.

Baseball, like most sports, gets a largely male viewing audience. And the San Diego Padres pull in, particularly in the bleachers, more attractive and scantily clad young women than just about any other park in baseball. Thus, the "leads."

In most baseball parks, the audience has a certain group personality. Though who goes to the ballgame varies from city to city, within each town fans have certain identifiable traits that seem to the outside observer, as immutable as the laws of nature. Thus Baltimore's fans are studious, and Yankee enthusiasts are manic and wild, while Milwaukee's stadium is a place where Archie and Edith Bunker would feel very much at home. Though the crowd at Jack Murphy isn't especially large, it's distinguished by the fact that two very different audiences turn out for Padres games at different times.

As a rule, night games tend to pull in fewer families and fewer kids than day contests in most cities. But in San Diego, it is not that way at all. Go to a night contest at Jack Murphy and you'll see Middle America personified. There

will be quite a few kids, many families, and a fair number of older fans—San Diego, for obvious reasons, is a retirement mecca. Overall, the audience will be well dressed, polite, and perhaps a bit too laid back: maybe it's because it's hard to fill this big stadium, and therefore get people really going, or maybe it's just the California character, but whatever it is, southern Californian fans just won't cheer themselves hoarse over a baseball game. Generally speaking, Padres fans would make no one's list of the most knowledgeable baseball fans, but the night crowd tends to be more baseball-oriented than the day crowd. You'll usually catch at least a few fans keeping score, and an occasional patron will have a walkman plug in his ear, listening to Padres' announcer Jerry Coleman's comments from the broadcasting booth.

The day crowd is another kettle of fish entirely. Early on in their history, the Padres noted that they were finding it almost impossible to compete for attendance with the nearby Pacific whenever the sun was out—which, in San Diego, is about 340 days a year. What to do? Finally, a bright person in marketing realized that the young people who were bypassing Jack Murphy and flocking to San Diego's benches rarely went in swimming; the water is often chilly. Rather, they were out lying on the sands principally with the idea of getting a tan and ogling the opposite sex, though not necessarily in that order. And so the thought occurred, why can't they do that at the ball game? After all, the Padres realized, they had thousands of comfortable seats located directly under the sun. What better place to get a tan? Thus, "baseball under the sun" was born. The slogan was coined, suntan lotions were offered in the concession stands, and promotions were wrapped around such items as beach towels, sunglasses, and tote bags. Annual concerts by the "Beach Boys," preceded by a ball game, were put on the schedule—and quickly became the team's most popular event.

Promoting the idea of coming to the ball game to get a tan may not seem to be the likeliest way to fill a park, but it has worked fairly well for the Padres. During most day games, the bleachers in particular fill up with young adults looking to all the world as if they were ready for an afternoon at the beach; as, indeed, most of them are, for the lion's share of these folks have either come from the ocean or will be headed back to it. This is an incredibly good spirited bunch of patrons. They sun themselves, cheer, bat around beach balls, do the wave, and, occasionally even watch the game. Mostly, though, they check out each other—and America, over the tube, checks them out.

You would think that the Padres, being one of the newer teams, would have developed little in the way of fan traditions, but that isn't quite accurate. The ocean crowd has made tossing beach balls and doing the wave popular, but fans like to do other things in the park, too. Tailgating is fairly popular here. Before each game, you'll see fans in the parking lot, roasting hots, grilling chicken, and tossing frisbees. Spectacular plays made by the Padres are greeted by Jerry Coleman's declaration that "You could hang a star on that one!" whereupon Coleman, to everyone's cheers and delight, extends a tinsel star out of his broadcasting booth at the end of a fishing pole. During opposition pitching changes, the organ blasts out "Hi di hi! Hi de hay!" and the crowd usually joins in. By contrast, the National Anthem, in this naval base city where thousands of military retirees live, is treated with special respect. This was partly why Roseanne Barr's obnoxious rendition of it, delivered in Jack Murphy in 1990, met such a vociferous response.

Overall, though, Padres fans go to the park to have fun, and, from all appearances, they do enjoy themselves. If you go, you'll probably have a fine time, too.

Getting There

Sunny California is the land of the auto. Accordingly, most visitors to Jack Murphy Stadium arrive by car or cab.

By car. Although traffic along I-8 can be a bit hectic near game time, Jack Murphy Stadium is a pretty accessible place. From almost any area in San Diego, you should be able to reach the Padres ballpark in thirty minutes or less. After the game is over, traffic backs up a bit as people try to get out of the stadium parking lot, but even here, the substantial number of exits and the easy access to the area's major freeways means that delays are minimal.

Those traveling to Jack Murphy from such *north* locales as Riverside and San Bernardino should take I-15 south to the Friars Road/Stadium exit and follow signs to stadium parking.

If you are coming from Tijuana, Mexico, or other *south* points, proceed along I-805 north after passing through customs to that road's intersection with I-15 north. Take I-15 north to the Friar's Road/Stadium exit and follow signs to parking.

By cab. If you are in town on business and don't want to bother with the hassle of renting a car, taking a cab to the game might be a good idea. Expect to pay $16 one way if you are coming from the airport, while a ride from downtown will be about $14. If you are staying in the "hotel circle" district in Mission Valley, you'll pay about half that.

At the stadium, convenient taxi stands are located at gates C, E, and G.

Parking

The Padres have thousands of parking spots, all uniformly priced at $3 for cars and pickups, and $6 for vehicles over 20'.

These prices seem pretty fair to us. However, you can avoid even this charge by finding neighborhood parking along San Diego Mission Road and walking to the game from there. Mission Road is to the east of the park, across I-15.

Tickets

You can get Padres tickets the usual ways: by mail, by phone, or you can pick them up at the advance ticket office.

To order by mail, write to the Padres at: San Diego Padres Ticket Office, PO Box 2000, San Diego, CA 92120.

Be sure to include the number of seats you want, the price category you are paying for, the dates, and the general locations you'd like your seats to be in. Also include payment in full, by check or money order, being sure to add on the Padres' $3 service charge. The Padres would also like you to enclose a self-addressed, stamped envelope with your order, which seems pretty chintzy to us.

Phone orders are accepted as well. To order by phone, call Teleseat in San Diego at (819) 283-SEAT. Be prepared with information on the date and the sort of seats you want and have a major credit card handy. Here you'll pay a service charge of $1.75 *per* ticket.

If you are in San Diego for a few days, you might want to stop by the advance ticket office for your seats. It's located at Gate C on the north side of the park (Friar's Road), and it is open Monday through Saturday from 9 A.M. to 6 P.M.

Availability. Jack Murphy Stadium, located in a town that has only a mild interest in the sport, is the fourth largest park in baseball. With yearly attendance rarely topping 2 million, that

means that there are always plenty of spots at every game. During games against such traditional rivals as the Giants and the Dodgers and especially during such popular promotions as "beach towel" night and the Padre's annual "Beach Boys" concert you may find it difficult to get good seats if you don't order in advance. On other occasions, you will probably be able to find something quite acceptable even on the day of the game.

Costs. Padres tickets are reasonably priced: $9.50 buys you the best spot in the house. In almost all cases, there's a fair correlation between the money you lay out for a seat and view you get.

The Padres 1990 ticket charges were: Field ($9.50); Plaza ($9.50); Press ($9.50); Loge ($8); Upper Reserved ($8); General Admission* ($4).

Rainouts. The last time a game was rained out at Jack Murphy was in 1983, which should give you some idea of how common game postponements are in sunny San Diego. If, by some remote chance, you should be in town and see the clouds gather threateningly, hop in your car, peel out, and *go to the game!* We have been informed by numerous people that the sight of the Padres' young staff trying first to find and then unroll the infield tarp as the rains come down is the funniest thing since the Keystone Cops.

Seating

Although Jack Murphy Stadium has its quirks, its seating arrangements are the soul of simplicity.

The best seats in the park, as well as the most expensive, are at the Field level ($9.50). Forming an arc along the baselines, these spots have uniformly fine views just about anywhere in the area (see chart p. 250). If you can find a Field spot in the baselines (aisles 23 to 37),

*Sold on game day only.

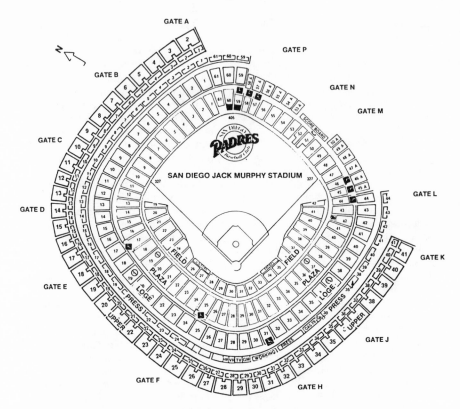

Seating chart, Jack Murphy Stadium.

great. If not, it's still hard to go really wrong with a seat in this area. If you do sit here, though, you'll find that you are quite far from the concession stands; specifically, they can be reached only by following a long dark corridor out of this level into the plaza area.

Seats at the Plaza level are the same price as those at Field, but they aren't quite so good. Located on the same tier as Field seats, they simply slope back further from the playing area. Within the baselines, (aisles 19 to 37) there's absolutely nothing wrong with these spots. On the other hand, chairs in 7 to 11 and 44 to 49 are little more than bleacher spots, and at this price ought to be avoided.

Some people enjoy the bird's eye

view available from the Press level ($9.50) boxes. These seats offer some privacy as well. However, in truth these spots are a bit far from the field, and only about a third of the spots are within the baselines (20 to 24). Unless this style of seating is really your thing, we'd suggest you go elsewhere if you can't get at least close to these aisles.

Loge seats ($8) are a level up from the Field seats, and, although we would have liked to have seen this deck set closer to the playing area, many of these spots still have pretty acceptable views. Baseline aisles here run from 19 to 37. Going for the same price, Upper Reserved seats are yet another level further up. Since, however, only the rows closest to the field are included in this designation, if you sit in the baselines here (21 to 35) you'll be able to see it all at a fair price.

There are thousands of General Admission ($4) seats in the stadium—in fact, over 18,000 in all. Two areas merit particular attention. Aisles 1 to 6 and 50 to 61 are the traditional bleachers. This is where many of San Diego's famed bathing beauties go to see and be seen. The view in this area is pretty good—and you can see the ballgame pretty well from here, too. General Admission aisles 27 to 32 fan out behind the batter's box, and though they are far from the action, you'll still be able to see the game without binoculars. If you are going to sit in General Admission, though, keep in mind that all these areas are pretty sunny. Bring lotion, sunglasses, and, if you are so disposed, a beach towel—everyone else does.

Special Needs

Parking. The Padres provide a special parking area and wheelchair entrance for the physically disabled at Gate H. When you pull into the stadium parking, show your plate or sticker and you'll be directed to it.

Seating. Inside, wheelchair seating is provided in several areas. Those at Plaza 44, 45, and 46 are among the most expensive, but they may not be the best—though they are located close to the field, they're set near the right field foul pole. Better in the same area is Plaza 17 (along left field line) and 25 (just to the left of home plate). The less expensive Loge area offers a fine location: aisle 31 is just to the right of home plate. In the bleachers, space has been set aside in sections 57 to 59, which is behind center field.

The Padres also offer two other types of special needs seating. There are two "family reserved" no alcohol, no smoking areas in the park, located at aisles 5 and 6 of the Press level. These are over-

priced spots far from the action; they are also, in our opinion, not needed as excessive drinking and rowdy behavior in the park outside the bleachers is pretty rare. However, the spots exist if you want them. There are also four "no smoking" sections, two set just past first base (Plaza and Loge 37) and two just past third (Plaza and Loge 19). As Murphy Stadium is well sheltered from the wind, smoking can be a pain here on occasion; accordingly, if cancer fumes are something that gets to you, you might want to book these spots.

Food and Features

Food. For some reason, California baseball parks, overall, knock themselves out to provide decent food to their fans. Jack Murphy Stadium is no exception to the rule. It may not have the best food in the majors (we'd give that honor to Montreal, with Anaheim a close second), but what it does have is pretty darned good.

Though San Diegans don't seem to consume many of them, the Padres' hot dogs are surprisingly tasty. They're big and meaty, and the price is right. Cotton candy is popular here, and you get a fair portion. Pretzels and Cracker Jacks (also a big hit) are on hand, too.

It's in the specialty areas that the Padres excel. "Churros," a kind of Mexican fried dough covered with cinnamon, are sold throughout the park and are deservedly popular. Cinnamon rolls, which are popular throughout southern California, are available, too. "Burgers and Fries," behind Plaza 26 and in other locations, serves, of course, burgers: however, theirs are charbroiled, and are well above the ball park standard. "Specialty Stands," at Plaza 15, Loge 17, and elsewhere, push "health foods" (this is California). Here's where you'll find turkey dogs (few nitrates, and little taste), fruit cups, "veggie sticks," and nonalcohol beer. You can feast on a whole buffet dinner at the *Sport's Club,* which is located behind Plaza 21. Among their specialties are B-B-Q dinner, turkey and swiss cheese sandwiches, fried chicken, and lasagna. Some fans come here to dine before the game.

We've saved the best specialty for last, and that's *Rubio's Fish Tacos,* found near Plaza 34, and at the "Upper Deck" restaurant (Upper 21), which also has a pleasant patio area with picnic tables where you can dine in the San Diego sunshine, before or after the game. Just what is a "fish taco"? It's a Tijuanan specialty, with real, Mexican-style soft tacos (not those hard Gringo horrors), a nice, flaky fillet, and a "special sauce" that really is special. Whatever the thing is, it's delicious. Be sure to try one.

Drinks. You'll certainly want something to wash all of the above down. Coke products are available throughout the park, and their prices are among the most reasonable in the game. "Bud" is the beer of choice with the younger set; white wine is available throughout the park, too, and seems popular here. Specialty places such as the *Top Deck* and *The Sports Club* serve better brands; *The Sports Club* also offers mixed drinks.

Features. Once upon a time, San Diego had the most popular feature in baseball—the San Diego Chicken. These days, though, the bird (now renamed "the Famous Chicken") has flown the coop and is just as likely to be seen in Kansas City as in California.

Since the fowl's departure, the feature scene at the park has been pretty quiet. There's no mascot. There is a "Speed Pitch" concession, located behind Plaza section 12. Outside the entrance to the Stadium Club elevators (Gate F), there are modest busts outlining the accomplishments of Jack Murphy, whom the stadium is named after, and Ray Kroc of McDonald's fame, who

once owned the team. Inside, of course, is good food, good times, and major league ball.

Assistance

The Padres' Customer Service office is located at Gate F, and is staffed by the usual friendly, able, long-suffering types. This is the place to look for lost tickets and lost kids.

Safety and Security

Safety. We wouldn't want to describe any park as absolutely safe, but Jack Murphy Stadium is just about as safe as they come. Occasionally, some one will drink a bit too much in the bleachers, but that's about the extent of the security problem in the facility. Outside, the parking lots and the surrounding neighborhood are about as secure as you could reasonably expect in today's world.

Health. Given San Diego's mild climate, neither extremes of cold nor heat present many difficulties for those who attend games. If you are going to an evening contest, bring a sweater. If you are coming to a day game, light and white is the style.

The sun, really, is the only significant health threat. Particularly if you plan to sit in General Admission, lotion, a cap, and sunglasses would be a good idea. If you forget to bring any of them, you'll find all available at the "Souvenir Shop" behind Plaza aisle 27. Should you come down with a burn or if you sould have any other health-related problems, you'll find the Padres' first aid office by Gate F, at Plaza 25.

Mementos

Souvenirs. Near Gate B, the Padres maintain a handsome gift shop which is accessible from both inside and outside Jack Murphy. There, a cap will cost $7 and up, while you can get a kids shirt for the same price. Also available are attractive posters of the classic ball parks of the past.

The gift shop is open during all games, of course, and also on Tuesday through Saturday, 11 A.M. to 5 P.M.

Foul Balls. You'll get a lot of competition from San Diego's future Ted Williams, but if you think you can outcatch the junior brigade, try sitting in Plaza level 20 to 23 and 34 to 35.

Autographs. Jack Murphy isn't one of the better parks for autograph hunters. Both the visitors and the Padres leave the park through a tunnel between Gates E and F and then go from there to a secured parking lot which has the visitors' bus and the Padres' cars — you can't even get near them. Every once in a while, one of the players will take the time to walk over and sign a few, but this isn't something you should count on.

SAN FRANCISCO GIANTS
Candlestick Park

What has been the most influential baseball park built in modern times?

A strong case could be made that it is Houston's Astrodome, that mammoth monument that represents the Lone Star spirit in all its expansiveness, extravagance, and excess. Not only was the Astrodome the first enclosed stadium, it was also, and probably just as significantly, the first round one. "Astroturf," that bane of baseball purists, also came to us courtesy of the Dome.

Yet San Francisco's Candlestick Park has equal claim to stadium preeminence. Opened in 1960, five years before the Houston complex, Candlestick was among the first baseball parks to be constructed as the result of public-private cooperation between a team (the Giants) and a government municipality (the City of San Francisco). Thus, like very few of the parks before and nearly all those since, Candlestick came into existence as much to satisfy urban pride as to provide a place

to play ball. By contrast, their more conservative fellow East Coast transplants the Dodgers insisted on keeping their new park a team-owned, private enterprise facility. As a result, the older Candlestick was a stadium that looked to — and prefigured — the future. Dodger Stadium was, and remains, a park that very much takes its cues from the past.

Candlestick was also the first park to take a serious look at the realities of postwar North American life and to try to adapt baseball around the changes that had taken place in the way people lived, and where they lived. Recognizing that many Americans had moved to suburbia after the war, Candlestick was the first park *not* constructed in an urban neighborhood. Rather, the place was put up on a vacant landfill on San Francisco Bay, close to the rapidly growing peninsula towns south of the city. Also seeing that nearly everyone now owned a car, Candlestick was constructed just off a major highway — and quite far from good public transportation. One of the ironies of a baseball visit to San Francisco, in fact, is that while you can't take the city's BART subway system to "The Stick," excellent train service is available to Oakland's Coliseum. Finally, grasping that the tremendous prosperity that occurred in the 1950s had brought with it a like increase in everyone's expectations, the Candlestick people built a park where the comfort and convenience of fans were among the planners foremost concerns.

When the Giants' new facility opened, it was the subject of unprecedented hoopla. Dignitaries from throughout the nation were invited to attend opening day, and many—including Ty Cobb and Vice President Nixon, who threw out the first ball—accepted. Major publications ran glowing articles on the new sports palace, and Charles Schultz issued a "Peanuts" panel about the park in which Charlie Brown is shown wishing he could manage a team in such a wonderful place. To promote interest in the stadium among San Franciscans, a contest was held to give people the opportunity to name the park. The term Candlestick was chosen, for reasons that no one really seems sure of. Just about everyone agrees, though, that somehow the term fits.

Candlestick's opening was greeted with rave reviews from just about all quarters. The *San Francisco Examiner* termed the park "A symphony of grey concrete and steel." The Stick was "A Dazzling Diamond Palace," trumpeted *The Sporting News*. Within months, traveling to San Francisco to see the wonders of the Stick (to say nothing of the wonders of the Willies, McCovey and Mays) became a popular journey for fans. In fact, had you asked baseball people what was the finest stadium in the early 1960s, the Giants' spanking new facility probably would have rated very high on the list. The popularity of the new park was so great that promoters of other forms of entertainment began to look to it as a place to stage their events. "The Great Wallenda" held thousands in the park awestruck one day as he walked across the field on a wire strung between the tiers of the top deck. The Beatles played in the Stick, too, in what would turn out to be their last appearance together.

Today, what was a generation ago among the most praised of ballparks is now one of the most routinely criticized. Pick up many a baseball book and you won't have read far before one player or another complains about how the Stick's infamous winds robbed him of a homer that was surely his. Baseball pundits, meanwhile, have seized upon the Stick as the prime example of everything that has been wrong with modern ballpark construction. Local newspaper articles frequently attack the park's bad traffic and lack of public transportation. Giants fans gripe about the park's coldness, while out-of-towners gripe about the Giants fans. Even the Giants themselves have turned on their once celebrated stadium. Citing all of these problems and more, the Giants have, in recent years, demanded that the citizens of San Francisco build them another stadium if they want to keep major league baseball in their town.

As if all this weren't enough, Mother Nature herself—never, in truth, a friend of the park—conspired to display Candlestick's age and deficiencies to the world when a major earthquake hit the stadium and the entire Bay area just before the third game of the 1989 World Series. Cracks appeared in the sports palace's concrete facings—and cracks widened in the already dwindling confidence fans and management had in the Stick.

Why was the park that was first so loved later so hated? The fact is that the way fans have, over the past generation, responded to the Stick has said a lot more about the changes that have taken place in their attitudes and priorities than it has said anything of real importance about this ballpark.

The truth is that Candlestick was never as great a place to play ball as it was initially said to be. Transportation into the facility was a problem from the earliest years, while the field in the 1960s was just as damp, cold, and windy as it is today. In fact, one of the funniest incidents in All-Star game history occurred in the Stick in 1961 when pitcher Stu Miller was actually blown off the mound by a gust while in the middle of his windup—and then was charged with a balk!

Just as Candlestick was never as great a stadium as people at first supposed, neither is the place quite as poor a baseball park as is now being said. Is it a park that represents the worst excesses of the newer stadiums? In some ways, yes. It's big and impersonal and many of its seats are too far from the action. On the other hand, the place also boasts a natural playing field, a blue sky, and committed fans who give the Stick much of the character that the building itself may lack. As for the supposed wind and damp air problems that are said to have a negative effect on play, what, we wonder, is the precise difference between obstacles such as these and Fenway's "Green Monster"? Don't both features add interest and excitement to the game? We can well understand why a player would be ticked when a ball he thought he'd hit clear to Oakland slows to a stop in the sky and falls into someone's mitt. But from the standpoint of the patron, such events give the contest an aspect of surprise. They supply the Stick that element of unpredictability that is one of the things most lacking from many of the newer facilities. Candlestick the *worst* baseball park? We don't think so.

All of which is not to say that it is particularly fine baseball facility, either. If you go to a Giants game, you'll have to put up with all the Stick's celebrated problems. All we can say about them is, bring your patience in order to handle the traffic, and a sweater (at least) to cope with the weather. On the other hand, you'll also get to see one of the sport's most famous and important teams play in one of North America's most beautiful and rewarding cities. That can make up for an awful lot.

The Team

In 1876, the National League was established. Seven years later New York was represented in the first of the major leagues when a new franchise, the "Gothams," signed up. This is the team we call the Giants today.

The Gothams were only an average team in their first quarter century of play. They managed to carry two pennants, but more typically they floundered around the middle of the standings. Still, they did field some outstanding players in these years, including such pre–1900 Hall of Fame pitching greats as Amos Rushie ("the Hoosier Thunderbolt") and Mickey Welch. They also acquired their unusual name. After a victory that put the unusually tall but little-heralded New York squad into a tight pennant race with Chicago, Jim Multrie, the team's excitable manager, ran out of the dugout to greet his players as they came off the field. "My big fellows!" he shouted, "My Giants! We are the people!" The name stuck.

In 1902, at the very beginning of the modern era, Baltimore Orioles manager John McGraw joined the Giants, and he quickly built in New York one of the most powerful baseball dynasties ever. Piloting the Giants to an incredible nine pennants in his thirty years with the club, McGraw may well have been the greatest manager of all time.

A profane, hard-nosed fellow, the Giants' helmsman favored tough play, tight baserunning, and using vociferous fans as a means of intimidating the opposition. Nor was McGraw averse to stretching the rules a bit if he had to in order to win. To him, such tactics were all part of the game.

The man had an incredible nose for baseball talent, and he was particularly adept at recruiting pitchers. Hall of Fame hurlers who served on the McGraw Giants during these years included Joe McGinnity, called "Iron Man" because of his habit of pitching both games of doubleheaders, Rube Marquard, and the great Carl Hubbell. Hubbell is particularly famous for his pitching feat in the 1934 All-Star game of striking out, consecutively, Babe Ruth, Lou Gehrig, Jimmy Foxx, Al Simmons, and Joe Cronin.

Without a doubt though, McGraw's greatest star was pitcher Christy Mathewson, one of the four original members of the Baseball Hall of Fame (the others were Ruth, Cobb and Walter Johnson). Currently third on the all-time wins list (373) and boasting the fourth-lowest ERA (2.13), Mathewson was a simply awesome hurler who specialized in control and guile rather than fastballs and force.

Matty, as everyone called him, was incredibly accurate. It was said he could throw a ball into a tin cup from the mound at pitching speed. He was also a master strategist, who, rather than waste his strength trying to burn down all before him would gauge his hurls to the hitter. This tendency to conserve his strength was the subject of one of the best tales about the man. Once, during a game against Boston, the Giants players had bet hundreds of dollars that they would beat the Beantowners. To their horror they watched as Matty, having held the Bostonians down throughout the game, proceeded to allow the bases to fill at the bottom of the ninth. Knowing that Mathewson was opposed to gambling and afraid that they were about to lose their money, the Giants held an impromptu

infield conference and then sent a delegation to the mound. Did Matty realize, they wanted to know, just what was at stake?

"Don't worry," he responded, gesturing to the Braves on base. "They aren't going to get any farther." Matty gunned down the next three batters in order.

Mathewson was also, in terms of personality, a total contrast to McGraw. A man who opposed drinking, swearing, gambling, and carousing, Christy denounced these things whenever he could. He also absolutely refused to play baseball on the Sabbath. Despising tobacco, Mathewson repeatedly refused lucrative offers to endorse cigars and cigarettes.

You would think that, given their obvious differences, McGraw and Mathewson would have often been at dagger points. Actually, it wasn't that way at all; the two were close friends. Mathewson, a baseball scientist of no mean skills himself, admired McGraw's comprehensive understanding of every nuance of the game. McGraw found in Mathewson the one characteristic he liked the most in anyone: he won.

Over three decades, McGraw took his team to the classic nine times (1905, 1911, 1912, 1913, 1917, 1921, 1922, 1923, 1924). Three times (1905, 1921, 1922) the Giants took the laurels. One of many memorable moments occurred during the 1923 losing effort when, during the first game, a young Giant won the contest in the ninth with a rare World Series inside the park homer. The player's name was Casey Stengel.

With McGraw's retirement, the Giants shrunk to human size, and became another good team—at least for awhile. Behind the fine pitching of Hubbell and the home run bashing abilities of Hall of Famer Mel Ott, the club made three trips to the classic in the 1930s (1933, 1936, 1937). They fell to the awesome Yankees in the last two contests, but beat the Washington Senators handily in the first.

After the thirties, the Giants seemed for a while to forget the lessons that McGraw had taught them. They slipped in the standings and attendance declined. In the early fifties though, thanks to such exciting new players as Willie Mays, pitcher Hoyt Wilhelm, and outfielder Monte Irvin, the Giants began to rediscover their winning ways. In 1951, the Giants returned to glory following an exciting and successful last minute dash for the pennant. They fell in the classic, however, to the Yankees in five games. Another pennant occurred in 1954, and this time the New Yorkers did not fall short. Charged up by Willie May's incredible catch of a 440′ drive off the bat of the Indians' Vic Wertz, the Giants went on to win the classic 4–0.

Through these years, though, attendance continued to be a problem for the team. Soon the Giants, like their Brooklyn brothers the Dodgers, began to listen to the blandishments of West Coast cities anxious to go "major league." In 1957, the team played in the celebrated Polo Grounds for the last time and headed out to San Francisco.

The Giants' thirty-year-plus sojourn in the cable car city has seen both the agony of defeat and the joy of victory. Sometimes the team has been great, sometimes it has been terrible, and during most years the Giants have stood solidly astride the middle of the standings.

Most longtime SF fans would identify the late fifties and early sixties as the best years for the West Coast club, even though the Giant's record during this period doesn't quite justify this assessment. What made the squad so popular then? To put it simply, Willie McCovey and Willie Mays.

Two of the most colorful and effective players of their day, both Willies were deeply loved by Bay Area fans, and, indeed, by baseball fans everywhere. A powerful slugger, McCovey currently stands at number ten on the all-time home run list. An even more awesome player, Mays' stats are astounding in a variety of categories. Willie is currently number three in total bases (6,066), number seven in RBIs (1,903), number three in home runs (660), and number nine in hits (3,283). He was also a fantastic fielder. Mays may not have been the greatest ball player that ever lived, but he was certainly one of the most versatile.

He was also fun to watch, and even more fun to listen to, for the man had an infectious enthusiasm. Poor at recalling names (a characteristic he shared with Babe Ruth), Mays would greet one and all with the expression, "Say, hey!" Pretty soon he was called the "Say, hey! Kid." A player who was never quite so happy as when he was suited up and on a field, people would visit Mays at his home when he lived in New York City only to find that he was out on the street, playing stickball with the neighborhood kids.

The combined talents of Mays, McCovey, and such other Giant giants as Juan Marichal and Orlando Cepeda conspired to bring the squad to the 1962 World Series against the Yankees. It was a heartstopping contest that went the full seven games. Finally, in the last contest at the bottom of the ninth Willie McCovey came to bat. The Yanks were one run ahead while the Giants had men in tying and scoring position. McCovey hit a powerful drive, but the Yankees' Bobby Richardson made a great catch and ended the Series with a Yankee victory. Years later, when McCovey was inducted into the Hall of Fame, he was asked how he would like to be remembered. He shook his head ruefully and said, "As the guy who hit the line drive over Bobby Richardson's head."

Following the 1962 Series, the Giants continued for a long while to field powerful teams that were, somehow, not quite powerful enough. For the next fifteen years, they were in the upper division nearly every year, but they went to the playoffs only once, in 1971. They folded in four games.

By the late seventies and early eighties the Giants' star fell further; last place finishes were not unknown, and attendance sank. For the first time since the club had moved to the West Coast people began to say that the Giants might have to move again.

Finally, thanks largely to two men, things began to change. Manager Roger Craig came on board in 1986, and things improved immediately. Slugger Will Clark joined at the same time and helped to put some steel in the club. In 1987, the team went to the playoffs for the first time in sixteen years. They lost to the Cards in a tight seven game contest. In 1989, the Giants participated in their second San Francisco World Series. However, they performed poorly, folding in four to their awesome cross-bay neighbors, the Oakland A's.

Currently, the Giants have a solid squad, boasting such stars as sluggers Clark, Kevin Mitchell (the 1989 MVP winner), and Matt Williams. The team performed credibly in 1990. There's no reason that they can't do even better in the years to come.

The Stadium

If you ever have occasion to fly into San Francisco and then take a car or cab into town from the airport, you will certainly pass Candlestick Park. Just as you make a right hand swerve up Route 101 headed for downtown you will see it looming up before you in gloomy solemnity, hugging the shores of San Francisco Bay.

If you are at all like us, two thoughts may occur. First, you'll say to yourself "How beautiful!" And it's true that, from the outside, Candlestick is an attractive park indeed. Next, though, you might wonder, "Just what the heck is this thing doing out here?"

It's a question we've often asked ourselves, for, though Candlestick is within the San Francisco city limits, it is nevertheless in the middle of nowhere. Occupying a paved over landfill sticking like a sore thumb into the Bay, the Giants' stadium isn't really near anything, except perhaps the highway. You can't get to it by the city's BART subway system; nor do regular bus routes pass by, though the city does run special buses for the games. In fact there is something disconnected about the place.

Traffic going to the game can be fierce. Once you do get to the stadium, though, you'll find yourself in a huge flat parking area with a large hill on one side and the stadium and the bay on the other. If it is a sunny day—something that is by no means guaranteed—you will find that the colors are brilliant: the shining white of the Stick, the greenish browns of the hillside, the pale blue of the surrounding ocean. The moment you step out of your car, moreover, you will be struck by other sensations. The famous Frisco wind will almost certainly graze your cheeks. Indeed, if you are heading into a night game, you might well decide that now is the time to reach for the sweater you brought along. You will also note the surf smell in the air, combined with the rich odors and sizzles of roasting sausages and hot dogs. Around you, in fact, you will see thousands of fans grilling franks, downing beers, playing frisbee and poker, and generally enjoying themselves. You might seriously consider throwing a grill into the back seat of your car and joining in the fun, for tailgating is very much a part of the Giants' experience.

Although the area is better landscaped than most baseball facilities, there is nothing outside the Stick to hold your interest. Inside, you will find out that you are, for the most part, outside, for most of the concourses are quite open to the wind, rain, and sun. Given that the weather at the Stick can be pretty raw at times, this lack of shelter is probably something of a negative. We confess to liking it, though, as it helps to maintain the feel of baseball as an outdoor sport.

Of the public areas of the park, there is little that can be said. Conveniently placed escalators take fans from the base level to the top deck. Corridors are wide and tall, but show signs of wear and tear: certainly that shouldn't be surprising when you consider that the place was hit with an earthquake a few years ago. Concession stands are attractive enough, without being exceptionally appealing. As far as the seating areas go, they feature comfortable chairs, decent legroom, and views that are not all they should be. At the beginning of a game everything is pleasingly tidy. That, however, soon changes. The wind whipping through the field and stands tends to pick up stray napkins, wrappers, and even beer cups and sends them swirling through the park. Soon litter is everywhere.

In Candlestick, it is such environmental factors as breeze and humidity that give a play its individuality rather than any peculiarities about the field. It is a pretty standard, natural surface playing area with moderate lines. The foul poles at the Stick are set at 335′ while deep center is 400′. Over the left field wall you will find a display of out of town baseball scores. The Nationals on the left, the Americans on the right. The Giants' scoreboard and video display hang above center field. On the right field wall is the park's most interesting display: its retired numbers. They are pitcher * Christy Mathewson and manager * John McGraw (playing before numbers were assigned are represented by an "*"); #3, hitter Bill Terry (the last National Leaguer to bat .400); #4, home run artist Mel Ott; #11, pitcher Carl Hubbell; #24, the great Willie Mays; #22, pitcher Juan Marichal; and #44, slugger Willie McCovey. Every one of these is a Hall of Famer, and they represent only a

selection of the Giants' greats. At present, the Giants have more players enshrined in Cooperstown than any other team, including the Yankees.

For fifty years the Giants made baseball history in New York. For three more decades they've made history at Candlestick. Whether the Giants remain in or leave their imperfect park, we expect that they will continue to live up to their name.

New Stadium

For the past several years, the Giants have been trying to get the City of San Francisco to help them build a new stadium to replace their aging and unpopular home. In 1989, the team succeeded in getting a proposition for a new park in downtown San Francisco placed on the ballot. In a close election, though, the idea was voted down.

As of this writing, the Giants' future in the Stick, and even in San Francisco, is unclear. The team's management has said that unless the town authorizes a new stadium, it will move elsewhere. The attitude in the cable car city seems to be divided between those who think the Giants are bluffing and those who say "So what?"

All of this has been complicated by the fact that cities in other parts of California and the nation have, sensing blood in the water, circled the team, offering stadiums, parking lots, and tax abatements if they will only move the Giants to their metropolis. Of these, Santa Clara, California, a town of about 100,000 people, has made a bid that is apparently receiving serious consideration. When you go to the park, you may very well see sweatshirts, as we did, that read "Santa Clara Giants."

The thought of the Giants leaving San Francisco seems to us, well, unthinkable. But, then again, there were lots of folks that believed the Giants and the Dodgers would never leave New York, either.

Highlights

The Stick is rich in highlights, and not all of them are connected with baseball. On July 11, 1961, viewers across the nation got a laugh as a gust of wind blew pitcher Stu Miller off the Candlestick mound during the All-Star game. A bit more than a year later, on October 15, 1962, all of San Francisco had a good cry when Willie McCovey hit his line drive to the waiting glove of the Yankees' Bobby Richardson, ending the Giants' Series hopes. June 15, 1963, marked the day Juan Marichal pitched the first Giant no-hitter in the Stick. On May 4, 1966, the "Say Hey Kid" blasted homer number 512, breaking the all-time National League home run record.

Events only tangentially related to sports have happened in the stadium as well. On May 8, 1977, "the Great Wallenda" took his tightrope walk across the park before an admiring throng. Pitching great Vida Blue established something of a local custom when he got married at the Stick on September 24, 1989. The Beatles made their last appearance together in concert at Candlestick on August 29, 1966. One of them is supposed to have said to the crowd "It's chilly here, isn't it?"

Fans

As we walked up to Candlestick for the first time, we saw the man. Perhaps thirty years old, he was dark and unshaven, and he had small, intense eyes. Wrapped over his shoulders was a Giants jacket. Pulled tightly over his head was a Giants hat. In one hand the fan was carrying the burnt stub of a half-lit cigarette. In the other he had a sign that read simply, "Go Giants." More placards were piled next to him, bearing the same message. If he was selling them, he never mentioned the price. As far as we could tell, he was giving them away.

"Wanna sign?" he asked as we passed by.

We wanted to pass on the offer, as we were both carrying clipboards and we had work to do. "No, thanks."

The fellow's small eyes got, if anything, beadier. He eyed us with intense suspicion.

"Wassa matter? Aren't you for the Giants?"

"Sure we're for the Giants."

"Well," said the guy, clearly not believing us, "you ain't no die-hards."

One thing we can guarantee you if you visit the Stick is that you will find no shortage of "die-hard" Giants fans at all. Whether you sit in the boxes or the bleachers, they will be all around you; and throughout the contest you will know exactly where they stand. Other California fans may be "laid back," but no one would even think of leveling this accusation against the crew that regularly attends San Francisco games. In fact, Giants fans so insist they are unlike other West Coast sport devotees that they make a point of not doing "the Wave," if only to show their utter contempt for those southern California wimps and yuppies who eat sushi, prefer white wine to beer, like "the Wave," and do not realize that baseball is war.

Many ballparks have a distinct "fan culture"; few have one as clear-cut as that which exists at Candlestick Park.

Every Giants game begins with a party. About two hours or so before each contest fans flock to the stadium parking lot in station wagons, pickups, vans, and RVs. Grills are lit, beers are cracked, sausages sizzle, and even volleyball nets appear. This tailgating scene is, on the whole, warm, good-spirited, and very friendly. People come to have a good time, and just about everyone does.

As batting practice wraps up within the Stick, people begin to pack up their things without. Just as the fans were all play outside the park, though, they become all business once they take their seats. Though they consume many beers, they make relatively few trips to the concession stands. Mostly, people watch the game and really get into it. Fans chant in unison and make the Stick's rafters shake with their roar. They shout a lot, boo the umps with abandon, and love to engage in rhythmic clapping and stamping. The playing on the stadium organ of the "1812 Overture," complete with a very realistic sounding trumpet call, will be responded to with a cry of "Charge!" that, we expect, can probably be heard in Oakland.

Some fans, it is true, get carried away by all of this. Rowdiness and obnoxious behavior directed toward opposing players and even fans who are for other teams is not unknown here. Fights happen occasionally, too, especially during contests against the Dodgers. These difficulties, however, are pretty rare. The lion's share of the "die-hards" direct their intense partisanshp into the appropriate channels.

Aside from tailgating and the "Charge!" cry, Giants fans don't have a lot of customs different from other baseball enthusiasts. Still, there are a couple you should be aware of. First, you will notice that the park's video display offers a feature called "Giants Juke Box," where fans get to pick what music is being played. This is very popular, and something we have not seen elsewhere. You will also note that "Take Me Out to the Ballgame" is played in a jazzy version, rather than in the traditional way. Finally, if you are lucky, you could catch a wedding ceremony just before or even during the game. Getting married in Candlestick is very popular with Giants fans. Usually, after the service is over, the bride and groom will make a tour though the stands followed by their wedding party as the audience takes a few seconds away from the game to applaud.

Who are the Giants fans? For one thing, they are not for the most part the sorts of folks outsiders associate with San Francisco. Yuppies, executives, computer specialists, and people of that ilk, while not totally absent from the Stick, make up only a fraction of the crowd. Most of the fans are working and middle class types. While they are divided fairly evenly among the age groups, there are quite a few more males than females, and the throng is pretty fairly representative of the ethnic mix that is the Bay Area. These folks know baseball fairly well, like the Giants real well, and get a kick out of being completely devoted to something; even if it is only a baseball team. The concept of the "die-hard fan" and what being one entails is something that is implicitly understood at Candlestick.

Getting There

Located directly south of San Francisco's downtown on the bay side of the peninsula, Candlestick isn't the easiest park in the world to get to. Mass transit opportunities to reach the Stick are limited. And while the place is easy enough to find by car, fighting traffic into the stadium's parking lots can be a daunting experience. Even so, car is your best choice to get to the park, followed by bus and then cab.

By car. There are only two things you need to know if you want to drive to Candlestick. The first is that the only really practical approaches to the park for out-of-towners are off Route 101, the main drag from San Jose to San Francisco. Next, no matter where you are coming from, you should leave for the game early: otherwise, you will almost certainly waste some time sitting in traffic.

If you are coming to the Stick from such *north* locales as Santa Rosa and downtown San Francisco, take Route 101 south to the Cow Palace/Brisbane exit (ignore the exit for Candlestick; it's much slower). From the exit, proceed to Third Street and turn left over the freeway. Then proceed north on Third to Candlestick parking.

Those coming from such *east* points as Sacramento and Reno should take I-80 west over the San Francisco Bay Bridge, and then follow Route 101 south to the Cow Palace/Brisbane exit. From that point, follow the above directions.

If you are driving from such *south* points as San Jose and Santa Barbara, take 101 north to the Third Street exit and follow Third to stadium parking.

By cab. Cab fares to Candlestick are fairly steep, but they might not be completely out of the question if you are traveling with friends. Expect to pay $13 to $15 if you are going to the park from downtown San Francisco. A ride from the San Francisco International Airport will run you $15 to $17.

By bus. MUNI, the San Francisco Municipal Railway, runs a variety of shuttle buses to the Stick. Their "9X" bus, for example, starts its route to the park at the corner of Sutter and Sansome in downtown San Francisco (near the Embarcadero), and then continues on to a number of other points picking up passengers before proceeding to the contest. The "47X" bus leaves from California and Van Ness, and then follows Van Ness (Route 101) to the stadium. There are other buses as well.

Particularly if you are staying in San Francisco, utilizing this service could be a good idea. If you call MUNI at (415) 673-MUNI and tell them where you are staying, they will be happy to point you toward the nearest bus and give you further details on schedules and current fares.

Parking

The parking situation at Candlestick is something of a mess. The park has 8,200 paved and lighted spots around the park, all uniformly priced at $4. For some games, however, that isn't enough. When the paved lots run out, the Giants open up dirt lots, some of which run half-way up a nearby mountain at odd and treacherous angles. After that runs out (thankfully not very often), it's every man for himself.

The only way to avoid this insanity is to arrive early; and when we say early, we mean ninety minutes or so before the contest. This need not be an onerous requirement. Candlestick has one of the liveliest pregame tailgating scenes in baseball, and you would really miss something of the Giants' experience if you were not a part of it.

We should at this point put out a caution. Some visitors to Candlestick are tempted to avoid the expense and chaos of stadium parking by parking their car in the neighborhood northwest of the facility. Don't try it. This is a high crime area, and when you come back to get your vehicle you may well find that it isn't there. Worse yet, it may be sitting where you left it — with someone crouched in the back seat just waiting for you to climb in.

Tickets

Giants tickets are available in two ways. You can phone in your order or pick them up in person at the Stick. Unless you are looking for season tickets, the organization does not encourage mail orders.

To get tickets by phone, call Bass-Ticketmaster at (415) 762-BASS within California and at (800) 225-BASS outside the state. Be prepared to state the number of tickets you'd like, the dates, and the locations. Also be sure to have your MasterCard or Visa ready. You will, of course, also be billed for a service charge.

You can avoid the service charge and also discuss seating on a one-on-one basis with someone who knows the park if you visit the Giants' advance ticket office, which is located outside Gate B at the Stick. It's open Monday through Friday from 9 A.M. to 5 P.M.

Availability. The Giants', overall, don't have one of the top attendance records in the Majors. It wasn't until the team's 1989 National League championship season that the squad passed the 2,000,000 attendance mark for the first time. Season ticket sales are also only moderate.

All of this means that, even if you show up at the Stick at the last minute, you will almost certainly find a seat. During games against such rival squads as the Mets and especially the Dodgers, people buying on the day of the game might well end up in the bleachers. Those attending less popular match-ups against teams like the Astros and the Expos may well find even box seats available a day or so before the contest.

Costs. Giants tickets follow an interesting pricing policy. If you want the best seat in the house or the worst one, you will find the prices very reasonable ($11 and $2.50). If, like most fans, you prefer something in the middle, you may be less pleased.

The oblong shape of the Stick presents pricing problems, too. If you get in-the-baseline spots at any cost level, you will probably be happy with your spots. The more you get out of the baselines, though, the less pleased you will be. This is one of those parks in which careful study of a seating chart before you buy could make a difference in the quality of your viewing experience.

In 1990, the Giants' ticket prices were as follows: Lower Box ($11); Upper Box ($10); Lower Reserved ($9); Upper Reserved ($7); Pavilion* ($5); General Admission (Adults [$2.50]); (14 and under** [$1]).

Rainouts. The Giants average less than one rainout a year. If your game is rained out, the club will exchange your ticket for a future game. If you have no plans to return to San Francisco, write a note to the Giants explaining this and enclosing your stubs, and they will refund your money.

Seating

Candlestick isn't one of baseball's most popular parks these days. That's because it has come to serve as a symbol of all the stadium design excesses of the 1960s and 1970s. It is true that the place, in common with many of the other "cookie-cutter" parks, has many seats that are too far from the action. It is also, as columnist George Will likes to point out, a place that's cold, both physically and psychologically. Even so, the Stick has good and even great seats as well as bad ones, its surface is natural grass, and its fans have given the whole Giants experience an individuality that's lacking in other stadiums. Sure the Stick isn't one of the better parks. But, contrary to what you may have heard, it isn't the worst, either.

Lower Box seats ($11) are the priciest spots in the park, and they're the best by far. Set on the lower of Candlestick's two decks, the Lower boxes wrap around the field from foul pole to foul pole. If you can stay in the baseline sections, which run from even 16 (third base) to odd 15 (first) you will have done very well. Even if you have to go a couple sections past these points, though, you will still get a view that's worth your money.

Upper boxes ($10) are a level higher and a buck cheaper. Most of the spots here are pretty good, but, since they are

*Special "no alcohol, no smoking" section.
**On nonholiday, nonconcert weekdays and Saturdays only. Must be accompanied by a paying adult.

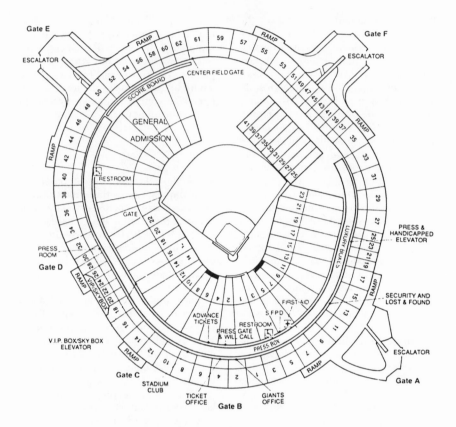

Seating chart, Candlestick Park.

farther from the field than the Lower boxes, staying in the baselines is more important here than there. The baseline section numbers are the same.

Lower Reserved spots ($9) present problems. Sitting on the lower deck in an area that's past the box seats, some of these spots have good views, some have bad views, and some have almost no views at all because they are situated behind poles. How can you protect yourself from disappointment? First, either get seats in a row lower than 9 or get the ticket office to sign a statement in blood that your spot in a row above that number does not have poles between you and the field. Next, try to

stay in the baselines, which—and we thank the Giants for the convenience of this—are represented by the same section numbers throughout the park. Finally, you might consider forking over the extra buck for an Upper box spot. In truth, seats in that area are considerably better than the ones in Lower Reserved.

By contrast with the above, spots in the cheaper Upper Reserved area ($7) have no obstructions at all, save the occasional gull that may come streaking down at you or the clouds that will, from time to time, roll between you and the pitcher's mound. If you sit up in this area, you will be far from the action;

but the same is true in the upper decks of most other parks.

The Pavilion area ($5) is a special "no alcohol, no smoking" area that has its own entrance (Gate E) and concession stand. Located over the right field wall, the area has decent enough views and it also offers a family atmosphere. However, there are some problems here with seating. Section 25 should be avoided altogether: it has a severe obstruction caused by the right field foul pole. Rows 36 and 37 in all sections have terrible views, and should be refused. Some spots in rows 25 and higher have pole obstructions, many others don't. If they try to put you here, ask about this before you buy.

General Admission seats ($2.50) are located behind the left and center field walls, and are certainly inexpensive. Indeed, if you take advantage of the special kids prices, a family of five can sit here for $8—which is the second lowest price in the majors (at Montreal, you can do this for slightly *less* than $5).

The question is, do you want to sit in the bleachers? The view isn't all that bad, particularly if you arrive early enough to secure seats in rows 1 to 5 or, failing that, at least to avoid spots in rows 5 to 10, from which you have to see home plate through two chain link fences. Moreover, the seating is composed of comfortable plastic-and-metal chairs, as opposed to the hard wooden benches the A's offer across the Bay for a buck more. So what's the problem with the area? The fans. For some time now, the Giant's bleachers crowd has had a reputation as being one of the rowdiest in the game. Though things seem to have improved in recent years, this is still an issue you should consider before you buy here.

Special Needs

Parking. Parking for the physically disabled is provided in the first row of spaces around the Stick. Simply show your plate or your disabled sticker to the attendants as you enter parking and you will be directed to this area.

The Giants also offer a special free car-to-seat wheelchair service. You can arrange for this by calling the Giants ticket office before you come to the game and getting details or you can try simply showing and flagging down one of the wheelchair shuttles you will likely see passing by.

Seating. Handicapped seating is provided in the park in Lower Reserved sections 1 and 19. The spots in section 1 are super; they are located right behind the batter's box. Section 19 is a ways down the right field line. It isn't great, but it is certainly acceptable.

Food and Features

Food. San Francisco is second only to New York City among the United States' fine dining towns. You certainly, however, wouldn't guess that fact from the food you are served at Candlestick. It's not that the food is bad; it isn't. It's just that there is almost nothing special about it at all. Even if the food is a bit blah, though, it must be admitted that Candlestick's prices compare pretty favorably with those at some of the other stadiums.

Standard ballpark fare is offered throughout the park. Choices include hot dogs, peanuts, polish sausage, popcorn (a good buy), "Giant" franks, chocolate malts, and pretzels.

There are some specialities, too. *Health Hut*, located behind section 11 on the main level, has such items as yogurt, juice, and blue tortillas with salsa—pretty good. They also serve a "health dog," which is an artificial wiener on a "whole wheat bun." This horror just serves to remind you that, while it may be true that there are many things not worth dying for, there are also some not worth living for.

Those who would like a full meal before the game will also find their needs satisfied at the Stick. In most stadiums the in-park restaurants are off-limits to all but members, which is why such places are rarely mentioned in this guide. Not so in San Francisco. Though you must pay a $5 fee for the privilege, you are welcome to enjoy drinks, dinner, and a fine view of the game at Candlestick's *Stadium Club*, which is located on the Mezzanine level behind section 10. Food at the Club is, overall, tasty if a bit expensive, while the place's wine list is surprisingly good. The atmosphere is friendly and relaxed. If you want to dine at the Club, come early. The restaurant begins table service two hours before the game and stops offering food at the beginning of the fourth inning.

Drinks. San Francisco may be the center of the American wine industry, but baseball fans in San Fran enjoy beer as much as fans anywhere; the principal brew is Miller's Dry. Those who'd like a bit wider selection in beers will find various imports offered at a selection of stands throughout the park. However, you must hunt them out; no one stand offers several.

Coke products are probably second to beer in popularity, and a smallish cup of wine (Paul Masson) is also available.

Candlestick's frozen night games make hot drinks more popular here than in most other parks. Coffee and hot chocolate both sell for a buck. Outside section 3 at the main level you can find a pretty fair cup of cappuccino.

Features. Like many of the West Coast parks, Candlestick has lots of features. Most of the fun takes place at the *Fantasy Fun* area, which is located off the main concourse, near Gate A. In this area you'll find a "speed pitch" concession; a "video fantasy" stand that allows you to star in your own short baseball video; a "Pose With the Stars" booth, where you can have photo taken

with a lifelike replica of, say, Will Clark; and a "Fantasy Club Card" concession, where a realistic baseball card featuring your kid (or you!) will be created before your eyes. Who says that California is no longer the land where dreams come true?

Assistance

The Giants' helpful "Guest Relations" office can be found on the Mezzanine level, behind section 13. In addition to providing such traditional services as helping you find lost seats and kids and answering questions, the office will also be happy to summon a cab for you after the contest.

Safety and Security

Safety. Safety is something of an issue at Candlestick. Rowdiness, fights, drunkenness, and illegal drug use are things that are all reported to have occurred from time to time in the park. When you visit the facility you will note that many of the security people carry billy clubs *and* guns. That is pretty unusual in a baseball stadium.

How bad is the problem? Outside the bleacher area, there seem to be few difficulties, except, perhaps, during games against the Dodgers, when things can get pretty raucous. Opinions seem to vary about how tough things are in the bleachers. One security guard told us that it's an area where "anything goes," and where difficulties occur at many games. Club officials insist that, while that may have been true in the past, the decision at Candlestick to cut off in-stand beer sales has provoked a general reformation.

Which view is correct? One of us sat in the bleachers during a contest, and, except for some foul language, there were no problems. That's more than we can say for a few of the other parks with better reputations. We can only hope that our experience at the Stick was typical.

Outside the park, you should encounter few difficulties in the parking areas. On the other hand, you should avoid the temptation to seek free parking in the neighborhood around the park; it's a high crime area.

Health. "The coldest winter I ever spent," said Mark Twain, "was July in San Francisco." Over the past century, millions of tourists from around the world who have visited the cable car city have had occasion to ruefully remember Twain's words. It does get cold in San Francisco during the summer, make no mistake about it. And it gets especially cold in Candlestick Park.

The Stick sits right next to San Francisco Bay, where it is subject to cold winds, bone-chilling dampness, and fog. No matter what the temperature may be outside your hotel as you head out to a day game, you can bet that it will be at least ten degrees colder at Candlestick. You should dress accordingly. As far as night games go, you should at least bring a jacket, no matter what. If it is at all chilly out, a coat and maybe even gloves would be a better idea. You'll be surprised how often they'll come in handy. You might also consider carrying along to the Stick a thermos of coffee or hot chocolate.

Though cold is the biggest health threat at Candlestick, sun is an issue too, particularly in the upper deck. If you plan on sitting in this area during a day game you should bring sun ban and wear a hat.

If you still find you've underdressed and need to warm up, or if you've gotten a headache from all the shouting of the Giants' "die-hard" fans, you'll find the stadium's first aid office located on the lower level behind section 7. Although this office accepts walk-ins, the Giants would prefer it if you would mention your problem to an usher first before heading down to this area.

Mementos

Souvenirs. Giants souvenirs are available throughout the park. You'll find a particularly large selection on the lower level at Gate B.

Foul Balls. Good places to snag strays at Candlestick include Lower Deck box sections 12 and 13 and the area behind home plate. If you want a foul though, you had better move quick. SF is the town where Joe and all the other little DiMaggios grew up, and you will find their spiritual descendants sitting next to you glove in hand, waiting to beat you to the catch.

Autographs. Both the Giants and the visitors' bus leave fromm Candlestick from the player's parking lot area, which is located between Gates A and F. You are pretty much kept away from your heroes here, but it isn't impossible to get signatures if team members are disposed to cooperate.

SEATTLE MARINERS
The Kingdome

Expansion franchises seem to follow a pattern. Once successful in gaining

admittance into one of the Leagues, they start out full of optimism. Players are signed, impressive stadiums are built, and at press conferences team officials confidently predict that, after a bad season or two, perhaps, pennants and trophies will soon be flocking their way.

Then reality sets in. Management finds out that all the great stars they've signed are either at the beginning of their careers or at the end; in either case, few prove to be at their peak of performance. Worse, whenever a new player does live up to the new squad's expectations, the team discovers that the big franchises—who had scorned the rookie in the first place—are now interested in signing him. It's at this point that management realizes the key role that deep pockets and prestige franchises play in the sport. As if all this weren't enough, as the team continues to perform poorly the fans start staying away in droves. Revenues decline, enthusiasm wanes, and owners who went into baseball expecting soon to be on network television accepting the Series trophy from Fay Vincent find that they are asking themselves, "How the heck did I get into this mess?"

New teams have responded to these problems in one of two ways. Some, like the Mariners and the Rangers, have changed managers and players frequently, trying to find the magic combination that will lead to victory. They've also refused in many cases to meet the offers of different teams for players who have served them well. Other expansion squads—the Blue Jays are one—have put funds into their farm systems and have tried to keep an ensemble of sound core players together, even when they've had to pay to do it. Which approach, overall, works better goes without saying. Both the Mariners and the Rangers now have new owners, and perhaps they'll learn from the mistakes of the past.

To this point the Mariners have been since their formation one of the worst teams in baseball. They not only have

yet to win a divisional championship; they've also never had a single winning season.

Which by no means means that you should by-pass attending Mariners games. To the negative side, if you're looking for an attractive, well-designed stadium or fine ball play in Seattle, chances are pretty good that you will find neither. Unless things change (which, actually, *is* a possibility), the Mariners will continue to fall short. As for the Kingdome, it might be better be called the "peasant dome," for it is a monument to penny-pinching functionality. Though the place serves its purpose, which is protecting sporting events from Seattle's often inclement weather, that is the limit of the Kingdome's attractions.

To the positive, you'll travel far to find a team management more committed to knocking itself out to please fans than that which currently runs the Mariners. The area around the Dome, too, offers opportunities for fan dining and partying that are first rate. In fact, only the Cubs and the Red Sox could be said to have a more vibrant pre- and postgame restaurant and nightlife scene than the Mariners. Then, of course, the team boasts the appeal of the Pacific Northwest itself, an area of beautiful cities, soaring mountains, and deep and inviting forests. Seattle is a town that you should visit, not just to attend a ballgame, but also to enjoy on its own behalf. If you make a trip to the Mariners games part of an extended visit to this beautiful area, you are sure to have a memorable vacation.

The Team

Seattlites have been playing baseball for a long time, and for just about as long, they have been trying to net a major league franchise. The Seattle Pilots, a triple A club from the Pacific Coast League, played in the minors for decades before getting a short-lived promotion to the majors. The team appeared briefly in the American League in 1969. Their performance was terrible, and their attendance was poor. After a single, pathetic season, they decamped and moved east to become the Milwaukee Brewers.

By 1977, Seattle was back in the majors as part of an American League expansion that also brought in the Toronto Blue Jays. Adopting the Mariners as their new name in order to honor Seattle's seagoing industries, the team took its place in the spanking new Kingdome, the second domed facility in the majors, and the second biggest.

Like most expansion clubs, the Mariners started in the cellar. Unlike at least some of the others, they've had some difficulty getting out of it. Over thirteen years of existence, the Mariners have never placed better than fourth. Thus, they've never won a divisional championship, or, in truth, even come close to winning one. They have also never had a winning season.

It's not that the Mariners have not had any good players. Pitchers Rick Honeycutt, Floyd Bannister, Mark Langston, and likely Hall of Famer Gaylord Perry have all worn the Mariners blue. So have such fine hitters as Gorman Thomas, Phil Bradley, Danny Tartabull, and Alvin Davis. The problem has been two-fold: money and management. Past Mariners officials never seemed willing to spend the bucks to get good players, and when, by happenstance, they did manage to find them, they quickly let them slip through their fingers. Overall, the team has just about had no vision for the future. As a result, several of the above players continue to turn in fine performances even today, but only one (Davis) is still on the team.

Today, as in the past, the Mariners have a number of good players. Included on the present squad are first baseman Davis, all-star second baseman Harold Reynolds, outfielder Ken Griffey Jr., and infielder Edgar Martinez. Along with an exciting young pitching staff, this represents enough talent to put the team in contention in the coming years. The question remains, though, if the Mariners do play well, will they still allow their best people to be bought away, as they have in the past? We'll see.

The Stadium

We should preface these comments with two truth-in-advertising disclaimers. First, your writers do not like round baseball parks. Second, they do not much care for domed facilities, particularly in towns which (unlike, say, Houston) have perfectly acceptable summer baseball weather, as Seattle does. You could draw the conclusion from the above that we do not much care for the Kingdome, and you would be correct.

Whoever planned the "King County Stadium" at least got the location right. Set just south of downtown Seattle, the place is convenient to all the major interstates, is a short bus or cab ride from the leading downtown hotels, and is right next to the "Pioneer Square" area, perhaps Seattle's most appealing dining and nightlife district. If you are the sort who likes to go out after the game, have a drink, and talk about the contest with other fans, this will be a big, big plus.

Beyond that, though, the Kingdome doesn't have much to recommend it. From the outside it looks like some sort of massive concrete lump; it really resembles a grey mushroom more than anything else, though a wavy roof saves the building from total functional sterility. Inside, the concourses are wide and well-lighted, but equally featureless and boring. You wonder why someone doesn't put some pictures up, or murals, or anything to relieve the greyness.

The seating arrangements are covered in some detail elsewhere (see *Seating*) so we won't belabor this aspect of the park. Suffice it to say that the facility's round design, here as elsewhere, doesn't serve to help fans get a good view of the game. On the other hand, the general availability of tickets at the Kingdome means that you are likely to get pretty good seats here despite this fact. As for the Dome itself, it's a leaden monstrosity, arching high over your head without the slightest glimmer of natural light or even any serious attempt to break up the area's vast grey monotony. The dugouts themselves, though, are kind of neat. There's a mural of the Seattle skyline over the bench area of the home team, while a big picture of Mount Rainer sits atop that of the opposition.

The surface of the field is astroturf, and it is a bit worn in places. Current field dimensions are 324' at the left field four pole, 314' at the right field one, and 410' is the maximum extent of center field. These settings are subject to change however. The Mariners are one of those outfits noted for moving their outfield walls in and out to suit the strengths of the team. On the left field wall you'll see plaques for the American League West clubs in order of their current standing. A similar area on the right hand side reports on the AL East. Above center field and a level higher are banners for each of the American League teams. Over left field is the Mariner's "diamond vision" while a display over right field carries the out-of-town scores.

The park has one feature giving it a bit of individuality. There is a rather large contingent of birds that lives in the park, who you'll catch flying around the Dome and the players from time to time. They live over the heating ducts in the Dome, and feed on that popcorn you didn't eat.

Other than this, though, if you had to describe the Kingdome in one word,

that word would be monotony. It provides fans with a air cooled shelter from the rain and an OK view of the contest, but it gives them little more.

Highlights

The Kingdome, having seen neither playoffs nor Series action, doesn't stand tall in the baseball highlights category. Still, a few moments of importance to the game have happened here. Gaylord Perry got his 300th win at the Dome while with the Mariners in 1981. In 1979 one of the most exciting of the All-Star games took place in the Dome. It resulted in the National League beating the Americans 7–6, thanks to a dramatic 8th inning homer followed by a 9th inning bases-loaded walk delivered by the Met's Lee Mazzilli. On June 2, 1990, Mariner Randy Johnson pitched the first no-hitter in the club's history.

Fans

Seattle is not one of the big baseball towns, and the Mariners, at least thus far, have been unsuccessful in turning locals into die-hard baseball devotees. For the past decade attendance at the park has been low, and that's been a constant problem for the team.

Accordingly, when Jeff Smulyan and his management group bought the club in 1989, just about the first issue they tackled was the question of what to do to get more people to go see the game. The program they've carried out thus far, which as resulted in a substantial surge in ticket sales, is really a model for what other poorly patronized teams could do to encourage interest.

First, realizing that people don't like to pay through the nose to see a team that may very well lose, Smulyan lowered ticket prices for those lower quality seats that are most likely to be bought by families and young people. Accordingly, a family of five can now attend a Mariners game for $16.50—a bargain by any standard. This move in and of itself went a long way toward boosting attendance among that portion of the audience that is the key to filling any stadium. In order to keep the little kids happy, a mascot (the Mariner Moose) was introduced, while (ugh!) video game machines were set up for teenagers.

Second, recognizing that Seattle is a city full of young professionals, the team began reserving some games for singles, staging a disco dance out on the field after the game, complete with live music. This worked, too, and now the Mariners get a pretty substantial dating crowd.

Next, the team saw that, whatever the prices or the attractions, Seattle fans weren't going to keep going to games if they didn't have fun. Since the team couldn't necessarily be counted on to produce a victory, other things had to be done. In order to create a festive feeling, a modest display of fireworks have been added to every game. Specifically, they are set off after the National Anthem, whenever the Mariners hit a home run, and whenever the team wins. The club has also put the video display screen to use, running a constant stream of contests and games to keep the fans amused during the contest. During an evening, you're likely to see on the "Diamond Vision" such offerings as "Baseball Jeopardy," "Baseball Wheel of Fortune," and even "Super Mario Brothers." More infamously, the club's management switches their video display screen to coverage of another ball game if their own contest is getting a bit boring. You have to wonder how the players react to that!

Finally, the Mariners' owners realized that even with these changes they could not be successful until people could be induced to come and check things out themselves. Accordingly, in 1990 the team pulled its most famous stunt. Declaring that they were anticipating a great game against Texas, the Mariners flatly predicted that if fans came to the contest, they would certainly see a no-hitter. If, by chance, the no-hitter didn't happen, then the Mariners would exchange the tickets for a later game. Needless to say, the fans flocked to the stadium, betting that the Mariners would be wrong—which they were, even though Nolan Ryan was pitching that night. Even so, the promotion accomplished exactly what the team wanted to achieve—it exposed thousands to "the New Mariners."

All of the above should give you an idea of what Seattle fans are like. To put it simply, they're a bunch of folks who don't always know a lot about baseball but who like to have a good time. They enjoy eating, talking, catching views of the sunset from the 300 level (and the view over Puget Sound is pretty), and even returning to their seats to see what the Mariners are up to from time to time. At this point this would have to be described as one of the most "laid-back" audiences in the sport. It would be interesting, though, to see what would happen if the team decided to really pour on some excitement.

Getting There

Located just south of downtown Seattle in the historic Pioneer Square area, the Kingdome is easily reachable by car, cab, trolley, and bus. You can also go by van or train.

By car. If you are traveling to the game by car, keep two things in mind. First, you are going to have to contend with Seattle traffic at least to some degree to get to the Dome, and it can be kind of hectic. Study a map before you leave and you'll keep to a minimum your chances of missing the Kingdome exits. Second, remember that the Mariners' parking lot is fairly small. If the game you are attending looks like it will be a crowded one, leave early to insure that you'll find a spot.

Those coming from such *south* points as Tacoma and Portland, as well as those arriving at the *Seattle-Tacoma Airport*, should take I-5 north to Exit 163 Spokane Street to Ferries. From there, turn right on 4th Avenue South and proceed to Kingdome Parking.

Candians driving down from such *north* areas as Vancouver, as well as Americans from Bellingham, will want to take I-5 south to Exit 164 Dearborn Street/Airport Way. From there, follow signs to Dearborn Street, make a right at the end of the ramp and follow signs to the Kingdome.

By cab. Cab fare from the downtown business district will run you $5 to $7 depending on your departure point. From the Sea-Tac airport, expect to pay $22.

By train. Amtrak's Seattle station sits in the Kingdome's parking lot. Accordingly, if you are so minded, you could book train travel from just about anyplace served by Amtrak and walk over to the game when you arrive. This would be a particularly attractive option if you are coming from Portland or even San Francisco.

By bus. Seattle's sophisticated public transit system offers good connections to the Kingdome. If you are staying in the downtown hotels, look for buses 174 or 194 going south and then ask to get off at 4th Avenue. You'll find that you are a short ways from the park. From the airport, seek out the same buses going north (they are outside the baggage claim area) and again ask to be let off at 4th Avenue. Prices vary on both routes, but the top fare either way is $1.85.

By van. If you are coming into town by air, van is a good option. If you call in advance at (800) 942-0711 or (206) 622-1424, *Airport Shuttle Express* will

have a van ready to take you to the Kingdome directly from the airport. The cost for this service is $12. If you arrive without having made a reservation, you might consider taking the regularly scheduled airport van to the Stouffer Madison Hotel ($6) and taxi to the stadium from there (about $5).

By trolley. The city runs an attractive and evocative old-fashioned trolley service from the downtown business district to the Pioneer Square area, which is very convenient if you are staying in the downtown hotels. For example, you could take the trolley from Seattle's intriguing Pike Place Market to South Main and Occidental, which is two blocks north of the Dome. Fares vary, but the maximum is $.75.

Parking

The parking situation at the Kingdome isn't all that great. The park is surrounded with spaces to be sure, but there are only about 2,200 of them. This is enough to accommodate fans at most games, but at popular contests (such as those against Toronto, New York, and Oakland) the parking lots can run out, and you could find yourself wandering the streets of Seattle looking for alternatives while the game is beginning. Particularly if you are planning to attend a contest against one of these teams, try to arrive early. Even if you don't want to walk into the park right away, there is nothing to stop you from strolling over to one of the many fine restaurants in the area for a bite to eat before the battle.

Whatever might be said about the lack of parking, though, it must be admitted that the price is right. Three dollars will give you a spot at the game and in one of Seattle's most interesting neighborhoods.

You should also be aware that the crush of cars getting into and out of the lots can be a problem. Before the game, the situation is often bad, but it is generally endurable. After the show, forget it! The whole area turns into a mass of crawling autos, beaming lights, and distracted motorists. We suggest that you take your time in leaving the Dome and wait until things settle down before going to your vehicle.

The Mariners' management is aware of these difficulties and is busily adding more spaces. Unfortunately, the city of Seattle is also busily putting up a new basketball arena just south of the Kingdome. Therefore, whether the parking situation will be better or worse by the time you read this is anyone's guess.

Tickets

You can mail for tickets, phone for them, or pick them up at the Kingdome in person.

To order seats by mail, write to the Mariners at: Seattle Mariners Baseball Club, PO Box 4100, Seattle, WA 98104.

Be sure to include the dates, the number of tickets, and the locations you'd like, as well as your check or money order for payment in full. The Mariners also assess a $2.50 "service charge."

Ticketmaster handles the Mariners' phone orders. Their number is (206) 628-0888. Be prepared when you call with your Visa or MasterCard and the usual information about the number of tickets you'd like and the dates. You'll be hit with a service charge here, too.

The Kingdome's advance ticket office is located near gate D, which is near the northwest corner of the park. Here, you can study a seating chart and argue with the ticket agent a bit before settling on your spots. The advance ticket window is open from Monday through Saturday from 8:30 A.M. to 5:30 P.M. and on Sunday from 12:00 P.M. to 5 P.M.

*Sold two hours before the game only.

Availability. Close to the bottom among all the major league teams in attendance, the Mariners have plenty of seats available at all games. Not only will you find a seat if you show up at the last minute; you will very likely also find a good one.

Costs. In the total scope of the game, the Mariners' prices are reasonable. Compared to other West Coast teams, though, at the top level they are a bit high. If you can get it, $11.50 buys you the best seat in Seattle. You pay $9 for the same spot in Los Angeles.

Overall, though, ticket prices at least correspond to the views you are paying for — so long as you keep in mind the fact that the Kingdome, like all the Domes, has many seats that are second rate.

In 1990, Mariner ticket prices were as follows: VIP Boxes ($11.50); Box Seats ($10.50); Club Seats ($8.50); View Seats ($5.50); (Kids 14 and under [$3.50]); General Admission* ($4.50); (Kids 14 and under [$2.50]).

Rainouts. Rainouts never happen in the Kingdome. On the other hand, rain in Seattle during the summer is pretty common, so if it looks threatening as you head to the game you might want to bring along an umbrella. Seattle is a great town to stroll around in, and it would be a shame to miss the chance to do it because you didn't come to the park prepared.

Seating

The Kingdome is a big (57,000 seats), round, multipurpose stadium, and it has all the seating problems associated with this design, which is essentially foreign to baseball. Happily, though, the Mariners' modest attendance record means that you are more likely to get a good seat here than in such similar parks as Riverfront or Busch.

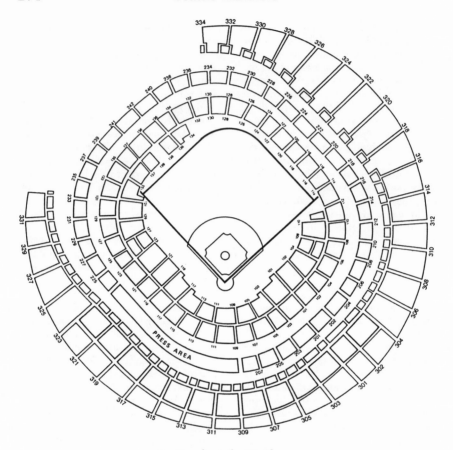

Seating chart, the Kingdome.

The Mariners' most expensive seats are designated VIP box ($11.50), and they are far and away the best in the park. Composed of the prime chairs wrapped around the infield at the field level, these spots could hardly be better. If you don't mind the price for one of these, you should snap it up: but hurry, these spots sell out fast.

Box seats ($10.50) are a buck cheaper and not nearly as good. Seats here are composed of good chairs running the baselines but set back from the field along with near-the-action spots off the baselines. Overall, these are still pretty good locations. We have a slght preference for the further back

baseline aisles, which run from 102 (first) to 119 (third), but low row seats in such beyond the baselines sections as 121, 123, 104, and 106 are probably just as good. If you sit here, however, try to stay in row numbers under 23 — and the lower the better.

Club seats ($8.50) are a level higher, and are set back a fair distance from the field. Still, they are not bad locations, particularly if you are careful to insure that your spot runs along the first base line in aisles 207 to 202.

Go up another level and you are among the View seats ($5.50). They have the advantage of being cheap, and if you can somehow manage to snag low row chairs (1 to 4) in aisles 307 to 315, you will find yourself in a very fine situation indeed. Beyond this section, though, things deteriorate pretty rapidly. If you sit here, try to stay in the baselines anyway (aisles 302 to 319) in the lowest rows possible.

General Admission ($4.50) is a huge area, the traditional "bleacher" style seats behind the outfield walls as well as many higher and less desirable spots. Here you are best off staying in the 100 section as opposed to going upstairs. Since the whole area has open seating, you would be well advised to come a bit early in order to nail down spots close to the action. If you get something near the field, you'll find that the view is fairly good.

Something needs to be said about the chairs in the park. In a word, they are not too comfortable. In the expensive sections, as well as in some of the better areas of the View level, you'll be seated in cramped plastic and metal chairs. In other places, the seating is principally composed of aluminum benches with metal backs. If you end up seated in one of these areas, plan on getting up every forty minutes or so to get the circulation going.

Special Needs

Parking. Handicapped parking is provided next to the Kingdome by Gate A. Show your sticker or plate to the attendant when you pull into the parking lot and you'll be directed to this area.

Seating. Four areas of the Kingdome offer seating for the physically disabled, and all are located at the 200 Club level. These sections are 204 (just past first), 206 (along the first base line), 220 (in General Admission), and 240 (also in General Admission). These places are good but not great.

There are "family reserved" no-alcohol seats in the Kingdome, but they are not very good ones. Spots currently set aside include portions of General Admission aisles 133 and 134. Aisle 112, in the Box section, has a few "family reserved" seats, too. Since the existence of these sections is mentioned nowhere in the Mariner's literature, you have to wonder why the team even bothered to set them aside in the first place. It seems to us that a "family reserved" area is something a team should either do right or not do at all; the Mariners do neither.

Food and Features

Food. The Mariners' poor attendance records have forced the squad's management to really think hard about what they have to do to attract fans, and one area that they've clearly done a lot of thinking about is food. Accordingly, food selection in the park is now excellent (that wasn't always the case in the past), quality is good, and the prices are at least no worse than at many another stadium.

Standard ballpark choices are hawked and offered throughout the stadium. These include hot dogs, popcorn (overpriced), pretzels, peanuts, bratwurst (fairly good), and Polish sausage. Pizza is big in the park, too, and will be delivered to your seat if you request the service.

There are specialty shops, too. The *Bar/Deli* located behind aisle 101 offers salads, chili, deli sandwiches, and strawberry shortcake. The *Specialty Stand* behind aisle 125 has hot items, salads, and tasty "Poor Boy" sandwiches (at the price, things must be looking up for the boy).

There are two places in the Kingdome where you can get a full meal. The *Top of the Dome* restaurant, at 215 on the Club level, offers a buffet dinner starting two hours before the game. Prices are high, but the food is decent and you have a nice view of the game. In theory, this place admits season ticket holders only. However, if you aren't too obvious about the fact that you don't belong, you'll probably be served; we were. At Gate B of the park, in a simple patio area with tables, the Mariners also run a tasty, unpretentious bar-b-que for any fan who cares to come. Specialties on the menu include baby back ribs with fries, salmon burgers (excellent), steerburger with onions, and bar-b-que chicken. If all of this sounds good, that's because it is. The bar-b-que opens when the gate does, which is about two hours before the game starts, and it stays open through the first inning. You may get a close view of the players in this area, too. The Mariners have a batting practice area nearby, and on occasion players will stroll out to get a few swings in before the contest begins.

Drinks. The Kingdome's patrons aren't the games biggest beer drinkers, but you can still get beer throughout the park.

Those seeking a more adventurous brew might want to seek the *Specialty Stand* behind aisle 125. Here you'll find a selection of "Micro Brewery" beers and Sharp's Nonalcohol beer. Those seeking cocktails or wine should look to the *Bar/Deli* behind 101 and 322. Smaller full service lounges can be found at 131, 216, and 319.

Coke products are sold throughout the facility, and the *Specialty Stand* also offers tasty pink lemonade.

Features. Given the Mariners' focus on providing a fan friendly experience at the Kingdome, you'd expect the place to have some features, and it does.

In the park's souvenir shop, which is located behind Gate D on the bottom concourse, you'll find the "Royal Brougham Museum." This is a collection of sports memorabilia from the personal collection of a well-known local sportswriter. Some of the stuff is related to baseball, and some of it isn't. Behind aisle 122 in General Admission is a small picnic area with tables and video games. Why one would want to come to a baseball game in order to play video games, we have no idea. We'll admit, however, that many Seattle teenagers were doing just that when we were there. The team has a mascot, too, the "Mariner Moose"; what a moose has to do with either baseball or seafaring is beyond us, but the fans seem to like him.

If you'd like to learn a bit more about the Kingdome, stadium tours are available. They leave Monday through Saturday from the Gate D advance ticket office at 11 A.M., 1 P.M., and, if no game is scheduled, 3 P.M. Just to be sure a tour is going, though, you should call the Mariners at (206) 296-3128; if few tickets are sold, tours are sometimes cancelled. Should you go, you'll visit the press box, the field, and, if the players aren't around, the dressing rooms. Tours also stop by the place outside the 300 level from where, on a clear day, you'll be able to see Mt. Ranier and Mt. Olympus. Among the things that the guides will point out will be the spot where the Kingdome's flock of birds lives. The charge for the tour is $2.50 for adults and $1.25 for kids and seniors.

Assistance

The Mariners' fan relations booth can be found—with some effort—at the ground level, behind Gate B. The staff is composed of the usual helpful types, but the location is terrible. You practically have to leave the stadium to get to this area no matter where you sit. Anyone who comes here with a problem, though he'll certainly be helped, will miss more of the game than he should have had to miss.

Safety and Security

Problems with rowdy fans at Mariners games are rare, except for one particular matchup. Whenever the Blue Jays are in town, hordes of Canadians stream down from the border to cheer on their compatriots. During these contests emotions can run high, abuse often occurs, and fights are not unknown. If you come to one of these games, you might want to avoid the bleachers.

The thought of maddened Canadians invading U.S. ballparks looking for trouble may seem funny, but we can attest that expatriot Blue Jay admirers were often the most aggressive fans we saw. The irony of it is that in Toronto itself, Blue Jay people are the soul of courtesy and calm disportment.

Many fans like to dine and party in the Pioneer district before and after the contest. Some also walk over to the Asian-oriented "International District." While both of these locales are well-patrolled and reasonably safe, they are not crime-free. Pioneer Square, in particular, is famed as the home of the original "skid row" (so named because logs used to slide through this district down to the harbor on wooden skids), and a large number of homeless people, drug abusers, and drunks hang out in this area, apparently feeling they have a tradition to uphold. You shouldn't let this stop you from enjoying this exciting neighborhood, but you should be aware of the problem and take such sensible precautions as staying on lighted streets and with the crowd.

Health. The climate controlled Dome is a pretty safe environment, if not to say sterile. Still, if you get nailed by a foul ball or have one "jumbo hot"

too many, you'll find the stadium's first aid offices located behind aisles 121, 220 and 319. The lower level office is always open, the other ones may be closed if the crowd is small.

Mementos

Souvenirs. The souvenir store attached to the "Royal Brougham Museum" has a wide selection of Mariner's goods, but the prices are a bit high. A cap costs $9 while shirts run $20 and up. The museum is located behind Gate D. If you don't mind walking a block north of the park, you'll find a selection with lower prices at *Superior Specialties*, 406 Occidental Street ([206] 624-8485).

Foul Balls. The Mariners' smallish crowds enhance your chances of getting a ball. If you'd like to see if you can nab one, try sitting behind and to the right of home plate, say in aisles 103, 105, 107, and 109.

Autographs. Visiting teams enter their buses just outside of Gate B. It isn't easy to get autographs here as the location is pretty well blockaded and security people will keep you well away from the players. However, every once in a while a visitor will walk over to the crowd to sign a few before boarding the bus.

Mariner signatures are easier to get. Members of the home team walk from Gate A to their private parking lot. In order to get there, they have to stroll past a large collection of fans. Frequently players will stop once or twice along the way to say hello and sign a few autographs.

TEXAS   RANGERS
Arlington Stadium

During World War II, the U.S. Army decided to send the Rangers, a special combat unit, into action in France. Intercepting the message, German troops decided that it was the *Texas* Rangers that were being sent against them. Thousands are said to have abandoned their positions and fled.

More than any other state, Texas is a place that has had to scrap and fight its way to greatness. Born in a bloody revolution against Mexico, it endured two more major wars in its first decades of existence. Interspersing these conflicts were bitter struggles with the Comanches and the Apaches, range wars between cattle ranchers and sodbusters, and the generalized violence of a lawless frontier. "God, Guts, and Guns Built America," declares a popular Lone Star state bumper sticker, "Let's Keep All Three." While these things may not have created the whole of the country, they certainly did build Texas.

It took a certain sort of person to settle Texas during these times. People had to be competent, self-reliant, and tough—able to endure privation without complaint, ready to make decisions and live with the consequences, and willing to work hard for, or take, if necessary, what they needed to survive. They often had to be men like Dunston in the John Wayne classic *Red River*, the sort of folks who could kill without compunction if you pushed them, but would always make sure to bury and "read over" the body before pushing on. The Lone Star state's famous police force, the Texas Rangers (the team is named after them), even today seeks out men and women who continue to convey the image of the rugged individualist.

Since the end of the frontier period, Texas has seen continued struggle as its economy has endured repeated booms and busts, from the wrenching effects of the 1930s "dust bowl," to the rise and collapse of oil prices in the 1980s, and now the savings and loan disaster. These repeated cycles of stress and giddy success have produced in Texans a personality more distinctive than that of any other state.

It's a personality that very definitely washes over into the sports world. Texans, for one thing, like their action to be rough and tumble. They love winners, dislike losers, and hate whiners most of all. They are willing to play by the rules, but if the rules have to be stretched a bit to produce victory, that'll be OK, too. Most of all, Texans like—and believe in—heroes, whether they be John Wayne, the post-assassination attempt Ronald Reagan, or even Oliver North.

Baseball, in truth, has had tough sledding in Texas for the simple reason that its dynamics do not fit the Lone Star psyche quite as well as the game of football. Accordingly, although minor league baseball has been active in Texas since the 1910s (Dizzy Dean played for years here), Texas baseball was strictly bush league for decades. Even with the creation of major league squads in Houston and in the Dallas–Ft. Worth area (the "Metroplex"), baseball has continued to run a poor second in the minds of Lone Star staters. Basically, Texans have had two things against the game. First, it isn't football, and second, and, more seriously, neither the Astros nor the Rangers have been able to produce many wins. As a result, attendance at both the Texas teams has been mediocre, interest has often flagged, and, at least in Dallas, you can easily run into people who haven't the foggiest idea where the Rangers play.

Now, however, things are starting to change. A Texan is in the White House, and he is a baseball enthusiast. And although George Bush himself is an Astros admirer, the fact that his son now co-owns the Rangers has not hurt Texas's AL franchise. Second, and most importantly, Texas baseball now has a genuine hero—Lynn Nolan Ryan—who is inspiring a generation of Lone Star staters to take a second look at the game as he moves toward the end of a long and distinguished pitching career.

The prime beneficiary of these changes has been Ryan's team, the Texas Rangers. An expansion franchise created in 1960, the Rangers moved from Washington to Texas in 1971. In the years since, the team has served almost as a case study of how to mismanage a new baseball franchise. The club has seen a bewildering array of managers, has made some incredibly bad trades, and has built for itself one of the most sun-exposed parks in baseball in what is one of the hottest regions of the country. As a result, the Rangers have never won a divisional title, let alone a pennant. During many of these years of frustration, Arlington Stadium featured almost as many fans cheering for visiting teams as would own up to being for the Rangers.

Now, visibly, the mood in the Metroplex is shifting. Ryan and an interesting young squad are starting to fill the park, and it's the Rangers that people are now cheering for. A good manager who looks like he'll be around for awhile (Bobby Valentine) and a competent ownership group have given the team stability for the first time ever. All of a sudden the pathetic Rangers look as if they could become winners, and the crowd can sense it.

It is true that the Rangers are not one of baseball's better teams. Nor do they play in a very good stadium. We can also report that all those things you may have heard about the ferocity of the Texas summer sun are all too true.

Still, going to Rangers games has its compensations. Food in the park is good, the Rangers staff is friendly, and the area around the stadium has just about everything you'd need in the way of accommodations, restaurants, and attractions to allow you to put together a great family vacation wrapped around a few games.

Nevertheless, from our perspective, the real interest at Arlington Stadium is what is happening on the field and how people are responding to it. For every baseball team, a point of time must come when the personalities of the audience and the club begin to merge; it's the time when people stop being attendees, and start becoming fans. At Arlington Stadium, that process is occuring now. Watching it happen is damned exciting.

The Team

The team we now call the Texas Rangers started out as the Washington Senators in 1961. It wasn't the famed Senators of the 1920s that Walter Johnson led to scores of victories; that team is now the Minnesota Twins. Rather, the 1961 Senators were a new franchise created by the American League to fill the vacuum left in the capital when the old Senators departed. The squad never really took hold in Washington. Its performance and its attendance were both poor—it boasted one winning season in a decade of play. In 1972 the Senators pulled up stakes and headed out to the booming Dallas–Ft. Worth area, changing their name to the Rangers.

In the Metroplex, the team has been more noted for its managers, and for managerial chaos, than for great play.

Over the years, a Who's Who of managing greats have traipsed through Dallas, trying their luck at turning the hapless Rangers around. Ted Williams, Billy Martin, Eddie Stankey, Don Zimmer, and Whitey Herzog are among the eleven leaders who have held the reigns at various points during the Ranger's eighteen-year history. During 1977, the team reached the low point in its game of managerial musical chairs when four people headed the squad. Eddie Stankey had the shortest reign. Hired over the phone one evening, he flew into Dallas–Ft. Worth the next day. After a pep talk with the team, Stankey looked around Arlington Stadium and decided he didn't like the place. "Take me back to the airport!" Eddie declared, ending the shortest managerial career on record. The Rangers won that night.

During these years the Rangers did not always do poorly. Under Billy Martin in 1974, the team scored second place in its division. They did nearly as well the next year, despite an incident in which Martin got involved in a fight in a local topless bar. When Martin was replaced by Frank Lucchesi, the Rangers came in second for him too, in 1977. The same courtesy was extended to managers Bill Hunter (1978), Don Zimmer (1981), and current boss Bobby Valentine (1986), during their first full years with the club. Unfortunately, the Rangers were never able to capitalize on good starts. After an initial good year with a succession of managers they usually slipped back into the loss column.

It wasn't that the Rangers didn't have good players; they often did. Fergie Jenkins, Bert Blyleven, Doyle Alexander, Rick Honeycutt, Al Oliver, and Rusty Staub are among the stars who wore the Ranger blue during these years. Somehow, though, it didn't all come together.

Maybe that's starting to happen now. Boasting one of their best squads ever, the Rangers currently have, in addition to Ryan, such solid competitors as pitcher Bobby Witt and sluggers Ruben Sierra, Rafael Palmeiro, and Julio Franco. Maybe 1991 will be the year when "impossible dreams" start to turn into reality.

The Stadium

Located midway between Dallas and Ft. Worth in the medium sized city of Arlington, the Rangers' stadium is convenient to both of the Metroplex's major population centers, and sits only a few miles south of DFW airport. The Rangers could have hardly picked a more ideal place from the standpoint of vacationers, for Arlington is something of a Texas tourist mecca. Surrounding the stadium are dozens of restaurants, nightspots, and hotels—several of which are within walking distance of the stadium. Directly east of the park (you can stroll over, if you like) is "Six Flags Over Texas," an amusement park that is one of the Midwest's biggest family tourist attractions. Within minutes of the facility are even more places to keep the kids, and yourself, amused.

As for Arlington Stadium itself, well . . . let's just say it isn't one of the nation's premier sports facilities. It isn't beautiful, God knows. With 43,508 seats, Arlington is the fourth smallest park in the majors, and is certainly among the most ungainly looking. Rising abruptly from the flat plains of Texas, it appears to the viewer as a vast mass of girders, sheet metal walls, and enormous billboards. The whole place has a temporary look about it. It's as if, when Dallas got the word that it would have a major league baseball franchise, someone at the celebratory party suddenly slapped a hand to his head and said, "Do you guys realize that we don't have a stadium?" whereupon everyone scurried out to see what they could do to throw one up before anyone else found out.

Actually, that's almost the way it happened. When the Senators moved to the Metroplex in 1972, there was a stadium on the site alright, a 10,000 seat steel-and-wood structure owned by the Dallas–Ft. Worth Spurs minor league squad. The Rangers simply took what the Spurs had and added to it, and added to it, and added to it, to produce the mishmash that exists today. Throughout the park, you get the sense that whole sections of the stadium came into existance simply because someone pointed and said "Hey, I think we can get in some more seats over there!" Which is exactly how the park did develop.

There's something else you should know about this place, which may help explain—at least for some people— some things about the Rangers' performance over the past two decades. Most baseball fans have heard about "the Curse of the Bambino," the idea that the Red Sox constant failure to take a Series is the result of a sort of divine retribution being enacted against the team for selling Babe Ruth to the Yankees after he won two games in the 1918 fall classic for them. In a similar manner, the Rangers are said to be afflicted by "The Curse of the Comanches," the result of Arlington Stadium's rumored construction over an Indian burial ground. Is the charge true? Management doesn't say. However, it is notable that less than a mile from the park are state historic signs pointing out the site of a major battle between, very literally, the cowboys and the Indians. So who knows? Maybe the Comanches *are* getting their revenge.

Outside the stadium there is nothing whatsoever to hold your attention. Inside, you walk up sunny staircases to get to the mezzanine level, which is where many of the food stands are and where fans go to chat or buy souvenirs. It's basically a wide, shaded aisle, reasonably clean but looking a bit worn. The concession stands placed

along it are not especially attractive, and the lines can and do get long. For the most part, though, they serve pretty good food.

From the mezzanine level you can see the whole of the stadium. It's your basic, simple bowl. Its expanses, in fact, are so rounded that this is the perfect park for "The Wave"—which, predictably, is very popular here. Between the foul poles, the vast majority of the seats slope back from the field, getting higher and steeper as they arch back. Nearly all are exposed to the hot Metroplex sun. Outlining the baselines area, but set way back from the field, is the park's single upper deck, a structure that looks like an architectural afterthought and probably was. Within the field area the seating is entirely composed of cheap plastic-and-metal chairs.

Beyond the outfield wall is one of the largest general admission areas in baseball, a place that's a vast, sun-beaten sea of aluminum benches. This area in turn is topped with an enormous row of billboard signs advertising such things as cigarettes, computers, and bourbon. We are assured that these boards are there principally to cut down on the wind; to us, they seem tacky and truly bush league.

In addition to the ads, though, are some things you should be aware of. Way above the left field pole you'll see a line of flags for teams in the American League East. You will note that they fly in order of the day's standings, from left to right. The end of the first base line has a similar display, in this case for the AL West. The order here runs right to left. You'll also note five electronic boards between the billboards. These record, from left to right, the day's AL scores, the NL scores, the park's Diamond Vision display, the scoreboard, and a combined time and temperature clock—during most summer evenings, the temperature display gets the most attention.

The field itself is strictly standard issue. It's a pleasant expanse of natural grass with moderate lines. The right and left field foul poles are set at 330', while the center field wall sits at 400'. Before the billboards, wind patterns made Arlington Stadium a tough place to get a home run in. Today, Nolan Ryan makes it a hard spot to nail a homer.

New Stadium

Although plans are only beginning to be developed, the Ranger's management has announced they will be building a new stadium, which they hope to have open by 1995. According to the officials, a variety of locations are being looked at throughout the Metroplex area.

It can only be hoped that in designing the new facility the Rangers will remember to preserve the good things about the current park (its natural grass field and its intimacy), while correcting the more obvious things that are bad. We would also hope that the team would give ample consideration to staying in Arlington. The location seems to us just about ideal.

Highlights

Though it's seen no World Series or Division Championship games, Arlington Stadium has been the scene of some memorable moments in baseball history. Nolan Ryan pitched his 5,000th strikeout in the park on August 22, 1989, putting Oakland's Rickey Henderson down on a list of Ryan's victims that now includes well over 1,000 different players, 19 of them members of the Hall of Fame. Mike Witt also hurled a "perfect game" for the Angels in the park on September 30, 1984.

Fans

When do attendees at baseball games truly start to become fans?

As anyone who has attended ball games in a variety of places knows, many of the old baseball towns — places like New York, Chicago, and Boston — have fans who are just that, enthusiasts who know the sport intimately and who share an emotional bond with their team and its fortunes. In other places, particularly in some of the expansion cities, it simply isn't that way. People in San Diego, for example, are certainly happy if the Padres win. But they don't lose any sleep about it if they don't, either. Pretty much the same could be said of fans in such places as Seattle, Houston, and Atlanta. Decades ago, New York, Boston, and Chicago adherents probably felt pretty much this way about the game, too. But, at some point in the past, something happened that galvanized these people and made them into true devotees of the sport.

We don't pretend to know who "created" the fans of Beantown and the Big Apple (though we suspect, in both cases, that his name was Ruth), but we can say with some certainty that the same process of transformation between attendee and fan is taking place in the Metroplex now. Will it be a permanent change? We couldn't begin to say. But in Dallas baseball is hot.

The agent of change is Nolan Ryan, the Lone Star state's hero of the hour. And, in truth, he seems perfect for the role. A native Texan who has never abandoned his home town of Alvin, Ryan is a strong man of few words and incredible will. He's the sort of pitcher who lets his on-the-field performance do most of his talking for him. Now near the end of his career, Ryan is as hot as he's ever been, in public recognition and adulation and in solid performance.

Every time Ryan is scheduled to pitch these days, Arlington Stadium fills. And all of a sudden people who two years ago couldn't have told you what an RBI was have memorized the Rangers' complete team stats and can argue persuasively (if incorrectly) that Ryan is the greatest pitcher ever. The Rangers' management is no doubt delighted that Nolan is rotating the turnstiles. But he's also providing for the team and the sport a far greater service; he's creating, in this baseball-beknighted state, a real baseball culture.

Who are these newly minted baseball fans? The Rangers draw a middle and working class family audience mostly. There are some young males out with their buddies, lots of kids with parents, a few oldsters, and even some teenagers out on dates. Most of these folks are, as you'd expect, Texans. However, you'll also see Oklahomans and lots of northern expatriates who've moved down to the sunbelt, with a particularly strong contingent of Michiganders, many of whom work at a nearby GM plant. Years ago, these GMers used to shout for the Tigers when they came to town. These days, like everyone else, they cheer for the Rangers.

This is a warm, friendly, and fun crowd—an audience that is, in the Texas sense of the term "neighborly." If fans around you perceive that you are an outsider, they will probably go out of their way at some point in the game to extend you a courtesy, even if it's just picking up an item you dropped or pointing out something about the park that you may have missed. As fans, Rangers people keep a pretty close eye on the game. They love to cheer the Rangers and down beers, are not averse to ragging the officials, and are almost always courteous to opponents. At times, the Texan sense of courtesy can result in genuine acts of graciousness. During a game we attended, we were privileged to see the White Sox's Carlton Fisk break the all-time record for homers hit by a catcher. The audience gave Fisk a long, appreciative

standing ovation. After the end of the game, the fan who'd caught Fisk's blast showed up at the clubhouse and presented him with the ball. That, of course, is not the way it would happen at every ballpark.

More than most sunbelt parks, Arlington Stadium has a sense of fan tradition. "The Wave" is popular here. So, too is a tune called "Cotten Eyed Joe," a Texas two-step that's played during the seventh inning stretch; just about everyone gets up and dances. Fans also enjoy watching the Lone Ranger on the video display—whenever the team gets close to victory, clips from the old TV show are run as the William Tell Overture blasts from the speakers and the audience yells "Charge!" In the past, the Lone Ranger (Clayton Moore) actually used to show up in person, and would gallop along the running track shouting "Heigh ho, Silver!" Threats of copywrite infringements by the owners of the rights to the character, though, put a stop to that.

Ryan's accomplishments, too, have added a new tradition to the Ranger fan's repertoire. As batters approach whenever the fastballer is on the mound, the audience will often start chanting "In ... the ... book!" What they want to see is a strikeout, knowing as they do that everytime Ryan racks up a "K" from now until the end of his career, that stikeout automatically goes "in the record book" as the most stikeouts ever—until Nolan gets his next one.

One of the great things about baseball is that it offers a variety of delights. If you attend a bad game, you might still find yourself among fun fans. If the attendees prove obnoxious, you might still get to see a hot contest. At Arlington Stadium, the fans are just great, and the team is getting better. Going to Rangers games may not be your highest baseball priority. But if you do go, be prepared to have a good time.

Getting There

Located midway between Dallas and Ft. Worth, Arlington Stadium is easy to reach by car and just about impossible to get to by mass transit. Your best (and just about only) options are car and cab, although Arlington Stadium can be reached by bus from Dallas–Ft. Worth Airport.

By car. From Dallas, Little Rock, and points *east*, take I-30 west to the Frontage Road exit. Follow Frontage Road to Copeland. Head west on Copeland to stadium parking.

From Ft. Worth, Abilene, and areas *west*, take I-30 east to Pennant Drive. Follow Pennant to stadium parking.

From Houston, Galveston, and sections *southeast*, follow I-45 north to I-30 west. Proceed along I-30 west to the Frontage Road exit. Follow Frontage Road to Copeland. Head west on Copeland to stadium parking.

From Wichita, Oklahoma City, and other *north* locales, take I-35 south to the exit for I-35W. Follow I-35W to I-30 east. Proceed along I-30 east to Pennant Drive. Follow Pennant Drive to parking.

From *Dallas–Ft. Worth Airport*, take International Parkway south to the Airport Freeway (I-183) west. Exit at Route 360 south. Proceed south to I-30 west. Exit I-30 at Copeland Road and follow signs to Arlington Stadium.

By cab. You can, of course, take a cab to the park — if you have a Texas-sized wallet. From either Dallas or Ft. Worth, the fare should be about $25 one way. From DFW airport, plan on spending $20. It's even worse if you are coming in from Dallas' Love Field; that will cost about $30.

Something you should be aware of is that some of the taxi drivers will have never heard of Arlington Stadium or the Rangers — to many Metroplex residents, the only park worth speaking of is Texas Stadium, where the Cowboys play. Just head these drivers down I-30 — they'll figure it out eventually.

By bus. There's a decent bus option available from DFW airport. Call for the Super Shuttle at (817) 329-2000, and ask it to take you to the Sheraton Centrepark Hotel in Arlington. From there, it's a short walk to the park. The charge is $9.50 per person.

Parking

Arlington Stadium has plenty of parking spots wrapped around the park, all uniformly priced at a very reasonable $3. With 12,000 spaces available, there's no likelihood at all of there not being enough spots to cover any crowd.

Those traveling in campers and recreational vehicles will find that the Rangers have provided spaces for them as well, but you will have to pay more.

Tickets

The Rangers make their tickets available in the usual ways, with one important exception: you can't get them by phone. They are available by mail, at the advance ticket office, or you can pick them up just before the game. Since seats are generally available for every game that Nolan Ryan is not pitching in, how you wish to order is basically a matter of what's most convenient for you.

Mail is probably the best option if you are planning a family vacation in the Arlington area. That's something that's a pretty good idea, really — kids will love the place. To get your Rangers seats, write down the number of tickets you want, the location you'd prefer and send your payment in full to: Ticket Office, Texas Rangers Baseball Club, PO Box 1111, Arlington, TX 76004.

Be sure to include the extra $3 service charge that the Rangers stiff you for.

Going to the advance ticket office is also a good idea. It's located at the stadium, and is open from 9 A.M. to 6 P.M. Monday through Friday, and from 10 A.M. to 4 P.M. on Saturday.

Availability. With 43,508 seats, Arlington Stadium isn't one of the bigger parks in baseball. On the other hand, the Rangers aren't one of the most successful franchises, either. It is a rare year when the Rangers hit the 2,000,000 attendance mark (they've topped it only once), and the club sells only 8,500 season tickets. During 1989, the Rangers sold an average of 26,000 spots per game—17,000 less than capacity—and that was their best ever. Therefore, even if you show up at the park at the last minute, there will almost certainly be a spot for you.

But what kind of seat? That's the question. Arlington Stadium has many bleacher spots and relatively few box chairs. If you want a good seat for one of the more popular match-ups (Detroit, Yankees, and Red Sox games are especially favored), you should order by mail or report to the advance ticket office fairly early. You should also be aware that whenever it's announced that Nolan Ryan is pitching, the place fills up fast. If you hear that the local hero is hurling, make sure to stop by the advance ticket office ahead of time.

Costs. Ticket prices at Arlington Stadium are moderate to inexpensive, and ticket prices generally match the relative value of the spots. It's possible to get "burned" in Arlington Stadium (indeed, it's likely), but it will be from the omnipresent sun, not from what you paid for your seats.

In 1990, ticket prices were as follows: Field and Mezzanine Box ($10); Reserved ($9); Plaza ($8); Reserved Grandstand ($5); General Admission (Adult [$4]); Child (13 and under [$2]).

Rainouts. Rainouts don't happen very often in Arlington. Still, if you should get caught in a downpour (which are usually Texas-sized), you can exchange tickets for a future contest. If you live outside the Metroplex area, write to the Rangers and they'll refund your money.

Seating

You'll find the biggest problem with seating at Arlington Stadium blazing right over your head—the sun. Avoiding its rays is just about impossible in the park; there's almost no shade. However, as a general rule the areas behind the outfield walls (Reserved Grandstand and General Admission) get the most sun. Among the box seats, those along the first base line get more shelter than those along third. If you are particularly sensitive to the sun, keep these things in mind as you book seats. However, no matter where you sit, if the day is bright bring lotion and a hat. You will probably need it.

The most expensive seats at Arlington Stadium are the Field and Mezzanine boxes ($10). Of these, the 100 level Field boxes are far to be preferred. You have to travel a long, hot, and dark corridor to reach them, and they use brown plastic chairs. (Why brown? A lighter color would retain less heat.) But they have decent legroom, and since this section is only twenty rows deep without any intervening aisles, the 100 level boxes offer outstanding views. If you can get them, the absolute best seats in the park are found in aisles 114 to 111, which are right behind the batter's box. They also have just about the only shade in the stadium. However, any seat located between aisles 118 (third) and 106 (first) would have to be rated exceptional. The only drawback to this area is that the only food to be found is in the corridors behind home plate, where the selection is poor and the lines are long. You would be better off to walk to the mezzanine level, where the selection is better.

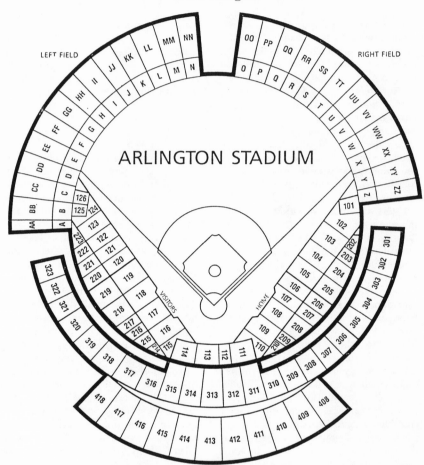

Seating chart, Arlington Stadium.

Level 200 box seats are set behind the 100 level seats. They're a bit further from the action but are still pretty acceptable. Since all are in the baselines, where you'll want to sit is more a function of whether you prefer first base or third base action.

Mezzanine boxes (300 level) are a secondary choice. They're the usual plastic chairs set up in longish rows fairly far from the field but pleasingly close to the food. For the money, these spots are acceptable, but they certainly can't be considered values. Happily, all aisles are in the baselines, which here

run from 320 (third) to 304 (first). Aisle 320 is a designated "no alcohol" family reserved area.

Reserved seats ($9) are the fewest in number in the park. That's because the Reserved spots are simply those portions of the 200 and 300 level boxes that aren't in the baselines. Of these, those located at the 200 level are fair values—you're still pretty close to the action. Those at the 300 level have the combined disadvantages of distance and an out-of-the baselines location. Rather than sit here, you might be better served to either pay the extra buck for a box seat or save four dollars by taking a spot in the Reserved Grandstand area.

Plaza level seats (400 level, $8) rest on an abbreviated upper deck that's set back fairly far from the field. The pitch of the deck is quite steep, the top spots are very high, and the whole structure has an unstable feel to it. The seats are fairly comfortable red plastic-and-metal chairs, but the rows are long, and the food selection is limited. Happily, though, all the seats in the area are within the baselines.

The key at this level is to sit in the lowest row possible (1 to 8 would be good) and as close to the batter's box as you can get (416 to 411 if possible). Frankly, seats aren't so great here. If you can't find a spot that's low and close in, you might want to consider someplace else.

The budget spots in the park are all located in the stadium's vast area behind the outfield wall. Reserved Grandstand seats ($5) occupy the first eight rows behind the wall and are great bargains. The view is good, the crowd is friendly, and the price is right. Section N is a "family reserved area." General Admission ($4) stretches forever behind these seats. This area is composed of hard aluminum benches with aluminum backs, and it gets a spirited crowd with lots of college students, kids, and young families. Though these are obviously not premier spots, you can find places with good views if you come a bit early and stake a claim to seats in the first few rows. Given the Rangers generous admission policy regarding kids, you can seat a family of five here for under $15 — slightly more than one good seat will cost you in Fenway or Wrigley Field.

There are a few things you should be aware of if you sit in these areas. First, food choices are limited, and you will not be able to get to the mezzanine level where the choices are bet-

ter. Second, you should try to stay out of sections XX, X, D, DD, E, and EE. Views in these areas are obstructed by the foul poles. Finally, you will find it difficult to see the electronic video-display board from much of this area, particularly in center field.

Special Needs

Parking. Handicapped parking is available next to the stadium entrance. Show your sticker or plate when you drive into the park and you'll be directed to the appropriate area.

Seating. There's good handicapped seating as well. On the field level, the handicapped seating section is at aisles 103 and 104. These are outstanding spots, just past first base and very close to the field. However, those who sit there should be aware that you are in some danger of being beaned by a foul ball. In the Reserved Grandstand area, the handicapped spots are in aisles A and Z. For the money, they're super spots, located at the far ends of the right (Z) and left (A) field lines.

Food and Features

Food. Although there are food stands throughout the park, the best concentration by far can be found at the mezzanine level. Though there are no fancy restaurants in the park, the dining situation is still pretty good. The selection is decent, the quality is good, and the prices are much better than usual.

An oddity about the park is that although it has the usual ballpark fare, no one seems to eat it. We'd bet that Arlington Stadium has the lowest per-capita hot dog consumption in the majors. Still, if you're a traditionalist, there are hot dogs, "super dogs," "corn dogs" (hot dogs covered in fried corn meal: a

real horror), and peanuts available, as
well as cotton candy, french fries, and
popcorn. Many locations also serve a
chicken breast sandwich.

There are specialties, too *Subs 'n'
Spuds*, located behind aisle 309 (first
base) has what its name implies. Here
you can snag a tasty baked potato with
toppings or a sizable sub. The place also
offers "fresh dough" pizza that—surprisingly—is very, very good. In fact,
although it's a tad expensive, it may be
the best pie in the ballparks.

More popular than any of these with
the fans, though, is Mexican chow.
Rangers fans, in fact, claim to have
popularized nachos in baseball—though
whether that's a plus or a minus is
something we'd rather not say! At any
rate, the best south-of-the-border
selections in the park (and in baseball)
can be found at *Mexican Fiesta*, which is
located bedhind aisle 318 (third base).
Selections available include meat and
bean burritos, tasty taco pie, Mexican
taco, and, of course, nachos. If you do
enjoy nachos, try buying them at *Mexican Fiesta* as opposed to other spots in
the stadium. You'll find that their version is an improvement on the usual
hard horrors.

Drinks. Coke products are offered
throughout the park, and Miller and
Bud Light are the primary brews served
in the park. You can also find an excellent selection of Mexican beers at *Mexican Fiesta*.

Features. The game is the sole
feature at Arlington Stadium. After all,
if you were interested in rides and the
like, you'd go next door to "Six Flags
Over Texas."

Assistance

If you are having problems with
rowdy fans, can't find your seats, or
have ideas on how the Rangers could
do things better, repair to the Personal
Services Office, which is located on the
mezzanine level behind aisle 314 (home
plate). Its friendly staff will be happy to
help iron out any difficulties.

Safety and Security

Safety. Within the park, occasional
rowdiness and drunkenness are the
only safety threats, and they are pretty
rare. Outside, in the parking lots and in
the surrounding neighborhoods, there
is no appreciable security problem. If
you decide to hoof it to such area
nightspots as the Atchafalya Cafe or the
bar at the Sheraton you should encounter no problems.

Health. Far and away the biggest
health threat in the park is the sun. It
can be fierce and unremitting. Even
when the sun goes down, oppressive
heat can continue far into the night:
during a recent game we attended, the
temperature started at 94, rose to 98,
and settled down to a brisk 89 by midnight!

The best way to avoid unpleasant
burns is to be prepared. Bring a hat and
suntain lotion with you to the stadium,
wear light (and light colored) clothing,
drink plenty of water and not so much
beer, and, if you know you are particularly sun-sensitive, stay out of the
outfield seating. If you find the sun getting to you, get out of it. It's better for
you to take a stroll to such air conditioned areas as the souvenir store or
first aid than for the ushers to have to
cart you out on a stretcher.

Should you find that the sun is getting
to be a bit much, or if you need other
assistance, the Ranger's first aid office is
located just inside Gate 8 of the stadium.
This is also a place where mothers can
find a quiet spot to nurse babies.

Mementos

Souvenirs. Rangers fans aren't big
paraphernalia wearers, though Nolan

Ryan shirts are popular. Still, the club has a nice in-the-park store called *The Dugout*, which is located on the mezzanine level behind home plate. Here you'll find a good selection of shirts, logoed hats, and other Rangers materials at the usual high prices. It's open during games, and also on away game weekdays from 10 A.M. to 4 P.M. during the season.

There is also a much smaller souvenir shop behind the General Admission area.

Foul Balls. Open to the elements, Arlington Stadium is a good place to catch them, though you'll have a lot of competition from the junior battalion. The 200 Field box seats seem to get the most balls. Try aisles 217 and 218 (left field) and 206 and 207 (right field).

Autographs. Arlington Stadium is a haven for the autograph hound if it's the visitors' singatures you are after. All the visiting teams stay at the Sheraton Centrepark, which is located perhaps four hundred yards southeast of the stadium. In order to get to it, most of the players will exit from Gate 1 and walk over after the game. This provides an exceptional opportunity for fans to get autographs. Please be polite; if autograph hunters get to be a nuisance, our guess is that the teams will sooner or later hire a bus to take them back to the hotel.

Getting Ranger signatures is considerably harder. The home team exits from Gate 7 and goes directly to their private parking lot, which is screened off from the fans. In order for you to get Ranger signatures, team members must stop their cars on the way out of the lot; most, of course, don't.

TORONTO BLUE JAYS
The Sky Dome

How do you spell success in baseball? These days it would be very tempting to spell it Toronto Blue Jays.

During the 1990 season, much of the attention of the baseball world was focused on the Jays due to the introduction of their stunning new Sky Dome stadium, which completed its first season of play during that year and attracted accolades and attention worldwide. Boasting a retractable roof, which allows the team's games to be played both indoors and out, a "Hard Rock Cafe," and a wonderful in-park hotel with rooms from which you can see all the action, the Sky Dome is far and away the most spectacular of all the baseball parks. It is little wonder that hundreds of thousands of fans have traveled hundreds and in some cases thousands of miles to see it.

Yet in a certain sense, the fabulous public acceptance of the Sky Dome has taken at least some of the spotlight away from the fine team that plays within it. The Blue Jays may not be the most successful of the expansion teams, though they are certainly close to being the most successful by now. If the yardstick, though, is popular acceptance, the Jays take the prize walking away.

One of the two newest teams in the major leagues (the other is the Mariners), the Blue Jays' attendance figures in their fourteen years of existence are little short of astonishing.

During their first season, despite an opener that was held in the middle of a snowstorm and a dismal last place finish that saw the new club dropping two games out of three, the Blue Jays still managed to shatter the all-time attendance mark for new expansion clubs. Indeed, that first year total of 1.7 million is more than a few long-standing clubs pull in to this day.

That record marked only the beginning of the prodigious growth in patronage that has distinguished the team since its inception. In 1984, though the club had still never led in the standings, it passed the 2,000,000 mark, a total that such historic and successful clubs as the Pirates and the Giants had never reached. Five years later, the Jays led the leagues as the team became one of the only five clubs in history (the others are the Dodgers, the Cards, the Mets, and the Twins) ever to sell over 3,000,000 tickets in a season. With 1990, Toronto picked up all the attendance marbles when the Sky Dome saw its first season turnstiles take in over 3.8 million people as the club established the all-time attendance mark. It's a statistic that's all the more impressive when you consider that the Blue Jays have yet to win a pennant, let alone a Series. As of this writing, it seems that the breaking of the 4,000,000 mark is well within the Blue Jays' sights. Indeed, there is every reason to believe that the Jays may turn out to be the hottest team of the 1990s.

Why has Toronto been so good at bringing in the fans? What has made the squad so incredibly successful in such a short period of time? Basically, the team's triumph has been built around three elements that other expansion teams would do well to emulate.

First, when the team came into existence in 1977, the organization recognized the primary essential truth about baseball attendance, namely that people go to a baseball game principally to see their home team win. In any sport, after all, victory is the aphrodisiac of attendance. The Blue Jays knew that if they wanted to build a powerful franchise, they were going to have to, sooner or later, give Torontonians something to cheer about.

Unlike some of the other expansion clubs, who optimistically anticipated reaping pennants within a year or two after their entry into big league ball, the Jays were wise enough to realize that they were probably not going to win in their early years in the majors. On the contrary, they knew they were almost certainly going to lose, and most likely were going to lose miserably—which, in fact, was exactly what they did.

Accordingly, instead of trying frantically to buy or trade for talent from existing organizations in a futile pursuit of immediate glory, the Jays concentrated on developing a plan for long-term success. They built one of the best farm team systems in baseball, and they spent time and money working with their minor league divisions to develop talent and skills. As talented players emerged in the minors, they were brought up one by one to Toronto, strengthening the team. Today, the current Blue Jay organization is largely composed of ex–Toronto minor leaguers.

The Jays also realized that potentially good players were not limited simply to the traditional locales. Accordingly, the squad developed an aggressive scouting division that was determined to hunt future Jays in places, most of them in Latin America, that other teams overlooked. Though Toronto is the second most northerly team in baseball, its ranks have been chock-full of competitive Latins who don't like to lose. Tony Fernandez, George Bell, and Junior Felix are only a few of the large contingent of Dominicans who have graced the club's rosters since its inception.

Finally, the team has, in the past, had

the sense not to trade away its stars. The result of all these policies has been that the Blue Jays have emerged over the past decade as one of the sport's most consistently outstanding teams.

The second key to the Jays' success has been built around their approach to the fans. The Toronto organization realized that, as much as people liked to go to see a winning team, they also wanted to go to a park where they could enjoy themselves and the game in comfort and safety. Though the organization's older Exhibition Stadium was pretty deficient as a ballpark, the place still lacked little that was required to make going to the game a pleasant experience. The park was easy to get to, particularly by public transportation, it had decent food, and it had a management that was "fan oriented" and that realized it was in the business of entertainment. The Sky Dome goes farther in all of these areas—indeed, in its dogged commitment to providing comfort, convenience, and cleanliness, the Dome is second to no park in baseball. Moreover, Toronto's management has always had the sense to realize that security is a very big issue in the minds of fans and their families. The team has accordingly been sure at both their parks to site them in totally safe neighborhoods and to police their facilities in such a way that problems such as drunkenness and rowdiness are practically nonexistent. This sensible approach has insured that families and kids, the largest segment of just about any team's potential audience, keep on coming to the games.

Lastly, the Blue Jays saw that fans don't come to the park just to enjoy a game of baseball. They also like to dine, have a drink, dance, take fun rides, and see the sights. Accordingly, and unlike San Francisco and New York, two other great towns that put their parks in the middle of no place, the Blue Jays built their spanking new stadium right in the heart of Toronto's vibrant and appealing downtown. Thus they made a trip to the game part of what the team like's to call "a total entertainment experience."

When you go to Toronto to watch the Jays and enjoy the Dome, you will also probably be taking a peak at baseball as it is likely to be presented in many cities during the next century. You will see a spectacular, high-tech, modern stadium that will literally take your breath away. You will enjoy efficiently served, standardized food, offered by smiling, friendly people. You will revel in an environment where everything is bright, convenient, immaculately tidy, and safe.

If the formula sounds familiar, it should. For our part, moreover, we are convinced that the parallel is no coincidence. The Sky Dome is the Disneyworld of baseball.

The Team

The Sky Dome may have assumed the roll of the "Magic Kingdom" in the sport, but the Blue Jays have certainly not deigned to play Mickey Mouse. Like every expansion team, the club got off to a terrible start. The Jays, however, turned things around fairly quickly.

The team came into existence in 1977, as a result of the 1976 American League expansion that also brought the Seattle Mariners into baseball. Consisting of a squad composed, as even the team admits, of "rookies, career minor-leaguers, and players other clubs didn't want," the new organization turned in the usual abominable first year performance, going 54-102. Still, despite a snowy first game, the fans came, which was something. During that desultory initial season catcher Ernie Whitt started what would be a long and productive career with the new club.

Over the next few years, the Jays

initial pattern maintained itself. The team performed poorly; the fan's waited patiently for improvement. In 1978 things brightened a little bit when star pitcher Dave Stieb signed on board.

The strike-ridden 1981 "split season" foreshadowed glories to come. The Blue Jays, as usual, stank up the circuit in the first fifty-eight games of the contest. After the strike, though, the squad astounded just about everyone by playing .500 ball until the last few weeks of the season. By God, Torontonians thought, they *can* do it!

The promise of 1981 was fulfilled in part in 1983, when the Jays found themselves in their first pennant race. They folded at the end, which, in truth, is something the team seems to specialize in. For the first time, however, they won more games than they lost. During the same year, shortstop Tony Fernandez and slugger George Bell joined the club and supplied excitement.

It all came together in 1985, when the Jays won their first Eastern Division title. Boasting such standout players as Bell, Fernandez, Stieb, and pitcher Doyle Alexander, the Jays were favored for the flag. It was not to be. The surging Kansas City Royals won the championship in seven games. In 1989, close to the same scenario repeated itself as the Jays nipped the Orioles in a last minute battle to again capture the AL East crown, only to lose the pennant to the powerful Oakland A's, 4–1.

Currently, the Blue Jays have a solid squad but one that is in a period of transition. A massive and atypical trade in 1990 sent such starts as Fernandez and slugger Fred McGriff packing while such potent players as Roberto Alomar and Joe Carter joined the Jays. The team should now have the people needed to go all the way. However, when you switch personnel you also affect the chemistry of personality, for

good or ill. How that will touch the Jays' prospects remains to be seen.

The Stadium

You have to go back a long way to recall a baseball stadium whose introduction made a bigger stir than the inauguration of the Sky Dome in 1989 and 1990. It is very likely, in fact, that no park ever built has been so expectantly awaited nor so warmly received as the Dome that, along with the nearby CN Tower, now dominates Toronto's already impressive skyline.

It's not that there haven't been other famous and influential baseball parks. There have. In its day, San Francisco's Candlestick was considered a model of modern design and convenience. It was praised by Presidents Nixon and Kennedy and patronized by the rich and famous. The Astrodome in Houston created even more of a stir with its revolutionary dome and its pioneering round structure, both based on the Roman Colosseum. So futuristic was the look of the place that is owners persuaded NASA to send Apollo astronauts over for a day or two for some impromptu moon walk training.

Nor were celebrated ballpark introductions limited to relatively modern times. In 1923, America "oohhed and ahhed" over Yankee Stadium, a simply enormous facility by the standards of its day, thrown up principally to accommodate fans brought in by the incredible drawing power of a single player, the Bambino himself. Babe Ruth obligingly hit the park's first homer on opening day. A generation earlier "The Old Roman," Charles Comiskey, put up the ballpark that for seventy years bore his name. Termed by one and all "the great sports palace of the world," it was probably the most influential ballpark of them all.

Even so, there has been nothing like the Sky Dome in terms of popular interest, for a simple reason: the park is spectacular in just about every way. Even if it is not the perfect place to play ball that its many boosters claim, few would question that the place is an incredible piece of sports architecture.

The need for a new ballpark was apparent in Toronto for some time. The team's pervious home, Exhibition Stadium, had the advantage of having a fine location in downtown Toronto near Lake Ontario. After that, however, there were not many good things you could say for the place. Seating in the stadium existed more to accommodate the needs of motorcycle races and track and field events than it did baseball. Many chairs were pointed, Montreal style, at the center of the field rather than toward the action. Cool and damp breezes from Lake Ontario had a negative impact on the game. Players who otherwise enjoyed Toronto came to dislike the idea of contesting a series at Exhibition.

Weather was a problem, too. Though Toronto gets much sun in the summer, both its springs and autumns are cold and damp. Not only did rainouts happen at Exhibition, fog outs and even snowouts happened, too.

Accordingly, the Jays began to look around for support for a new stadium, at the same time placing some parameters on their search. First, they wanted to build a park specifically for baseball. If the place could serve other sports, that was fine, too, so long as its principal purpose was to accommodate bats and balls. That requirement automatically eliminated round and "brick" designs, both popular with "multipurpose" planners. Next, the team wanted to preserve the downtown Toronto location that had proved so popular with their Exhibition Stadium fans. They were looking to build a place that would be adaptable to the club's philosophy of baseball as part of a "total entertainment experience." Finally, the Blue Jays sought a design that would

make it possible for fans to enjoy Toronto's sunshine and avoid its fog and rain. The Sky Dome, the product of a unique public-private partnership, represents the wholly successful attempt of Toronto and, indeed, of Canada, to meet and exceed all of these requirements.

As soon as you drive into downtown Toronto you will see the Sky Dome. The place is just about impossible to miss. Almost smack in the middle of the business district, the Dome is the building immediately adjacent to the CN Tower, which just happens to be the tallest freestanding building in the world (you can take a ride to the top). At first glance you will notice two things about the Dome. First, even in comparison with the CN Tower, the concrete and blue glass stadium is unusually tall. In fact, the place is high enough to enclose a 31-story building. Your eyes will also be drawn to the roof. If the building is closed, it will seem a much less interesting place, a kind of enormous oval egg with the ends somehow squared. But if the dome is open you will be intrigued as we were by the flashes of white, green, and blue in the park's concrete vastness.

Walking to the building you discover that the Dome is indeed in the heart of everything in Toronto. Within a two or three minute stroll of the park are restaurants, hotels, the headquarters of some of Canada's largest corporations, and the attractive concert hall of the Toronto Symphony. Immediately south of the dome is "Harbourfront," a highly appealing area of nightspots, theatres, shops, and restaurants on Lake Ontario. It's very suitable for a meal before the game or a drink after. Get ambitious and decide to hike a bit farther and you will see attractive urban parks, historic sights, and, on University Avenue, Ontario's attractive Provincial Capitol.

We suspect, however, that you came to town mainly to see the Sky Dome.

The best view is probably along Front Street, and it is undeniably impressive. The Jays, in fact, just love to publish statistics about how big and magnificent the place is, and we thought you would like to know a few of them. For example, what is the roof made of? Plastic and steel. How much did the place cost to build? About a half billion dollars, or three times as much as the most costly park in the U.S. How long does it take to close the roof? Twenty minutes, which can be something of a pain during a ball game. That, in part, is why the open or closed decision is usually made before the contest. How much does the roof weigh? Eleven thousand tons. Just in case you were dying to know, the Jays helpfully point out that is as much as 3,734 automobiles, though whether those cars are Toyota Tercels or Cadillacs the club does not say.

Walking around the Dome there is a fair amount to see. High above your head at both north corners of the park you will see some wonderful reliefs that are delightful caricatures of baseball fans. If there is better art in the ballparks, we don't know of it. Directly to the back of the stadium on the north side are the entrances for the Hard Rock Cafe, the Windows on the Skydome restaurant, the Sightlines lounge, and, finally, the first class Sky Dome Hotel. All of these facilities offer fine views over the outfield inside the park. In particular, many of the bedrooms in the hotel have windows facing about forty thousand fans. During the 1990 season, this occasioned as much looking in on the part of fans as it did looking out on the part of patrons.

Walk counterclockwise around the building from here, you will see the next sight, a modest birch Indian tepee located directly northwest of the hotel in a pleasant and quiet park area. Purportedly, this is a monument to "Native Americans," and espcially to their notion of man living in harmony with nature. Why this tribute is in front of a massive, 31-story climate-controlled concrete sports arena escapes us. Is someone trying to be funny? If this were New York, we might suspect that. Irony, however, is not numbered among the Canadians' many virtues, and we think this is simply a humble if somewhat misplaced tribute to these people.

The west side of the building, while it provides good views, has few features of interest. Accordingly, this is a good point to talk about the principal building material of the dome, which is concrete. According to the club, the building used 210,000 tons of the stuff, which could have formed a sidewalk from Montreal to Toronto. Within the concrete and through the park are 120 miles of electrical cable that supply the facility enough electricity to meet the needs of the Canadian province of Prince Edward's Island.

The south part of the park is where the advance ticket office is, and you will see lines in this area as well as some scalping activity. Don't think of taking advantage of the latter though, as the practice is heavily policed in the area. To the east are a number of sights. The two floor "Skyplace" souvenir shop has not only a wide selection of goods but also stars on the floor honoring Blue Jay players and a variety of other entertainment stars. The McDonald's in this area is one branch of what is the largest division of the chain in North America.

Once inside the Sky Dome, the resemblance between the public areas of the place and a shopping mall are unmistakable. The air conditioning is comfortable, concession stands beckon, and pleasant music surrounds you. Restrooms are everywhere, and they are something the Jays seem to be especially proud of. Team literature informs us that there are 88 bathrooms, 1,280 toilets, and 119 electric hand dryers. Altogether, all this septic activity creates a flood of truly gargantuan proportions. According to the team, if every toilet in the Sky Dome were flushed simultaneously it would equal the amount of water that would flow over Niagra Falls for three seconds. We are also told that, in the scope of a single year, the park uses enough toilet paper to stretch to the moon.

The seating areas are impressive. Composed throughout of comfortable blue platic chairs, a very large proportion of the park's seating is situated on either the front or sides of the stadium. A relatively small proportion of the chairs are behind the outfield walls. Overall, the patron's area of the park is composed of three levels; one at the field, which is pleasingly proximate to the action, another termed "club" above that, and a final upper deck which is, as far as we are concerned, pretty distant from the game, particularly when you consider that as much as $12 is charged for some of the seats.

The astroturf field at the Blue Jay park is big. In fact, it is so big that you could fit the Roman Colosseum on it or (again from club literature) 516 elephants of the African variety, or 751 Indian elephants. We dread to think of what the team had to go through to pin down these precise numbers.

As impressive as the area is in terms of pachyderms, its dimensions are otherwise pretty ordinary. The foul poles are set at a mid-range 328′ while the center field wall is set at 400′. Close the roof and you have a kind of pitchers park. Open the roof and, depending on the wind, just about anything can happen.

In the Dome, the area behind the field has attracted the most attention. You will certainly see the windows of the various Sky Dome hotel rooms; hopefully, that is all you will see. If you are really eagle-eyed and look over the right field wall you may spot dancers at the Hard Rock and diners at Window on the Sky Dome. You will be peering at them and they will be peering at you.

Besides the roof, the most impressive thing about the dome is the enormous scoreboard, which features at its center a huge Sony video display area. A high-tech wonder 115′ × 33′, the videoboard runs contests, ads, Blue Jay messages, and, especially, live action shots of the game and replays with incredible clarity. The larger than life view of the game you get on the screen is so good that you are forced to wonder why anyone bothers to watch the action on the field.

What is one to make of this incredible stadium? We are not fans of huge sports palaces. We like a more natural game than we saw in Toronto. We prefer our ballparks intimate and human rather than sepctacular and sterile. Nevertheless, we would be the first to admit that if one really wants to build a "bigger is better" ballpark, the one that has been constructed for the Blue Jays is about as impressive a place as we can conceive of anyone putting up in the near future.

There is much that can be said in favor of the Sky Dome, and its vast popularity comes as no surprise to us. The park is awe-inspiring, convenient, clean, and comfortable. We are glad the place is around and look forward to visiting it again.

Still, when people speak to us of the Sky Dome as the model for the future, that makes us a bit uneasy. Right now the Dome is unique. We'd just as soon it stayed that way.

Highlights

The newest park in the major leagues, the Sky Dome has as yet seen no significant baseball highlights. Given the general excellence of the team that plays in the dome, though, that is a deficiency that we imagine will be corrected in short order.

Fans

If the Sky Dome itself is spectacular, the fans who come to watch the Blue Jays play in it are unexceptionable. They are pleasant, decent, well-dressed middle class sorts, the kind of folks you would find at a PTA meeting, in church, or headed for "Pirates of the Caribbean" at Disneyworld. They are mostly white, represent all age groups, and are fairly homogeneous.

Many Blue Jay fans seem to be tourists, and you will find fairly large numbers of people showing up at the dome an hour or two before the game. They walk around the park and like you are impressed at the sights and, probably, a bit annoyed about the prices. Perhaps an equal number of attendees will be regular Blue Jays people. They'll watch the contest intently, cheer the plays, and discuss what's going on quietly with their friends. You will see very few scorecards in evidence, for these are not baseball scholars. Talk with these fans, though, and you will find them quite up to date on how the teams are doing, who is hitting well and who is not, and what the Blue Jays' prospects are.

This is an exceptionally polite audience. Good plays performed by the opposition are routinely applauded, officials are treated with respect, and people in the stands generally treat each other well. Swearing is rare, drunkenness rarer, and folks will usually go a bit out of their way to help if you are lost or need any sort of help.

Mostly, the emphasis in the dome is on entertainment. Blue Jays fans like "the Wave," and the stadium is built especially well for it. They also enjoy getting up during the seventh inning stretch and doing exercises, which are led by a bevy of gymnasts who charge out onto the astroturf the moment the players leave the field. Personally, we would rather sing "Take Me Out to the Ballgame." If things get interesting, the audience get into the game. Cheers will mount, the "Charge!" will be hollered much louder, and feet stamping will begin. If, on the other hand, things go poorly you will see some people head for their cars starting at about the eighth inning.

People who enjoy the more dynamic audiences of such baseball towns as Boston or New York may find these Blue Jay fans unexciting. On the other hand, if you have spent all day touring Toronto's many sights, you might appreciate the opportunity to rest your feet and lungs and enjoy a game of baseball admidst a group of folks who are friendly and civilized.

Getting There

Located downtown just west of Lake Ontario, the Sky Dome, which sits next to the CN Tower, makes an impressive addition to the Toronto skyline. The place is fairly easy to reach by car, which may be the most practical option for those coming in from out of town. However, if you are staying in the Toronto area, subway and even walking are even better ways to get to the Dome. Cab service to the facility is also available.

By car. Those traveling to Toronto from such *south* points as Hamilton, Niagra Falls, and Buffalo should take the Queen Elisabeth II Expressway (Route 2) to downtown Toronto. From there, follow the signs to the Sky Dome and start looking for parking.

Those arriving at *Toronto International Airport* should take the Airport Road to Route 427 headed south. At the junction with the Queen Elisabeth Expressway, head toward downtown Toronto and pick up the directions given above.

If you are coming to the game from Montreal, Kingston, and other cities to the *east*, take the Macdonald-Cartier Highway (Route 401) west to the point where it meets the Don Valley Parkway (Route 404). From there, follow the Don Valley, which soon joins the Gardiner (Route 2) toward downtown Toronto. Once in downtown, follow the Sky Dome stadium signs and start hunting up a parking spot.

Americans headed in from Detroit as well as Canadians coming from London and other points *west* should follow the McDonald-Cartier Highway (Route 401) east to the Don Valley Parkway and then follow the directions above.

Northerners driving to the game from such points as Barrie should proceed on Route 400 south to the MacDonald-Cartier (Route 401) going east. From that point they should proceed as outlined above.

By cab. From any place in downtown Toronto, cab is an acceptable option. Within the central business district, expect to pay $6 to $7 for a ride to the park.

Cabs from Pierson Airport are prohibitively expensive; the airport limo to the park is a steep $35. A much better way to get to the Dome from this area is to take the hotel limo to L'Hotel, and simply walk to the Sky Dome from there. You will find the limo outside the baggage claim area. The charge is $8.75.

By subway. Toronto's fast and efficient subway system is by far the best way to get to the game if you are staying in the Toronto area. You will find the trains uniformly clean and safe. To get to the Sky Dome by subway, simply take the train to the Union Station on the Yonge Street line and walk to the Dome from there. If it's raining, you will certainly want to utilize the covered Skywalk that takes you from Union Station to the facility. Since there are only two subway lines you will have to change trains only one time at most. If you are traveling to the stadium from within the city, the charge is $1.20.

It is also possible to get from the airport to the Dome by mass transit, though it's difficult. To do this, go to terminal #2 and from there take the #58A Malton bus to the Lawrence West train station. At that point, take the subway from Lawrence West to Union Station. The combined charge for bus and train is $2.60.

By foot. If you are staying in any of the downtown hotels, walking is a pleasant option. Simply take a look at the horizon, pick out the biggest building around (the CN Tower) and start heading toward it! The Sky Dome sits at the corner of Front and John Streets.

Parking

Unfortunately, there is no regular stadium parking at the Sky Dome. Instead, you must wander around a bit in the streets near the park looking for a place to put your car.

Actually, there are a fair number of lots around, particularly in the Harbourfront area, which is directly south of the Dome near Lake Ontario. If you arrive in at the stadium an hour or so before the game you should have little difficulty locating a space reasonably close to the Dome. If you show later, be prepared for a walk.

Prices could be better. If you don't mind a hike you might find a spot for as cheap as $5. More typically, you will pay $8.

If this all sounds like something of a pain, it is. Thus we recommend, if you have the option, that you do as the Torontonians do and take public transportation to the game.

Tickets

You can get Blue Jays tickets by mail, by phone, or you can pick them up in person. Whichever option you choose, though, we urge you to buy your tickets early.

Mail ticket orders are handled by the Blue Jays at: Toronto Blue Jays, 300 The Esplanade Way, Box 3200, Toronto, Ontario M5V 3B3.

When you order by mail, be sure to enclose the dates and locations you want, along with your payment in full by check or money order. You should also include the team's $3 service charge. The Blue Jays will also allow you to charge tickets to MasterCard, Visa, or American Express if you enclose your account number and expiration date.

U.S. fans wishing to order tickets should be sure to pay in Canadian funds. You can do this either by getting a money order in Canadian funds from your bank, or, more simply, by paying by credit card.

Phone orders are accepted by the club as well. To order by phone call the Blue Jays at (416) 341-1234 between 9 A.M. and 6 P.M. Monday through Friday and from 9 A.M. to 4 P.M. on Saturday. Be prepared to relate the number of tickets you want, the dates you would like them for, and the locations you prefer. Also keep your major credit card close at hand. You will pay a service charge if you buy this way, also.

You'll avoid the charge and have a better chance of getting a good seat if you pick your spots up in person at the Jays' advance ticket office, which is located on the Esplanade level of the stadium between Gates 9 and 10 on the south side of the edifice. If you do buy there, be sure to check out your spots on a seating chart before you plunk your money down. Although the club contends that its "view" pricing policy guarantees that you will get your money's worth on seats, you will nevertheless find that even within the given view areas all seats are not created equal.

Availability. The Sky Dome has replaced Dodger Stadium as the most patronized park in baseball. The club led the leagues in attendance in 1989.

In 1990, the Sky Dome smashed baseball's all-time attendance record, bringing in over 3.8 million fans and selling out all seats on well over half their home games. There is no reason to believe that the Jays won's do even better in the future.

All of this means that Blue Jays tickets are very hard to come by. No matter what the match-up, the further you order tickets in advance, the better your chance of getting a decent seat, or of getting any seat at all. Should you arrive in town at the last minute and decide you'd like to go to a game, you would be well-advised to call the ticket office to see what is available before heading to the stadium. Otherwise, you might find that you have wasted a trip.

Costs. It's a basic rule of economics that when something is in demand, prices rise. Right now and for the foreseeable future, Jays' tickets are very popular. Accordingly, tickets are set at prices that are quite popular with the club.

As expensive as Toronto seats are, though, there is at least one compensation. In setting its rates, the club adopted a "view" pricing policy. You pay, at least in theory, in accordance with your proximity to the action. We think this is a good way to go about things, and it is a practice that some of the other teams would do well to emulate.

In 1990, Blue Jay ticket prices were as follows: Esplanade ($15); Skyclub Level, Outfield ($15); Esplanade, Outfield ($12); Skydeck, Infield ($12); Skydeck, Red ($9); Skydeck, Green ($4).

These charges are in Canadian funds. Fans coming to the game from the U.S. will usually, depending on the exchange rates, find that prices will be about 10 percent lower.

Rainouts. When the rain starts to come down the dome closes. Hence, there are no rainouts in Toronto.

Still, you could get a little wet. While the club is allowed to either open or

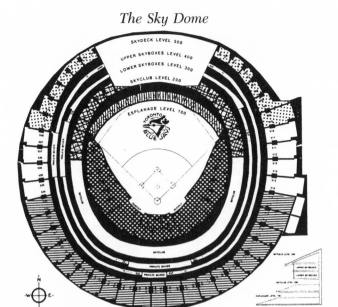

Seating chart, the Sky Dome.

close the dome before a contest, only the umpires can order it shut in the middle of a battle. Sometimes, no matter how hard it pours, they will wait until a full inning is finished before they decide that the dome should be shut. If you find yourself caught in one of these rare situations, it might be a good opportunity to pick up another order of "Chicken McNuggets."

Seating

Overall, the "view" seating system does work this way in the Sky Dome. Yet despite this philosophy, all spots at the dome in the various view areas are not created equal. A little study of a seating chart as you order could well prove rewarding in making your visit to the Blue Jays a fully satisfying and memorable baseball experience.

Esplanade ($15) and Skyclub Level Outfield seats ($15) are the most expensive spots in the park. The Esplanade seats are wonderful. Composed of handsome blue plastic chairs set in fairly longish rows, these spots hug the action from foul pole to foul pole. Those seat in the baselines sections, which run from 117 (first) to 127 (third) have the best views, of course. However, the other chairs are all set close enough to the action that you feel a part of it, particularly if you are able to snag spots in the lower rows, particularly 1 to 20.

If you are planning on sitting in The Esplanade, though, there are some things you should know about this area. First, if you are seated in rows beyond 30, you may not be able to see all of the pop flies. In certain areas, you won't be able to tell if the dome is open or closed either. Some of the chairs at the far end near the foul poles cannot see the full outfield, though they do not miss very much. Overall, we would still rate Eplanade very highly.

We can be less positive about the Skyclub seats. These are comfortable chairs set above the outfield walls, with a commanding bird's eye view of the proceeding. And that's just the point; you'd have to have bird's eyes — particularly eagle eyes — to get a great view from an area where the closest seats are over 300 feet from home plate. In many parks seats with this kind of view would be termed bleachers. We can't see why such spots are worth $15, even in the Sky Dome.

Esplanade Outfield seats ($12) are just what the Skyclub seats pretend not to be; they are glorified bleacher spots, with nicer reserved chairs. As far as we are concerned the view in this area is just as good as the one in the Skyclub seats and the price, while not great, is better. Set at the same price, Skydeck Infield seats have, overall, less to offer. Resting on the top deck of the park, chairs in this area are smaller and have less legroom. Spots here in the base-lines (518 to 529) and in the lowest rows possible are your best bet.

There really are no best bets in the next two areas, Skydeck Red ($9) and Skydeck Green ($4). Located high above the field and past the baselines, just about every seat in both areas is fairly far from the action. In fact, on a day when the dome is open, you are more likely to get a close view of feathered blue jays up here than of the bat-carrying kind. The deck at this level also has a very steep pitch, which is something the elderly and those with heart conditions should consider be-fore booking. Still, the Jays' limited ticket availability means that you may have to take seats in these sections. What should you do?

Our best advice is to go only with the reds if you can get something in a very low row. If they are going to put you up in the rafters anyway, why pay the $5 difference in prices between the sec-tions? If you can find very low row spots in any of the green sections that might be the best bet of all.

Special Needs

Parking. The Sky Dome offers very convenient in-stadium parking for the physically disabled. You must, how-ever, reserve a spot in advance in order to be able to take advantage of this ser-vice. To do this, call Ticketmaster at (416) 872-1111.

Seating. Handicapped seating is offered in a wide variety of places throughout the park. Sections 120 to 124 are a particularly good area to re-quest seats in, as these are spots along the first base line on the lower level.

There are a widely scattered variety of no-alcohol "family reserved" seating rows set aside in the Sky Dome. The location of these spots changes, and, in any case, most of these chairs are reserved for groups. Still, if you want this sort of seating, you could ask about it when you call or write to reserve your ticket. The Sky Dome is a very civilized stadium, and we know of no area of the park in which families would be likely to encounter any problems.

Food and Features

Food. Though it is only a few years old, the Sky Dome already boasts a well-known first in the dining area. That achievement is that the stadium currently encloses under its sliding roof the largest *McDonald's* outlet in North America.

McDonald's!? You read that right. The "Big Mac" has finally come to base-ball. Not only does McDonald's of Canada—the same friendly folks who brought the "Mac" to Moscow—run hamburger stands in the Sky Dome. It also runs the parks' "baseball food" con-cessions. Thus you get not only a "Quarter Pounder" and a "Big Mac." You also buy a McDonald's hot dog, pretzel, nachos, pizza, and Italian sausage. Shades of the future!

Like all ballparks, the Sky Dome has the usual favorites, albeit with the McDonald's twist. Selections include hot dogs, "deluxe" hot dogs, pizza, pop-corn, nachos, Italian sausage, and pretzels. All we can say about these is that Ronald M. might be better off sticking to beef.

The standard McDonald's fare is available, too, and it all tastes the same as it did in Vancouver, Albany, or West Podunk. The prices charged for the stuff, though, are likely to give you a "Mac Attack" of a different sort. As you would expect, the McDonald's outlets are all spic-and-span, and smiles are everywhere. If we were getting those prices, we would be smiling, too.

Those seeking something a bit more interesting than burgers will also find opportunities to indulge their taste buds in the dome. *The Sky Club Bar*, a watering hole located on the club level behind home plate has a nice patio dining area overlooking Lake Ontario that serves a tasty buffet before and during the early innings of each game. On the night we attended it offered a choice of steak or BBQ chicken with a selection of salads. In theory, you need a club level ticket to enjoy this service, but, in practice, if you are coming from elsewhere and are discrete, you will be served.

Drinks. Beer and soft drinks are popular with Blue Jay fans and are available throughout the park. They include Coke products, Labatt's beer, and some wine coolers.

Features. During the contest, the main "feature" is the Sky Dome itself. For most spectators that is feature enough.

Fans who are especially interested in the Dome might want to take the *SkyDome* Tour. Departing every weekday from 9 A.M. to 6 P.M. from "Skyplace," which is located at the northeast corner of the park, the tour gives participants a unique behind-the-scenes look at how the Dome was built and how it is operated. The trip is interesting and informative, but it is also quite costly. Adults are charged $7, while kids and seniors pay $5. If you want to go, be sure before you head out to the park to call Ticketmaster (416) 872-1111 to reserve a place and to guarantee that your tour has not been preempted by other Sky Dome events.

Assistance

Should you be unable to find your kids or your seat, or if you just want more information on the Blue Jays or the stadium, you will find the club's "Customer Services" office behind section 135 on the lower concourse level. Its staff is composed of friendly and helpful people.

Safety and Security

Safety. If you are one of those people who is paranoid about his personal safety and you have to decide whether to stay home and go to bed or go to a Blue Jays game, come to the contest. You will almost certainly be safer. There is no security threat in the park whatsoever.

The same could be said of downtown Toronto. We see no reason why you would want to hang around the park until 2 A.M. and then walk back to your hotel, but if you are so disposed, feel free to do it. Toronto, like any big city, has some tough neighborhoods. They are nowhere near the Sky Dome.

Health. The biggest health threats in the dome come from fast flying stray balls, stumbles, and too many "Big Macs." If Ronald's Revenge strikes you, head for the stadium's first aid office, which is behind section 134 of the lower concourse.

Across from the first aid office you will also find a "Family Washroom," a special area set aside for diaper changes, cleaning scrapes, and similar tasks. We think this is a great idea.

Mementos

Souvenirs. Torontonians love to wear Blue Jay paraphernalia. Within the park, you will find an outstandingly large collection of the stuff at the *SkyPlace* souvenir shop on the northeast side of the park. The selection is excellent, but the prices are daunting.

If you prefer to pay a bit less, try visiting *Athletic Supply*, 156 Front Street West ([416] 971-5222), which is about a two minute walk east of the stadium. There you will find as wide a selection of goods as are available in the Dome and better prices. The place also has an interesting "Canadian Baseball Hall of Fame" display. *Athletic Display* is open from 10 A.M. to 6 P.M. on Monday through Thursday and from 10 A.M. to 8 P.M. on Friday and Saturday.

Foul Balls. The Sky Dome is a good place to snag stray balls, provided you can find seats in those sections where fouls are most liable to wander. The best areas by far run from Esplanade sections 114 to 129. Unfortunately, season ticket holders have virtually all the spots in these sections. Occasionally high pop-ups reach the Skydeck Infield area. If you buy a spot in 522 to 526 it is possible you might catch one.

Autographs. The Sky Dome is one of the worst places in the majors to get autographs. Blue Jays and visitors enter and leave the park from a private lot under the stadium that you cannot get to. Nevertheless, some hopeful fans will still gather outside the exit from the players parking lot (it is near Gate 8) in hopes that one of their heroes will slow down and sign a few before peeling out. You stand a better chance of getting run over by a star here than you stand of getting his signature.

Index